A CHATTO & WINDUS PAPERBACK
CWP 57

SHAKESPEARE'S HISTORY PLAYS

Awarded to

ANDREW BRADLEY

for

Fourth Form Prize: 7th

Headmaster

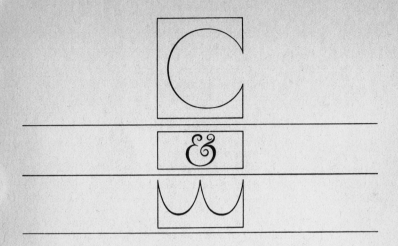

SHAKESPEARE'S
HISTORY PLAYS

E. M. W. TILLYARD

CHATTO & WINDUS

LONDON

Published by
Chatto & Windus Ltd
40 William IV Street
London WC2N 4DF

*

Clarke, Irwin & Co. Ltd
Toronto

First published 1944
Reprinted 1948, 1951, 1956, 1959, 1961,
1964, 1969 and 1974
First issued in this paperback edition 1980
© Stephen Tillyard 1944

British Library Cataloguing in Publication Data
Tillyard, Eustace Mandeville Wetenhall
Shakespeare's history plays.
1. Shakespeare, William – Histories
I. Title
822.3'3   PR2982
ISBN 0-7011-2495-4

Printed and bound in Great Britain by
Redwood Burn Ltd
Trowbridge & Esher

Contents

v

Preface

THE main intentions of this book are set forth in its last pages, while the table of contents shows its scope and proportions. I wish here to acknowledge some of my main debts to other authors.

Shakespeare's History Plays are political writings, and there are several ways of taking Shakespeare's treatment of politics. For pointing out what I now think the right way (and this way applies to Elizabethan literature generally) I owe most to Edwin Greenlaw's *Studies in Spenser's Historical Allegory* and his article in *Kittredge Anniversary Papers* on *Sidney's "Arcadia" as an Example of Elizabethan Allegory*. Greenlaw sees how seriously the great Elizabethans took politics and how much general political lore they put into their works but he stops short of finding in them elaborate allegories of recent political events. Agreeing with Greenlaw, I have much to say about Shakespeare's ideas on politics and on the Tudors but nothing, for instance, about Shakespeare and the Earl of Essex.

For my treatment of Shakespeare's earliest History Plays (the three parts of *Henry VI*) and of Shakespeare's early years I owe much to J. S. Smart and Professor P. Alexander. It is Alexander's book on *Henry VI* and *Richard III* that has given me warrant for an opinion long entertained: that Shakespeare wrote all three parts of *Henry VI*. I have thus been emboldened to pass over the large amount of writing based on what I am convinced is the false and unnecessary theory that Shakespeare was but part-author and reviser of these plays. I find myself too in close accord with these two writers' general way of thinking about the early years of Shakespeare.

Professor Dover Wilson has so far published editions of two of the History Plays: *King John* and *Richard II*. To the erudition and vivacity of his prefaces to these plays I owe a debt, and as much when I disagree (which is not seldom) as when I agree. The same is true of this writer's *Fortunes of Falstaff*.

For Elizabethan ideas on history I have found the work of Miss Lily Campbell very useful.

vii

For criticism of the plays themselves I have got great benefit from Mr. A. P. Rossiter's penetrating article on *Richard III* and from talk and correspondence with him. I regret that his edition of *Woodstock* has not appeared in time for me to consult. I look forward to his extending his researches to the whole body of Chronicle Plays. I have found some of the best criticism in Professor Mark Van Doren's studies of the plays in his *Shakespeare*; and in a few passages from Mr. Middleton Murry's *Shakespeare*, a book about which I have very mixed feelings. I have derived benefit and probably annexed ideas from unpublished papers by Miss Enid Welsford and Miss U. M. Ellis-Fermor.

I have omitted *Henry VIII*, not being convinced that Shakespeare wrote it all. The case of this play is quite different from that of *Henry VI*. In youthful work resemblances to predecessors or contemporaries are to be expected and are no argument for divided authorship; in mature work they are surprising and demand an explanation. Moreover in *Henry VI* resemblances to other writers may crop up anywhere, while in *Henry VIII* there is a stylistic contrast between whole scenes. Anyhow, *Henry VIII* is so far removed in date from the main sequence of History Plays that its omission matters little to the argument of this book.

E. M. W. T.

JESUS COLLEGE,
CAMBRIDGE

PART ONE

The Background

CHAPTER I

The Cosmic Background

1. INTRODUCTORY

SHAKESPEARE'S Histories have been associated with Holinshed's chronicle and with the Chronicle Plays: and rightly. Holinshed is shorter than the more thoughtful Hall and he includes more matter. Hall dealt with a single stretch of English history from Richard II to Henry VIII; Holinshed goes back to the very beginnings of British legend and includes the history of Scotland. Shakespeare found Holinshed useful as an omnibus volume.

Shakespeare's Histories belong to the class of English Chronicle Plays, and that class, like Holinshed, was practical and not very thoughtful. It was rarely performed at the Inns of Court and was enjoyed by the populace. It exploited the conscious patriotism of the decade after the Armada and instructed an inquisitive public in some of the facts and legends of English history. In formal ingenuousness it resembled the Miracle Plays.

It is easy, and up to a point true, to think of Shakespeare as transforming by his genius the material of Holinshed and the dramatic type of the Chronicle into something uniquely his own. But to leave one's thought at that is a large error; for what Shakespeare transformed was so much more than Holinshed and the Chronicle Play. If Shakespeare went to Holinshed for many of his facts, he had meditated on the political philosophy of Hall and of his own day; and if he imparted much historical information in the manner of the other Chronicle Plays, he was not ignorant of the formal pattern of *Gorboduc*. Shakespeare's Histories are more like his own Comedies and Tragedies than like others' Histories, and they not so much try out and discard a provincial mode as present one of his versions of the whole contemporary pattern of culture. It was not his completest version, but behind it, as behind the Tragedies, was that pattern.

In this chapter I shall describe some parts of that pattern which have most to do with the Histories.

3

Now this pattern is complicated and was the possession only of the more learned part of society. It can be to the point only if Shakespeare too was learned. There is still a prejudice against thinking of him as such. That prejudice must be overcome if the substance of my first two chapters is to be relevant. To overcome it one can point out that a man can be learned in more ways than one and that at least one of those ways fitted Shakespeare; and then one can produce concrete examples of his learning.

For different ways of being learned, consider how Shakespeare might have dealt with the academic doctrine of the Three Dramatic Unities, which he respected in the *Tempest*. He might have studied it in Aristotle and in Aristotle's Italian commentators; he might have read of it in Sidney; he might have heard it discussed. If the first way is improbable, it is equally improbable that he could have avoided acquaintance with it in the other two ways. We may fairly conjecture that he was in fact learned; not in an academic way but in the way Johnson conjectured for Dryden:

> I rather believe that the knowledge of Dryden was gleaned from accidental intelligence and various conversation, by a quick apprehension, a judicious selection, and a happy memory, a keen appetite of knowledge, and a powerful digestion; by vigilance that permitted nothing to pass without notice, and a habit of reflection that suffered nothing useful to be lost ... I do not suppose that he despised books, or intentionally neglected them; but that he was carried out, by the impetuosity of his genius, to more vivid and speedy instructors; and that his studies were rather desultory and fortuitous than constant and systematical.

For proofs, take for example Lorenzo on music in the fifth act of the *Merchant of Venice*:

> Look how the floor of heaven
> Is thick inlaid with patines of bright gold:
> There's not the smallest orb which thou behold'st
> But in his motion like an angel sings,
> Still quiring to the young-eyed cherubins;
> Such harmony is in immortal souls;
> But whilst this muddy vesture of decay
> Doth grossly close it in, we cannot hear it.

This has been called "an unlearned man's impression of Plato's sublime dream"; this dream being that "upon each of the heavenly spheres is a siren, who is borne round with the sphere uttering a single note; and the eight notes compose a single harmony." Shakespeare, it is alleged, gets Plato wrong in attributing song to the whole host of heaven instead of to the single spheres into which they were fitted. But more recently a specialist in Greek philosophy asserted that Shakespeare was in fact quite surprisingly knowledgeable and accurate. It is true that he garbled the above passage from the *Republic* by substituting cherubim for sirens and vastly enlarging the range of the heavenly music, but Lorenzo's general doctrine shows an accurate knowledge of a part of Plato's *Timaeus*. In that dialogue it is said that the planetary motions of the heavens have their counterpart in the immortal soul of man and that our souls would sound in accord with the grander music of the cosmos were it not for the earthy and perishable nature of the body. Shakespeare reproduces the gist of this doctrine.

Twice in the tragedies Shakespeare mentions the seeds or "germens" of nature: when Macbeth says to the Witches

> though the treasure
> Of nature's germens tumble all together,

and when Lear, addressing the storm, bids it

> Crack nature's moulds, all germens spill at once
> That make ungrateful man.

It seems that behind these brief references is the whole doctrine of the λόγοι σπερματικοὶ or *rationes seminales*: the doctrine that God introduced into nature certain seminal principles that abide there waiting to be put into action. It is most apt to the passage in *Macbeth* because there was the further doctrine, found in Augustine and Aquinas, that angelic and demonic powers have the gift, under God's permission, of speeding up these natural processes and producing apparently miraculous results.

If anything, we are apt to underestimate what such passing references mean in a dramatist who (unlike Jonson) is not in the least anxious to parade his learning. No one can doubt that Shakespeare knew the outlines of orthodox Christian theology. Yet how few are the precise references to it in the plays. But what there are become significant in inverse proportion to their brevity. Here is one passage: Angelo and Isabella arguing about Claudio's condemnation in *Measure for Measure*—

> *Ang.* Your brother is a forfeit of the law,
>   And you but waste your words.
> *Isab.*   Alas, alas!
>   Why all the souls that were were forfeit once;
>   And He that might the vantage best have took
>   Found out the remedy.

The reference is of the slightest, yet it reveals and takes for granted the total Pauline theology of Christ abrogating man's enslavement to the old law incurred through the defection of Adam. Now we can be certain that living in the age he did and having the intelligence he had Shakespeare must have known the outlines of orthodox Christian theology. To this theology there are few references in the plays. Do not these two facts make it *probable* that behind other correspondingly scanty references there is a corresponding abundance of knowledge? When Brutus talks of the state of man, like a little kingdom, suffering the nature of an insurrection, he implies not merely the bare commonplace analogy between the human body and the body politic but the whole mass of traditional correspondences between the heavenly order, the macrocosm, the body politic, and the human body or microcosm.

The argument gains in strength, if we compare the cases of Shakespeare and of Montaigne. Montaigne, an expansive and discursive essayist, is free to give as much of his background and derivation as he wishes. And he makes full use of this freedom by constant quotation. His most famous essay takes off from and partly denies the *Natural Theology* of Raymond de Sebonde. Before having his say about the state of man and his relation to the beasts, he tells how his father asked him to translate de Sebonde's book from the Latin and how gladly he complied. Had Montaigne been exclusively a dramatist, he might have given little or no sign of having read de Sebonde. His meditations on de Sebonde's material would certainly have got into his plays in some form or other. He would in fact have given us something not unlike Hamlet's pronouncements on the nature of man or Lear's and Timon's broken references to the relation of man and beast. Take in turn one of Hamlet's pronouncements:

> What a piece of work is a man: how noble in reason; how infinite in faculty; in form and moving how express and admirable; in action how like an angel; in apprehension how like a god; the beauty of the world, the paragon of animals.

This is Shakespeare's version of the very precise, traditional, orthodox encomia of what man was in his prelapsarian state and of what ideally he is still capable of being. Raymond de Sebonde himself, a mainly derivative writer, has such an encomium in the ninety-fifth to the ninety-ninth chapters of his *Natural Theology*. How Shakespeare got hold of this material matters little; he could have got it from plenty of places, the pulpit included. It is the stuff's somehow being there, behind Hamlet's sentences, that matters. The equivalent of Montaigne's discursiveness is implied.

Shakespeare, then, had much the same general equipment of learning as his more highly-educated contemporaries, Sidney and Spenser for instance, though it may have been less systematic, less detailed, and less derived from books. How does this equipment bear on the Histories?

2. THE CONTEXT OF HISTORY

The picture we get from Shakespeare's Histories is that of disorder. Unsuccessful war abroad and civil war at home are the large theme; victory abroad and harmony at home are the exceptions, and the fear of disorder is never absent. Henry V on the eve of Agincourt prays that the ancestral curse may be suspended, and the Bastard qualifies his patriotic epilogue in *King John* with an *if*: if England to itself do rest but true. And by *resting true* he meant not, displaying the English characteristics but avoiding internal treachery and contention. But to allow disorder to stand as the unqualified description of Shakespeare's Histories would be no truer than to call the *Fairy Queen* a study of mutability. Throughout his poem Spenser shows the alertest sense of the instability of earthly things. But as a nondramatic, philosophical poet Spenser has both the space and the obligation to make his *total* doctrine clear. So, in the two cantos that survive from a seventh book he turns Mutability into a goddess and makes Nature judge her claims to absolute domination. This is Nature's pronouncement on the evidence:

> I well consider all that ye have said
> And find that all things stedfastness do hate
> And changed be; yet, being rightly weigh'd,
> They are not changed from their first estate
> But by their change their being do dilate,
> And, turning to themselves at length again,
> Do work their own perfection so by fate.
> Then over them Change doth not rule and reign,
> But they reign over Change and do their states maintain.

Even on earth then there is an order behind change, an order which makes Spenser think of a heavenly order and

> Of that same time when no more change shall be,
> But stedfast rest of all things, firmly stay'd
> Upon the pillars of Eternity,
> That is contrare of Mutability.

The case is the same with Shakespeare. Behind disorder is some sort of order or "degree" on earth, and that order has its counterpart in heaven. This assertion has nothing to do with the question of Shakespeare's personal piety: it merely means that Shakespeare used the thought-idiom of his age. The only way he could have avoided that idiom in his picture of disorder was by not thinking at all, like the authors of *Stukeley* or *Edward I*; for to go against the contemporary thought-idiom is to make it rather more than usually emphatic. Witness Marlowe's Tamburlaine, who, because he so very emphatically does *not* crash from Fortune's wheel, proclaims his affinity with all the traditional victims who lament their falls in the *Mirror for Magistrates*.

If a Spenserian analogy suggests that there is a general (and predominantly religious) doctrine behind the mass of particular events transacted in Shakespeare's Histories, the chronicles themselves point just the same way. Many of these kept to the religious setting which was common in medieval days. For instance, Grafton's *Chronicle at Large* (1569), though purporting to be British only, begins with the creation of the world and of paradise in the full medieval fashion. Now the medieval chronicler in writing of the creation habitually inserted the commonplaces of orthodox theology: the nature of the Trinity

and of the Angels, the fall of Satan, the question of free will,
and so on. Higden, for instance, writing in the first half of the
fourteenth century, spends a large portion of the second book of
Polychronicon on theology, before finally settling to chronicle the
events of the world. History in fact grows quite naturally out
of theology and is never separated from it. The connection was
still flourishing after Shakespeare's death. A work that illustrates it to perfection is Raleigh's *History of the World*. The
frontispiece shows History, a female figure, treading down
Death and Oblivion, flanked by Truth and Experience, supporting the globe; and over all is the eye of Providence.[1] And
the first book deals with the creation and is as full of Augustinian
theology as any medieval book of world history. Further,
Raleigh's preface contains not only a disquisition on history but
an account of English history from Edward II to Henry VII.
This account is no mere summary but a view of this stretch of
history in a definite pattern; and the pattern resembles Shakespeare's. Now, if these purely historical patterns are similar,
it is most probable that behind both of them are similar philosophical or theological axioms, and that Raleigh's theological
preface and first book instruct us in the commonplaces upon
which not only his own but Shakespeare's historical writings
were founded.

A sketch of English history very like Raleigh's occurs in a
much less likely place, the *Microcosmos* of John Davies of Hereford. His chief poems, *Mirum in Modum, Summa Totalis,* and
Microcosmos (written in the Spenserian stanza with a deca-
syllabic substituted for the final Alexandrine) are to the age of
Shakespeare as the work of Soame Jenyns is to the mid-
eighteenth century; they epitomise the commonplaces of the
time's serious thought, all the better for being the product of a
second-rate mind. Davies himself is especially to my purpose
because he is Shakespeare's slightly younger contemporary,
because his social status was almost identical with Shakespeare's, and because on the certain evidence of an epigram and
the possible evidence of two marginal notes he knew Shakespeare personally. He came of middle-class parents, was
educated at the local grammar school but did not attend the

[1] To an Elizabethan a picture of the eye of Providence would first suggest,
not, as to a Victorian, the eye remorselessly recording the minutest sin of the
individual but the instrument of the power that sustained the world's vitality and
prevented its slipping back into chaos.

university, became a writing-master much patronised by the
nobility, and ended by being writing-master to Prince Henry.
He addressed short poems to most of the important and intelligent Englishmen of or near the court circle, and his serious
poems epitomise just that knowledge the possession of which
was taken for granted in that class of person. He writes of God
and creation, the universe and the influence of the stars, the
soul and body of man; man's mind and its passions. And from
his repetitive and indifferently arranged stanzas as completely
as from any single source I know of can be extracted the contemporary notion of order or degree which was never absent
from Shakespeare's picture of disorder in the Histories. That
Davies inserts his very Shakespearean version of English history
into *Microcosmos* strongly confirms that belief.

3. THE ELIZABETHAN WORLD ORDER

Most readers of Shakespeare know that his own version of
order or degree is in Ulysses's speech on the topic in *Troilus and
Cressida*; not all would grant that it states the necessary setting
of the Histories; and few realise how large a body of thought
it epitomises or hints at. (May I here ask the reader to have
before him a text of this speech?)

Its doctrine is primarily political but evidently goes far
beyond mere practical politics. First, we learn that the order
which prevails in the heavens is duplicated on earth, the king
corresponding to the sun; then that disorder in the heavens
breeds disorder on earth, both in the physical sublunary organisation and in the commonwealth of men. When Shakespeare
calls degree the ladder to all high designs he probably has
another correspondence in mind: that between the ascending
grades of man in his social state and the ladder of creation or
chain of being which stretched from the meanest piece of inanimate matter in unbroken ascent to the highest of the arch-
angels. The musical metaphor in "Take but degree away,
untune that string, and hark what discord follows" is far more
than a metaphor; it implies the traditional Platonic doctrine
that (in Dryden's words)

> From harmony, from heavenly harmony
> This universal frame began,

and that at the world's last hour

> Music shall untune the sky.

Finally, when an Elizabethan audience heard the words "chaos, where degree is suffocate," the educated element at least would understand chaos in a more precise sense than we should naturally do. They would understand it as a parallel in the state to the primitive warring of the elements from which the universe was created and into which it would fall if the constant pressure of God's ordering and sustaining will were relaxed.

The above references are fragmentary but they show that Shakespeare had in mind a complete body of doctrine. Having made this the subject of another book, I need give no more than a short summary in this place.

The Elizabethan conception of world-order was in its outlines medieval although it had discarded much medieval detail. The universe was a unity, in which everything had its place, and it was the perfect work of God. Any imperfection was the work not of God but of man; for with the fall of man the universe underwent a sympathetic corruption. But for all the corruption the marks of God's perfection were still there, and one of the two great roads to salvation was through the study of created things. But though the idea of unity was basic, the actual order of the world presented itself to the Elizabethans under three different, though often related, appearances: a chain, a series of corresponding planes, and a dance to music.

As a chain, creation was a series of beings stretching from the lowest of inanimate objects up to the archangel nearest to the throne of God. The ascent was gradual, no step was missing; and on the borders of the great divisions between animate and inanimate, vegetative and sensitive, sensitive and rational, rational and angelic, there were the necessary transitions. One of the noblest accounts of the chain of being is by Sir John Fortescue, the fifteenth century jurist:

> In this order hot things are in harmony with cold; dry with moist; heavy with light; great with little; high with low. In this order angel is set over angel, rank upon rank in the Kingdom of Heaven; man is set over man, beast over beast, bird over bird, and fish over fish, on the earth, in the air, and in the sea; so that there is no worm that crawls upon the ground, no bird that flies on high, no fish that swims in the depths, which the chain of

this order binds not in most harmonious concord. God created as many different kinds of things as he did creatures, so that there is no creature which does not differ in some respect from all other creatures, and by which it is in some respect superior or inferior to all the rest. So that from the highest angel down to the lowest of his kind there is absolutely not found an angel that has not a superior and inferior; nor from man down to the meanest worm is there any creature which is not in some respect superior to one creature and inferior to another. So that there is nothing which the bond of order does not embrace. And since God has thus regulated all creatures, it is impious to think that he left unregulated the human race, which he made the highest of all earthly creatures.

The last sentence illustrates to perfection that same striving for unity and for correspondences that was so strong among the Elizabethans. Expediency was the last reason for justifying the laws of England: Fortescue justifies them because they are a necessary piece in the great jig-saw puzzle of the universe. For Shakespeare too the justification of that political order with which he is mainly concerned is the same.

For the way one large class is linked with another in the chain of being take a passage near the beginning of the second book of Higden's *Polychronicon*. Higden's evidence is of exactly the right kind. He can be trusted to give the perfect commonplace and he was extremely popular not only in his own day but well into the Tudor period. The opening of his second book is for a brief summary of "degree" as good as anything I know:

In the universal order of things the top of an inferior class touches the bottom of a superior: as for instance oysters, which, occupying as it were the lowest position in the class of animals, scarcely rise above the life of plants, because they cling to the earth without motion and possess the sense of touch alone. The upper surface of the earth is in contact with the lower surface of water; the highest part of the waters touches the lowest part of the air, and so by a ladder of ascent to the outermost sphere of the universe. So also the noblest entity in the category of bodies, the human body, when its humours are evenly balanced, touches the fringe of the next class above it, namely the human soul, which occupies the lowest rank in the spiritual order. For this reason the human soul is called the horizon or meeting-ground of corporeal and incorporeal; for in it begins the ascent from the lowest to the highest spiritual power. At times even, when it has been cleansed of earthly passions, it attains to the state of incorporeal beings.

It was this key-position in the chain of being, not the central position of the earth in the Ptolemaic astronomy, that made man so interesting among the objects of creation. Subject to lunar vicissitudes unknown in higher spheres and by its central position the repository of the dregs of things, the earth was not happily situated. But from before Plato till beyond Pope man's amazing position in creation—a kind of Clapham Junction where all the tracks converge and cross—exercised the human imagination and fostered the true humanist tradition; and at no period of English history so powerfully as in the age of Elizabeth. Here is a typical account of man's position between angel and beast, his high capacities and his proneness to fall, from Sir John Hayward, Shakespeare's contemporary:

> Thou art a man, endued with reason and understanding, wherein God hath engraven his lively image. In other creatures there is some likeness of him, some footsteps of his divine nature; but in man he hath stamped his image. Some things are like God in that they are; some in that they live; some in their excellent property and working. But this is not the image of God. His image is only in that we understand. Seeing then that thou art of so noble a nature and that thou bearest in thine understanding the image of God, so govern thyself as is fit for a creature of understanding. Be not like the brute beasts, which want understanding: either wild and unruly or else heavy and dull. . . . Certainly of all the creatures under heaven, which have received being from God, none degenerate, none forsake their natural dignity and being, but only man. Only man, abandoning the dignity of his proper nature, is changed like Proteus into divers forms. And this is occasioned by reason of the liberty of his will. And as every kind of beast is principally inclined to one sensuality more than to any other, so man transformeth himself into that beast to whose sensuality he principally declines.

But if man is allied to the beasts in sensuality and to God and the angels in understanding, he is most himself in being social. This passage, translated from the Italian about 1598, would have been accepted without question by every educated Elizabethan:

> Man, as he is in form from other creatures different, so is his end

from theirs very diverse. The end of other creatures is no other thing but living, to generate those like themselves. Man, born in the kindgom of nature and fortune, is not only to live and generate but to live well and happily. Nature of herself provideth for other creatures things sufficient unto life : nature procureth man to live, but reason and fortune cause him to live well. Creatures live after the laws of nature : man liveth by reason prudence and art. Living creatures may live a solitary life : man alone, being of himself insufficient and by nature an evil creature without domestical and civil conversation, cannot lead other than a miserable and discontented life. And therefore, as the philosopher saith very well, that man which cannot live in civil company either he is a god or a beast, seeing only God is sufficient of himself, and a solitary life best agreeth with a beast.

It is with such a doctrine in mind that Shakespeare's Ulysses speaks of

> communities,
> Degrees in schools and brotherhoods in cities,
> Peaceful commerce from dividable shores,

standing by degree in authentic place. Such things are the organisations and activities proper to man in his place in the scale of being.

Although the Middle Ages found the doctrine of the chain of being useful they did not elaborate it. For the full exercise of medieval and Elizabethan ingenuity we must turn to the sets of correspondences worked out between the various planes of creation. These planes were God and the angels, the macrocosm or physical universe, the body politic or the state, and the microcosm or man. To a much smaller degree the animals and plants were included. The amount of intellectual and emotional satisfaction that these correspondences afforded is difficult both to picture and to overestimate. What to us is merely silly or trivial might for an Elizabethan be a solemn or joyful piece of evidence that he lived in an ordered universe, where there was no waste and where every detail was a part of nature's plan.

Shakespeare touches on one of the fundamental correspondences in Ulysses's speech on degree when he speaks of

> the glorious planet Sol
> In noble eminence enthron'd and spher'd

> Amidst the other, whose medicinable eye
> Corrects the ill aspects of planets evil,
> And posts like the commandment of a king.

But *le roi soleil* is only a part of a larger sequence of leadership, which included: God among the angels or all the works of creation, the sun among the stars, fire among the elements, the king in the state, the head in the body, justice among the virtues, the lion among the beasts, the eagle among the birds, the dolphin among the fishes. It would be hard to find a single passage containing the whole sequence (and there may be items I have not included), but at the beginning of the *Complete Gentleman* Peacham gives a very full list, itself intended to illustrate the universal principle of order and hierarchy. To most of those already mentioned he adds the oak, the rose, the pomeroy and queen-apple, gold and the diamond.

For the general notion of correspondences I know of none better than a passage from an abridgement of de Sebonde's *Natural Theology*, a passage quite valid for the Elizabethan age. It expresses admirably the cosmic order into which the human order was always set. De Sebonde's theme here is the number and the ordering of the angels.

We must believe that the angels are there in marvellous and inconceivable numbers, because the honour of a king consists in the great crowd of his vassals, while his disgrace or shame consists in their paucity. Therefore I say that thousands of thousands wait on the divine majesty and tenfold hundreds of millions join in his worship. Further, if in material nature there are numberless kinds of stones herbs trees fishes birds four-footed beasts and above these an infinitude of men, it must be said likewise that there are many kinds of angels. But remember that one must not conceive of their multitude as confused; on the contrary, among these spirits a lovely order is exquisitely maintained, an order more pleasing than can be expressed. That this is so we can see from the marvellous arrangement among material things, I mean that some of these are higher, others lower, and others in the middle. For instance the elements and all inanimate things are reckoned in the lowest grade, vegetative things in the second, sensitive in the third, and man in the fourth as sovereign. Within the human range are seen different states from the great to the least: such as labourers merchants burgesses knights barons counts dukes kings, and a single emperor as monarch. Similarly in the church there are curates deacons archdeacons deans priors abbots bishops archbishops patriarchs, and one Pope, who is their head. If then there is maintained such an order among low and earthly things, the force of reason makes it necessary that among these most noble spirits there should be a marshalling unique, artistic, and beyond measure blessed. Further, beyond doubt, they are divided into three hierarchies or sacred principalities, in each of which there are the high middle and low. But this well-ordered multitude leads up to a single head: in precisely the same way as we see among the elements fire the first in dignity; among the fishes the dolphin; among the birds the eagle; among the beasts the lion; and among men the emperor.

Of all the correspondences between two planes that between the cosmic and the human was the commonest. Not only did man constitute in himself one of the planes of creation, but he was the microcosm, the sum in little of the great world itself. He was composed materially of the four elements and contained within himself, as well as his rational soul, vegetative and sensitive souls after the manners of plants and animals. The constitution of his body duplicated the constitution of the earth. His vital heat corresponded to the subterranean fire; his veins to rivers; his sighs to winds; the outbursts of his passions to storms and earthquakes. There is a whole complex body of doctrine behind the account of how Lear

> Strives in his little world of man to outscorn
> The to and fro conflicting wind and rain.

Storms were also frequent in another correspondence, that between macrocosm and body politic. Storms and perturbations in the heavens were duplicated by commotions and disasters in the state. The portents that marked the death of Caesar were more than portents; they were the heavenly enactment of the commotions that shook the Roman Empire after that event. Irregularities of the heavenly bodies duplicate the loss of order in the state. In the words of Ulysses,

> but when the planets
> In evil mixture to disorder wander,
> What plagues and what portents, what mutiny,
> What raging of the sea, shaking of earth,
> Commotion in the winds, frights changes horrors,

> Divert and crack, rend and deracinate
> The unity and married calm of states
> Quite from their fixture.

Last may be cited the correspondence between microcosm and body politic. It can take the form of Brutus in his agony of doubt comparing his own little world to a city in insurrection. But its most persistent form was an elaborate analogy between the various ranks in the state with different parts of the human body.

The picture of the universe as harmony or a dance to music is met with less often than the other two, but Shakespeare knew it as he shows by Ulysses's words once again:

> Take but degree away, untune that string;
> And hark what discord follows.

It was a notion that appealed especially to the more Platonic or mystically minded. It was dear to Milton, and in Elizabethan days it was the theme of Sir John Davies's *Orchestra*. This poem is a kind of academic disputation between Penelope and Antinous, most courtly of the Ithacan suitors, on the dance. Penelope will not dance, but Antinous seeks to persuade her that the universe and all it contains is one great dance-pattern and that she is going against the cosmic order by refraining. Finally he gives her a magic glass in which she sees Queen Elizabeth, the mortal moon, presiding over the dance-measures of her courtiers. Repeated at last in the polity, the dance-pattern, which has ranged through the whole order of nature, is complete. *Orchestra* is one of the most lovely and most typical of Elizabethan poems. It is also very apt to the present argument. Not only does it contain nearly every one of the commonplaces I have touched on, but it presents the cosmic as the background of the actual. The Elizabethan political order, the Golden Age brought in by the Tudors, is nothing apart from the cosmic order of which it is a part. If this is Davies's faith, is it not contrariwise the more likely that when Shakespeare deals with the concrete facts of English history he never forgets the principle of order behind all the terrible manifestations of disorder, a principle sometimes fulfilled, however imperfectly, even in the kingdoms of this world?

4. SHAKESPEARE'S ACCESS TO THE DOCTRINE

If the total doctrine of order is indeed there behind Ulysses's speech, what were the means by which Shakespeare came to learn of it? Little can be said for certain, for we are now dealing with a mass of material which was part of the collective consciousness of the age, material so taken for granted that it appears more in brief reference than in set exposition. The doctrine of the chain of being was ignored by readers of Elizabethan literature till Lovejoy wrote his book on it; now, our eyes being open, we find it all over the place. If Shakespeare knew it, there can be little question of a single source. He could have got it from a hundred sources. The fountain-heads of general cosmic doctrines were the *Book of Genesis* and Plato; but the material derived thence is handled and rehandled with infinite repetitions and small modifications till it becomes a kind of impersonal ballad-lore, and the question of sources is ridiculous. A book has been published in America on the hexemeral literature, in other words, on the literature that has accumulated round the account in *Genesis* of the six days of creation. As there appears to be no copy of it in this country, I have not read it; but it is said to imply that most of the alleged sources of Milton, for instance in the Kabbala or Augustine, are in fact doubtful because all the stuff is already there in the early commentaries on *Genesis* and must have formed a body of oral tradition that would have survived in sermon and talk independent of any written record. The theory is extremely plausible; and to seek the exact sources of the Shakespearean doctrine of degree is futile in just the same way. But there is one detail of derivation which admits of greater certainty. Of all the passages I have read dealing with "degree" one of the closest to Ulysses's speech is in the original book of Homilies published in 1547 when Edward VI was king. It is worth quoting, not only for its likeness to Shakespeare, but for its beauty, and for the greater amplitude with which it states ideas that are only hinted at by the poet. Contrary to my custom in this book I give the original spelling and punctuation; for the 1547 book of Homilies is a fine piece of printing and was produced with a care that earns the right of accurate transcription. The passage is the opening of the *Sermon of*

Obedience, or *An Exhortation concerning good Ordre and Obedience to Rulers and Magistrates.*

Almightie God hath created and appoyncted all thynges, in heaven, yearth, and waters, in a moste excellent and perfect ordre. In heaven he hath appoynted distincte Orders and states of Archangelles and Angelles. In the yearth he hath assigned Kynges, princes, with other gouernors under them, all in good and necessarie ordre. The water aboue is kepte and raineth doune in dewe time and season. The Sonne, Moone, Sterres, Rainbowe, Thundre, Lightenyng, cloudes, and all birdes of the aire, do kepe their ordre. The Yearth, Trees, Seedes, Plantes, Herbes, and Corne, Grasse and all maner of beastes kepe theim in their ordre. All the partes of the whole yere, as Winter, Somer, Monethes, Nightes and Daies, continue in their ordre. All kyndes of Fishes in the sea, Rivers and Waters, with all Fountaines, Sprynges, yea, the Seas themselves kepe their comely course and ordre. And Man himself also, hath all his partes, bothe within and without, as Soule, Harte, Mynd, Memory, Understandyng, Reason, speache, with all and syngular corporall membres of his body, in a profitable necessarie and pleasaunt ordre. Euery degree of people, in their vocacion, callyng, and office, hath appointed to them their duetie and ordre. Some are in high degree, some in lowe, some Kynges and Princes, some inferiors and subjectes, Priestes and Laymen, Masters and Servauntes, Fathers and Children, Husbandes and Wifes, Riche and Poore, and euery one haue nede of other, so that in all thynges is to bee lauded and praised the goodly ordre of God, without the whiche, no house, no citee, no common wealthe, can continue and endure. For where there is no right ordre, there reigneth all abuse, carnall libertie, enormitie, synne, and Babilonical confusion. Take awaie Kynges, Princes, Rulers, Magistrates, Judges, and suche states of God's ordre, no man shall ride or go by the high way unrobbed, no man shal slepe in his awne house or bed unkilled, no man shall kepe his wife, children, and possessions in quietnesse, all thynges shall be common, and there muste nedes folowe all mischief and utter destruccion, bothe of soules, bodies, goodes and common wealthes.

This passage and Ulysses's speech are close enough together to make it likely that at least an unconscious act of memory took place. It is also possible that it was first through this homily that Shakespeare had the idea of degree impressed on his mind. Alfred Hart has pointed out that Shakespeare was six years old when the great rebellion broke out in the north of England. His father as alderman would have shared responsibility for the local militia; Shakespeare himself would have seen the troops marching through Stratford to the north. The homily in question deals with civil obedience and was directed against civil war. At the time of the rebellion it must have had special point and been read with a special emphasis that Shakespeare, granted that he shared the precociousness of other Elizabethan children, was not likely to have missed. Four years later another and longer homily on the same topic, but with specific reference to the late rebellion, was added to the original collection. When Shakespeare was ten, he would have heard a part of a homily on order and civil obedience nine Sundays or holy-days in the year. Hart has added to the meagre stock of reasonable probabilities in the life of Shakespeare. Early experience of rebellion and of the detestation in which it was held may help to account both for his seriousness in speaking of order and for the attraction he felt towards the theme of civil war.

CHAPTER II

The Historical Background

1. MACHIAVELLI

EARLY in the last chapter I said that behind the disorder of history Shakespeare assumed some kind of order or degree on earth having its counterpart in heaven. Further, that in so assuming he was using the thought-idiom of his age and could have avoided doing so only by not thinking at all, like the authors of *Stukeley* or *Edward I*. This is not strictly true, because there is another alternative. Shakespeare could have ignored some of his age's basic assumptions by following the doctrines of Machiavelli. I noticed that Marlowe by the very ostentation with which he keeps Tamburlaine poised on Fortune's wheel does homage to the traditional theme of the fall of princes. Plainly he had asked questions and worried his head about the answers. Machiavelli is quite different. He disbelieves so completely in a natural law and a fixed order that he just passes them by. The result is that his basic doctrines lie outside the main sixteenth century interests: "Calvin and Hooker might be almost unaware of Machiavelli's existence." Thoughtful Elizabethans agonised over the terrible gaps between the "erected wit" and the "infected will" of man and between the majestic harmony of an ideal state and the habitual chaos of the earthly polity. Machiavelli spared himself such agonisings by cutting out the "erected wit" altogether, thereby making irrelevant the questions that most disturbed men's minds. In the third chapter of the first book of the *Discourses on Livy* he makes his plain statement on the basic proneness of man to evil. There can be no question of a fall, because the seeds of evil were there from the start ready to germinate: there had never been a state from which a fall was possible. Disorder was the natural state of man, and civilisation a matter of pure expediency. Such a way of thinking was abhorrent to the Elizabethans (as indeed it always has been and is now to the majority), who preferred to think of order as the norm to which disorder, though lamentably common, was yet the exception.

The above cool statement of Machiavelli's irrelevance to the age of Elizabeth does not mean that I am trying to prove that the educated man of Shakespeare's day did not know or heed him, or that the semi-educated did not distort his image in a very queer way. What I mean is that the age, while making much use of certain details of his writing, either ignored or refused to face what the man fundamentally stood for. It may even be that the whole fraudulent edifice of anti-Machiavellianism, based on a misunderstanding of his meaning and on a wrenching of his maxims from their contemporary context, was the unconscious means of punishing him for a fundamental heresy men hated too much to face and attack openly. Not till the age of Hobbes was the same heresy subjected to frontal attacks. Machiavelli among the Elizabethans is in some points like Wilde among the late Victorians. The plain man smelt out something fundamentally wrong in both of them: in Machiavelli his lack of idealism or, better, his psychological error in ignoring it; in Wilde his snobbery and esotericism. And he took his revenge as he could, turning Machiavelli's specific political remedies for Italy in the year 1513 into eternal principles and turning Wilde's homosexuality into the mainspring of his whole life. Stupid as his expression may have been, he was right enough in his unconscious conviction that they both tried to set false limits to the human spirit. It is interesting that the two authors should each have written one superb, intellectual, a-moral comedy.

With what lordly carelessness the Elizabethans could ignore the Machiavellian essentials while using him in details can be seen from the two great authors most clearly indebted to him, Spenser and Raleigh. Spenser must have known Machiavelli young. His college friend, Gabriel Harvey, says he was much read at the universities. When Spenser came to deal with practical politics as secretary of Earl Gray in Ireland he used Machiavelli as his guide; for his *View of the present State of Ireland* is founded on Machiavelli's recommendations for achieving the most difficult task of ruling a country where language and religion are different from the rulers'. Yet the use of Machiavelli does not prevent Spenser's devotion to a Platonic idealism which for Machiavelli was quite without meaning. The case of Raleigh is rather different. In his youth he was mixed up in the charges of atheism brought against Marlowe and others. Baines, a professional informer concerned in these charges, reported Raleigh's statement that "the first beginning of religion was only to keep men in awe," which might easily be derived from Machiavelli. Large parts of Raleigh's *Maxims of State* are taken from him direct. But Raleigh never seems to have been irreligious, though he plainly enjoyed baiting the conventionally orthodox. The statement recorded by Baines is just like the little essay called the *Sceptic*, where Raleigh copies Montaigne in asking what right human beings have to exalt their opinions over those of the animals. In both he advances a challenge, not states an opinion. In the *Maxims of State* Raleigh combines isolated Machiavellian sentiment with denial of Machiavellian generalisation in a most instructive way. On one page he recommends a ruler to borrow a small sum and repay it so that later he may borrow a large sum and keep it. But on the next page he gives it as a first general rule of the statesman to maintain the true worship of God: and for most un-Machiavellian reasons. For the worship of God is the *end* of all government, not, as for Machiavelli, the means of maintaining order. And when he gets down to the unadulterated Machiavellianism of his Rules of politic Tyrants he adds "rather to be known than practised."

If Spenser and with him the Sidney circle, and if Raleigh and with him the "School of Night," knew Machiavelli at first hand, it can hardly be doubted that the Southampton circle and with it Shakespeare knew Machiavelli too. And it cannot reasonably be doubted that Shakespeare took Machiavelli much as Raleigh did. It is true that if Raleigh used Machiavelli to make a challenge, Shakespeare too may have done so, and more thoroughly. It may well be that his challenge to orthodox opinions on order in *Troilus and Cressida* became temporarily an opinion. But never again. In his most violent representations of chaos Shakespeare never tries to persuade that it is the norm: however long and violent is its sway, it is unnatural; and in the end order and the natural law will reassert themselves. With Bacon it is another story, with which this book need not be concerned.

The conclusion is that in trying to picture how the ordinary educated contemporary of Shakespeare looked on history in the gross we do not need to give much heed to Machiavelli. His day had not yet come.

2. THE MEDIEVAL NORM

But if to heed the true doctrines of Machiavelli is to anticipate the future, we must not fall into the other error of neglecting the past. Although a new conception of history began with the Tudors and was sedulously fostered by them, it was usually compounded with older ideas.

The Tudor innovation was to see a portion of English history in a certain pattern, a pattern highly convenient to themselves. And the innovation consisted not in the fact of a pattern but in adding a new pattern to the old. In the Middle Ages a pattern was not lacking but it was single: the theological; the drama of the revolt of the angels, the creation and fall of man, the incarnation, the redemption of man, and the Last Judgment. Indispensable parts of history outside this scheme, when they were taken seriously, had somehow to be brought within it. For instance, the members of the Greek and Roman Pantheon had such excellent credentials and had interfered so repeatedly and effectively in human history that they could not simply be dismissed as fictions. Instead, they were attached to the theological scheme by the discovery that they were the old crew of Satan under a new disguise. But though in its serious mood medieval orthodoxy referred the events of history to a theological scheme, it tolerated a great mass of quite unrelated events, where the sequence of cause and effect was just not required. Aquinas laid it down that play was necessary to the human spirit; and "honest mirth" was encouraged. Just so the mere happenings of history might legitimately be recorded with no further object than to satisfy man's natural curiosity and his delight in a good story. History could also be justified on grounds more serious yet short of the fully theological. It could preserve the memory of worthy deeds and provide a store of moral examples.

Higden, the monk of Chester active in the first half of the fourteenth century, can illustrate many of the qualities of the late medieval chronicler of English history. His *Polychronicon* deals with history from the creation to Edward III, becoming more and more confined to English history as he approaches his own day. Higden is modest in his pretensions. He treats history as a pure memorial. He disclaims all originality, calling himself a mere compiler from others; and he makes no effort to give a shape to history. His first book is mainly geographical and describes the *mappa mundi* on the traditional lines familiar to many from the pages of Mandeville and the medieval map in Hereford Cathedral. He ends on England and shows an absence of patriotic feeling that would have sounded as queer to an Elizabethan as to a modern. He considers the national faults of the English coolly and sets them down with an almost brutal candour. In his second book Higden leaves the physical world for the little world of man. He begins with an elaborate account of the correspondence between the macrocosm and the microcosm (part of which I quoted in my first chapter). In speaking of the creation he becomes theological and gives a fine account of the pre- and post-lapsarian states. Then, coming to the multiplicities of earthly events, he grows excessively disjointed and anecdotal. He is deeply interested in Noah's ark and gives a picture of it and of its internal arrangements, lavatory included. When he comes to Britain, he repeats the legends of the Trojans in Britain popularised by Geoffrey of Monmouth. Virgil, when mentioned, is a magician in the medieval manner. Not that Higden was entirely uncritical. He discounts much Arthur lore and writes in high praise of Alfred the Great. But he shuns the difficult task of relating the events of history to the great theological drama. This, however, is utterly different from that drama's being absent. It is there, solidly enough, in the background and *could* be applied, if required, at any moment. However much was added to history in the interval, the qualities of *Polychronicon* persisted right up to the time of Shakespeare.

No more need be said about the medieval chroniclers as such. The next concern is with any signs of innovation that appear in the Middle Ages and with the actual changes brought in under the early Tudors.

3. FROISSART AND TITO LIVIO

If we may include Froissart among the English chroniclers, then something was added during the fourteenth century. To Froissart's original French the English writers owed very little, but as translated by Lord Berners in the reign of Henry VIII Froissart became one of the recognised authorities for the reigns of Edward III and Richard II. In tone Froissart is medieval.

He aims at recording the deeds of chivalry so that they may be remembered, serve as examples, and give pastime and pleasure. He is also pious, saying in his preface:

> But, or I begin, I require the Saviour of all the world, who of nothing created all things, that he will give me such grace and understanding that I may continue and persever in such wise that whoso this process readeth or heareth may take pastance pleasure and example.

What Froissart adds to history is what Chaucer adds to poetry, an unsleeping psychological curiosity. Not only does he live through the happenings he describes, thus raising the bare story to a high degree of vividness, but he is deeply concerned with the mental springs of action. Not that he always draws definite conclusions but he has the art of keeping all the actors in the picture, so that we have the option of allowing an act to work with all sorts of ramifications on the minds of those it can affect. For instance, near the very beginning he describes how Isabel, wife of Edward II, leaves England with her son, later Edward III, to take refuge with the French king, her father. At first the king supports her but later, influenced by his advisers whom Edward's agents have corrupted, he turns against her, and she flies for help to John of Hainault. Froissart says nothing of the effect of all this on the prince then aged fifteen, yet by the way he tells his story he makes us feel that the prince is there and allows us to conjecture the kind of effect the experiences must have had on him. How far, we ask ourselves, were the French wars of Edward III wars of personal revenge? In other words Froissart is a dramatist, interested not only in action but in the springs of action. In his later work he allows his characters longer speeches and discusses motives more openly. He says for instance that Bolingbroke would have been faithful, if Richard II had recalled him from exile and allowed him his title and lands at the death of John of Gaunt his father. But if Froissart is a dramatist of genius he exercises his genius on the medieval material without at all anticipating the more philosophical and moralised way of looking at history that came in with the Tudors. He records for instance how Edward III consented to having his uncle, the Earl of Kent, put to death; but he does not suggest that this crime had to be visited on the next generation. He is so near to what he describes and so absorbed in it that he has no desire to do more than exploit the immediate happening to its uttermost. And to have done that was achievement enough for one man. How this dramatic strain was continued in the chronicles will be seen later.

In the reign of Henry VI an Italian, Titus Livius de Frulovisiis or Tito Livio da Forli, came to England to seek the patronage of Humphrey Duke of Gloucester, at whose suggestion he wrote what can be called the official biography of Henry V. An anonymous writer translated this biography from the Latin with some additions from other sources and some of his own comments, in 1513; and this translation has been edited by C. L. Kingsford under the title of *The First English Life of Henry V.* Tito Livio's method of narrating events is pretty much that of the medieval chronicler. His innovation is to isolate, in a frame as it were, a single king from the ceaseless flux of events as normally recorded. Kingsford thinks that the traditional view of Henry V as hero-king has its origin in Tito Livio. This is doubtful. Tito Livio indeed praises Henry for his piety and courage, but the full copy-book picture of the hero-king was a later creation. Still, Tito Livio added something to the formula of Higden.

4. MEDIEVAL ANTICIPATIONS

It can be said that the status of literature in men's lives varied inversely with that of the Church. While the hold of the Church was very strong, the moral value of literature counted for less than the amusement value. But when the hold of the Church relaxed, something of the lost awe was transferred to letters; and the doctrine of didacticism, always present, now became overpoweringly strong. In the long medieval narrative, didacticism is mainly illustrative. The narrator tells his story for what it is worth, and then, if he likes, he illustrates a specific act by a general moral. Take, for instance, this episode in Barbour's *Bruce.* When Bruce was in great straits, his hostess on Arran prophesied a happy issue. Bruce was encouraged without quite believing her; whereupon Barbour inserts a short sermon on the right and wrong use of prognostication. Similarly the medieval rhetorician was expected to have a repertory of *exempla*, anecdotes or fables, ready to illustrate or to point a moral. Chaucer's *Monk's Tale* is a series of such *exempla*, which really had no business to be huddled together apart from the morals they should have served to illustrate. But in the late Middle Ages the *exemplum* was given a new status, being elevated from an illustration to an autonomous piece of didacticism. The protagonist of the moral story becomes less a man doing things than one who in doing them embodies certain virtues and vices in such a way that he stands as a great example, a figure of solemn didacticism. This new didactic solemnity can be seen most clearly in Boccaccio's *De Casibus Virorum Illustrium.* There was also a difference in the audience to which the two kinds of didacticism were addressed. In the earlier Middle Ages the audience was not so specialised; a change came when Church control began to weaken and when with the rise of nationalism the actual character of the princely ruler became more crucial than before to the welfare of a country. Then, more and more, the great didactic examples of virtue and vice were directed to educating the growing prince or swaying the policy of the actual ruler. This notion of the great example continued strong till well after the age of Elizabeth. The main means of its dissemination in England was Lydgate's translation of Boccaccio's *De Casibus.*

This general literary trend hardly had its counterpart in strictly historical writing till the sixteenth century but it is reflected in at least one chronicler; and his reference is so typical and so anticipates the future that it calls for mention.

Hardyng was a man of affairs employed by Henry IV and Henry V. He fought at Agincourt, but in the next reign ended by becoming a Yorkist. He wrote a verse chronicle extending from the Trojans in Britain till just after the accession of Edward IV. On the whole he is informative merely and medieval, but when he speaks of the divisions of Britain at the time of Cadwallader, he shows the influence of the new didacticism. Addressing himself to the Duke of York, father of Edward IV, he acknowledges his claims to the throne but talks of the evils of internal division with clear didactic reference to the present. Henry I grew strong because France was divided internally; Carthage and Rome fell for the same thing in themselves:

> Wherefore, good lord, think on this lesson now
> And teach it to my lord of March, your heir,
> While he is young; it may be for his prow
> To think on it, when that the weather waxeth fair

And his people unto him doth repair
And little hath them to relieve and pease:
Then may it hap with it his people ease.

While he is young, in wisdom him endow,
Which is full hard to get without labour;
Which labour may not be with ease now,
For of labour came king and emperor.
Let him not idle shall be your successor,
For honour and ease together may not been:
Wherefore writhe now the wand while it is green.

Behold Boccace what princes have through pride
Been casten down from all their dignity.

There is the doctrine: history not the record of events or the
mere homage to a man's worthy deeds, but a repertory of
solemn lessons useful above all as a practical guide for the
princes of to-day, with Boccaccio cited as the main authority.

5. THE TUDOR MYTH

With the accession of Henry VII the practice of historical
writing becomes more complicated, for not only did the
methods of history follow their natural growth, but the Tudors,
to suit their ends, encouraged their people to look on the events
that led to their accession, in a special way. This special view
was of the greatest importance to Elizabethan literature, and I
shall speak of it before noting the more general contributions to
historical writing made by More and Polydore Vergil.
Not too happy about his title to the crown, Henry VII
fostered two historical notions that became great national
themes. The first was that the union of the two houses of York
and Lancaster through his marriage with the York heiress was
the providential and happy ending of an organic piece of
history. The second was that through his Welsh ancestry he
had a claim to the British throne unconnected either with his
Lancastrian descent or his Yorkist marriage. Not only did he
claim through his ancestor Owen Tudor, husband of Henry V's
widow, direct descent from Cadwallader, last of the British
kings, but he encouraged the old Welsh superstition that Arthur
was not dead but would return again, with the suggestion that

he and his heirs were Arthur reincarnate. The first notion is so obviously crucial to an understanding of Shakespeare's Histories and will come up so often in the course of this book that I do not wish to spend time on it here. With the second notion Shakespeare was less directly concerned, though he must always have had it at the back of his mind. So I shall have less to say about it later on. For that reason and because readers may allow its fantasy to minimise its importance in their minds, I shall say a little about it now. Had Henry VII's claim to be *Arthurus redivivus* been confined to himself as a temporary and perhaps a rather desperate expedient to strengthen his claim to the throne, it might merit little heed. But it showed the most astonishing persistence and had a strong hold on the imaginations of men. Henry sought to extend the fiction by naming his eldest son Arthur; but the unfortunate death of this prince did not prevent the other Tudors making the Arthurian claim. In the ancient legends the return of Arthur was to bring back the age of gold; and the age of Elizabeth was sedulously called golden not in mere unrelated praise but to imply that the golden age of prophecy had indeed come in. Nor did the house of Stuart upset the myth. On the contrary it brought with it an additional claim; for James was furnished with Arthurian credentials not only through his Tudor ancestors but through his ancestor Fleance, son of Banquo, who married the daughter of Griffith Llewelin, himself a descendant of Arthur and last of the Welsh kings. How the idea of Arthur reincarnate stirred men's imaginations a single passage of Spenser will illustrate well enough. The third canto of the third book of *The Fairy Queen* is one of those historical sections that meant so much more to Spenser and his contemporaries than they mean to us. It contains Merlin's prophecy to Britomart concerning the British kings that were to spring from the union of herself and Artegal, in other words Spenser's version of British history from after the time of Arthur to the present. This history is presented entirely from the British as against the Saxon side. The Saxons are lawless invaders whom God has allowed to prevail for a time to punish the Britons for their sins:

> Ne shall the Saxons selves all peaceably
> Enjoy the crown, which they from Britons won
> First ill, and after ruled wickedly.

Then Merlin refers briefly to the Danish and Norman invasions, and, missing out the entire history of the Plantagenets, prophesies the restoration of the British lineage to the crown through the Tudor dynasty:

> Tho, when the term is full accomplished,
> There shall a spark of fire, which hath long while
> Been in his ashes raked up and hid,
> Be freshly kindled in the fruitful isle
> Of Mona, where it lurked in exile;
> Which shall break forth into bright burning flame
> And reach into the house that bears the style
> Of royal majesty and sovereign name.
> So shall the Briton blood their crown again reclaim.
>
> Thenceforth eternal union shall be made
> Between the nations different afore,
> And sacred peace shall lovingly persuade
> The warlike minds to learn her goodly lore
> And civil arms to exercise no more.
> Then shall a Royal Virgin reign, which shall
> Stretch her white rod over the Belgic shore
> And the great Castle smite so sore withal
> That it shall make him shake and shortly learn to fall.

In other words the House of Tudor is the blossoming of the seeds of British royalism that had been lying dormant in the remotenesses of Mona or Anglesea for many centuries and at the same time the means of reconciling the agelong feud between Briton and Saxon. And the crowning Tudor achievement is Elizabeth, who shall humble the pride of Castile. It will be noticed that there is no *direct* reference to the Tudors being the reincarnation of Arthur. And for a very good reason, namely that this is itself one of the main themes of the total poem. Prince Arthur's successful quest for Gloriana, which would have been the master-theme of the completed poem, has for one of its meanings the reincarnation of Arthur in Elizabeth. Spenser indeed makes the most extravagant claims for Elizabeth. Ignoring the Tudor union of York and Lancaster as a mere episode in the great sweep of British history, Spenser pictures the golden age of Elizabeth as the providential consummation of a vast process that had its beginning in the remote and fabulous past when the Trojans landed in Britain and subdued its giant-brood. It is in pictures of this kind that the close relation between history and the world-order as described in my first chapter can be seen. The age of Elizabeth is golden, corresponding to the dawning of the Great Year when all the heavenly bodies have returned to their rightful positions in the firmament. Spenser's imagining will also serve to prove that Davies's picture of Elizabeth and her court duplicating in their dance the dance of the universe is more than a mere fancy.

So much just now for the two special notions of history encouraged by the Tudors. I return to the normal growth in the practice of historical writing under Henry VII and Henry VIII.

6. POLYDORE VERGIL

In 1501 an Italian scholar, Polydorus Vergilius of Urbino, came to England as sub-collector of Peter's Pence for Pope Alexander the Sixth. Polydore was the friend of Erasmus and had a reputation as author of a work on the inventors of arts and culture. He had a recommendation to Henry VII, possessed influential friends, and came to enjoy various ecclesiastical offices in England, where he spent most of his life. Some six years after his arrival in England Henry VII asked him to write a complete English history. By 1517 he reported his history nearly finished; but it was not printed till 1534, and not till 1555 did he bring it to its conclusion with the events of 1538. Polydore's history was very popular and it was early translated into English as far as the death of Richard III. Of this translation the bulk is still in manuscript, but the first eight books dealing with British history from the fabulous beginning to the Norman Conquest and the twenty-third to twenty-fifth books dealing with the period from Henry VI to Richard III were published by the Camden Society. Polydore Vergil is an innovator among English chroniclers because he writes in conscious competition with the classical historians and because he has the critical spirit. His descriptions of character and the reported speeches emulate the vividness and conciseness of Livy and Tacitus. More important for its effect on the Elizabethan drama is his writing up of Henry V after the manner of Tacitus's *Agricola* but in full accord with the contemporary vogue of the "example." Relaxing for the moment his usual critical coolness, Polydore gives a heightened and to a modern a very unpleasant and unconvincing picture of a paragon of courage and piety. He opens his account of Henry's reign by saying that Henry is almost alone among princes in recognising that a king should be such in spirit wisdom seriousness vigilance and good faith, that he should look on his kingdom as a burden rather than as an honour, and that good counsellors are needed to help him bear it. And he goes on to general moralising about the effect of a prince's example in his own land:

> As Cicero says, it is not so great an evil that a prince should go astray, though that is indeed a big evil in itself, as that he corrupts others and brings it about that as his own life is changed so are the morals of his people.

A prince acquires honour only in so far as he oversees the morals of his people and keeps free from the vices of the mob. Any prince who has not learnt this lesson is not grown up, even if he is a man in years; he does not rule but is ruled. Richard II was an adolescent of this kind. He was not naturally vicious but he was incapable of taking good advice and in the end was ruined by bad counsellors. Edward II was the same, and both suffered miserable deaths. Very likely Henry learnt from their example, when he realised that he must beware of his hangers-on and that he must choose men of the highest capacity, from whom to learn the art of government. Polydore makes Henry piously proclaim, before invading France, his God-justified right to the French throne. On his campaigns Henry punishes with death any sacrilege attempted by his troops. There can be no doubt which side will win, for, while the French had broken promises, Henry had founded monasteries. It is Polydore who first made Henry oratorical before Agincourt, and it is interesting that his Henry says much the same as Shakespeare's. In sum, Polydore in dealing with Henry V ceases to be a critical historian and becomes a classicising cleric, who feels it his duty to write up a human being into a cheap royal pattern of all the virtues. Why he should have done this I do not know. It may be that Tito Livio's mild portrait of Henry V had been harshly stereotyped in the interval, and Polydore could not but acquiesce in what had become a national myth. Quite as likely the combined traditions of medieval hagiography and of the moral biography of the ancients—Plutarch and Tacitus—tempted Polydore to a venture that was quite out of keeping with his normal sobriety.

C

Polydore's critical spirit shows itself in three things : a sincere attempt to state the truth impartially, a reasonable and kindly judgement of men's motives, and a desire to understand the causes of events.

On the first of these I can be brief, as it concerns the historian more than the literary critic. In the nineteenth book, describing the truce between Edward III and the French in 1366, Polydore says that he will tell the truth although French and English historians quarrel over it much as their armies fought in battle. The rights and wrongs as between Richard II and Henry IV he discusses with the most sympathetic impartiality. He recognises Richard's two great crimes in doing away with his uncle, the Duke of Gloucester, and in confiscating the Lancastrian property. He also recognises that Henry IV acted moderately in the circumstances and refuses to believe that he could have been personally responsible for putting Richard to a cruel death. Yet he is emphatic that Richard was not naturally vicious, and though he praises Henry's character, never lets us forget that he was a usurper and that he was a criminal in letting Richard die. Polydore was a kindly but quite unsentimental Latin, who knew the mixed motives of human nature but judged them tolerantly. He can therefore hold the balance between the two kings deftly and without muddle. This balance became traditional in later men's treatment not only of Richard II and Henry IV but of Edward II and those who deposed him. But it did not suit the more violent and romantic taste of the Anglo-Saxon and lost the clear delicacy with which Polydore maintained it.

The last sentences have encroached on the second quality of Polydore's critical spirit, his reasonable and kindly judgment of men's motives. But it is remarkable enough to deserve further illustration. He has, for instance, a comment on the guilelessness and innocence of ordinary people. Edward IV, returning from abroad after the restitution of Henry VI, found that men were generally against him. He then gave it out that he did not want the crown but only his dukedom of York. On the effect of this pretence Polydore writes :

And it is incredible to be spoken how great effect that feigned matter was of, such is the force of righteousness generally among all men ; for when they heard that King Edward minded nothing less than to require the Kingdom and sought simply for his inheritance they began to be moved either for pity to favour him or at the least not to hinder him at all from the attaining of that dukedom.

Most interesting of all is Polydore's comment on Anglo-French dissension after the final loss of France under Henry VI. Polydore blames above all the unyielding nationalism of the French, which refused to accept the English as their kin.

There were [in France] even from the beginning who would say that one consideration was to be had of citizens another of the residue, and thereby concluded that none was to be had of strangers. Whereby it came to pass that the common society of mankind was broken and a certain natural hatred mutually bred of itself in both peoples. This venom therefore hath already a good while since infected much people, so as that (to be silent of others) it cannot be brought to pass by any mean that a Frenchman born will much love an Englishman or contrary that an English will love a Frenchman. Such is the hatred that hath sprung of contention for honour and empire; and that hath been these many years increased by mutual bloodshed and slaughter. Wherefore this was the very cause of the utter ruin that came to the English affairs beyond the seas.

This passage is relevant to Elizabethan drama and hence to this book only because of its contrariety, for such tolerance is remote from the perfervid patriotism of the later age. But the picture of this internationally minded Italian regretting the rise of the new national spirit is too interesting to omit.

But of the three manifestations of Polydore's critical spirit his desire to understand the causes of events is by far the most important for its effect on the drama; for, by being the first chronicler of English history to be seriously concerned with cause and effect, he made that history the potential material not only for the bare recording of events in dramatic form but for the authentic human drama where the bare event is subordinated to the event's significance. I am not concerned with any historical question of Polydore's sources or the measure of his originality. What does matter in this context is that, whether or not the writers of Elizabethan History Plays read him, they did read chroniclers who were ultimately indebted to Polydore for a way of writing history that gave a new kind of help to the historical play. The above does not mean that

Polydore referred every word he wrote to some great logical scheme of human events, that he anticipated Gibbon's unrelaxing hold on his single great theme. Polydore's history is a sane, concise, and reasonable account of the events of British history, punctuated by sensible reflections on the way things happen and containing in its later parts the dim outlines of a pattern in whose form the historical events leading up to the Tudor monarchy are presented. As this pattern was ultimately inherited by Shakespeare it is of the first importance to the plan of this book.

As an example of Polydore's occasional reflections on the way things happen, take the opening of his sixth book. Here he enunciates an evolutionary idea of history and explains how it fits the case of Britain. States, like men, have their youth manhood and decay, but unlike men they are not confined to a single life. England was in its old age in the eleventh century, but the Norman conquest renewed its youth and began the old rhythm once more. Again, in the preface to book four he hints at the doctrine, so widespread in the Renaissance, of history specifically repeating itself. He considers the age of the Saxon princelings with its civil wars as a providential prelude to union under monarchy. There is little doubt from his tone that he is thinking also of the Wars of the Roses and the extinction of the feud under Henry VII. Polydore is also careful to mark specific cases of cause and effect. For instance in book twenty he gives a vivid account of Richard II's kidnapping his uncle the Duke of Gloucester and then notes that it was because of this crime that the Dukes of York and Lancaster withdrew their support from Richard, which withdrawal was the chief cause of Richard's overthrow.

The specific pattern in which Polydore sees English history concerns the period from Richard II to Henry VII. That stretch is seen in a solemn moral light; it shows the justice of God punishing and working out the effects of a crime, till prosperity is re-established in the Tudor monarchy. How far this pattern was Polydore's idea, how far it was inspired officially by Henry VII, I do not know. This is a matter for the historian; the mere fact of Polydore's giving sanction and literary currency to the idea is what here concerns us. Not that Polydore is nearly so emphatic as Hall was to be later. The full consequences of Henry IV's usurpation are not suggested at the time but they are stated retrospectively. The crucial passage occurs in the twenty-fourth book after the issue of the Wars of the Roses had been finally decided by the Battle of Tewkesbury. Polydore there comments on the amazing luck of Edward IV. But he checks himself and ascribes Edward's success not to his personal good fortune but to God's punishment of the Lancastrian crime:

> Yet it may be peradventure that this came to pass by reason of the infortunacy of the house of Lancaster, which wise men thought even then was to be ascribed to the righteousness of God; because the sovereignty extorted forcibly by Henry IV, grandfather to King Henry VI, could not be long enjoyed of that family. And so the grandfather's offence redounded unto the grandson's.

Other misfortunes are referred to their appropriate crimes. The princes may have been murdered in the Tower because of the false oath their father Edward IV took before the gates of York, to confine his claims to his dukedom and not to attempt the kingdom again. When Margaret of Anjou laments her misfortunes after the Battle of Barnet, Polydore says she might have remembered that all her sorrows originated in her obtaining the death of the regent, Humphrey Duke of Gloucester. And he adds,

> Would to God many would well weigh the causes of such events, who measure equity and right according to their power and will.

Henry V had Richard II reburied to expiate the ancestral curse caused by his death. When Henry V discovered at Southampton on the eve of sailing to France the plot of Richard Earl of Cambridge against him, he did not realise its full import. The conspirators pretended that they had been corrupted by the King of France to screen what was really a Yorkist plot. Polydore comments:

> But if Henry had set his eye on this fire which was burning even now, he might have seen a terrible torch kindled from it threatening the walls of his own house; and perhaps he would have quenched it on the instant.

Alongside the ancestral curse of the house of Lancaster is set the hope in the line of Tudor. Owen Tudor, who married the widow of Henry V, is called "a gentleman of Wales, adorned with wonderful gifts of body and mind, who derived his pedigree from Cadwallader, the last king of Britons." Henry VI, restored to his throne, on seeing the future Henry VII then aged nine, is made to say "This truly, this is he unto whom both we and our adversaries must yield and give over our dominion." Finally Henry VII's exile in Brittany as Earl of Richmond and the various hazards he there experienced are told very fully and with an emphasis that suggests throughout the guidance of God. The Tudor myth is in fact there in outline, although it could be stated with much stronger emphasis.

Polydore writes as a moralist but he is not particularly dramatic. Earlier I referred to Polydore's vivid account of how Richard II kidnapped his uncle, the Duke of Gloucester. It is indeed vivid, but put it by the side of Froissart's superb rendering of the same event (from which it is certainly derived), and it is clear that Polydore's dramatic sense was but mediocre. But that does not matter, for he supplied the stuff which others, more gifted dramatically, were to put to finer use.

7. SIR THOMAS MORE

In the year 1513, while Polydore was writing his English history, Sir Thomas More, then one of the undersheriffs of London, wrote his unfinished history of Richard III. This work, like parts of the *Book of Kings* and of Thucydides, is one of those pieces of history that transcend the noting of events and the sorting of evidence and abide as classic records of fundamental human nature. As More's history begins long past where Froissart left off, there can be no internal evidence of More's having read Froissart. And there is no external evidence. There is however external probability. Polydore Vergil comes within the More circle through his friendship with Erasmus; he read Froissart and used him for his history; and it is probable that Froissart in the original was known to his friends. Anyhow More imports into English chronicling Froissart's sense of drama and closeness to the actual event. The episode of Edward IV's widow, in sanctuary at Westminster, being persuaded by the Archbishop to give up her younger son to the care of his uncle, the Protector, is more tragic than anything the English drama produced till the great age. And on the comic side the episode of Dr. Shaw's sermon goes right outside Froissart's range. Dr. Shaw was put up to preach a sermon in which he was to accuse Edward IV's children of bastardy and to contrast with it the patent resemblance of the Protector Richard to the duke his father. And as he said the words, "This is the father's own figure, this is his own countenance, the very print of his visage, the sure undoubted image, the express likeness of the noble duke," Richard was to have appeared in the congregation, "as though the Holy Ghost had put the words in the preacher's mouth and should have moved the people even there to cry King Richard, King Richard, that it might have been after said that he was specially chosen by God and in manner by miracle." But the timing went wrong; the words were spoken before Richard appeared: and when he did, the preacher hurriedly repeated them quite out of their context and with a ludicrous effect. After the service "the preacher gat him home and never after durst look out for shame but kept him out of sight like an owl."

As well as being dramatic like Froissart, More judged kindly of human nature like Polydore. Excusing himself for introducing so slight a person as Jane Shore in his work on the plea that she illustrates instructively the fall from weal to woe, he outlines her history and character with the most delicate sympathy.

But More differs from Froissart by adding a measure of classical formality to Froissart's informal realism. It is indeed just this blend—like the blend of medieval and Petrarchian in Wyatt's lyrics—that gives More's history its distinction. More's opening of Edward IV on his deathbed has the immemorial touch of a fairy story, but the elaborate dying oration he puts into his mouth is in the full style of classical rhetoric. And the blend is complete and convincing.

More, like Polydore, accepts and makes evident the contemporary moral of history: that solemn insistence on the great example which Hardyng introduced into chronicle writing. But he does not obtrude it or let it interfere with his primary interest in the human drama. It is not till Hall that this morality receives its first full expression.

The effect of More's history was very great and largely incalculable. Through being incorporated in later chronicles it escaped the anti-Catholic feeling that might have prejudiced its popularity if it had been lumped with the rest of his work. I should guess that it not only set the pattern of Shakespeare's *Richard III* but was a direct incitement to him to write dramatically rather than anecdotally. Anyhow there it was, one of

the two pieces of original English historical writing apt actively
to incite an Elizabethan dramatist to get close to his matter and
to treat it primarily as human happenings and only secondarily
as a repertory of morals or a mere series of events. I said
original English historical writing, because there was also
Berners's translation of Froissart to help towards the same
thing.

The piece of original historical writing thus to be coupled
with More's *Richard III* is Cavendish's *Life of Cardinal Wolsey*,
written under Queen Mary but not printed till 1641. Shakespeare had probably read it in manuscript before he wrote
Henry VIII; but we cannot tell how long before, or whether it
helped him to form his early notions of history or his early
practice of writing History Plays. It is in some ways more
vivid than More's *Richard III*, for Cavendish was Wolsey's most
trusted servant and witnessed almost all he describes. But as
its service to Shakespeare is so uncertain, it cannot get more
than this brief mention in this place.

8. HALL

I must preface my remarks on Hall, whom I shall make out
to be very important, with an apology to the general reader.
Hall's complete works are difficult to get and when got so heavy
and so hard to manipulate that they do not make reading easy.
Apart from the originals there is only one complete edition,
that of 1809, and it is a bulky and forbidding volume. There
is an edition of the reign of Henry VIII limited to 350 copies.
So the general reader is ill provided for and may well complain:
why do you try to interest me in a man whose writings are out
of my reach? To this there is no good answer. However, it
would be easy to reprint Hall's *Chronicle* from the opening to
the end of the reign of Henry V. This part is not a large proportion of the whole but it covers all the material for Shakespeare's most interesting History Plays, and includes the essential prefatory matter telling us Hall's intentions. Moreover
his account of Richard III is mainly a reprint of More's
history, which is easily accessible. The portion mentioned
would really suffice for the general reader, and it would not
make a long book.

Edward Hall came of good family. His great-grandfather

had been personal adviser to the Duke of York (father of Edward IV) and appointed by him captain of Caen, which may be the reason why in his chronicle Hall softens Polydore's picture of the Duke. He was educated at Eton and King's College Cambridge. He studied law and became a judge and a member of Parliament. His active career is entirely within the reign of Henry VIII, except that he just survived into Edward VI's, to whom he dedicated his history. He was lucky not to live on into the reign of Mary, for his uncompromising Protestantism and his unshaken support of Henry VIII in all his acts would have brought him persecution. As it was, his book was burnt. Anyhow he lived under Henry VIII and was the true spiritual child of that age. Intellectually and emotionally he believed in Protestantism and the new autocracy of the Tudors. He delighted in Henry's taste for show as well as in his new position as head of the English church. But he was much more than the supporter of Henry VIII and the recorder of his progresses and tournaments; and it is a pity that the incomplete notion had its life prolonged by Charles Whibley and the authority of the *Cambridge History of English Literature*. Hall's *Chronicle* deals with English history from Henry IV to Henry VIII; and the reign of Henry VIII is nearly half the whole book. Whibley thinks the first half a mere compilation and the last half, when Hall was writing about his own day, the real vivid stuff. He also thinks that the first half deserves the charge made by Ascham against the book of being written in "indenture English," while the last half escapes it. By "indenture English" Ascham meant that habit of using synonyms and equivalent phrases practised in legal documents and raised to beauty in the Prayer Book. Hall certainly used it freely, and here is an extreme example (showing incidentally the ancestry of Euphuism):

> As fire being enclosed in a strait place will by force utter his flame and as the course of water astricted and letted will flow and burst out in continuance of time; so that cankered crocodile and subtle serpent could not long lurk in malicious hearts nor venomous stomachs, but in conclusion she must according to her nature appear and show herself.

But though "indenture English" occurs freely in the first half it is by no means absent from the second. And when it does occur it often serves an end by ennobling the rhythm, or as in

this quotation marking an emphasis. The "cankered croco-
dile" is sedition, and Hall here, at a very emphatic place in his
chronicle and at the beginning of a new chapter, wants to tell
the reader how terrible and ineradicable a thing sedition is.
His "indenture English" has a high moral purpose. Nor is it
true that Hall's vitality is confined to the later part. Actually
it is spread throughout. Even in the matter of pageantry the
descriptions of the preparations for the tournament between
Bolingbroke and Mowbray or of Henry VI's coronation in
Paris are as brilliant as any of the more famous descriptions
from the reign of Henry VIII. But to call, as Whibley does,
the first half of Hall's history a piece of medieval chronicling is
a very gross error and one that needs showing up because it is
all of a piece with the traditional reluctance to perceive how
much was owed to Hall by Shakespeare. Several people, beginning with C. L. Kingsford, have shown up the error, but I
doubt if Hall's great importance not only as an influence on
Shakespeare but as a shaper of Tudor historical thought, not to
speak of his considerable literary merit, has ever been recognised as it should.

Hall's chief importance is that he is the first English chronicle-
writer to show in all its completeness that new moralising of
history which came in with the waning of the Middle Ages, the
weakening of the Church, and the rise of nationalism. And the
special literary importance of this feat is to have introduced a
sense of drama into his manner of expression. I do not mean
the sense of drama in the actual event, the special gift of
Froissart and of More (though Hall has his share of it) but the
sense of the moral concatenation of great events: moral as
against psychological drama. It was this moral drama in Hall
that inspired the authors of the *Mirror for Magistrates*; and to
the influence of the *Mirror* on the literature of the great Elizabethan age it is difficult to set a term. Hall's other great
importance is that he developed and settled the Tudor historical myth; for if he moralises history he does so through the
particular organic stretch of it that issues into the "Triumphant
Reign of Henry VIII." This second importance is thus so
closely joined with the first that I shall deal with both together.

Hall made his intentions clear from the start. His title-page
to the earliest surviving edition (1548) calls his work not a
chronicle of English history from Henry IV to Henry VIII but
The Union of the two noble and illustre Families of Lancaster and

York, thus claiming unity for his subject as clearly as Gibbon for his. But the whole title-page needs quoting:

> The union of the two noble and illustre families of Lancaster and York, being long in continual dissension for the crown of this noble realm, with all the acts done in both the times of the princes, both of the one lineage and of the other, beginning at the time of King Henry the Fourth, the first author of this division, and so successively proceeding to the reign of the high and prudent prince King Henry the Eighth, the indubitable flower and very heir of the said lineages.

It is then the marriage of Henry VII with Elizabeth daughter of Edward IV that is the unifying event of this stretch of history, "for," as Hall says in his preface, "as King Henry the Fourth was the beginning and root of the great discord and division, so was the godly matrimony the final end of all dissensions titles and debates." How dramatically he conceived his subject appears from the very headings of his chapters. He calls his prologue an introduction into the division of the two houses of Lancaster and York; and the titles of the actual chapters are the following:

   i. The unquiet time of King Henry the Fourth.
  ii. The victorious acts of King Henry the Fifth.
 iii. The troublous season of King Henry the Sixth.
 iv. The prosperous reign of King Edward the Fourth.
  v. The pitiful life of King Edward the Fifth.
 vi. The tragical doings of King Richard the Third.
vii. The politic governance of King Henry the Seventh.
viii. The triumphant reign of King Henry the Eighth.

Hall knew and rejoiced that this list can provide more than one pattern. There were four successful and four unsuccessful kings in his list and they fall into a sort of stanza form. Call the unsuccessful *a* and the successful *b*, and you get the form *a b a b a a b b.* It was not for nothing too that the *victorious acts* of Henry V are matched by the *tragical doings* of Richard III. *Acts* or *doings* are confined to these two kings, whose history is presented in a quite exceptionally dramatic manner: Hall may even intend the word *acts* as well as *tragical* to have reference to the drama. I shall revert to this exceptional treatment later.

His preface done, Hall announces the great theme of his

work with all the pomp and circumstance he can command. It is the great theme of disorder (in this case civil war) and of union and "degree" ensuing on it.

> What mischief hath insurged in realms by intestine division, what depopulation hath ensued in countries by civil dissension, what detestable murder hath been committed in cities by separate factions, and what calamity hath ensued in famous regions by domestical discord and unnatural controversy, Rome hath felt, Italy can testify, France can bear witness, Bohemia can tell, Scotland may write, Denmark can show, and especially this noble realm of England can apparently declare and make demonstration. . . . What misery, what murder, and what execrable plagues this famous region hath suffered by the division and dissension of the renowmed houses of Lancaster and York my wit cannot comprehend, nor my tongue declare, neither yet my pen fully set forth.

But although other dissensions continue, this most terrible one has been healed for ever by the union of Henry VII and Elizabeth and by the issue of that union in Henry VIII. And Hall would have us see this event as symbol of an order greater than itself. This union was achieved, he writes,

> so that all men, more clearer than the sun, may apparently perceive that as by discord great things decay and fall to ruin, so the same by concord be revived and erected. In like wise also all regions which by division and dissension be vexed molested and troubled be by union and agreement relieved pacified and enriched.

Hall does not stop here but sees in his theme a correspondence with unions more sacred still:

> By union of the Godhead to the manhood man was joined to God, which before by the temptation of the subtle serpent was from him segregate and divided. By the union of the catholic church and the outworn synagogue not only the hard ceremonies and deadly pains of the Mosaical law were clearly abolished and made frustrate, but also Christian liberty is inferred and Christ's religion stabilised and erected. By the union of man and woman in the holy sacrament of matrimony the generation is blessed and the sin of the body clean extinct and put away. By the union of marriage, peace between realm and realm is exalted, and love

between country and country is nourished. By conjunction of matrimony malice is extinct, amity is embraced, and indissoluble alliance and consanguinity is procured. What profit, what comfort, what joy succeeded in the realm of England by the union of the fore-named two noble families you shall apparently perceive by the sequel of this rude and unlearned history.

There was no novelty in exalting the sacrament of marriage or of seeing other conjunctions as an analogy of it, but there was one in putting so solemn an emphasis on what was after all primarily a political event, on exalting not Marriage but the wedding of two clearly specified human beings, to such mystical heights. Polydore had indeed stated the Tudor myth but he was far from dramatising and hallowing it. Here in Hall we get the full transfer of historical drama from the sacred to the secular, while what is lost from sheer worship of God is used to make sterner the pious morality governing profane events. Many details apart, there is not a great deal of difference in the ways Hall regards Henry VIII and Shakespeare's contemporaries Elizabeth.

Having given his theme as union, Hall says that the preceding dissension must first be dealt with : that will be his beginning. Not that he implies with Machiavelli that dissension is the natural state of man. On the contrary, after the briefest reference to Henry III and his children for purely genealogical reasons he comes to Edward III and solemnly lists his seven sons. More than ourselves the people of Hall's day would think of seven as the lucky number; and it cannot be doubted that he meant us to think that the reign of Edward III was the norm of order from which the subsequent history of England was diverted. Certainly Shakespeare did not doubt it when he copied Hall in putting even stronger emphasis on the seven sons of Edward III. From this same detail can be seen how Hall differs from Polydore. An impartial historian rather than a dramatist, Polydore discusses whether Edward had seven sons or six and is content to leave it in doubt without seizing on the possibilities of the number seven. Having explained the genealogies of Lancaster and York, Hall begins actual history precisely where Shakespeare was to begin it when he wrote his major historical tetralogy, the quarrel of Bolingbroke and Mowbray and the estrangement of Bolingbroke from his cousin Richard II. From this episode the trouble began, and Hall is at pains to give the reason why one event led on to another right through to the Battle of Bosworth. And the cause of events is usually a crime and God's vengeance on it. Hall does not forget that in presence of the nobles who met him when he landed from Brittany in England Bolingbroke swore an oath that he would do no bodily harm to Richard II. And this oath, we are made to feel, redoubles the punishment Bolingbroke underwent for Richard's actual death, being later made one of the main motives of the Percies' rebellion. When disaster comes, Hall often moralises and implores other statesmen to beware by the example. Here is a typical passage about the Duke of Exeter, brother to Richard II, who raised a revolt against Henry IV to have his brother put on the throne again:

> When the Duke of Exeter heard that his complices were taken and his counsellors apprehended and his friends and allies put in execution, he lamented his own chance and bewept the misfortune of his friends but most of all bewailed the fatal end of his brother King Richard, whose death he saw as in a mirror by his unhappy sedition. And so, wandering lurking and hiding himself in privy places, was attached in Essex and in the lordship of Plashy, a town of the Duchess of Gloucester, and there made shorter by the head, and in that place especially because that he in the same lordship seduced and falsely betrayed Thomas Duke of Gloucester and was the very inward author and open dissimuler of his death and destruction. So the common proverb was verified: as you have done so shall you feel. Oh Lord, I would wish that this example of many highly promoted to rule might be had in memory, the which mete and measure their own iniquity and ill doings with force authority and power, to the intent that they by these examples should avert their minds from ill doings and such ungodly and execrable offences.

No wonder if the authors of the *Mirror for Magistrates* found Hall to their taste.

Some of Hall's moralisings and statements of cause and effect are borrowed from Polydore, but even so they are put with a heightened emphasis. Here is an instance of very close copying but with a rhetorical underlining. The passages refer to the death of the Earl of Salisbury at the siege of Orleans and to its being the turning-point of the whole war.

Polydore. Truly from that day forth the English foreign affairs began to quail; which infirmity though the English nation as a most sound and strong body did not feel at the first, yet afterward they suffered it as a pestilence and sickness inwardly by little and little decaying the strength: for immediately after his death the fortune of war altered.

Hall. What detriment, what damage, what loss succeeded to the English public wealth by the sudden death of this valiant captain not long after his departure manifestly appeared. For high prosperity and great glory of the English nation in the parts beyond the sea began shortly to fall and little by little to vanish away; which thing although the English people like a valiant and strong body at the first time did not perceive yet after that they felt it grow like a pestilent humour, which successively a little and little corrupteth all the members and destroyeth the body. For after the death of this noble man fortune of war began to change and triumphant victory began to be darkened.

This is Hall at his most inflated, yet if he adds no new fact or sentiment to Polydore, he does add melodrama. Often Hall inserts comments of his own. In describing the Battle of Towton, Hall is close to Polydore, but this comment on the battle is his own addition:

This conflict was in a manner unnatural, for in it the son fought against the father, the brother against the brother, the nephew against the uncle, and the tenant against the lord.

It was this addition, not in Holinshed, which may have suggested one of the finest scenes in Shakespeare's *Henry VI*.

But it is also by his larger additions and especially his speeches that Hall makes a different effect from Polydore and comes closest to the drama. An instance is the speech of the Duke of York when after the battle of Northampton he returned to England from Ireland and claimed the throne from Henry VI in the House of Lords. Polydore merely says he pronounced himself king, but Hall inserts a long oration in which past history is reviewed and the interest in the main theme thereby kept up. After the speech he writes:

When the duke had thus ended his oration, the lords sat still like images graven in the wall or dumb gods, neither whispering nor speaking, as though their mouths had been sewed up.

The sentence is as good as many others to show that Hall did

not always write "indenture English." When Hall comes to
the events leading to the Battle of Bosworth he follows Polydore
closely but in one place he greatly heightens the solemnity. It
is where the Duke of Buckingham confides to Morton, Bishop
of Ely, his plan of marrying Henry Earl of Richmond to Princess Elizabeth. Polydore recounts his story coolly; Hall gives
Buckingham a long speech in which he suggests the inspiration
of the Holy Ghost prompting his idea and talks eloquently on
true and false titles to the crown. Buckingham is highly
dramatic when he recounts how he goes back on his own claims
to be the heir of the House of Lancaster.

> But whether God so ordained or by fortune it so chanced, while
> I was in a maze either to conclude suddenly on this title and to set
> it open amongst the common people, see the chance: as I rode
> between Worcester and Bridgnorth I encountered with the Lady
> Margaret, Countess of Richmond, now wife to the Lord Stanley,
> which is the very daughter and sole heir to Lord John, Duke of
> Somerset, my grandfather's elder brother. Which was as clean
> out of my mind as though I had never seen her, so that she and her
> son the Earl of Richmond be both bulwark and portcullis be-
> tween me and the gate to enter into the majesty royal and getting
> of the crown. And when we had communed a little concerning
> her son and were departed, she to Our Lady of Worcester and I
> toward Shrewsbury, I then, now changed and in a manner
> amazed, began to dispute with myself. . . .

And the dispute, which is over the claims of monarchy by
election or by inheritance, is settled very emphatically on the
side of inheritance. Hall is writing with an eye on his own time
and his own king, "the very indubitate flower and very heir of
both the said lineages."

In talking thus about Hall's dramatic qualities I must not
imply that he succeeds in dramatising his whole history. He
could not do this with all the details of the French wars under
Henry VI and is forced to relapse for stretches into the mere
chronicler, though he does what he can to keep the main issue
before the reader. But two entire reigns he does dramatise in
an unusual way, so that they stick out from the whole structure:
the reigns of Henry V and Richard III. For Hall these two are
not so much historical personages as Good King and Bad King
respectively. His Henry V he takes from Polydore and vastly
improves. Polydore, a peace-loving internationally minded

Italian, makes his Henry V a faintly disgusting copybook hero;
Hall, a full-blooded English patriot, creates a not particularly
pleasant, equally dehumanised, but at least exaggeratedly vital
portrait. The finest of all Hall's additions is the debate between Henry's counsellors about what war he should undertake.
The Archbishop speaks on Henry's right to the French crown
and the Salic Law, Westmoreland opposes with a plea for war
against Scotland, Exeter speaks third in favour of France.
The three speeches are Hall's invention and are his highest
reach of eloquence. They have been rewarded by oblivion and
by partial assimilation into Shakespeare through the medium of
Holinshed.

To dramatise the reign of Richard III and to make it stick
out from the rest Hall took the easy but effective course of using
More's unfinished history with a few, unimportant interpola-
tions. He completes the reign with something of the elaboration he had spent on Henry V. More's style is of course more
direct than Hall's and, as said above, he is nearer to the event;
but the classicising rhetoric of his speeches makes him like
enough Hall for his fragment not to appear more exceptional
in its context than Hall himself had planned the reign of the
wicked Richard to be. And I say "planned" confidently,
because as a preface to Richard's reign Hall goes out of his way
to say that he "abhorrs to write" Richard's "miserable
tragedy" but that he will persist in his plan for the high moral
value that Richard's example has for princes. Hall's little
preface is a deliberate device to get Richard very specially into
the limelight.

From Polydore I quoted two passages to show the man's
sympathetic and anti-nationalist temper: the first commenting
on the trustfulness of the ordinary man, the second deploring
the strong nationalism of the French that refused to treat
citizens and others alike. Hall omits both. He has less delicacy
of feeling than Polydore and no great love for foreigners.

Hall's artistry has not had its due. In an age when coherence
was not demanded in a long work it was something of a triumph
to impose so powerful a pattern on his theme. And the pattern
was complex: the working out of a long chain of nemesis to its
happy expiation, varied by two astonishing moral examples,
teaching princes the one to pursue virtue the other to eschew
the punishment of vice. And, formally not unlike the last
movement of a symphony or the last act of *Prometheus Unbound*,

there follows the consummation of the process in the triumphant reign of Henry VIII. It is no wonder that the influence of
Hall was double: on history and on poetry. The second
influence must wait till the next chapter.

9. HOLINSHED

After the reign of Henry VIII writers of history had wide
choice of imitation. They could imitate the pedestrian chronicling of Fabyan, or the intimate and vivid humanity of More
and Berners's Froissart, or the moral drama of Hall. The first
method remained the rule; the second was practised by
Cavendish in his *Life of Wolsey*; the third method passed to the
poets, though the later chroniclers made great use of Hall's
material. The exception to this statement is Sir John Hayward,
whose *History of Henry IV* is in the true spirit of Hall and should
be associated with Shakespeare's Histories and Daniel's *Civil
Wars*. But as he is cousin and not in any way parent of Shakespeare he does not concern me now. The man who matters
here is Holinshed.

By "Holinshed" is usually meant the second edition of
Holinshed's *Chronicle* published in 1587, for this was the edition
Shakespeare used. I have called it "an omnibus volume," and
it does include much varied matter. In plan it rather resembles
Higden's *Polychronicon*, for as Higden begins with geography so
does Holinshed include as a preface Harrison's *Description of
Britain*. Higden begins with the Creation and Holinshed with
Noah. Both include the matter of Geoffrey of Monmouth and
both take English history down to their own day. Holinshed
includes the histories of Scotland and Ireland. The resemblance to Higden extends also to ability. Holinshed was
not greatly gifted (his contribution to the *Mirror for Magistrates* is quite the worst thing in that collection of tragic poems)
and he was not the man to turn his ablest predecessors to good
account. He is indeed a compiler, whose crime is to miss the
point of the more distinguished of his sources. Much of the
motivation of Polydore and Hall was borrowed by Holinshed
but only parrotwise and with little understanding. Holinshed
has not indeed the space to be as ample as Hall was in his restricted area of history, but his abbreviations and omissions are
unintelligent. He neither rewrites entirely nor has the tact to

discern and anthologise the essentials. He blurs the great
Tudor myth. Hall in describing the coronation of Henry VII
says that he "obtained and enjoyed" the kingdom

> as a thing by God elected and provided and by his especial favour
> and gracious aspect compassed and achieved. Insomuch that
> men commonly report that seven hundred and ninety-seven years
> past it was by a heavenly voice revealed to Cadwallader, last king
> of the Britons, that his stock and progeny should reign in this land
> and bear dominion again. Whereupon most men were persuaded
> in their own opinion that by this heavenly voice he was provided
> and ordained long before to enjoy and obtain this kingdom,
> which thing King Henry VI did also show before, as you have
> heard declared.

Holinshed omits this, although he had copied from Polydore
and Hall the myth of Henry VI's prognostication. He often
corrects Hall's "indenture English," but does not scruple to
follow up such corrections by repeating one of Hall's speeches
verbatim, thereby making it look silly in the simpler context.
How he misunderstands Hall can be seen from his comment on
the Duke of York's speech mentioned (p. 47) above:

> Master Edward Hall in his chronicle maketh mention of an ora-
> tion which the Duke of York uttered, sitting in the regal seat there
> in the chamber of the Peers, either at this his first coming in
> amongst them or else at some one time after, the which we have
> thought good to set down; though John Whethamsted, the Abbot
> of St. Albans, who lived in those days and by all likelihood was
> there present at the Parliament, maketh no further recital of any
> words which the duke should utter at that time.

It takes no very sharp eye to detect that the Duke of York's
speech is entirely fictitious and purely dramatic, but Holinshed
has not got beyond an uneasy feeling that perhaps it isn't all
genuine. Holinshed here copies Hall verbatim but sometimes
he summarises in indirect speech. The great debate before
Henry V's French expedition is thus treated and of course
ruined. On the other hand Holinshed was extremely useful to
his contemporaries. His style is simple, and his sense at once
understood on a quick reading. He was more ample and more
up to date than Polydore or Fabyan or Grafton, he covered far
more history than Hall. And through his usefulness he has
enjoyed a fame beyond his deserts.

To describe further the differences between Polydore or Hall and Holinshed would be tedious, but some actual instances will be less so. I have selected one or two events common to several chroniclers and quote their versions side by side. They will illustrate a number of points I have made in this chapter.

Here first are some accounts of the death of the Earl of Salisbury at the siege of Orleans and its consequences.

Caxton (1483). And this same year the good Earl of Salisbury laid siege unto Orleans, at the which siege he was slain with a gun that come out of the town: on whose soul God have mercy. Amen. For sith that he was slain, Englishmen never gat nor prevailed in France.

Fabyan (1516). But sorrow it is to tell and doleful to write, while one day the said good earl rested him at a bay-window and beheld the compass of the city and talked with his familiars, a gun was levelled out of the city from a place unknown, which brake the timber and stone of the window with such violence that the pieces thereof all to-quashed the face of the noble earl in such wise that he died within three days following, upon whose soul and all Christen Jesu have mercy. Amen. This, after divers writers, was *inicium malorum*, for after that mishap the Englishmen lost rather than wan, so that little and little they lost all their possession in France; and albeit that somewhat they gat after, yet for one that they wan they lost three.

Hall. In the tower that was taken at the bridge end there was a high chamber having a grate full of bars of iron, by the which a man might look all the length of the bridge into the city; at which grate many of the chief captains stood diverse times, viewing the city and devising in what place it was best assautable. They within the city perceived well this tooting hole and laid a piece of ordnance directly against the window. It so chanced that the Earl of Salisbury Sir Thomas Gargarve and William Glasdale and divers other went into the said tower and so into the high chamber and looked out at the grate. And within a short space the son of the master gunner perceived men looking out at the window, took his match, as his father taught him (which was gone down to dinner), and fired the gun, which brake and shivered the iron bars of the grate, whereof one struck the earl so strongly on the head that it struck away one of his eyes and the side of his cheek. The earl was conveyed to Meung upon Loire where he lay being wounded eight days, during which time he

received devoutly the holy sacraments and so commended his
soul to almighty God.

And there follows the comment on Salisbury's death quoted on
p. 47 above. Holinshed repeats Hall's account of Salisbury's
death with a few minor verbal alterations but tones down his
comment as follows:

> The damage that the realm of England received by the loss of this
> noble man manifestly appeared; in that immediately after his
> death the prosperous good luck which had followed the English
> nation began to decline and the glory of their victories gotten in
> the parts beyond the sea fell in decay.

It is the unpretentiousness of Caxton, sticking to mere chronicling and the barest comment, and the consistent picturesque-
ness and amplitude of Hall that come out best from among
these versions.

When Orleans was at the point of surrender the French com-
mander decided to offer the town to the Duke of Burgundy,
then the ally of England. The Duke was willing to accept the
town and asked the English, who were investing the town, if
they agreed. The English debated the matter, but the Regent,
the Duke of Bedford, was against the proposal as a bad precedent. What followed is thus described by Polydore, Hall,
and Holinshed.

> *Polydore.* This [sc the Duke of Bedford's] sentence took place;
> and the ambassadors were answered that the wars were kept for
> King Henry, and likewise the victory ought to be his. With this
> answer the duke dismissed the ambassadors. But upon little
> occasion cometh often great alteration; for two mischiefs fell out
> thereupon. First, the Duke of Burgoigne, angry in mind, sup-
> posed that the Englishmen did envy his renowm and therefore
> even then begun to be evil affected towards them. Secondly the
> Englishmen were forced afterward to leave the siege.

> *Hall.* This reason took place, and the Regent answered the duke's
> ambassadors that it was not honourable nor yet consonant to
> reason that the King of England should beat the bush and the
> Duke of Burgoigne have the birds. Wherefore sith the right was
> his the war was his and the charge was his, he said that the city
> ought not to be yielded to no other person but to him or to his
> use and profit. By this little chance succeeded a great change in
> the English affairs, for a double mischief of this answer rose and

sprang out.   For first the Duke of Burgoigne began to conceive a certain privy grudge against the Englishmen for this cause, thinking them to envy and bear malice against his glory and profit; for the which in continuance of time he became their enemy and cleaved to the French King.   Secondly, the Englishmen left the siege of Orleans, which by this treaty they might have had to friend or to have continued neuter, till their lord the Duke of Orleans or the Earl of Angulosie his brother were delivered out of the captivity of the English people.   But if men were angels and foresaw things to come they like beasts would not run to their confusion.   But fortune which guideth the destiny of man will turn her wheel as she listeth, whosoever saith nay.

Holinshed.   Hereupon the Regent answered the Burgoignian ambassadors that after so long a siege on his part and obstinate resistance of theirs he might not receive rendering and conditions at their appointment.   At this answer the duke hung the groin, as conceiving that our side should envy his glory or not to be so forward in advancing his honour as he would have it.

Here Polydore is simple and clear and is interested in cause and effect; Hall adds the picturesque to the episode and moralises on the cause and effect; Holinshed reverts to the simplicity of Polydore yet without his emphatic clarity.

10. THE USES OF HISTORY

As this book is on Shakespeare, I need say no more about separate chroniclers, for the sort of chronicle material Shakespeare used has now been described.   Details of any other chroniclers he used would add nothing to the general picture. But something remains to be said about the notions of history and of politics taken for granted in his day.   As in the first chapter I shall aim at stating the commonplace, the kind of thing Shakespeare could not have avoided knowing and heeding.   Some of the commonplaces have occurred already in relation to this or that chronicler but they need some supplementing.

For many years the text-books have stated that when Shakespeare began his Histories there was a strong popular desire to be instructed in the facts of history and that this desire was due in part to the rise in the patriotic temperature of England after the defeat of the Spanish Armada. The truth of the statement still seems to be admitted; and indeed Shakespeare with his career to make would hardly have risked so much in the chronicle form without a strong demand for history. But the taste of a mixed audience would not be the only thing that swayed him; he would also have an eye to the status of history among the better sort or the ordinary educated man. What then were the chief ends of history for the Elizabethans?

In the sixteenth century the distinction between useful and useless knowledge had hardly been drawn; to learn was the specific human function, and facts were accumulated as the White Knight accumulated things. They *all* might come in useful. History was valuable because it was a great accumulation of facts. It was also valuable because it had certain immediate practical uses. This double value corresponds to what can be called for short Higden and Hall, and explains why the Elizabethans had a use both for the mere compilation and for history moralised. About these practical uses the writers show a unanimity that both astounds a modern and makes illustration difficult by the very abundance of the alternatives available. The gift of saying the old thing as if it had all the excitement of a new birth was common in the sixteenth century. It surprises us, because we have been brought up to look on new discoveries as interesting and the repetition of old truths as dull and superfluous; and when we find positive excitement expressed just because the thing said has been incorporated into tradition, the difference between that world and this hits us with peculiar force. Two of the finest accounts of the uses of history are in Berners's preface to his translation of Froissart and in Raleigh's preface to his *History of the World*; and though the doctrine is similar and had many decades between the two prefaces in which to go stale, Raleigh puts it with unfaltering energy and conviction.

In Raleigh's preface more emphatically and splendidly than elsewhere we find one of the ruling ideas about history, namely that it repeats itself. Raleigh believes that the same pattern shows itself in Jewish, in French, and in English history. If this idea is granted, it follows that we have it in our power to foresee the future and therefore in some way to provide for it. And that is one of history's great practical uses. A second use of history is that it preserves worthy deeds from oblivion. And this leads to a third: since men desire glory, they are incited to

great deeds by thinking of the glory these deeds will bring
through being perpetuated in historical writing. For other
practical uses of history a short summary of Berners's preface
will serve, followed by one or two illustrations from elsewhere
of his main points. History, says Berners, shows the reader "by
example of old history" what we should desire and pursue and
contrariwise what we should shun. It is of the highest practical
value. History also knits together people separated by time
and space: the acts of history become as it were

> of one self city and in one man's life. Wherefore I say that history
> may well be called a divine providence, for, as the celestial bodies
> above complect all and at every time the universal world, the
> creatures contained therein and all their deeds, so doth history.
> Is it not a right noble thing for us by the faults and errors of other
> to amend and erect our life into better?

By reading history young men acquire the wisdom of age.
History incites the spirit of virtuous emulation; it promotes
high deeds and great discoveries. It also works through glory,
for history is the only sure pledge of the immortality of noble
acts. History is of special worth to the Prince, who can gather
from it the home truths a friend dare not give him.

Berners's first point, that history teaches us what to imitate
and what to shun, has occurred earlier in the chapter. It is the
commonest of all comments on history. The individual example in history is indeed dwelt on much more often than the
example of a whole stretch of history repeating itself. History
provided innumerable examples of men who fell from prosperity, and especially of men who fell because of a single passion
or error; and it is from them that we may best learn a practical
lesson. Above all it is necessary that princes should learn these
lessons. The reverence in which princes were held in the sixteenth century did not prevent humbler men preaching at
them: indeed to have to endure such preaching seems the price
they had to pay for their more autocratic position. As a specimen of this preaching—this time to pursue the example of a
virtuous man, not to beware the example of an unfortunate—
here is part of an address to Henry VIII which forms the preface to the English translation of Tito Livio's life of Henry V:

> To this end I have been moved to the enterprise hereof, that his
> Grace [i.e. Henry VIII], hearing or seeing or reading the virtuous

manners the victorious conquests and the excellent sagess and wisdoms of the most renowned prince in his days, King Henry V his noble progenitor (of whose superior in all nobleness manhood and virtue to my pretence it is not read nor heard amongst the princes of England since William of Normandy obtained the government of this realm by conquest), his Grace may in all things concerning his person and the regiment of his people conform himself to his [*i.e.* Henry V's] life and manners which he used after his coronation, and be counselled by the example of his great wisdom and discretion in all his common and particular acts. And secondarily the principal cause of this my pain (forasmuch as we then laboured in war) was that our sovereign lord by the knowledge and sight of this pamphlet should partly be provoked in this said war to ensue the noble and chivalrous acts of this so noble and so excellent a prince, which so followed he might the rather attain to like honour fame and victory.

It is not only the Prince who can benefit by the example of history. Here is a passage showing how it applies to all kinds of men. It comes fron Grafton's *Chronicle at large* published in 1569 and is part of the second preface entitled "Thomas N. to the Reader." Thomas N. has been identified as Thomas Norton, part author of *Gorboduc* and translator of Calvin. Among the benefits conferred by Grafton's history, he says, are the following:

Kings may learn to depend upon God and acknowledge his governance in their protection: the nobility may read the true honour of their ancestors: the ecclesiastical state may learn to abhor traitorous practices and indignities done against kings by the popish usurping clergy: high and low may shun rebellions by their dreadful effects and beware how they attempt against right, how unable soever the person be that beareth it: we all may be warned to thank God for the most virtuous wise and peaceable government that we now enjoy in comparison of terrible times heretofore. Each man may have a glass to see things past, whereby to judge justly of things present and wisely of things to come; to behold the beauty of virtue and deformity of vice, what sweetness remaineth after well doing, what stings of repentance evil doing leaveth. Men of elder honour may learn not to deface their forefathers' praise; the newer sort may seek to bring light and dignity to their houses. And finally all men in seeing the course of God's doings may learn to dread his judgments and love his providence: may see how good doings be defended; evil doings and wrongs revenged, blood with blood, violence with violence, injuries with miseries: and so grow into an affection to give each matter his right judgment, to each superior his right duty, to each other that which justice or charity willeth, and to all well doers and among others to this setter forth of so many well doings such thankful acceptation as his whole life employed to common benefit hath deserved.

Stow, author of the *Chronicles of England* published in 1580, after making a similar statement, ends:

So that it is as hard a matter for the readers of chronicles to pass without some colours of wisdom, invitements to virtue, and loathing of naughty facts, as it is for a well-favoured man to walk up and down in the hot parching sun and not be therewith sunburned.

This is a large claim, which does not find an echo in the bosom of every person who has had occasion or been compelled to read more than a very little in such chroniclers as Stow. Such a one may like to remember that just about the time of Stow's *Chronicles of England* Sidney in his *Apology for Poetry* makes good-natured fun of the claims of history, the more to exalt the Muse of his choice.

The historian, loden with old mouse-eaten records; authorising himself for the most part upon other histories, whose greatest authorities are built upon the notable foundation of hear-say; having much ado to accord differing writers and to pick truth out of partiality; better acquainted with a thousand years ago than with the present age and yet better knowing how this world goeth than how his own wit runneth; curious for antiquities and inquisitive of novelties; a wonder to young folks and a tyrant in table talk; denieth in a great chafe that any man for teaching of virtue and virtuous actions is comparable to him.

Shakespeare can hardly not have read and enjoyed this passage, but that does not mean that he did not accept the high contemporary regard for the practical virtues of history. Sidney's excepted, every single sentiment on the subject that has been presented in this section is pure Tudor commonplace, and whether Shakespeare liked it or not he could no more escape them than the late Victorians could escape popular presentations of evolution or the between-war generation the current perversions of Freud.

11. ELIZABETHAN NOTIONS OF RECENT ENGLISH HISTORY

Part of the extract from Thomas Norton will serve to introduce the next topics: the special shape in which the age of
Elizabeth saw its own immediate past and its present political
problems. Norton spoke of "traitorous practices and indignities done against kings by the popish usurping clergy"; he
denounced rebellion against "right" or the lawful ruler, "how
unable soever the person be that beareth it"; and he advises
men "to thank God for the most virtuous wise and peaceable
government that we now enjoy in comparison of terrible times
heretofore." The horror of civil war was common to the whole
of western Europe at the time, but it took a special form in
England; where the conception of what civil war meant was
founded both on memories of the Wars of the Roses and on the
spectacles of the Peasants' Revolt in Germany and the wars of
religion in France. Over against those memories was a lively
gratitude that under the Tudors rebellions had been comparatively small matters. But there remained the terror that the
Wars of the Roses might be fought again; and it was Catholic
intrigue that the Elizabethans most feared as likely to start
them. The monarchy was the safeguard against civil war and
must at all costs be upheld. In this section I will deal with the
shape in which the Wars of the Roses appeared to Shakespeare's contemporaries.

Something indeed I have said already when referring to the
Tudor myth; but not enough, for the matter is crucial to
Shakespeare's Histories. And there are two things to bear in
mind at the start: the first that the history before Henry VII
could be made to evolve in somewhat different versions; the
second that a sharp division exists between the select few who
saw a dramatic and philosophical sweep in this part of history
and those who saw it merely as a welter of misery and a rich
repertory of lessons on the fickleness of fortune and the inevitable punishment of the peccant individual. It can be said
categorically that Shakespeare was among the select few; and
it is with the versions current among these that I am concerned.
The differences in the versions are not great, and they have to
do mainly with where the trouble began. In Hall, Edward III
is a prosperous and satisfactory king, or at least this can be
inferred from Hall's silence and his mention of Edward's seven

sons; and the beginning of the trouble was the quarrel of
Bolingbroke and Mowbray and Richard II's inability to cope
with it. Little is made of Richard's procuring the death of his
uncle Woodstock, Duke of Gloucester, though it is mentioned.
Over against Richard's inability is set Henry IV's crime, first
in usurping the throne and secondly in allowing Richard to be
killed against his oath. God punished Henry by making his
reign unquiet but postponed full vengeance till a later generation, for Henry (like Ahab) humbled himself. But Henry was
none the less a usurper and this was a fact universally accepted
by the Elizabethans. Hall notes the immediate jealousy of the
house of York when Richard was deposed. Henry V by his
politic wisdom and his piety postpones the day of reckoning.
He learns from the example of past history and chooses good
counsellors; he banishes his evil companions; he does his best
to expiate his father's sin by having Richard reburied in Westminster. But his wisdom does not stretch to detecting the
danger from the house of York. With Henry VI the curse is
realised and in the dreaded form of a child being king—"woe
to the nation whose king is a child." Not that disaster comes
immediately, but the few years of the new king and later his
retiring disposition allow the sin of pride to show itself in various
places and ultimately to ruin the kingdom. The pride of
Cardinal Beaufort is a reason for the English being hated in
France; the arrogance of the Duke of Bedford offends Burgundy, England's ally. Above all the pride of Margaret of
Anjou, wife to Henry VI, hastens the process. She envies the
strength and wisdom of the late regent, Humphrey Duke of
Gloucester, and she encourages the pride of de la Pole, Duke of
Suffolk, whom she lets intrigue against Humphrey. The weakening in Lancastrian rule caused by Gloucester's death gives
the pride of the house of York its chance; and the curse reaches
its full issue in the Wars of the Roses. The position of the house
of York was dubious: it had the better title but, to establish it,
had to upset the precedent of three generations. But Edward
IV settled the balance of right against himself by swearing a
false oath, when he returned to England, that he sought no
more than his dukedom of York. A second perjury was that of
Edward's brother, Duke of Clarence. He swore to help Warwick to restore Henry VI and then sided with his brother. He
and his other brother, the Duke of Gloucester, incriminate
themselves by murdering Edward son of Henry VI after the

Battle of Tewkesbury. Meanwhile Providence is taking good care of Henry Tudor, Earl of Richmond, and sees that he is out of the Yorkists' reach in Brittany. Edward IV is a good king and like Henry IV earns the postponement of the punishment incurred by perjury. But it is visited on his sons. His brother, Richard Duke of Gloucester, is a villain in his own right just as Henry V was a perfect king in his own right: there was no question of his crimes proceeding from the excess of any one passion. He had meant ill from the start, and it was probably he who had contrived to get his brother the Duke of Clarence out of the way during Edward's reign. Clarence, of course, was justly punished for his perjury. Richard's murder of the two princes is sheer wickedness. Shortly after this culminating crime of the whole civil war the Holy Ghost puts the Duke of Buckingham, now alienated from Richard and beginning to hatch claims for the crown, in mind of Henry, Earl of Richmond. Buckingham concludes that Henry is the true heir of Lancaster and with Morton, Bishop of Ely, makes plans for recalling him from Brittany and marrying him to the daughter of Edward IV. The delicate question of how Henry has the right to raise sedition against Richard, the rightful heir by succession and the actual possessor of the crown, is not discussed. It is merely assumed that Richard is exceptional, a monster for whose case the ordinary rules simply do not hold good. Henry returns, wins the Battle of Bosworth, and providentially heals the old division by marrying the heiress of York. He is a successful politic king. Full fruition of the new order can only come from the issue of the union of the two houses. In Henry VIII the process is complete, and his reign is triumphant.

Such is Hall's picture and, as we shall see, Shakespeare's was nearly the same. But it is the general notion with its minor variations we are now after. To Hall's account I will add Raleigh's and Davies of Hereford's, already referred to in my first chapter. Davies, as usual, is particularly apt because he is so perfectly conventional a person. The three versions together must give a pretty faithful account of how the educated and more thoughtful Elizabethan took the matter. Raleigh's is the less like Hall's. Writing under James I, he is of course less obliged to make everything lead up to the Tudors or to flatter them. He is more interested in history's iterative pattern than in the Tudor myth. He sees the beginning of England's period of disaster in the murder of Edward II. The issue of this blood, "though it had some times of stay and stopping, did again break out, and that so often and in such abundance as all our princes of the masculine race (very few excepted) died of the same disease." The dominant rhythm of history Raleigh sees in the crime of a king visited on his grandson; and in English history it begins with Edward III. Edward put to death his uncle the Duke of Kent, for which crime his grandson Richard II had to suffer. Henry IV was a faithbreaker with similar consequences to his grandson Henry VI. Henry VII, though a wise and politic prince and the immediate instrument of God's justice on Richard III, sinned in having Lords Stanley and Warwick executed, with the result that his grandson Edward VI was punished with early death.

Davies of Hereford combines elements found in Hall and in Raleigh and adds new ones. He begins with William the Conqueror, and like the translator of Tito Livio sets him up as one of the model kings. With barest mention of the interim he goes on to John, whom he treats as the bad king justly punished for usurpation not as the virtuous resister of popish rapacity. Edward I was a model king. Edward II was led astray by parasites; his son Edward III was responsible for his murder, punishment for which was reserved for his grandson Richard II, who like Edward II was incompetent. Richard might have prospered if he had dealt rightly with Bolingbroke when Mowbray accused him of treason. Henry IV was a usurper but efficient. After Henry V the nemesis of Richard's murder makes itself felt again and provides another instance of the grandson suffering for ancestral sin. Henry VI was a saint but politically a fool. Davies dwells on the havoc of civil war as a central event in his scheme of history and then digresses on the wisdom of Elizabeth. He commends her for equivocating about her successor and for frowning on all claims. Elizabeth had a "sharp sight into events" and had learned by the example of the Wars of the Roses, when claimants were the curse of the land. In this way Davies brings out the main theme of Hall: the dreadful disorder of the Wars of the Roses and the blessed order of the Tudor peace. Going on with history, Davies makes the crime of Edward IV the murder of his brother Clarence, and then moralises on the dangers of an undisciplined people: once they become such, all unattached adventurers with the vaguest claim to the throne are a menace;

and the legitimate king in self-defence is apt to get rid of them and thus to go from one crime to another. Richard III is shown in his traditional part of utter villain. Henry VII was "God among men, no king but demi-god," and Davies rejoices that Tudor now succeeds Plantagenet. Henry VIII, another demi-god, made Europe tremble before him. There is little about Edward VI and Mary, but much praise of Elizabeth. Davies ends his survey with the doctrine that to obey a bad king is better than to run into civil war. He then recapitulates and adds his criticism of some of the kings, and some morals that can be drawn from history. William I shows how easy it is to conquer a divided state; how wise to be stern at first and then to soften; how wise to rule in person and not to trust the allegiance of deputies. Under William "degree" was properly observed:

> Now are the kings and the nobility
> True friends and fathers to the commonweal;
> The common now obey unfeignedly.

Edward I made the state "an entire monarchy," as states are meant to be. Edward II, Richard II, Henry VI, and Edward V are kings childish either in years or in character and they give the opportunity to unscrupulous ambition. They are "mirrors to kings negligent." Kings must be strong and active like the sun: Edward III, Henry IV, Henry V, and Edward IV were successful, circumspect kings:

> These princes were of fortune ne'er forsook,
> Because they governed with due regard.

Kings cannot afford to be over trustful, because in every state there are ambitious men, and of all the qualities ambition knows no mean. Richard III is ambition embodied. Henry VII was the nation's Solomon. He saw that foreign conquest did not suit an island and he combined firmness with sound policy: and he knew the advantages of trade. Henry VIII showed strength and the peculiar kingly virtue of munificence.

There must be other varieties in this general pattern of Tudor history but they are much less important than the pattern itself. We can gauge that importance best by thinking of another great pattern of English history, which might be called the Whig pattern and which probably began to take shape after 1688. It is only its simpler and cruder versions that can justly be compared with the Tudor pattern of Hall and Davies of Hereford: I mean those found in the children's history books of the Victorian age and now popularly referred to as "1066 and all that." Those versions anthologised and interpreted history with an assured prejudice against which the ordinary person had no defence, and had an incalculable influence on men's minds. The Tudor pattern had the same kind of power but with the important differences that it was not instilled by systematic educational means and that it did not spread nearly so wide. It was in fact the possession not of the average school-boy but of the more thoughtful portion of educated Elizabethan society. In that restricted portion it must have been a dominant idea. How restricted its vogue was is plain from its complete absence from nearly all the Chronicle Plays. It is this absence from them and its presence in Shakespeare that should teach us to link him not with the less educated writers of plays but with the best educated and most thoughtful writers outside the theatre as well as within.

12. THE DOCTRINE OF REBELLION

Two of Davies's sentiments (one of them found in Thomas Norton) anticipated this section. He said it was better to obey a bad king than to run into civil war and that a state ought to be an entire monarchy, thereby changing the topic from the form under which a stretch of history was seen to political theory. Being no historian I hesitate to follow Davies in this change, but if I am to attempt any true picture of the ideas behind Shakespeare's Histories I cannot avoid saying something about the general opinion on rebellion and the status of the Prince. Luckily the true theorising on monarchy belongs to the seventeenth century, and the sources from which this general opinion derived are popular and not technical. Moreover it is so clear what men thought, and the thought itself is so simple, that there is not much to do beyond stating the obvious and trying to make it emphatic. The evidence is much fuller than it was in the last section. There we found that only a minority saw recent history in a clean and connected pattern, but the orthodox doctrines of rebellion and of the monarchy were shared by every section of the community. Whereas the Chronicle Plays usually show no pattern of history, they are full of the other doctrines. And if we are looking for orthodoxy we could not find it in a more certain place than in these plays. R. U. Lindabury has extracted this orthodoxy (and noted very rare exceptions to it) from the Elizabethan drama. It can be found just as well in the *Mirror for Magistrates*. But not everyone went to the theatre or read the *Mirror for Magistrates*; and I prefer to go for the same doctrine to a still more popular source of dissemination, the Book of Homilies of the English Church.

Far from being pieces of abstract theology, relatively timeless, the Church Homilies were largely written, as occasion arose, to meet a present need. For instance, the sermon on the fear of death, one of the first series published in 1547, was written to calm the minds of many men who, though nominally Protestant, retained the Catholic fear of dying without shrift. They are thus good evidence of contemporary opinion. They were also intended for a popular audience; "to be declared and read by all persons vicars and curates, every Sunday and Holy Day in their churches, and by her Grace's advice perused and overseen for the better understanding of simple people." And they voiced an official opinion certain to be accepted by the theatrical world, which owed its very existence to the unbroken support of the court and its periphery. There are twelve homilies in the first series (1547); twenty in the second (1563); and in 1571 the long homily *Against Disobedience and wilful Rebellion* was added to the rest. I spoke of Shakespeare's probable debt to the Homilies in my first chapter and of Alfred Hart's important essay on them.

After the passage (quoted on p. 19 above) that begins the *Exhortation concerning good Ordre* and sets forth the doctrine of "degree" in heaven, universe, and state, comes an expression of thanks to God "for our most dear sovereign lord King Edward the Sixth with a godly wise and honourable council, with other superiors and inferiors in a beautiful order and goodly." Not only is this order the counterpart of the heavenly order but that portion of it which rules does so through the direct appointment of God:

> as it is written of God in the Book of Proverbs 'Through me kings do reign; through me counsellors make just laws; through me do princes bear rule and all judges of the earth execute judgment.'

Princes and other rulers must therefore "reknowledge themselves to have all their power and strength not from Rome but immediately of God most highest." Vengeance is God's, but they may use it as God's vice-gerents. Such is the nature of rulers: the duty of the subject was laid down once and for all by St. Paul in the thirteenth chapter of *Romans*:

> Let every soul submit himself unto the authority of the higher powers: for there is no power but of God: the powers that be, be ordained of God. Whosoever therefore resisteth the power, resisteth the ordinance of God: but they that resist shall receive to themselves damnation.

And the homilist ends his argument by stretching Paul to threaten all disobedient persons with everlasting damnation "forasmuch as they resist not man but God; not man's device and invention but God's wisdom, God's order power and authority." This rule of obedience applies to evil as well as to good rulers. Christ said to Pilate, "Thou couldest have no power against me, except it were given thee from above," thus proving that even this "wicked judge" had his authority from God. Thus all rulers must be obeyed except when they order us to do acts against God's commandment. Subjects must bear patiently with the oppression of an evil ruler. David was oppressed by Saul yet "though he were never so much provoked, he refused utterly to hurt the Lord's anointed." This is the true doctrine; sedition is never justified;

> but the bishop of Rome teacheth that they that are under him are free from all burdens and charges of the commonwealth and obedience towards their prince, most clearly against Christ's doctrine and St. Peter's.

Here is the simple doctrine of the Tudors, highly convenient to themselves but quite in keeping with the trend of the times and strong accordingly. It corresponds indeed with that transfer, already noted, of earnestness from religious contemplation to the morality of the secular event. The Tudor age was still intensely religious, and the religious feeling that had found its expression in the complexities of the medieval faith and ritual was not fully absorbed by the simplified Protestant order. The surplus of the spirit of worship had to be accommodated; and if a part found its home in the new veneration of the Scriptures, a part too went to intensify the feelings of the common people towards their rulers and especially their prince. It was this religious respect for their rulers that caused the English to accept and even to approve the drastic curtailments of their old liberties made definitive by Henry VIII and continued by Elizabeth, her Parliament admitting that her prerogative could override any laws made by them, and the active rule of the country being kept in the hands of herself and of the Privy Council. It was the same thing too that made the adoration of the queen an active power in men's minds and kept it from the obvious danger of absurdity. She was head of the church not by mere formality but in the hearts of most Englishmen. To serve her was not to carry out the arbitrary and perhaps hastily or lightly improvised orders of a hot-tempered and sharp-tongued woman but to act in accordance with the will of God, when to obey was a privilege and to question not to be thought on.

With the sanctity of monarchy thus heightened, the enormity of rebellion was likewise swollen. And when in 1569 the execrable event happened and was dealt with, no wonder if the authorities added a new and exceptionally long homily to the already existing. It is called *An Homily against Disobedience and wilful Rebellion*, it is in six parts, and it ends with "a thanksgiving for the suppression of the last rebellion." Though the second homily does little more than elaborate the sense of the first, using the same passages of Scripture for the argument, the tone is different. The tone of the first was collected, measured, magisterial, and eminently thoughtful; in the second the tone is greatly heightened, there is the active fear that rebellion may recur, a still strong horror at the recent event, and a dramatic style that lets us into the world of Hall's Chronicle and the *Mirror for Magistrates* and anticipates the world of Shakespeare's earlier historical tetralogy. The most interesting expansion of doctrine has to do with men's duties under a bad king. The homilist explains the dangers attached to *any* condonation of rebellion, however bad the ruler may be. Who, first, are subjects that they can judge if he is bad? They may easily mistake, for there are always wicked men around, very ready to take advantage of a prince vulnerable whether through too great kindness, or the wrong sex, or too few years. And there will always be difference of opinion; so that if rebellion is once allowed against a bad prince, how can it in the end be prevented against a good? Moreover it is not blind chance but God who sends a bad prince, and he does it to punish a people's sins. To revolt is to add new sin to sin not yet expiated. The proper acts are to pray for the prince's amendment and to live better lives that God may forgive us and remove the scourge. The anti-Catholic theme is also greatly expanded. The main causes of rebellion are ambition and ignorance; and in European history the ambition of the Papacy for temporal power using the ignorance of simple folk as its tool. The homilist gives many instances from history of papal arrogance and exaction. Especially he enlarges on papal interference in England under King John, the foreign invasion and native defection it caused, and asks, "Would Englishmen have suffered this had they in those days known and understanded that God doth curse the blessings and bless the cursings of such wicked usurping bishops and tyrants?" This interpretation of the reign of John was by now a Protestant tradition, but it is interesting that its rendering in the Homilies greatly resembles its rendering in the *Troublesome Reign of King John.*

Active fear that rebellion may recur can be detected in the violence with which the homilist denounces it, as in this passage near the beginning of the third part:

> How horrible a sin against God and man rebellion is cannot possibly be expressed according unto the greatness thereof. For he that nameth rebellion nameth not a singular or one only sin, as is theft robbery murder and such like, but he nameth the whole puddle and sink of all sins against God and man, against his prince his country his countrymen his parents his children his kinsfolks his friends and against all men universally; all sins, I say, against God and all men heaped together nameth he that nameth rebellion.

Again, this passage near the end of the first part shows by its mention of England and Englishmen that the homilist has the recent rebellion in mind:

> What shall we say of those subjects? May we call them by the name of subjects who neither be thankful nor make any prayer to God for so gracious a soveriegn, but also themselves take armour wickedly, assemble companies and bands of rebels, to break the public peace so long continued and to make not war but rebellion, to endanger the person of such a gracious sovereign, to hazard the estate of their country for whose defence they should be ready to spend their lives, and bring Englishmen to rob spoil destroy and burn in England Englishmen, to kill and murder their own

neighbours and kinsfolk, their own countrymen, to do all evil and mischief, yea and more than foreign enemies would or could do—what shall we say of these men, who use themselves thus rebelliously against their gracious sovereign, who, if God for their wickedness had given them an heathen tyrant to reign over them, were by God's word bound to obey him and to pray for him?

The dramatic touch is felt from the start. The homily begins with a splendid picture of original obedience and order in the Garden of Eden and of its upsetting by the first and the greatest rebel. The virtue of David in forbearing to rebel against Saul, that figured so strongly in the earlier homily, is treated with deliberate drama in a long imaginary dialogue between himself and "men desirous of rebellion." In the fourth part there is a most interesting reference to the English chronicles, which is especially appropriate to the dramatic renderings of history in Hall's Chronicle and the *Mirror for Magistrates*, then at the very height of its popularity and influence:

Turn over and read the histories of all nations; look over the chronicles of our own country; call to mind so many rebellions of old time and some yet fresh in memory; ye shall not find that God ever prospered any rebellion against their natural and lawful prince, but contrariwise that the rebels were overthrown and slain and such as were taken prisoners dreadfully executed. Consider the great and noble families of dukes marquises earls and other lords, whose names ye shall read in our chronicles, now clean extinguished and gone: and, seek out the causes of the decay, you shall find that not lack of issue and heirs male hath so much wrought that decay and waste of noble blood and houses as hath rebellion.

But the most eloquent part of the whole homily is in the third part, where all the excesses and miseries of civil war are described. Just as the earlier homily gave one of the noblest accounts of order or degree and served to illustrate the background of Ulysses's speech in *Troilus and Cressida*, so the later homily gives a picture of disorder and civil war that gives a better background to the four history plays Shakespeare first wrote than any passage I know. It is profoundly commonplace, and the commonplace it tells is stale to the humblest student of Shakespeare or of Elizabethan history: that horror of civil war which haunted the Elizabethans till the succession

was peacefully and firmly established.   But it brings this horror
to life and really makes us feel it as the comment on history that
mattered most to the Elizabethan age. By ending this chapter
with a quotation from it I may get a right emphasis and end at
a place to which the subjects of my next chapters must inevitably be referred:

> Now as I have showed before that pestilence and famine, so is it
> yet more evident that all the calamities miseries and mischiefs of
> war be more grievous and do more follow rebellion than any other
> war, as being far worse than all other wars. For not only those
> ordinary and usual mischiefs and miseries of other wars do follow
> rebellion, as corn and other things necessary to man's use to be
> spoiled, houses villages towns cities to be taken sacked burned and
> destroyed, not only many very wealthy men but whole countries
> to be impoverished and utterly beggared, many thousands of men
> to be slain and murdered, women and maids to be violated and
> deflowered: which things when they are done by foreign enemies
> we do much mourn, as we have great causes; yet are all these
> miseries without any wickedness wrought by any of our own
> countrymen. But when these mischiefs are wrought in rebellion
> by them that should be friends, by countrymen, by kinsmen, by
> those that should defend their country and their countrymen from
> such miseries, the misery is nothing so great as is the mischief and
> wickedness when the subjects unnaturally do rebel against their
> prince, whose honour and life they should defend, though it were
> with the loss of their own lives: countrymen to disturb the public
> peace and quietness of their country, for defence of whose quiet-
> ness they should spend their lives; the brother to seek and often
> to work the death of his brother, the son of the father; the father
> to seek or procure the death of his sons . . . and so finally to make
> their country, thus by their mischief weakened, ready to be a prey
> and spoil to all outward enemies that will invade it, to the utter
> and perpetual captivity slavery and destruction of all their
> countrymen their children their friends their kinsfolks left alive,
> whom by their wicked rebellion they procure to be delivered into
> the hands of foreign enemies, as far as in them doth lie.

CHAPTER III

The Literary Background: Non-dramatic

1. A MIRROR FOR MAGISTRATES

IN my first chapter I described the general conception of order prevalent among the educated men of Shakespeare's day; in my second the more special Tudor conceptions of history and politics that Shakespeare must have known through certain chronicles, in particular Hall's, and through the Church Homilies. It is just possible that Shakespeare got his conception of history from these alone: the stuff was there. But it is unlikely; for the same ideas quickly found their way into a very popular if quite different, type of writing. They were adopted, many of them, by the rising young poets and through them obtained an unquestioned currency in the early and middle days of Elizabeth. It is difficult to see how the youthful Shakespeare, who must have been interested in contemporary poetry, could have missed this particular mediation of the above ideas. The poets I mean are the authors of that great composite work, *A Mirror for Magistrates*, which was the chief creative effort after the age of Wyatt; the one poetical composition which Sidney in his *Apology for Poetry* thought fit to mention between the lyrics of Surrey and the *Shepherd's Calendar*.

There is no reason why the common reader should have a first-hand knowledge of the whole of *A Mirror for Magistrates*, when there is so much else to read. But at least he had better not fall into an error frequent among those who have merely read about it: that it is reactionary, a recrudescence of an outmoded medieval form; an unnecessary piece of obfuscation after the tentative dawn of Wyatt and Surrey and before the authentic dawn of the *Shepherd's Calendar*. This error is easily explained. The preface to the *Mirror* recounts how the printer wished this work to continue that series of doleful stories, Lydgate's *Fall of Princes*, beginning in point of time where Lydgate had ended. In the popular mind Lydgate suggests dullness and a lapse from the sweetness and light of Chaucer into monkish obscurantism; things not at all worthy of a long sequel. Actually, the *Mirror* is a sequel to Lydgate more by accident than in essence. Its main intention was not to swell

an already long list of tragical narratives but to point a very
solemn contemporary moral, namely to educate the prince or
magistrate by a series of exemplary stories that would teach
him to shun vice. The connection with Lydgate was a matter
of advertisement, for, strange as it may seem, Lydgate was still
popular in the middle of the sixteenth century. Further, even
if the *Mirror* had essentially continued Lydgate it would not
thereby have been out of date; for the morality that Lydgate
preaches, though less poetical, is more of the Renaissance than
Chaucer's. Lydgate was translating Boccaccio, and Boccaccio
was the first great author to expound the kind of morality
preached in the *Mirror*. It was Boccaccio who first altered the
older, mainly fortuitous, type of tragic story to one governed by
a close moral law of cause and effect. In deriving from
Boccaccio the *Mirror* was progressive not reactionary.

I cannot avoid writing at some length on *A Mirror for Magistrates*. Not only does it deal with the same events as Shakespeare's Histories but in spirit it is much closer to them than are
the Chronicle Plays. It must be added to Hall's Chronicle and
the Homilies as one of the important formative influences of
Shakespeare's youth. As the facts about the *Mirror* are slightly
complicated and not too well known, I had better set them out
briefly. Readers who want to get on to Shakespeare himself
and to avoid preliminaries can find a summary of my conclusions about the *Mirror* at the end of this chapter (p. 89).

A Mirror for Magistrates is a series of imaginary monologues
by the ghosts of certain eminent British statesmen who came to
unfortunate ends. They are pictured as speaking to a group of
men (namely the actual authors of the stories) of whom William
Baldwin is the leader. Between the stories the authors make
their comments in prose. They discuss the stories themselves,
their notions of ethics and politics, the details of their craft, and
in so doing reveal themselves as a group of friends eagerly concerned with the problems of their own day and with the future
of poetry; not unlike such groups as the Scriblerus Club or the
Preraphaelite poets. The *Mirror* went into many editions,
several of them containing new matter. In its first form it consisted of nineteen short stories or "tragedies" of an average
length of under two hundred lines. It was printed in 1555
under Queen Mary, but publication was not allowed till 1559
under Elizabeth. The historical period covered is from
Richard II to Edward IV. In an edition in 1563 eight stories

were added, longer and much more dramatic, of about the same bulk as the original nineteen. They mainly concern the reign of Richard III and include the sections now best known: Sackville's tragedy of the Duke of Buckingham with its Induction and Churchyard's Tragedy of Jane Shore. There were smaller additions in 1578 and 1587, taking history down to the reign of Henry VIII. All these additions, though often more ambitious and more dramatic, are in keeping with the political principles of the original nucleus. But in 1574 John Higgins published a quite independent series of tragedies dealing with British history from Brut to the Christian era; and in 1578 Blenerhasset a second series from Caesar to William the Conqueror. These quite lack the political earnestness of the tragedies staged by Baldwin, which keep strictly within the period covered by Hall's Chronicle. Nevertheless in 1587 Higgins's series was incorporated with Baldwin's and became henceforward the standard edition, the total volume being in composition not unlike the second edition of Holinshed, published in the same year. In referring to *A Mirror for Magistrates* I mean only the stories collected by Baldwin between 1555 and 1587; not the additions of Higgins and Blenerhasset; in fact the *Mirror* as edited by Miss Lily Campbell.

The authors of about half the stories are known. Sackville, Lord Buckhurst, was socially the most eminent; but nearly all were of good birth and had positions at court. Politically they were not extremists, having survived the changes of four reigns. They were men highly educated and very much in the stream of things. Their work lives because artistically it is experimental and exploratory and because it expresses ideas about which men at that time felt very strongly.

The artistic interest appears through the metrical variety of the tales and the literary discussions in the prose end-links. Though the prevailing stanza is the rime-royal, its rhythmic character varies from the extreme regularity of Sackville's *Induction* and Churchyard's *Jane Shore* to an alliterative lilt based on Langland or to the measures of Masefield's *Cargoes* and Meredith's *Love in a Valley*: from

> The wrathful winter proaching on apace
> With blust'ring blasts had all y-bar'd the treen,
> And old Saturnus with his frosty face
> With chilling cold had pierc'd the tender green,

to

> Read well the senténce of the rat of renown
> Which Piers the Plowman describes in his dream,
> And whoso hath wit the sense to expoun
> Shall find that to bridle the prince of a realm
> Is e'en as who saith to strive with the stream.

or to

> In the rueful register of mischief and mishap,
> Baldwin, we beseech thee with *our* name to begin,
> Whom unfriendly fortune did train unto a trap,
> When we thought our state most stable to have been.

For an example of the author's interest in an artistic problem take the end-links before and after the story of the poet Collingbourne, where the company is perplexed by the poet's difficulty of uniting imaginative freedom with correct belief. They have just heard Sackville's story of Buckingham. One of the company thinks that the setting of this story in Hell, where a number of eminent and respectable people are found along with Buckingham, raises difficulties of doctrine.

> Whereas he faineth to talk with the princes in Hell, that I am sure will be misliked, because it is most certain that some of their souls be in Heaven. And although he herein do follow allowed poets in their description of Hell, yet it savoureth so much of Purgatory, which the Papists have digged thereout, that the ignorant may thereby be deceived.

Baldwin retorts that by "Hell," the poet meant merely the grave and that thus Protestant decorum is observed. To which quibble one of the company retorts:

> Tush, what stand we here upon? It is a poesy and no divinity; and it is lawful for poets to feign what they list, so it be appertinent to the matter. And therefore let it even pass in such sort as you have read it.

And the company agree that the poet ought to have the utmost freedom, and that King Richard was a tyrant for making Collingbourne suffer for his verses.

It is a pleasure to reconstruct from the *Mirror* the picture of an intelligent group of men creating for themselves the shape of their own works of literature. The results may seem crude to us; but it is a good sort of crudity, that of something new, full of promise for the future. To Shakespeare, at the age say of twenty, when the *Mirror* was at its most popular, these results would not have seemed crude, and the promise would have been much more interesting.

So much for the technical and experimental side of the *Mirror*. I come now to its more general ideas.

First, although politics are the poem's main ethical concern, the sense of a cosmic setting is not absent. The setting of the erring magistrates is not only the state but, as in Elyot's *Governor* and the Church Homilies, God's ordered universe. The chaos they cause is allied to the chaos that would ensue if God relaxed his pressure on creation. In Baldwin's first preface (addressed "to the nobility and all other in office") he says that the office of magistrate

> is God's own office, yea his chief office. For as justice is the chief virtue so is the ministration thereof the chiefest office.

Here in brief space are brought together and in a way equated God, the ruler, and justice. We shall not be wrong to think of all three in their traditional setting of primacies: God among the angels, the ruler among men, justice among the virtues. Owen Glendower (whose story was written by Phaer, translator of Virgil) moralises on the nature of man and beast in a way that shows him well versed in the chain of being and in man's position along it.

> Each thing by nature tendeth to the same
> Whereof it came and is disposed like:
> Down sinks the mould, up mounts the fiery flame;
> With horn the hart, with hoof the horse doth strike;
> The wolf doth spoil, the subtle fox doth pike;
> And generally no fish flesh fowl or plant
> Of their true dam the property doth want.
>
> But as for men, sith severally they have
> A mind whose manners are by learning made,
> Good bringing up all only doth them save
> In virtuous deeds, which with their parents fade.
> So that true gentry standeth in the trade
> Of virtuous life not in the fleshly line;
> For blood is brute but gentry is divine.

Again, when Lord Hastings speaks of the unnatural treachery of his servant Catesby, whom he had trusted utterly, he wishes this chaos of human relationship to be duplicated in the universe.

> Fly from thy channel, Thames, forsake thy streams;
> Leave th' adamant, iron; Phoebus, lay thy beams;
> Cease, heavenly spheres, at last your weary work,
> Betray your charge, return to chaos dark;
> At least some ruthless tiger hang her whelp:
> My Catesby so with some excuse to help
> And me to comfort that I alone ne seem
> Of all dame nature's works left in extreme.

Most frequent and emphatic of all cosmic references are those to the stars, and they bring us to the centre of the *Mirror's* ethics and to its importance as a shaping agent of Elizabethan drama. As in this drama, there is a terrible sense of the stars' power combined with a precise orthodox doctrine of that power's limit. The stars play havoc; yet, if they do, it is because man allows it. The problem of fortune and the stars is raised and answered by Jack Cade (a choice of expounder so inappropriate as to call forth the comment of the company,

> By Saint Mary, if Jack were as well learned as you have made his oration, whatsoever he was by birth, I warrant him a gentleman by his learning. Now notably and philosopherlike hath he described fortune and the causes of worldly cumbrance!).

Cade explains that the planets working on the constitutions of men's bodies may incline their minds to ill, but the ultimate choice is free and God is above fortune.

> It may be well that planets do incline,
> And our complexions move our minds to ill;
> But such is reason that they bring to fine
> No work unaided by our lust and will:
> For heaven and earth are subject both to skill.
> The skill of God ruleth all, it is so strong;
> Man may by skill guide things that to him long.

There remains however the question why God, who controls the stars, allows them, though they need not impair man's moral welfare, to subject the good as well as the bad to such impartially hard fates. There is more than one answer.

Thomas Earl of Salisbury, before telling his own death by a
cannon ball at the siege of Orleans, does a very interesting piece
of thinking aloud about fortune.   In realistic self-argument he
fluctuates between conflicting notions before coming to a hesi-
tating conclusion.   It is stupid for a statesman to set store by his
high deserts or his fame, for not only does time devour but
fortune makes them uncertain.   All the same the princely mind
is right in seeking fame, even though fame is not dealt out in
accord with desert.   Then he gives his father's reputation as an
instance.   His father died in a just cause and yet got death and
obloquy for a reward.   Why does fortune often reward the
unworthy with fame and deny it to the good?   The Earl's
father joined with the Duke of Exeter to get the rightful king,
Richard II, put back on the throne usurped by Henry IV.
The plot was betrayed, and Salisbury executed, an unjust end.
"And God doth suffer that it should be so."   But then the
speaker thinks that there may be a reason after all:

> The cause why mischiefs many times arise
> And light on them that would men's wrong redress
> Is for the rancour that they bear, I guess.
>
> God hateth rigour though it further right,
> For sin is sin however it be used,
> And therefore suffereth shame and death to light,
> To punish vice, though it be well abused.
> Who furthereth right is not thereby excused,
> If through the same he do some other wrong:
> To every vice due guerdon doth belong.

In other words evil means may corrupt what was at first a pure
motive; the ways of fortune, against all appearances, may be
just after all.   Not that the speaker applies this doctrine of
resignation to himself, for he soon breaks out:

> O fortune, fortune, cause of all distress,
> My father had great cause thy fraud to curse,
> But much more I, abused ten times worse.

But though through dramatic propriety the Earl of Salisbury
reaches no fixed conclusion about the sufferings of good men,
the full doctrine does occur elsewhere.   Once again there is
dramatic propriety, for the doctrine is put in the mouth of
Henry VI, who knew so much misfortune but whose saintliness

enabled him to reflect dispassionately upon it. He enumerates
the causes usually assigned to misfortune. Astronomers blame
the stars, physicians the humours, while divines bring in God's
will and man's sin. It is folly and wickedness, says Henry, to
separate the stars from God's will and make them first causes.
Then he examines these different agents. The body's humours
are insufficient in themselves: they can only minister to mental
proclivities already existing.

> For through our lust by humours fed all vicious deeds begin:
> So sin and they be one, both working like effect.

Nor can you separate the stars and fortune from God's will.

> Thus of our heavy haps chief causes be but twain,
> Whereon the rest depend and underput remain.
> The chief the will divine, called destiny and fate;
> The other sin, through humours holp, which God doth highly
>   hate.

> The first appointeth pain for good men's exercise,
> The second doth deserve due punishment for vice:
> This witnesseth the wrath and that the love of God;
> The good for love, the bad for sin, God beateth with his rod.

And Henry goes on to analyse his own case, saying that though
his many sins have merited the chastisement of God's wrath, he
has striven after virtue and believes that part of his afflictions
are a token of God's love and approval. Anyhow Henry has
advanced a theory of why misfortunes befall men, and in particularly good men, that will cover every case. It supplements
and completes the wavering statements of the Earl of Salisbury.

I have dwelt so long on the ethics of *A Mirror for Magistrates*
because they present the sort of problem that could hardly not
have attracted the young Shakespeare. He did not indeed
agonise over such problems till later, but he was interested from
the first in the apparent vagaries of fortune. Shakespeare could
have got these ethical solutions from sermon or treatise. But
that they came home to him with special force as presented in
the most popular modern poem of his youth can hardly be
doubted.

It remains to discuss the more purely historical side of the
Mirror: its derivation from the chronicles and its affinities with
Shakespeare's conception of history.

The *Mirror* both derives from the English chronicles and has very decided opinions on what chronicles should be like. How Baldwin and his friends took the chronicles can be seen by the introduction to the story of Lord Rivers, the first of the eight to be added in 1563. Baldwin reports to the company, which had broken up after hearing the first section of the poem and is now supposed to have reassembled to hear the next, that he has a number of tales with him.

"I pray you," quoth one of the company, "let us hear them." "Nay soft," quoth I, "we will take the chronicles and note their places and as they come so will we orderly read them all."

It was not seemly then to depart from the order of history as set out in the chronicles. What a good chronicler should be is set forth by Sir Nicholas Burdet.

> A chronicler should well in divers tongues be seen
> And eke in all the arts he ought to have a sight,
> Whereby he might the truth of divers actions deem
> And both supply the wants, correct that is not right.
> He should have eloquence and full and fitly write,
> Not mangle stories snatching here and there,
> Nor gloze to make a volume great appear.
>
> He should be of such countenance and wit
> As should give witness to the histories he writes;
> He should be able well his reasons so to knit
> As should continue well the matter he recites;
> He should not praise, dispraise, for favour or despites;
> But should so place each thing in order due
> As might approve the stories to be true.

In fact the authors of the *Mirror* both use the chronicles as their basis and mind very much what the chronicles are like as history.

It has already been remarked that the period of history into which the fallen statesmen are set in the *Mirror* is precisely that covered by Hall's Chronicle. This is partly accidental, partly not. Baldwin in his second preface (to the reader) tells us that he will begin with the reign of Richard II (where Hall begins) because the printer wanted him to follow on where Lydgate had stopped. There were, he says, just as many exemplary stories of unfortunate statesmen in the earlier stretches of

English history. But the period from Richard II on was good
enough; and the printer was allowed his wish. But, the period
having thus been chosen, it is Hall and not the other chroniclers
that the authors of the *Mirror* follow. They were probably glad
to keep within Hall's historical limits, just because they valued
his interpretation of history above any other. Not only is it
plain from internal evidence that the tales are mostly taken
from Hall, but the text acknowledges the debt. The link between the stories of Lord Mowbray and Richard II mentions
that in the preceding story Hall was mainly followed. Much
more interesting is the disquisition on history, put in the mouth
of John Tiptoft, Earl of Worcester, which praises Hall at the
expense of Fabyan and indeed sums up the aims of the authors
of the *Mirror*.

> But story writers ought for neither glory
> Fear nor favour truth of things to spare.
> But still it fares as always it did fare:
> Affection fear or doubts that daily brew
> Do cause that stories never can be true.
>
> Unfruitful Fabyan followed the face
> Of time and deeds but let the causes slip;
> Which Hall hath added, but with double grace,
> For fear, I think, lest trouble might him trip:
> For this or that, saith he, he felt the whip.
> Thus story writers leave the causes out
> Or so rehearse them, as they were in doubt.
>
> But seeing causes are the chiefest things
> That should be noted of the story writers,
> That men may learn what ends all causes brings,
> They be unworthy the name of chroniclers
> That leave them clean out of the registers
> Or doubtfully report them; for the fruit
> Of reading stories standeth in the suit.

Hall then is better than Fabyan but imperfect because apt to
be equivocal for fear of getting into trouble. The chain of cause
and effect, not the unrelated fact, is the essence of history.
And, to complete the argument from other parts of the *Mirror*,
the good of tracing cause and effect in the past is practical:

statesmen may avoid, by past example, the commission of the old errors.

Now in examining the chroniclers I found that Polydore was first concerned with cause and effect and that Hall greatly enlarged that concern. The *Mirror* (in spite of the complaint that Hall equivocates and is not emphatic enough) does really follow Hall, does transplant into poetry one of the very important things that had taken place in the province of history. The story of Thomas Woodstock, Duke of Gloucester, by Ferrers illustrates well enough the affinities with Hall. Like Hall and later Shakespeare and Hayward (and unlike Polydore) Ferrers mentions the seven sons of Edward III, of whom Woodstock was one:

> Brothers we were to the number of seven,
> I being the sixth and youngest but one.
> A more royal race was not under heaven,
> More stout or more stately of stomach and person,
> Princes all peerless in each condition.

And like Hall Ferrers seeks the causes of a king's troubles in some act of folly or wickedness:

> And cruelty abused the law of kind
> When that the nephew the uncle slew.
> Alas, King Richard, sore mayst thou rue,
> Which by this fact preparedst the way
> Of thy hard destiny to hasten the day.
>
> For blood axeth blood as guerdon due
> And vengeance for vengeance is just reward.
> O righteous God, thy judgements are true;
> For look, what measure we other award,
> The same for us again is prepar'd.
> Take heed, ye princes, by example past:
> Blood will have blood, either first or last.

In talking above of the ethics of fortune I gave instances from the *Mirror* of more elaborate chains of cause and effect than this simple example of blood having blood. There is nothing in Hall so elaborate as Henry VI's search for the causes of his own trials, and we can understand why the authors of the *Mirror* thought they had gone beyond him.

In one matter however they did not follow Hall. There is

nothing at all in the *Mirror* of Hall's master-theme, the working
out of destiny over the stretch of history from Richard II to the
Tudors.   The opportunity to speak of Providence bringing back
Henry Earl of Richmond from Brittany to get the throne and
then end civil war by the marriage of the two houses was there
in the story of Richard III, but it was not taken.   The authors
of the *Mirror* omit the Tudor myth.   Not that there is not the
idea of a family curse with its origin in a single definite act
showing itself in a series of tragic events.   In the story of
Humphrey Duke of Gloucester (again by Ferrers) the Plantagenets are made to owe all their misfortunes to Henry II's
grandmother being a *succuba*.

> It is for troth in an history found
> That Henry Plantagenet first of our name,
> Who called was King Henry the Second,
> Son of dame Maud the empress of high fame,
> Would often report that his ancient grandame,
> Though seeming in shape a woman natural,
> Was a fiend of the kind that *succubae* some call.

The undutifulness of his children Henry, Richard, and John
confirmed this, and on his deathbed he foretold that the Plantagenet stock would be destroyed by internal strife.

> This king, some write, in his sickness last
> Said, as it were by way of prophecy,
> How that the Devil a darnel grain had cast
> Among his kin to increase enmity,
> Which should remain in their posterity,
> Till mischief and murder had spent them all.

And Humphrey maintains that events have quite borne this
prophecy out.

> Which to be true if any stand in doubt,
> Because I mean not further to digress,
> Let him peruse the stories throughout
> Of English kings whom practice did oppress;
> And he shall find the cause of their distress
> From first to last unkindly to begin
> Always by those that next were of the kin.

It is interesting that Ferrers widens the context of this English
curse into that of the Senecan drama by saying that the rage of

the Erinyes "was never half so wood." But he is at the same time narrower than Hall in not allowing the long process of the curse to issue into such an Aeschylean reconciliation as Hall found in the union of the two houses of York and Lancaster.

Other historical matter that figures in the *Mirror* has nothing specially to do with Hall but consists of those general doctrines about educating the rulers by the example, about the king's status, about obedience to him, and about civil war, which were common throughout the Elizabethan age to all sections of the community. These doctrines, however, the *Mirror* expounds or discusses so emphatically and with so much detail—much of it recurring in Shakespeare—that something must be said of them.

The first topic, the education of the ruler through the example, is inherent in the whole plan of the book, and the statesmen themselves are constantly bidding their successors take heed to behave better and avoid their own fate. The gist of Baldwin's first preface is that the health of a state depends on its rulers, that bad rulers suffer God's vengeance, and that the erring statesmen utter their complaints to make contemporary statesmen heed their example and act the more justly.

> The goodness or badness of any realm lieth in the goodness or badness of the rulers. And therefore not without great cause do the holy Apostles so earnestly charge us to pray for the magistrates; for indeed the wealth and quiet of every common weal, the disorder also and miseries of the same, come specially through them. I need not go either to the Romans or Greeks for proof hereof, neither yet to the Jews or other nations: our own country stories, if we read and mark them, will show us examples enow—would God we had not seen more than enow.

And speaking to "the nobility and all other in office" Baldwin defines the aim of his book:

> For here as in a looking glass you shall see, if any vice be in you, how the like hath been punished in other heretofore; whereby admonished I trust it will be a good occasion to move you to the sooner amendment. This is the chiefest end why this book is set forth, which God grant it may attain.

But though the bad ruler is execrated, the actual office is exalted in complete accord with the contemporary Protestant doctrine, that the ruler derives his authority from God direct;

the *Mirror* in fact shares the impulses that prompted the *Homily Of Obedience*. This from Baldwin's first preface is close to the portions of the Homily quoted or described above (p. 66). The office of magistrate, he says,

> is God's own office, yea his chief office. For as justice is the chief virtue, so is the ministration thereof the chiefest office. And therefore hath God established it with the chiefest name, honouring and calling kings and all officers under them by his own name, gods. Ye be all gods, as many as have in your charge any ministration of justice.

Now as God appoints the magistrate, so it is God's business to decide whether his nominee shall be good or bad. This is stated in emphatic prose not only in Baldwin's preface but in the comment made after the story of Jack Cade.

> For indeed officers be God's deputies and it is God's office which they bear; and it is he which ordaineth thereto such as himself listeth: good when he favoureth the people and evil when he will punish them. And therefore whosoever rebelleth against any ruler either good or bad rebelleth against God and shall be sure of a wretched end, for God cannot but maintain his deputy.

The repentant Cornish blacksmith, who led a rebellion in Henry VII's reign, is entirely orthodox on the subject.

> For kings by God are strong and stoutly hearted
> That they of subjects will not be subverted.
> If kings would yield yet God would them restrain,
> Of whom the prince hath grace and power to reign,
> Who straightly chargeth us above all thing
> That no man should resist against his king.
>
> Who that resisteth his dread sovereign lord
> Doth damn his soul by God's own very word.
> A Christen subject should with honour due
> Obey his sovereign though he were a Jew.

The last couplet is as orthodox as the rest.

This question of the loyalty owed to a bad or indifferent king was urgent for the authors of the *Mirror*. To men who had lived through the changing loyalties of four reigns it was complicated and perplexing; and in the political tangles of the fifteenth century they saw exemplified the same questions of

loyalty that troubled themselves. Thus the ethics of the deposi-
tions of Richard II and Richard III were matters not of mere
historical interest but had an immediate bearing on the present
time. And they remained so throughout the Elizabethan age.
The *Mirror* was popular for so long largely because it never
relaxes its earnestness about these living political issues.

For the king himself, apart from God's choice, the first thing
is that he should be a grown man of strong character. Edmund
Duke of Somerset, who plotted against Humphrey Duke of
Gloucester and was killed at St. Albans, gives the conventional
doctrine.

> True is the text which we in Scripture read,
> *Ve terrae illi cuius rex est puer:*
> Woe to the land whereof a child is head,
> Whether child or childish, the case one is sure:
> Where kings be young we daily see in ure
> The people, aweless, wanting one to dread,
> Lead their lives lawless by weakness of the head.
>
> And no less true is this text again,
> *Beata terra cuius rex est nobilis.*
> Blest is the land where a stout king doth reign,
> Where in good peace each man possesseth his,
> Where ill men fear to fault or do amiss,
> Where the prince prest hath alway sword in hand
> At home and abroad his enemies to withstand.

The prince's strength must be sure to show itself in checking
the excesses of his subordinates. Only so can he be free from
rebellion. If he omits this duty God will stir up rebellion to
inflict on the corrupt officers the punishment omitted by the
prince. Such is the doctrine deduced from the story of Jack
Cade, who, though a rebel, was set on by God to kill Lord
Saye, a corrupt magistrate not yet brought to justice.

From the king's divine office and its being a part of God's
order comes the abhorrence of civil war. The ubiquity of that
abhorrence at the time does not prevent one of the company
exclaiming at the end of Lord Clifford's story, as if he were
uttering an original thought,

> O Lord, how horrible a thing is division in a realm; to how many
> mischiefs is it the mother! what vice is not thereby kindled, what

virtue left unquenched? For what was the cause of the Duke of York's death and of the cruelty of this Clifford save the variance between King Henry and the house of York, which at length besides millions of the commons brought to destruction all the nobility?

Now if the prince is God's deputy and rebellion even against a bad king or a Jew is forbidden, does loyalty to him admit of any exception? The doctrine is that, though loyalty must be carried very far, there is a point beyond which it must not go. The problem of a personal loyalty is dealt with in the story of Edmund Duke of Somerset. He knew his master, Henry VI, was a childish and feeble king and as such destined to bring his country to ruin. Yet he sticks to him, and this loyalty is his comfort when he reviews his past:

> Yet one thing to me is comfort and relief:
> Constant I was in my prince's quarrel.

> What though fortune envious was my foe,
> A noble heart ought not the sooner yield
> Nor shrink aback for any weal or woe
> But for his prince lie bleeding in the field.

But Henry did not order Edmund to do any crime. If a king gives such an order, he must be disobeyed. Tiptoft Earl of Worcester utters this doctrine. Edward IV had ordered him to murder the innocent sons of the Earl of Desmond, and he obeyed. He knew that if he had disobeyed he would have been beheaded as a traitor. But even so God did not exonerate him and confine the guilt to the king, but punished him in the end. And the final word is this:

> let none such office take
> Save he that can for right his prince forsake.

It is this problem of personal loyalty to a bad king that recurs as the master motive of Shakespeare's *King John*.

Then there was the question not of personal but of national loyalty. Was there *any* exception to a nation's fidelity to the actual ruler? There were two. If the rightful king had been deposed, it was lawful to rise against his usurper and reinstate him. Thus, as mentioned above (p. 77) in another context, the Earl of Salisbury was right in joining the plot to restore

Richard II after Bolingbroke's usurpation. But even this principle must not be carried too far. It was agreed that the house
of York had a better claim to the throne than the house of
Lancaster, but that claim had weakened and become less
cogent than the three generations of actual reign enjoyed by
the Henries. As Edmund Duke of Somerset pronounced:

> Some haply here will move a farther doubt
> And for York's part allege an elder right.
> Oh brainless heads that so run in and out!
> When length of time a state hath firmly pight
> And good accord hath put all strife to flight,
> Were it not better such titles should sleep
> Than all a realm for their trial to weep?

But though York may have been wrong to rebel against
Henry VI, there is never any doubt that Henry IV, the first
Lancastrian king, was a usurper. That is constantly stated, and
most emphatically by Henry Earl of Northumberland, himself
largely responsible for Richard II's deposition. Northumberland had followed the evil doctrine that he was justified in
rebelling against a bad king.

> Because my king did shame me wrongfully,
> I hated him and indeed became his foe.
> And while he did at war in Ireland lie
> I did conspire to turn his weal to woe;
> And through the Duke of York and other moe
> All royal power from him we quickly took
> And gave the same to Henry Bolingbroke.
>
> Neither did we this all only for this cause,
> But, to say truth, force drave us to the same;
> For he, despising God and all good laws,
> Slew whom he would, made sin a very game.
> And, seeing neither age nor counsel could him tame,
> We thought it well done for the kingdom's sake
> To leave his rule that did all rule forsake.

But the rebellion brought no good with it for

> when Sir Henry had attain'd his place
> He straight became in all points worse than he:
> Destroy'd the peers and slew King Richard's grace
> Against his oath made to the lords and me.

And the final moral is

> Wherefore, good Baldwin, will the peers take heed
> Of slander malice and conspiracy.

Richard II, however, was not the worst kind of king. His deeds were bad, but his heart was not utterly corrupted. Thus it was a sin to rebel against him. But if a king is quite bad, and especially if he has attained the crown by violence, then rebellion is justified. The words constantly used to describe the quite bad king are *tyrant* and *tyranny*, whose connotations in the sixteenth century must have been even worse than they are now. When the oracle in the *Winter's Tale* calls Leontes a tyrant, the meaning is not merely that Leontes is unwarrantably arbitrary but that he is not fit to be a king: it is a terrible accusation. Normally a tyrant is past praying for. Such was Richard III; and in the *Winter's Tale* Shakespeare may well have meant to express the power of his belief in the possibilities of forgiveness by showing the repentance even a tyrant is capable of. Anyhow there is no doubt that Richard III was a tyrant. A minor instance of his tyranny was his putting the poet Collingbourne to a most cruel death for having written the satirical couplet,

> The Cat, the Rat, and Lovel our Dog
> Do rule all England, under a Hog.

And Collingbourne is made to complain of the enormity of punishing a trifle with such cruelty.

> If Jews had killed the justest king alive,
> If Turks had burnt up churches, Gods, and all,
> What greater pain could cruel hearts contrive
> Than that I suffered for a trespass small?
> I am not prince nor peer, but yet my fall
> Is worthy to be thought upon for this:
> To see how canker'd tyrants' malice is.

As well as being a tyrant Richard had got the crown by force and could thus not command loyalty. This exception to loyalty is made quite clear in the long prose passage after the story of the rebellious blacksmith:

> Whatsoever man, woman, or child is by the consent of the whole realm established in the royal seat, *so it have not been injuriously*

procured by rigour of sword and open force, but quietly by title either
of inheritance, succession, lawful bequest, common consent or
election, is undoubtedly chosen by God to be his deputy.

It was then just to revolt against a tyrant, but discontented man
was only too apt to class as tyrant a merely bad king appointed
by God to punish his impious subjects.

But if the subject owed an almost inescapable loyalty to the
king, the king had obligations to his subjects, too often un-
fulfilled. He had of course to be just, but the *Mirror* mentions
also the qualities, traditionally so valued in England, of being
accessible and ready to listen to advice. Lord Hastings, for
instance, tells princes that they must not shut themselves off
but imitate God in condescending to impart their favour even
to the lowest.

> Disdain not, princes, easy access, meek cheer.
> We know than angels statelier port ye bear,
> Of God himself: too massy a charge for sprites.
> But then, my lords, consider: He delights
> To vail his grace to us, poor earthly wants,
> To simplest shrubs and to the dunghill plants.
> Express Him then in might and mercies mean:
> So shall ye win, as now ye wield, the realm.

And in the prose that follows the story of the poet Collingbourne
the company is enthusiastic on the liberty that should be
allowed the artist and the benefit a king can get from frank
speech.

If King Richard and his counsellors had allowed or at least but
winked at some such wits, what great commodities might they
have taken thereby. First, they should have known what the
people misliked and grudged at and so mought have found mean,
either by amendment (which is best) or by some other policy, to
have stayed the people's grudge, the forerunner commonly of
rulers' destruction.

Kent in *King Lear* is a character perfectly in keeping with the
teaching of *A Mirror for Magistrates*. He is doggedly loyal yet
quite free in speaking his mind to his master.

I will repeat in summary the historical doctrines of the
Mirror in the order in which they occurred in my chapter on the
general Tudor conception of history. The *Mirror* fully approves

of the powerfully didactic as against the factual or anecdotal practice of history. It is first concerned with instructing the prince or the magistrate through the example of the past. It is almost silent on the Tudor myth: on the great themes of the union of the two houses of York and Lancaster, on the descent of the Tudors from King Arthur, on the Golden Age of Elizabeth. It copies and enlarges the process of moralising history by that close tracing of cause and effect, begun by Polydore Vergil and developed by Hall. It is entirely orthodox and most emphatic in its ideas about history repeating itself and hence being a most valuable practical study, about the importance of obedience to the king and the wickedness and misery of civil war. It is also (and this I mention for the first time) up to the average of the time in nationalist not to say Jingo sentiment, witness the story of Sir Nicholas Burdet.

From this brief summary we may deduce the chief importance of *A Mirror for Magistrates*. It is that it assembled so many current political ideas and gave them a quite new animation by putting them into a poetical form, not indeed at all polished, but on the whole sincere and extremely popular. The *Mirror* indeed shifted the centre of sixteenth century poetry. In the age of Henry VIII didactic poetry had been less alive than the lyric: Hawes could not compete with Wyatt and Surrey. But now, new and living ideas raised the status of didactic poetry. The new strenuous alliance of politics morality and religion that marked the Reformation had been given literary form, and one that persisted till near the end of the century. There are three great products of the high age of Elizabeth with a strong political intention: Spenser's *Fairy Queen*, Sidney's *Arcadia*, and Shakespeare's History Plays. All three should be thought of together, and behind them, the most authoritative earlier exponent in poetry of the ideas on which they are founded, is *A Mirror for Magistrates*.

2. SPENSER, SIDNEY, WARNER

Although *A Mirror for Magistrates* was the essential prelude of the *Fairy Queen*, *Arcadia*, and Shakespeare's Histories, these works do not exploit equally the same political themes. Spenser's debt was general: he could write political poetry with far greater assurance when his public had been brought up on the

Mirror. In detail he worked differently. His aim was positive and epic: to fashion a gentleman by examples of what to do not to discipline one by examples of what not to do. Nor is he concerned with Plantagenet history: he is far more interested in Arthur and the resurrection of Arthur in the Tudors. In this he is allied to one of the most popular verse-chronicles of the age of Elizabeth: Warner's *Albion's England.* This poem was published in part in 1586 and expanded in subsequent editions. It epitomises history from Noah to Elizabeth. But though it includes the epoch of Hall's chronicle and of the *Mirror* it mainly lacks their moralising of history. There is no sense of cause and effect: the house of Lancaster is the victim of mere fortune. Only with the Tudor myth the case is different: Providence was greatly concerned with establishing Henry VII on the throne. Warner makes much too of the Tudors' royal ancestry. In the twenty-ninth chapter of Book Six he describes how Queen Katherine, widow of Henry V, courted Owen Tudor "a brave esquire of Wales," who modestly states that he has his pedigree from King Cadwallader. And they go on to talk a lot of Ovid together in the most handsome Elizabethan style. Spenser and Warner, therefore, though generally encouraged by the *Mirror* to write verse on high political matters, go for one of their great themes behind the *Mirror* to Hall.

Arcadia, which Sidney and his age regarded as an epic though in prose, is related to the *Mirror* not only after the general manner of the *Fairy Queen* and *Albion's England* but in having civil war one of its main themes.

These three works, however, lie off the main road of my enquiry, which now must leave the modes of narrative and monologue for the drama proper.

CHAPTER IV

The Literary Background: Dramatic

1. THE MORALITY PLAY

ALTHOUGH the Morality Play was an essential stage in the evolution of English drama, although it may have prompted the structure of *Henry IV*, and although as a pervasive influence on all Shakespeare's History Plays it was of the first importance, it had not a great deal to do with the ideas about history, so far the theme of this book, on which those plays were built. Those ideas get first into the drama less through the Morality than through the theme of the last chapter, *A Mirror for Magistrates*, of which *Gorboduc*, the first play with a philosophy of history, is an offshoot.

The main moralities with a historical turn are Skelton's *Magnificence*, *Respublica* (possibly by Udall), Lyndsay's *Satire of the Three Estates*, and Bale's *King John*. The first three are substantially the same play, though poetically Lyndsay's is vastly superior. The ruler or the state is substituted for Everyman and subjected to Everyman's temptations. He is corrupted by one or other Vice, falls into misery, repents, and is rescued by divine aid. Lyndsay adds to the Everyman theme much direct reference to contemporary Scotland. But none of the plays sees history in a pattern. Skelton indeed exhorts his audience to "remember the turn of Fortune's wheel" and to look on his play as a "mirror"; but with the minute historical circumstance of *A Mirror for Magistrates* he has nothing to do nor with Hall's philosophy of history. His play is not a History Play but a Morality with a princely turn.

Respublica is social rather than political, with Avarice the chief Vice. It does, however, contain in the prologue this interesting passage about God's bringing the state periodically back to order out of disturbance; yet without citing any particular stretch of history. There is no application of the doctrine to the Wars of the Roses and the Tudors.

> But though these vices by cloaked collusion
> And by counterfeit names, hidden their abusion,

Do reign for a while to common weals' prejudice,
Perverting all right and all order of true justice,
Yet time trieth all and time bringeth truth to light,
That wrong may not ever still reign in place of right.
For when pleaseth God such common weals to restore
To their wealth and honour wherein they were afore,
He sendeth down his most tender compassion
To cause truth go about in visitation.
Verity, the daughter of sage old father time,
Showeth all as it is, be it virtue or crime.
Then doth justice all such as common weal oppress,
Tempered with mercy, endeavour to suppress;
With whom anon is linked tranquillity and peace
To common weals' joy and perpetual increase.

Bale's *King John* is different. Though John is a kind of
English Everyman, the life of the play is contemporary Protestant propaganda, and allegorical characters are constantly
turning into actual historical ones. Dissimulation turns into the
Monk of Swinstead who poisons John, Usurped Power into the
actual Pope. Little bits of actual history too appear in the more
general Morality procedure. But, again, there is no reflection
whatever on the way historical events take place, no philosophy
of cause and effect, while political theory does not go beyond
ordinary royalism as intensified by Protestant interpretations
of St. Paul, the royalism found in the Homilies.

I therefore pass over the Morality and go on to speak more
fully of *Gorboduc*.

2. GORBODUC

It is not too easy to put a label to *Gorboduc*, but it is certain
that the usual one of "first Senecan tragedy in English" is mis-
leading. The classical regularity of construction must indeed
have been novel and exciting to the young intellectuals of the
time and it may have been taken from Seneca's example as
well as from anywhere else. But in spirit the play is an offshoot
of *A Mirror for Magistrates* and in content it is a Chronicle Play.
Taken as a tragedy, to be judged by its universal human appeal,
it is a dreary affair; taken as a piece of solemn contemporary
didacticism and, in point of literary history, as extending the
historical and ethical doctrines of Hall and the Homilies into
the drama, it is a most interesting composition. *Gorboduc* has

also many traces of the Morality Play; but that is a topic sufficiently treated elsewhere and with no direct bearing on Shakespeare's Histories.

Once more the novelty of *Gorboduc* must be insisted on. The rigid decorum of the play with its choruses, its long sententious speeches, its avoidance of all violence on the stage, its unity of action, and the blank verse now first used in the drama must have had for the young intellectuals of the time something of the glamour of *Poems and Ballads* in 1866 or the *Waste Land* in 1922. Behind it were the recent formulations of Italianate neo-classicism corresponding to the poetical novelties of Baudelaire and Laforgue behind Swinburne and Eliot respectively. Only by realising a certain awe which this novelty must have created in the audience can we estimate the effect that the play's content must have produced.

The doctrinal affinity of *Gorboduc* with *A Mirror for Magistrates* is close. It is just what one would expect. One of its authors, Sackville, was part-author of the *Mirror*, the other, Norton, published in 1561, the year *Gorboduc* was produced, a translation of Calvin's *Institutes*, the political doctrines of which, agreeing as they do with the Homilies, may have left their mark on the *Mirror*. The motive behind them both is identical; and the first chorus in *Gorboduc* actually uses the word *mirror* in setting it forth. Commenting on Gorboduc's intention to divide his kingdom between his sons Ferrex and Porrex, the chorus says,

> And this great king, that doth divide his land
> And change the course of his descending crown
> And yields the reign into his children's hand
> From blissful state of joy and great renown,
> A mirror shall become to princes all,
> To learn to shun the cause of such a fall.

But in one matter *Gorboduc* differed from the *Mirror*. Though the *Mirror* was thoroughly up to date it was addressed not to any named statesmen then living but to men in office generally. *Gorboduc*, on the other hand, in a production by the gentlemen of the Inner Temple on 18 January 1561, was not so much played before, as directed at, Queen Elizabeth. This particular mirror was intended to enlighten no less a person than the queen. For something so solemn the austerities of the new classicism were the fitting vehicle.

Corresponding to this particularity of address is one particularity of substance. Most of the substance indeed is general,
applicable to all princes; but the references to the succession
are plainly directed at Elizabeth. They are gathered together
in the last speech of all, when Eubulus, the king's secretary and
the counsellor who is always in the right, comments on the
whole action and foretells the future course of events. The
country's case is disastrous, for

> No ruler rests within the regal seat;
> The heir, to whom the sceptre 'longs, unknown.

The result is anarchy. How terrible, therefore, is the ruler's
responsibility to settle the succession while he lives. Anarchy,
he says,

> doth grow, when, lo, unto the prince,
> Whom death or sudden hap of life bereaves,
> No certain heir remains, such certain heir
> As not all only is the rightful heir
> But to the realm is so made known to be.

Once the prince is dead, parliament lacks the authority to back
up its nomination of a successor.

> No, no: then parliament should have been holden
> And certain heirs appointed to the crown,
> To stay the title of established right
> And in the people plant obedience,
> While yet the prince did live; whose name and power
> By lawful summons and authority
> Might make a parliament to be of force
> And might have set the state in quiet stay.

Presumably in the production the actor who took the part of
Eubulus, speaking with the authority of the Inns of Court
behind him, would have come forward and spoken straight at
the queen. Such didacticism, as stated on p. 56 above, was
quite in the Renaissance tradition. The exalted position of the
prince in the sixteenth century was certainly paid for by the
weight of good advice he was expected to endure.

In general political doctrine *Gorboduc* is orthodox and close
to *A Mirror for Magistrates*. It is even more emphatic than the
Mirror on the theme that political order is a part of a larger
order, natural and divine. When in the second scene of the

play the counsellors debate on Gorboduc's project to divide the
kingdom they agree on the basis of what is fitting in the larger
realm of the universe. Philander argues that it is against nature
or degree that Gorboduc should abdicate in favour of his sons.

> But now the head to stoop beneath them both,
> Ne kind ne reason ne good order bears.
> And oft it hath been seen, where nature's course
> Hath been perverted in disordered wise,
> When fathers cease to know that they should rule
> And children cease to know they should obey.

Not that Philander has anything against the King's sons:

> Only I mean to show by certain rules,
> Which kind hath graft within the mind of man,
> That nature hath her order and her course,
> Which being broken doth corrupt the state
> Of mind and things, ev'n in the best of all.

Whatever the practical errors of Gorboduc, there is no doubt
of his divine status as king. In explaining his intentions in the
second scene of the play he begins:

> Ye know, the gods, who have the sovereign care
> For kings, for kingdoms, and for common weals,
> Gave me two sons in my more lusty age;

and no one would dream of contradicting him. The duty of the
subordinate officer to give good advice to the prince is one of
the play's reiterated themes, conveyed with special force in the
dumb show before the second act, where the good counsellor
is likened to wine in a glass and the evil to poison in a cup of
gold.

A further likeness to Hall and the *Mirror* (which is also one of
the beauties of the play) is the carefully worked out sequence of
cause and effect. Gorboduc's initial mistake leads surely from
one misfortune to another. It is in this motivation too that the
human interest of the play is mainly found. Thus Ferrex, the
elder son, not in himself a bad person, fears that Gorboduc may
have influenced Porrex's ambition by giving him equal rights
with himself. He resists Hermon's wicked suggestions of making war on Porrex but decides to arm secretly in self-defence.
Porrex hears of these secret preparations and decides to invade
before it is too late. In its ending *Gorboduc* is more like Hall

than like the *Mirror*, for it maintains that order will emerge from chaos once more:

> Of justice, yet must God in fine restore
> This noble crown unto the lawful heir:
> For right will always live and rise at length,
> But wrong can never take deep root to last.

Not only is the notion that history repeats itself implicit in the whole exemplary trend of the play but it is preached explicitly within the play. Eubulus, soliloquising at the beginning of the second scene of act five, laments that the people are quite unable to learn the obvious lessons of history. In his long speech in the play's second scene, dissuading Gorboduc from parting with the crown, he cites the disastrous precedent of Brut.

> The mighty Brut, first prince of all this land,
> Possess'd the same and rul'd it well in one.
> He, thinking that the compass did suffice
> For his three sons three kingdoms eke to make,
> Cut it in three, as you would now in twain.
> But how much British blood hath since been spilt
> To join again the sunder'd unity,
> What princes slain before their timely hour,
> What waste of towns and people in the land,
> What treasons heap'd on murders and on spoils,
> Whose just revenge ev'n yet is scarcely ceas'd,
> Ruthful remembrance is yet raw in mind.
> The gods forbid the like to chance again.

The authors of *Gorboduc* are orthodox on their notions of rebellion. Though Gorboduc made mistakes, that was no justification for the people, fickle and irresponsible, to rise and kill him:

> Though kings forget to govern as they ought,
> Yet subjects must obey as they are bound.

For this great crime there must be punishment; but wise rulers will confine it to the ringleaders. And when in his last speech of all Eubulus pictures the horrors of civil war he might be anticipating the 1574 homily, *Against Disobedience and wilful Rebellion*.

> With fire and sword thy native folk shall perish,
> One kinsman shall bereave another's life.

The father shall unwitting slay the son,
The son shall slay the sire and know it not.
Lo, guiltless blood shall thus each where be shed.
Thus shall the wasted soil yield forth no fruit,
But dearth and famine shall possess the land.
The towns shall be consum'd and burnt with fire,
The peopled cities shall wax desolate.
These be the fruits your civil wars will bring.

In sum, the authors of *Gorboduc* transferred into the dramatic medium and expressed in blank verse most of the ideas about history on which Shakespeare's History Plays were founded. They may well have encouraged Shakespeare, against what we shall see was the trend of the Chronicle Plays, to dwell on historical principles and not merely dramatise historical events.

3. THE ENGLISH CHRONICLE PLAY

The English Chronicle Play is an ambiguous name. *Gorboduc*, at its first publication, was called a tragedy; yet it takes its plot from the English chronicles. *King Lear*, when published in quarto in 1608, was called a "true chronicle history," however little subsequent years accepted it as such. Greene's *James IV* was printed with the title *The Scottish History of James IV slain at Flodden*. The same title goes on to say that the play was "intermixed with a pleasant comedy, presented by Oberon King of the fairies"; while the main plot is actually an Italian story. The chronicling consists in the title. I shall not try to define the English Chronicle Play, but shall confine myself nearly to plays related very obviously by their subject matter to the plays of Shakespeare denominated Histories by the editors of the First Folio: that is, to plays treating mainly of English history after the Conquest.

That Shakespeare owed something to some of these plays is obvious. That he owed less than is sometimes thought I shall try later to prove. Meanwhile it will be granted that he owed enough for it to be necessary to include the English Chronicle Play among the topics I deal with before coming to Shakespeare himself: among the literary productions that helped in some sort to make Shakespeare's History Plays what they are.

It can be stated with some confidence that by 1580 men

began to write plays that had as a main concern the facts of history, that sought to instruct their audience in the matter of the prose chronicles. But it can be stated dogmatically that Shakespeare grew up along with an increasing trend to write plays of this kind, until in 1592 Nashe in his *Pierce Penniless*, writing in defence of plays, says

> First for the subject of them, for the most part it is borrowed out of our English chronicles, wherein our forefathers' valiant acts, that have lien long buried in rusty brass and worm-eaten books, are revived, and they themselves raised from the grave of oblivion and brought to plead their aged honours in open presence.

It was a trend away from a play like *Gorboduc*, where the political morality came first and the facts of history counted for little as mere information; and it duplicates the trend of the chronicles themselves. Just as Holinshed seizes on the factual side of Hall and ignores his philosophy, so most of the English Chronicle Plays ignore the steady moral bent of *Gorboduc* and exploit the mere accident of successive events. And further, just as Holinshed revives the medieval simplicities of Higden, so the plays on English history go behind the severer form of the Morality to the factual and accidental forms of some of the Miracle Plays. Of these one of the best examples is *Mary Magdalene* in the Digby Mysteries, where no less than fifty-two scenes set forth in simple charade style the supposed facts of Mary's life and death. Another contemporary parallel is the revival of the medieval pulpit in the Puritan preachers. Like the Miracle Plays the English Chronicle Plays were popular and they were rarely if ever performed before the sophisticated audiences of the Inns of Court.

The nature of the factual element will appear most plainly in an extreme example. The *True Tragedy of Richard III*, published in 1594 but written some years earlier, not only contains much chronicle matter in its bulk but has informative prologue and epilogue. The prologue represents Truth and Poetry meeting the Ghost of the Duke of Clarence. Truth informs Poetry she will "add bodies" to Poetry's "shadows" and proceeds to give an exact historical account of the events leading up to Richard III's reign. At the end, after Bosworth and Henry VII's departure to London to marry the heiress of York, four of the play's characters stay behind to tell the audience what happens later; and very minutely informative they are,

as here for example on the subject of Henry VIII and his
children:

> When he had reign'd full thirty-eight years,
> Nine months and some odd days, and was buried in Windsor,
> He died and left three famous sprigs behind him.
> Edward the Sixt:
> He did restore the gospel to his light
> And finish'd that his father left undone;
> A wise young prince giv'n greatly to his book.
> He brought the English service first in use
> And died when he had reign'd six years five months
> And some odd days and lieth buried in Westminster.
> Next after him a Mary did succeed,
> Which married Philip King of Spain.
> She reign'd five years four months and some
> Odd days and is buried in Westminster.
> When she was dead, her sister did succeed.

It was only a very serious desire for facts that could have
tolerated such writing when the play's business was done.

In other ways too the English Chronicle Play (like Holinshed)
continues the practice of the medieval chronicle, whose functions, as I recorded in my second chapter, were to provide a
repertory of recreational anecdote, to serve as memorial of
great men, and to convey separate moral lessons. The recreational anecdote, existing just for itself and of no organic virtue,
is so much a part of all inferior Elizabethan drama that it
hardly needs special mention here; but at least its so frequent
occurrence serves to link the Chronicle Play with the less rather
than with the more thoughtful type of historical writing. Examples are Prince Henry's sticking his coat full of needles before
going to see his father in the *Famous Victories of Henry V* and
Queen Eleanor being swallowed up by the earth for having put
to death the virtuous Lady Mayoress of London in Peele's
Edward I. The Chronicle Plays also bring certain great men
into prominence. Illustration is superfluous. The matter of
conveying separate moral lessons will be sufficiently dealt with
when I come to these plays' general doctrinal content.

Where the Chronicle Play differs most from the medieval
chronicle is in the matter of patriotism.

There is a hard-dying habit of putting down the vogue of the
English Chronicle Plays to the Spanish Armada, but it is un-

founded. At most, that event encouraged a process already in full working. Peele's *Battle of Alcazar*, Lyly's *Midas*, Greene's *Orlando Furioso*, and Robert Wilson's *Three Lords and three Ladies of London* are sometimes called Armada plays. But in the first three the references are scanty or uncircumstantiated, and in Wilson's play they occur abruptly in a setting that has nothing to do with the chronicles but is inherited from the Moralities. Indeed it is likely that the publication of a second edition of Holinshed's Chronicle in 1587 did more to forward the growth of the English Chronicle Play than the defeat of the Armada in 1588.

This does not mean that the Chronicle Play did not spring out of the patriotism, not to say jingoism, that was gathering such force in the middle years of the Queen's reign. On the contrary, this national self-satisfaction is an animating principle of these plays and is often directly expressed in it. And it is something new: different from the aggressive, nationalist, but nervous protestantism of the early Homilies and Bale's *King John*, and far wider spread over the whole community than the earnest didacticism about the succession found in *Gorboduc*.

This patriotism can take rather agreeable forms. Here for example is a piece of rhetoric from *Locrine*, which, we must remember, is a chronicle of early British history as well as a revenge tragedy. After the defeat of the invading Scythians, Corineus and Locrine have this conversation:

> *Cor.* And thus, yea thus, shall all the rest be serv'd
>   That seek to enter Albion gainst our wills.
>   If the brave nation of the Troglodytes,
>   If all the coal-black Ethiopians,
>   If all the forces of the Amazons,
>   If all the hosts of the Barbarian lands
>   Should dare to enter this our little world,
>   Soon should they rue their overbold attempts
>   That after us our progeny may say:
>   There lie the beasts that sought to usurp our land.
> *Loc.* Aye, they are beasts that seek to usurp our land
>   And like to brutish beasts they shall be serv'd;
>   For mighty Jove, the supreme king of heaven,
>   That guides the concourse of the meteors
>   And rules the motion of the azure sky,
>   Fights always for the Britons' safety.

Peele in finer verse says much the same near the end of Act
Two of the *Battle of Alcazar*, putting these words in praise
of Queen Elizabeth into the mouth of Sebastian King of
Portugal:

> Were every ship ten thousand on the seas,
> Mann'd with the strength of all the eastern kings,
> Conveying all the monarchs of the world
> To invade the island where her highness reigns,
> 'Twere all in vain, for heavens and destinies
> Attend and wait upon her majesty.
> Sacred imperial and holy is her seat,
> Shining with wisdom love and mightiness.
> Nature, that every thing imperfect made,
> Fortune, that never yet was constant found,
> Time, that defaceth every golden show,
> Dare not decay remove or be impure;
> Both nature time and fortune all agree
> To bless and serve her royal majesty.

More attractive, for being more human, are the scenes in
Wilson's *Three Lords and three Ladies of London* describing the
threat of the Spanish invasion. Though the play in which
they occur is close to the Morality (with London, though she
appears only to speak a prologue, substituted for Respublica
as heroine), they faithfully represent the best side of the
patriotism that animated the English Chronicle Plays. The
three lords of London are Policy Pomp and Pleasure, the
three ladies Love Lucre and Conscience. After much moral
traffic between the various allegorical characters Diligence
announces to the three lords that the Spaniards are about
to invade.

> The Spanish forces, lordings, are prepar'd
> In bravery and boast beyond all bounds
> T' invade, to win, to conquer all this land.
> They chiefly aim at London's stately Pomp,
> At London's Pleasure Wealth and Policy,
> Intending to despoil her of them all,
> And over all these lovely ladies three,
> Love Lucre Conscience, peerless, of the rarest price,
> To tyrannise and carry hardest hand.

Policy refuses to be rattled and orders shows and rejoicings in London as well as preparations for war.

> Well, Diligence, go get in readiness
> Men and munitions: bid our pages ply
> To see that all our furniture be well.
> My Lords, I would I might advise ye now
> To carry, as it were, a careless regard
> Of these Castilians and their accustom'd bravado.
> Lord Pomp, let nothing that's magnifical
> Or that may tend to London's graceful state
> Be unperform'd; as shows and solemn feasts,
> Watches in armour, triumphs, cresset-lights,
> Bonfires, bells, and peals or ordnance.
> And, Pleasure, see that plays be published,
> May-games and masques with mirth and minstrelsy,
> Pageants and school-feasts, bears and puppet plays.
> Myself will muster upon Mile End Green,
> As though we saw and fear'd not to be seen;
> Which will their spies in such a wonder set
> To see us reck so little such a foe,
> Whom all world admires, save only we,
> And we respect our sport more than his spite,
> That John the Spaniard will in rage run mad
> To see us bend like oaks with his vain breath.

Later three Spanish characters, Pride Shame and Ambition, come in and are duly routed by the English lords. Ambition has as his "impress," *non sufficit orbis*. Reading these scenes at the present time, one cannot help substituting *morgen die ganze Welt* for the motto and for Policy's defiance the advice to be grim and gay.

A constant piece of patriotic convention is that every English king or queen, whether good or bad, is made to appear noble in presence of foreigners. There is a good example in Peele's *Edward I*. Queen Eleanor, Edward's wife, is a proud and luxurious Castilian. She represents Spanish pomp and would like to corrupt English simplicity. She puts to death the virtuous Lady Mayoress of London; and the earth swallows her up for the crime. It disgorges her, however, so that she may confess to having committed adultery with her brother-in-law. But in the scene when Edward I, lately victorious over Baliol King of Scotland, hands him back his kingdom, Eleanor is the

stately English queen, the loyal supporter of her husband and
properly enamoured of him:

> Now brave John Baliol, Lord of Galloway
> And King of Scots, shine with thy golden head.
> Shake thy spears in honour of his name
> Under whose royalty thou wear'st the same.
> The welkin, spangled through with golden spots,
> Reflects no finer in a frosty night
> Than lovely Longshanks in his Eleanor's eye;
> So Ned thy Nell in every part of thee.

This Ned-ing and Nell-ing is quite alien to the wicked Castilian
princess and shows that we here have for the moment to do not
with specific characters but with An English King and An
English Queen in their traditional parts of forthright hearty
English monarchs. And when the heir to the throne is about
to be born, they address each other in the same way. Eleanor,
however wicked, must not be allowed to let the English monarchy down.

I come now to the general doctrinal content of the Chronicle
Plays. How many of the ideas set out in my first two chapters
get into them?

First, although most of the writers of these plays must have
known the theory of degree and the hierarchical conception of
the universe, they seem little interested in them. They are
mainly practical playwrights writing for a popular audience,
with small inclination to philosophy. The portion of the hierarchy that interests them is the social one, but that interest
takes the form of preaching by example that a sensible man
sticks to his position in society; it makes no suggestion that by
so doing a man was taking his own part (small perhaps yet none
the less necessary) in the great cosmic harmony. At the end of
the *Pinner of Wakefield*, which though called a comedy contains
traditional ballad lore acceptable enough as historical to an
Elizabethan audience, George the Pinner refuses the knight-
hood offered him by King Edward; but in a thoroughly
matter-of-fact way.

> *Ed.* Kneel down, George.
> *Geo.* What will your Majesty do?
> *Ed.* Dub thee a knight, George.
> *Geo.* I beseech your Grace, grant me one thing.

Ed. What is that?

Geo. Then let me live and die a yeoman still:
   So was my father, so must live his son;
   For 'tis more credit to men of base degree
   To do great deeds than men of dignity.

Ed. Well, be it so, George.

The *Tanner of Tamworth* in the first part of Heywood's *Edward IV* has the same hearty contentment with his station in life. Every now and then, as an exception, a small piece of cosmic lore will get through. In this same play the king talks to Jane Shore about himself and the court in terms of sun and stars, implying the correspondence between macrocosm and body politic; and in *Nobody and Somebody*, a play dealing with the early British material of Geoffrey of Monmouth, Somebody stands generally for chaos and absence of degree.

The case is pretty much the same when we come to the body of doctrine set forth in my second chapter. On the whole the writers of Chronicle Plays show little thought, though bits get through every now and then. And the simpler and less philosophical the thought, the more likely it is to get through.

In the *Famous Victories of Henry V*, Peele's *Edward I* and *Battle of Alcazar*, the *Life and Death of Jack Straw, Look about You*, and the *Famous History of the Life and Death of Captain Thomas Stukeley* there is hardly any thought about history at all. Other plays may have a touch here and there. For instance in *Lord Cromwell* the Chorus before Act IV says to the audience,

> Now sit and see his highest state of all;
> His height of rising and his sudden fall,

showing an analogy with the theme of the *Mirror for Magistrates*. In the second part of Heywood's *Edward IV* the Queen and Jane Shore have a conversation in which the instance of Henry II and Rosamond is recalled in a way that suggests the doctrine of history repeating itself. Yet in the same play there is not the slightest reflection on Edward's death. He simply dies: there is no suggestion of cause and effect, that his early death may have been a punishment for his false oath sworn before York to seek no more than his duchy, and for his impolitic marriage.

The political theorising that occurs most often is about loyalty to the king and rebellion, with which Protestantism and Catholicism are often connected respectively. The *Troublesome Reign of King John* provides illustrations. John, referring to Lewis's expected invasion, says

> Though John be faulty, yet let subjects bear;
> He will amend and right the people's wrongs.
> A mother though she were unnatural
> Is better than the kindest stepdame is.
> Let never Englishman trust foreign rule.

And the Bastard gives the orthodox doctrine that only God may punish an erring king.

> Why, Salisbury, admit the wrongs are true,
> Yet subjects may not take in hand revenge
> And rob the heavens of their proper power,
> Where sitteth he to whom revenge belongs.

The *True Tragedy of Richard III*, while not seeing history as an organic process, is typically emphatic on the evils of civil war and on the benefit of Richmond's marriage in averting it. The anarchy of civil war is like brambles choking the authentic saplings in a grove, while the abuses of the commonwealth at such a time are like the waters of the Nile overflowing its banks. The *Life and Death of Jack Straw* is conventionally sound on the evils of rebellion, the doctrine being put in the mouth not only of those in authority but in that of Nobs, who, though one of the rebels, comments chorically on their excesses. In Heywood's *Edward IV* there is the detestation of civil war in plenty.

So much for the general run of the Chronicle Plays. A few (apart from Shakespeare's) stand out so clearly from the norm and are so much more thoughtful that they call for separate treatment. These are Marlowe's *Edward II*, *Sir Thomas More*, *Edward III*, *Woodstock*, and *Sir John Oldcastle*.

Edward II does contain political reflection but it is confined to two themes. These are hinted at in the play's complete title —*The troublesome Reign and lamentable Death of Edward II, King of England, with the tragical Fall of proud Mortimer*—and they are the status of the king and the punishment of overweening political ambition.

Little need be said about the second theme. Young Mortimer is a character in the tradition of the *Mirror for Magistrates*.

He is persistently violent and ambitious and arranges for the king's death with Machiavellian craft.

> The king must die, or Mortimer goes down,
> The commons now begin to pity him;
> Yet he that is the cause of Edward's death
> Is sure to pay for it when his son is of age.
> And therefore will I do it cunningly.
> This letter, written by a friend of ours,
> Contains his death yet bids them save his life.
> *Edwardum occidere nolite timere, bonum est;*
> Fear not to kill the king, 'tis good he die.
> But read it thus, and that's another sense:
> *Edwardum occidere nolite, timere bonum est;*
> Kill not the king, 'tis good to fear the worst.
> Unpointed as it is thus shall it go,
> That, being dead, if it chance to be found,
> Matrevis and the rest may bear the blame,
> And we be quit that caus'd it to be done.

After Edward's death and Prince Edward's resolute bearing, the *Mirror* motive comes out. The queen exclaims to Mortimer,

> Ay me, see where he comes, and they with him.
> Now, Mortimer, begins our tragedy.

And Mortimer, ordered to his death, speaks appropriately:

> Base fortune, now I see that in thy wheel
> There is a point to which when men aspire
> They tumble headlong down. That point I touch'd,
> And, seeing there was no place to mount up higher,
> Why should I grieve at my declining fall?
> Farewell, fair queen, weep not for Mortimer,
> That scorns the world and, as a traveller,
> Goes to discover countries yet unknown.

This is the matter of the *Mirror for Magistrates* but, instead of the moral that other statesmen should learn by his example, the typical Marlovian defiance.

There is no such defiance in Marlowe's doctrines of kingship and loyalty. He never confuses the legitimate cutting off of princely parasites with the illegitimate lifting of the hand against the Lord's Anointed. However much our personal sympathies with Edward as human being may fluctuate according to his behaviour or his sufferings, the political sentiments remain impeccable. Moreover they are treated so fully that Marlowe must have been interested in them. Early in the play the Archbishop of Canterbury says,

> But yet lift not your swords against the king.

Later Lancaster, heading the barons, answers the queen's question whether they seek the king,

> No, madam, but that cursed Gaveston:
> Far be it from the thought of Lancaster
> To offer violence to his sovereign;
> We would but rid the realm of Gaveston.

The characters show different degrees of loyalty. Matching in his loyalty the treachery of Mortimer and setting the standard of right, is Prince Edward. He never wavers and is always on the lookout for the least disloyalty to his father. When young Mortimer, joined with the queen at Hainault, says that he lives to advance the prince's standard, Prince Edward at once says,

> How mean you, and the king my father lives?

Edmund Earl of Kent, the king's brother, remaining loyal while among the English peers, yields to the proposals of John of Hainault to make war on his brother, and repents after the battle in violent self-curses:

> Vile wretch, and why hast thou of all unkind
> Borne arms against thy brother and thy king?
> Rain showers of vengeance on my cursed head,
> Thou God, to whom in justice it belongs
> To punish this unnatural revolt.

And later he deplores the fate of the commonwealth

> Where lords keep courts and kings are lock'd in prison.

The queen changes from violent loyalty to disloyalty equally violent.

In spite of these two political themes *Edward II* shows no prevailing political interest: no sense of any sweep or pattern of history. What animates the play is the personal theme: Edward's personal obsession, his peculiar psychology, the humour and finally the great pathos of his situation. Marlowe shows no sense of national responsibility: he merely attaches two current political orthodoxies to a play concerned nominally but not essentially with historical matter. This is not to decry the play; it is only to suggest of what kind the play is or is not.

In spite of its multiple authorship *Sir Thomas More* shows a recurrent interest in cosmic or political matters alien to the norm of the Chronicle Play and much wider than the political themes just discussed in *Edward II*. Not that there is any steady development of a single great idea; only a number of separate instances or touches show that some of the authors thought of More's career as a part of a cosmic process and as an example of the kind of thing that happens in states. And though these instances are conspicuous in the lines that may be by Shakespeare they are by no means confined to them.

First, More's speeches to the rioters in the Shakespearean passage bring out to the full the traditional Elizabethan notion of degree as described in my first chapters: they take us quite away from the mere doctrine of resting contented with your station to the religious setting of Elyot's *Governor* and the Homilies.

> Let me set up before your thoughts, good friends,
> One supposition, which if you will mark,
> You shall perceive how horrible a shape
> Your innovation bears. First, 'tis a sin
> Which oft th' apostle did forwarn us of,
> Urging obedience to authority.
> And 'twere no error if I told you all
> You were in arms against your [God himself].
> For to the king God hath his office lent
> Of dread, of justice, power and command,
> Hath bid him rule and will'd you to obey.
> And, to add ampler majesty to this,
> He hath not only lent the king his figure,
> His throne and sword, but given him his own name,
> Calls him a god on earth. What do you then,
> Rising gainst him that God himself installs,
> But rise gainst God? What do you to your souls
> In doing this? O, desperate as you are,
> Wash your foul minds with tears; and those same hands,
> That you like rebels lift against the peace,
> Lift up for peace; and your unreverent knees
> Make them your feet to kneel to be forgiven.

In a later speech, after he has fallen from favour, More philosophises on the fact of degree.

> I conceive that nature
> Hath sundry metals, out of which she frames
> Us mortals, each in valuation
> Outprizing other. Of the finest stuff
> The finest features come: the rest of earth
> Receive base fortune even before their birth;
> Hence slaves have their creation, and I think
> Nature provides content for the base mind.
> Under the whip the burden and the toil
> Their low-wrought bodies drudge in patience.

The phrase "each in valuation outprizing other" shows that the author knew the doctrine of the chain of being, where every creature was at once inferior and superior to another. In little touches too the idea of "degree" comes out. Faulkner, the long-haired ruffian who breaks in on More as Lord Chancellor, seeking justice, says

> I thought it stood not with my reputation and degree to come to my questions and answers before a city justice.

More throughout is perfectly aware of the vagaries of fortune and of the temptation, when she is favourable, to make a man forget his degree. This is his soliloquy after he has been made Lord Chancellor.

> It is in heaven that I am thus and thus;
> And that which we profanely term our fortunes
> Is the provision of the power above,
> Fitted and shap'd just to that strength of nature
> Which we are born [withal]. Good God, good God,
> That I from such an humble bench of birth
> Should step as 'twere up to my country's head
> And give the law out there! I, in my father's life,
> To take prerogative and tythe of knees
> From elder kinsmen and him bind by my place
> To give the smooth and dexter way to me,
> That owe it him by nature!

For general political interest there is the debate in IV. 2 on how to deal with France and the German Emperor and the doctrine (traditional but presented with great emphasis in the prose comment on the tragedy of Collingbourne in the *Mirror for Magistrates*) that counsellors must keep the king informed of what is going on. Cholmley blames some of the king's counsellors for not telling him about the people's hatred of the aliens.

> Now, afore God, your honours pardon me.
> Men of your place and greatness are to blame,
> I tell ye true my lords, in that his majesty
> Is not informed of this base abuse
> And daily wrongs are offer'd to his subjects;
> For, if he were, I know his gracious wisdom
> Would soon redress it.

These instances, with others that could be quoted, make *Sir Thomas More* quite unusually thoughtful for an English Chronicle Play and remove it far from mere brick-on-brick narration.

Edward III for all its brightness and glitter is one of the most academic and intellectual of the Chronicle Plays. In the first scene the Black Prince is still a student, and his father says to him,

> And, Ned, thou must begin
> Now to forget thy study and thy book
> And use thy shoulders to an armour's weight.

The Earl of Warwick must certainly have been trained in university disputation to have argued so thoroughly on both sides of the question whether his daughter, the Countess of Salisbury, should yield to the king's love-making. The Black Prince, threatened with death before Poitiers, is not melodramatic but reflective and intellectual. His tone is that of Seneca the moralist. The Countess of Salisbury, conventionally chaste, is clever and witty too, as when she argues that the law of marriage is older than that of kingship:

> In violating marriage sacred law
> You break a greater honour than yourself.
> To be a king is of a younger house
> Than to be married. Your progenitor,
> Sole reigning Adam of the universe,
> By God was honour'd for a married man
> But not by him anointed for a king.

There are a number of references to the order of creation. Warwick for instance, arguing with his daughter to yield to

Edward, uses the traditional comparison of the king to the lion and the sun,

> The lion doth become his bloody jaws
> And grace his foragement, by being mild
> When vassal fear lies trembling at his feet.
> The king will in his glory hide thy shame;
> And those that gaze on him to find out thee
> Will lose their eyesight, looking in the sun.

The author of the play had a lively awareness of the great cosmic correspondences. For instance he uses the correspondence between heaven and body politic when he compares the countess defying her Scottish besiegers from the battlements of her castle with angels repelling devils from the battlements of heaven, making her

> Breathe from the wall an angel's note from heaven
> Of sweet defiance to her barbarous foes.

And at one of the high moments of the play, when the entrance of the Black Prince and his troops begins to recall King Edward from his infatuation with the countess, there occurs the comparison of the world and microcosm:

> Lust is a fire, and men like lanthorns show
> Light lust within themselves even through themselves.
> Away, loose silks of wavering vanity!
> Shall the large limit of fair Brittany
> By me be overthrown, and shall I not
> Master this little mansion of myself?
> Give me an armour of eternal steel:
> I go to conquer kings.

Such writing is alien to the norm of the Chronicle Plays.

There is political reflectiveness also. The author takes Edward's title to the French throne seriously. Robert of Artois in the opening scene is in exile from France because he believes Edward his true lord and John King of France a usurper, whom he is thus quite correct in styling a tyrant. He says to Edward:

> You are the lineal watchman of our peace,
> And John of Valois indirectly climbs.
> What then should subjects but embrace their king?
> Ah, wherein may our duty more be seen

> Than striving to rebate a tyrant's pride
> And place the true shepherd of our commonwealth?

The French know themselves to be in the wrong. King John
has qualms and communicates them to his son Philip.

> *John.* Now tell me, Philip, what is thy conceit
>   Touching the challenge that the English make?
> *Phil.* I say, my lord, claim Edward what he can
>   And bring he ne'er so plain a pedigree,
>   'Tis you are in possession of the crown,
>   And that's the surest point of all the law.
>   But were it not, yet, ere he should prevail,
>   I'll make a conduit of my dearest blood
>   Or chase those straggling upstarts home again.
> *John.* Well said, young Philip.

But the French people are not so brazen. One Frenchman confesses to another that

> 'tis a rightful quarrel must prevail.
> Edward is son unto our late king's sister,
> Where John Valois is three degrees remov'd.

The limits of obedience to the king, so important a theme in
the *Mirror for Magistrates*, are redefined in *Edward III*. Lord
Villiers, the Earl of Salisbury's prisoner, has been released on
parole to procure a promise of safe conduct for the earl from
Charles Duke of Normandy. Charles both refuses the promise
and advises Villiers to break his parole on the plea that loyalty
to his king overrides it; he should not go back to Salisbury but
stay with him. Villiers retorts with the correct doctrine.

> *Cha.* Thine oath? why, that doth bind thee to abide.
>   Hast thou not sworn obedience to thy prince?
> *Vil.* In all things that uprightly he commands.
>   But either to persuade or threaten me
>   Not to perform the covenant of my word
>   Is lawless, and I need not to obey.

There is even a unifying principle in the play: the education
of the two main characters, Edward III and the Black Prince.
Edward III, tempted to lust by the beauty and wit of the
Countess of Salisbury, learns to "master this little mansion of
myself," and later, tempted to indulge his rage at having been

thwarted so long by putting the burghers of Calais to death, he yields to Queen Philippa's plea for mercy and submits his passions to reason.

> Insomuch it shall be known that we
> As well can master our affections
> As conquer other by the dint of sword,
> Philip, prevail; we yield to thy request:
> These men shall live to boast our clemency;
> And, tyranny, strike terror to thyself.

When Edward refuses to send help to his son in great danger at Cressy he does so on a policy of education. The prince must learn to find himself. His education is completed when before Poitiers the great force of the enemy hedge him and his army in on every side and threaten them with certain death. He rejects all French offers to save his life and then turns to the aged Audley for advice and help.

> Thyself art bruis'd and bit with many broils,
> And strategems forepast with iron pens
> Are texted in thine honourable face.
> Thou art a married man in this distress;
> But danger woos me as a blushing maid.
> Teach me an answer to this perilous time.

Needless to say, Audley complies, emptying a sackful of aphorisms *de contemptu mortis*, which entirely succeed in educating the prince in the proper fortitude.

> To live or die I hold indifferent,

is the prince's last word.

On the whole *Edward III* is the most steadily thoughtful of all the Chronicle Plays outside Shakespeare.

Woodstock, though one of the best Chronicle Plays, is little read. It exists in a single manuscript version and was not printed till the nineteenth century. In 1870 Halliwell printed an edition of eleven copies under the title of *A Tragedy of King Richard the Second* and in 1899 Wolfgang Keller republished it in the current *Jahrbuch der deutschen Shakespeare-Gesellschaft*. It was republished in 1929 in the Malone Society Reprints. Even so it has remained not too accessible to the common reader: a popular version in modern spelling is overdue.* The play is sometimes called the *First Part of Richard II*, but I prefer the less

---

*But see note to this page on p. 327.

ambiguous title *Woodstock*. The play deals with the earlier events in Richard's reign: his trouble with his uncles, his marriage with Anne of Bohemia or Ann-a-Beame as she is called in the play, his farming out the kingdom to his parasites, and finally his procuring the murder of his uncle Woodstock and his ultimate repentance. Shakespeare's play, in which Woodstock's murder is a main motive, pretty well takes the story up where *Woodstock* drops it. Thomas Duke of Woodstock is the most important character in the play, although the action centres in Richard, who, like the central character in a Morality Play, is acted on by his uncles on the one side and his favourites on the other.

Though less academic and theoretically ethical than *Edward III*, *Woodstock* is more fully permeated with the doctrines set forth in my two first chapters than any History Play outside Shakespeare.

First, there are enough references to details of the cosmic order to show that the author knew the whole outline. Richard's parasites use the traditional repertory of primacies to flatter him.

> *Bushy*. Your uncles seeks to overturn your state,
>   To awe ye like a child, that they alone
>   May at their pleasure thrust you from the throne.
> *Scroop*. As if the sun were forced to decline
>   Before his dated time of darkness come.
> *Green*. May not the lion roar, because he's young?
>   What are your uncles but as elephants
>   That set their aged bodies to the oak?
>   You are the oak.

As so constantly in Shakespeare the idea of order is expressed through its opposite, chaos. When Richard dismisses his uncles and appoints his parasites to office, the action is part of a general reversal of the natural order. Woodstock exclaims:

> What transformation do mine eyes behold,
> As if the world were topsy-turvy turn'd?
> Shall England, that so long was governed
> By grave experience of white-headed age,
> Be subject now to rash unskilful boys?
> Then force the sun run backward to the east,
> Lay Atlas' burden on a pigmy's back,
> Appoint the sea his times to ebb and flow:
> And that as eas'ly may be done as this.

Nimble, the corrupt Chief Justice's man, expresses the same cosmic chaos through the comic picture of the scholars put on to whip their schoolmaster:

> And for my school-master, I'll have him march about the market-place with ten dozen of rods at's girdle the very day he goes a-feasting; and every one of his scholars shall have a jerk at him.

The author of *Woodstock* uses the traditional correspondences between the different levels of creation. This is how Cheney and Woodstock talk while Anne of Bohemia lies sick before her death.

> *Che.* The lights of heaven are shut in pitchy clouds,
>   And flakes of fire run tilting through the sky
>   Like dim ostents to some great tragedy.
> *Wood.* God bless good Ann-a-Beame! I fear her death
>   Will be the tragic scene the sky foreshows us.
>   When kingdoms change, the very heavens are troubled.

And Arundel sets up the correspondence between the human body or microcosm and the body politic or state when he says of Green, the king's favourite:

> Cut but this ulcer off, thou healst the kingdom.

Finally, the metaphor of the ladder which Woodstock uses to express the way one so exalted as Richard must be approached implies the whole doctrine of creation figured under the same image.

> Soft, soft.
> Fruit that grows high is not securely pluck'd.
> We must use ladders and by steps ascend,
> Till by degrees we reach the altitude.

Although *Woodstock* uses Holinshed as its main source, it treats history much more thoughtfully. In fact there is no main doctrine among those described in my second chapter that does not occur explicitly or implicitly in *Woodstock*. First, the play is constructed on a pattern and not as a heap of historical anecdotes. Though he brings in much history, thereby showing himself the serious chronicler, the author does not scruple to take great liberties with his material, subordinating the sequence of events to his two main patterns: Richard fought for by wise and corrupt counsellors, yielding disastrously to the corrupt, punished by the death of his queen, and turning to repentance; and Woodstock, the blunt honest yet scrupulously moderate counsellor, never faltering in loyalty and always hoping, even up to his death, that Richard may mend his ways. The play is powerfully didactic and exemplary in the first place and factual only in the second; in full accord with the tradition of the *Mirror for Magistrates*. There is a fine passage where the actual chronicles are quoted, and with the plain acceptance of their didactic value. It is fine largely because it is ironic. Richard is induced to interpret the chronicles one way, when only too plainly they point another. Richard's parasite, Bushy, is seeking to persuade him to assert his independence and dismiss his old counsellors, and he uses the chronicles for this purpose:

> *Rich.* How now, what readst thou, Bushy?
> *Bush.* The monuments of English chronicles, my lord,
>   Containing acts and memorable deeds
>   Of all your famous predecessor kings.
> *Rich.* What finds thou of them?
> *Bush.* Examples strange and wonderful, my lord,
>   The end of treason ever in mighty persons.
>   For here 'tis said your royal grandfather,
>   Although but young and under government,
>   Took the Protector, then young Mortimer,
>   And on a gallows, fifty foot in height,
>   He hung him for his pride and treachery.

And afterwards Bushy reads of the Battle of Poitiers, which for a moment makes Richard want to emulate his father. Bushy of course argues falsely, for Woodstock the Protector was not in the least like young Mortimer. And the irony is that the chronicles of that very time were a perfect precedent for the very state of affairs now holding: the ruin of a king by his flatterers. But though Bushy argues amiss, there is no place in all the Chronicle Plays that points to the didactic value of history so well and the lessons that can be learnt from the tendency of history to repeat itself. Coming to the Tudor myth, to the forms in which the most thoughtful Elizabethans saw the pattern of history, we find the author of *Woodstock* much closer to Hall than to the *Mirror for Magistrates*. Though there is no account of how history evolved after the time of Richard II, there are hints that the whole pattern was there. First, like Hall and unlike Holinshed, the author of *Woodstock* speaks emphatically of the seven sons of Edward III. He plainly looks on Edward's reign as a norm of good luck and prosperity, the swerving from which brings in a long succession of disasters. This comes out in one of the principal scenes, the murder of Woodstock at Calais by order of Richard. Before the murderers enter, Woodstock sleeps and sees the ghosts of his brother the Black Prince and of his father Edward III. The Black Prince's ghost, fearing the worst, says to Woodstock:

> Thy blood upon my son will surely come:
> For which, dear brother Woodstock, haste and fly.
> Prevent his ruin and thy tragedy.

The ghost of Edward III speaks of his seven warlike sons and of his victories in France and laments the present case of England. He tells how Woodstock's other brothers, Lancaster and York, are up in arms and begs Woodstock to join them to prevent the kingdom's further ruin. Then, after Woodstock's murder, when he faces his uncles' forces, Richard says:

> O my dear friends, the fearful wrath of heaven
> Sits heavy on our heads for Woodstock's death.
> Blood cries for blood, and that almighty hand
> Permits not murder unreveng'd to stand.

I have no doubt that the author of *Woodstock* saw English history from Edward III to Henry VII as Hall saw it: a state of prosperity broken by a great crime and only recovered after a terrible chain of criminal disasters.

On the matters of civil war and obedience to the king, the author of *Woodstock* is ample, explicit, and scrupulously orthodox. Richard II, though vicious in act, is never quite a tyrant, and Woodstock behaves with perfect propriety in always opposing rebellion even under the bitterest provocation. This speech of Woodstock pretty well sums up the whole matter:

> So many wild boars roots and spoils our lands
> That England almost is destroy'd by them.
> I car'd not if King Richard heard me speak it.
> I wish his grace all good, high heaven can tell.
> But there's a fault in some, alack the day;
> His youth is led by flatterers much astray.
> But he's our king and God's great deputy.

And if ye hunt to have me second ye
In any rash attempt against his state,
Afore my God I'll ne'er consent to it.
I ever yet was just and true to him,
And so will still remain: what's now amiss
Our sins have caus'd, and we must bide heaven's will.

But the limits of obedience to the king are also set. Lapoole,
ordered to have Woodstock murdered at Calais, has a struggle
between conscience and loyalty to the king. He wrongly dis-
obeys his conscience, arguing that either he or Woodstock is
bound to die: so why not Woodstock rather than he? The
author of *Woodstock* plainly accepts the orthodox doctrine that
a man must not obey the king to the danger of his immortal soul.

Sir John Oldcastle is the least important of the group. As a
whole it is pleasant hearty and not very thoughtful: a good
specimen of wholesome Elizabethan stuff. But there are scenes
in it exceptional in their weightiness. This is not surprising, as
according to Henslowe's Diary the first part of this play (which
alone survives) had four authors: Munday, Drayton, Wilson,
and Hathway. With Drayton part-author some heightening of
tone is to be expected. The first scene of the third act, where
the Earl of Cambridge, Lord Scroop, and Lord Gray plot
against Henry V, is in this conspicuous. The first lines in their
high style are typical of the whole scene.

Scroop. Once more, my Lord of Cambridge, make rehearsal
How you do stand entitled to the crown.
The deeper shall we print it in our minds
And every man the better be resolv'd,
When he perceives his quarrel to be just.

And there follows a long weighty genealogical passage. The
proposed revolt takes its place in the logical sequence of historical events, for Cambridge says:

Besides, you must persuade ye, there is due
Vengeance for Richard's murder, which, although
It be deferr'd, yet will it fall at last,
And now as likely as another time.
Sin hath had many years to ripen in,
And now the harvest cannot be far off,
Wherein the weeds of usurpation
Are to be cropp'd and cast into the fire.

It was not till some time after I had picked out these plays from the other Chronicle Plays as of exceptional seriousness that I saw that all of them but one, *Edward II*, had something in common other than their thought-content: some close connection with Shakespeare. In seeking the effect of the Chronicle Play on Shakespeare I had found something much more like the effect of Shakespeare on the Chronicle Play. The single exception is not of much account, for, as stated above, *Edward II*, though enlarging on two special political themes, shows no prevailing political interest. Where such interest occurs, Shakespeare too comes into the case. In other words, the norm of the Chronicle Plays is the factual treatment of Holinshed. When exceptionally the superior thoughtfulness of Hall is found, then Shakespeare is found too. It is not easy to resist the conclusion that Shakespeare was mainly responsible for giving the Chronicle Plays any superior thoughtfulness or sophistication they may contain. But such a large conjecture needs more detailed backing. I will take the relevant plays in turn and see what their affinities with Shakespeare amount to.

Whether or not we accept Act II Scene 3 lines 1-172 of *Sir Thomas More* as being by Shakespeare and in his own hand, we cannot deny the Shakespearean affinities of the scene and indeed of the whole play. Schücking went so far as to think the play an imitation of Shakespeare written 1604-5. He is probably wrong about the date, but that does not mean he is not right about the play's general Shakespearean character. No one would deny the likeness between the mobs in the above passage and in the Cade scenes of *2 Henry VI*; and it is commonly accepted that the Cade scenes come first in point of time. For Shakespearean analogies outside the 172 lines there is the scene in More's house when he entertains the Lord Mayor, and the Lord Cardinal's players come to offer their services. They are a humble troupe with a repertory of Morality Plays. More is kind to them in just the tone in which Theseus is kind to Bottom and the rest. Anyhow no one is likely to deny that Shakespeare had his influence on *Sir Thomas More*.

For myself I think one can go farther. The authors of *Shakespeare's Hand in the Play of Sir Thomas More*, though they have not proved their case, have established so high a probability of the 172 lines being by Shakespeare, that it is less rash to accept than to be sceptical of their findings. But in one matter the authors give the wrong turn. They believe that the players after getting into difficulties with the censor, to whom the play in its first form was submitted, "turned to an 'absolute Johannes factotum' who had previously had no part in the play." This theory was prompted by the traditional falsehood,[1] derived from a misinterpretation of Greene's attack on Shakespeare (where the "absolute Johannes factotum" occurs), that Shakespeare began as a professional botcher of other men's work. What more natural, was the line of unconscious argument, than for the botcher of genius to be called in when things miscarried? Actually by 1593, the date which A. W. Pollard assigns to the play, Shakespeare was an independent playwright of high repute, and on the face of things it is far more likely that Shakespeare was directing or helping a team than that he was in the subordinate position of repairer. Greg recognised six different handwritings in the manuscript, two of which have been identified as Munday's and Dekker's. Munday's portion contains the bulk of the play, but the style shows he did not write it all himself. He was probably the copyist of the work of several authors, himself included. There is nothing to prove Shakespeare was not one of these. The play is not well plotted; it has no formal unity. But it has a pervasive charm; the charm of humour and tolerance. It is the work of a group of writers, of whom Shakespeare was one; and he infected them a little with his own spirit. When there was trouble with the censor, he helped once more.

This cannot be proved, but I believe it the most plausible notion.

So much has been written on Shakespeare's possible share in *Edward III* that its Shakespearean affinities cannot be doubted. For all the variety of opinion, the play presents a much simpler problem than *Sir Thomas More*. A mind gifted with a little common sense and clear of preconceptions should not find it hard to see the sort of play it is. Much unnecessary trouble arose from the notion that the episode of Edward's making love to the Countess of Salisbury was not by the author of the rest of the play. Tucker Brooke has pretty well disposed of this error, but I think what I have noticed above about the plot-motive, the education of Edward III and his son, strengthens the case for single authorship. I doubt if any serious critic to-day would credit Shakespeare with the whole play. It was popular for some years, and, had it been entirely Shakespeare's, its absence

---

[1] See below, pp. 131-3.

from the First Folio is unthinkable. On the other hand Alfred Hart's detailed analysis of its language proves it to be much more Shakespearean as a whole than is usually supposed. I noted above that the author was academic as well as brilliant: the play is exceedingly thoughtful. In style its Shakespearean affinities are more with the poems, the sonnets, and the courtly wit of *Love's Labour's Lost* than with the Histories, though the more lyrical, static qualities of *Richard II* sometimes come to mind. The duplication of "lilies that fester smell far worse than weeds" in this anonymous play and in Shakespeare's sonnets is indeed symbolic. We may guess that the author was an intellectual, probably young, a university man, in the Southampton circle, intimate with Shakespeare and deeply under his influence, writing in his idiom. In a much smaller degree he was indebted to Chapman, chief poet of the School of Night, the rival circle to that of Southampton, witness the cloudily rhetorical description of the battle of Sluys.

If a courtier and scholar wrote *Edward III*, a don or a schoolmaster or a lawyer wrote *Woodstock*. Nor is there anything to suggest that the author was intimate with Shakespeare. Nevertheless he gets a great deal from him, though he has another debt. That other debt is Marlowe's *Edward II*. The picture of Richard pulled this way and that by lords and parasites is copied from that play, of which there are a number of verbal echoes. But this same picture also goes back (and far more emphatically) to the Morality pattern of the main character acted on by the Virtues and Vices. Indeed Richard's "bravery" when he has taken the kingdom in his own hands is far more like the similar situation when Magnificence or Respublica gets rid of the tiresome restraints of Reason than like anything in *Edward II*. Further, the varied and earnest political interest goes quite beyond anything in Marlowe. More important than the debt to *Edward II* is the debt to Shakespeare: especially to *Henry VI Part 2*. The author of *Woodstock* may have read *Richard III* but for his most important character, "plain" Thomas of Woodstock, and for his main theme he goes to Shakespeare's picture of the "good" Duke Humphrey of Gloucester, Protector of England in the minority of Henry VI, whose fall is one of the main episodes of the second part of Shakespeare's trilogy. Another clear piece of derivation is the lawless talk of Richard's parasites when they have got the kingdom into their hands. It comes from the boastings of Jack Cade and his fellows in Shakespeare's play. This is how the parasites talk after the royal dukes have been turned out of their offices and have left:

> *Scroop.*   Old doting greybeards!
> Fore God, my lord, had they not been your uncles,
> I'ld broke my council-staff about their heads.
> *Green.* We'll have an act for this. It shall be henceforth counted high treason for any fellow with a grey beard to come within forty foot of the court gates.
> *Bagot.* Aye, or a great-bellied doublet. We'll alter the kingdom perforce.
> *Green.* Pox on't, we'll not have a beard amongst us. We'll change the country and the city, too.

There are signs too of Shakespearean comedy. I doubt if Woodstock would have talked to the courtier's horse he is given to hold unless Launce had previously talked to his dog; while in the same scene the courtier's speech about the pike of his shoe is in the exaggerated courtly style of some of *Love's Labour's Lost*.

With all these debts it would be surprising if the play's political earnestness, described above, did not go back to Shakespeare likewise. The whole doctrine is in Shakespeare's first historical sequence.

The case of *Sir John Oldcastle* is even plainer. Tucker Brooke wrote in his introduction to the *Shakespeare Apocrypha*:

> The first part of *Oldcastle* was beyond question composed for the Lord Admiral's Company as a reply to the successful Falstaff plays which the Lord Chamberlain's servants had been acting. The character of Falstaff, originally called Oldcastle, is certainly aimed at in the slur of the prologue:
>
> > It is no pamperd glutton we present
> > Nor aged Councellor to youthfull sinne.
>
> The gambling scene between the disguised King and Sir John of Wrotham suggests *Henry V*, IV, 1; while the reference to the thieving exploits of the King's youth is a clear allusion to the first part of *Henry IV*, and the two mentions of Falstaff by name are reminiscences of the same play.

This does not exhaust the lists of debts. Harpoole making the Bishop's Sumner eat the warrant he brings is an obvious variant of Fluellen making Pistol eat the leek. From all this it becomes even plainer than it would otherwise be that the historical and genealogical solemnity of the scene described above comes from Shakespeare too: from the serious scenes in the two *Henry IV's* and *Henry V*.

For any ideas on history, then, Shakespeare was indebted to the Chronicle Plays very little. He may have got his jingoism mainly from them but that is all. In other matters he was the medium of ideas derived from outside the Chronicle Plays to the authors of a few exceptional examples of that mode.

But the bare habit of using drama for history was for Shakespeare of the highest moment. He was, as we shall infer, warmly interested in history from an early age. That there existed a form of drama ready made into which he could infuse without violence the thoughts that were troubling his mind was a rare piece of luck. Had he been born a Frenchman or an Italian he would have had no native Chronicle Play with which to experiment.

CHAPTER V

Retrospect

HAVING had my say on the background of Shakespeare's Histories, I must explain why I have included so much and no more: why, for instance, I have mentioned Tito Livio and not Seneca, who certainly was a part of that background. My first business has been to find out whence Shakespeare got his ideas on history generally and on English history in particular. This search and its results were the subject of the second chapter. But the Elizabethans, as I showed in my *Elizabethan World Picture*, never departmentalised life but always saw the connections between things and insisted on the total cosmic context of a single phenomenon. Thus, to dwell solely on Shakespeare's ideas of history would make a false impression, and it was necessary, before coming to history, to set forth some of the more general, cosmic, notions with which, for the Elizabethans, history was inseparately connected. These were the subject of the first chapter. Though Shakespeare went direct to some of the historians for his ideas, he also could have found them in certain non-historical writers, who themselves had borrowed from these historians. These writers were not only additional sources for Shakespeare's ideas of history but gave him warrant and encouragement to use historical material for creative work. They too formed a part, though a different part, of his historical background; and these were the subject of chapters three and four.

I have not included Seneca or Ovid or Virgil in the background, even though they figure plainly in Shakespeare's earliest History Plays, because they have nothing to do with ideas about English history and because the reader can find plenty already written on them as Shakespearean influences. I should like, however, to record my sympathy with the trend of opinion away from Seneca. F. L. Lucas some years ago warned us against seeing the influence of Seneca whenever the lights burned blue in Elizabethan drama. And recently Howard Baker in his *Induction to Tragedy* has reconsidered the whole matter. He argues that much so-called Senecan stuff is either medieval or Virgilian, while he considers *A Mirror for Magis-*

trates as important in forming early Elizabethan tragedy as I consider it important in mediating to later writers the Tudor notions of history. This however is mentioned only in passing. My present point is that thus far I have tried to confine myself to historical influences. But this restriction does not mean that in dealing with Shakespeare's actual History Plays I shall deny myself a wider scope.

PART TWO
Shakespeare

CHAPTER I

The Early Shakespeare

I HAVE set forth the general ideas and the special historical principles behind Shakespeare's Histories. I have also suggested some of the means through which Shakespeare might have got to know them. The next step would seem to be to expound these principles as found in Shakespeare himself. But my true theme is Shakespeare's Histories, the plays themselves, and not an account of Shakespeare's historical thought abstracted from the Histories. This thought, though interesting in itself and in its derivation, is also a part of the plays. I shall deal with it then less as an abstracted totality than as it occurs in this or that play.

But it might easily be objected that I have been going too fast; that I am assuming without warrant a connection between a certain body of thought and Shakespeare himself; and that to talk of the ideas contained in Froissart's chronicle or in *A Mirror for Magistrates*, for instance, and then to omit any concrete evidence that Shakespeare knew these works, offends against logic. My answer is that in these matters probability founded on common sense weighs more than any available evidence of direct borrowing. Recently opinion has swung round to thinking that *Richard II* is partly founded on Froissart; and when in the same play Richard says

> For God's sake, let us sit upon the ground
> And tell sad stories of the death of kings,

critics have seen a definite reference to *A Mirror for Magistrates*. But the recently claimed derivation of Shakespeare's Gaunt from Froissart's Gaunt has been denied by someone learned in the chronicles, while Richard's sad stories may refer to Lydgate's *Fall of Princes* equally well. Indeed, it is only a small proportion of source-hunting that reaches a certain conclusion. On the other hand the probability that Shakespeare had read Berners's Froissart and *A Mirror for Magistrates* and *Gorboduc* is overwhelming. To doubt it is like doubting whether Browning had read Gibbon and Byron.

Yet there are still some who would refuse to accept the above analogy, because obsessed by the assumption that Shakespeare was comparatively ill-educated. To counter such sceptics (and to introduce my detailed study of Shakespeare's early History Plays) I will say something about his formative years, seeking to answer the question whether from the things he wrote and his manner of writing he was or was not likely to have encountered and assimilated the above works. In so doing I shall be continuing the plea made briefly near the beginning of my first chapter that Shakespeare was in his own way learned. But this applied to the mature Shakespeare. It could still be maintained that in his middle years he redeemed an illiterate youth by keeping his ears open and picking up knowledge from the better educated, to whose company he was now admitted.

In my impression of the young Shakespeare I agree very cordially with the late J. S. Smart, whose *Shakespeare, Truth and Tradition* I think one of the most valuable books on Shakespeare recently published. Peter Alexander, Smart's pupil, has developed many of Smart's embryonic ideas in his admirable *Shakespeare's Henry VI and Richard III*. And to him too I wish to acknowledge my debt.

Though Lamb in *Sanity of True Genius* said "it is impossible for the mind to conceive of a mad Shakespeare," it has been possible for generations of critics and readers to accept a Shakespeare who offends against verisimilitude and common sense. They have made him an exception from the usual pattern of great poet, denying him the attributes of learning and of originality in his early years. They have pictured him as a youth of poor education and one who began his dramatic career by mending the work of others. It is a picture so contrary to the usual order of things that one is confounded both by the ease and by the satisfaction with which men accepted it. That in an age when learning was so highly prized, when the capacity to learn was considered the great human attribute, a person of Shakespeare's inquiring disposition should have been quite indifferent to his studies is an improbability it would take the most irrefragable evidence to establish. That he did not learn exactly in the manner his teachers wished is possible, but this is not the same as being indifferent. And would Shakespeare have made Lord Saye in *2 Henry VI* address Cade's rebels in these words,

And seeing ignorance is the curse of God,
Knowledge the wing wherewith we fly to heaven,

if in his youth he had been averse to learning?

Many scholars have been ingenious in detecting other hands in the plays attributed to Shakespeare by his colleagues and intimates who first edited his works: apparently without being worried by the staggering initial improbability. A man whose "mind and hand went together," "who flowed with that facility that sometime it was necessary he should be stopped," was the least in need of others' help. Shakespeare in his youth was not more likely to accept help than the most precocious schoolboy in a dormitory is likely to get others to eke out his compositions. If the disintegrators of Shakespeare had asked themselves what is apt to happen in the dormitory, they might have concluded that the particular game to which they were addicted would stand a better initial chance of success, if it were played the other way round: if they sought the hand of Shakespeare in the works supposed to be by others.

Many people must have revolted against the above improbability, but Smart in *Shakespeare, Truth and Tradition* went to the root of the matter by proving that Stratford was a civilised little town, by exposing an utter error in the traditional interpretation of Greene's attack on Shakespeare as an upstart crow, and by claiming that the anonymous play which Shakespeare was supposed to have touched up to make the third part of *Henry VI* was not other men's work but merely a bad quarto or garbled version of Shakespeare's play. Alexander extended and proved the last claim, while Miss M. Doran, of the University of Iowa, had reached the same conclusion independently.

To expose the error in interpreting Greene's attack was a work of major importance, for from it came most of the trouble. If it had not been for this error, men might never have denied Shakespeare the sole authorship of *Henry VI*. As the error is still widely prevalent, I had better repeat its correction.

Greene wrote his *Groatsworth of Wit bought with a Million of Repentance* on his deathbed. It concerns the follies of his youth and his last repentance. Among the short pieces of writing appended to the end of his account is a letter to his old acquaintance "that spend their wits in making plays." He addresses three in particular, who can be identified as Marlowe Nashe and

Peele, and warns them against the whole tribe of actors and one actor in particular:

> Base-minded men, all three of you, if by my misery you be not warned: for unto none of you, like me, sought those burs to cleave—those puppets, I mean, that spake from *our* mouths, these antics garnished in *our* colours. Is it not strange that I, to whom they all have been beholding, is it not like that you, to whom they all have been beholding, shall, were ye in that case as I am now, be both at once of them forsaken?

Greene, the author, hates the actors as mere puppets, as mere parrot-renderers of the dramatists: an inferior class. Further, they are ungrateful. These actors at one time sought his company (as they did not of the other three) yet they did nothing to help him when he was in trouble. Smart conjectures that Greene had applied for help to a company to which he had sold one of his plays but had been refused as the piece had already been paid for. Then Greene goes on to his specific attack.

> Yes, trust them not: for there is an upstart crow, beautified with our feathers, that with his "tiger's heart wrapp'd in a player's hide" supposes he is as well able to bombast out a blank verse as the best of you; and being an absolute *Johannes Factotum* is in his own conceit the only Shake-scene in a country.

One cannot be quite certain what Greene meant by his reference to the crow. He certainly refers to the fable, found in Caxton's Aesop and elsewhere, of the jackdaw or raven or crow which, being undistinguished, begs plumes from the other birds and then boasts of his finery. The other birds in anger reclaim their feathers, and the crow is left naked. And the moral is that the crow stands for man, who is prone to acquire various extrinsic help such as riches and fine clothes. Stripped of these he is naked and miserable, and exposed to the wrath of heaven. It is thus likely that Greene was thinking not only of the impudence of this actor in assuming the properties that do not belong to him but of the worldly backing which Shakespeare enjoys: without his patrons—the "divers of worship" mentioned by Chettle in apology for Greene's attack—Shakespeare would be nothing. But I fancy Greene chose also to refer to this fable from the aptitude of the crow or jackdaw, the bird that will repeat without understanding, to the actor: Shakespeare, not content with being a mere jackdaw like the other players, has had the impudence to dress up like a nightingale or a swan, to put on singing-robes, and utter his own original compositions. And Greene contemptuously misquotes a line from one of Shakespeare's big scenes,

O tiger's heart wrapp'd in a woman's hide,

addressed by captive York to Queen Margaret after the battle of Wakefield just before she murders him (*3 Henry VI*. I. 4). He hates Shakespeare for a would-be universal genius (as the *New English Dictionary* explains the *absolute Johannes Factotum*) or, as we might now say, a little Johnny Know-all. Greene's words express hatred and jealousy of a popular and successful author.

Unfortunately Malone initiated, and through his great authority disseminated, a wrong interpretation. The line Greene misquotes appears both in *Henry VI* and in the *True Tragedy of Richard Duke of York*. Malone concluded that the latter play was by Greene, that Shakespeare stole Greene's play to turn it into *3 Henry VI* and therefore that "beautified with our feathers" meant "given habitually to plagiarism." The whole interpretation, forced in any case, collapses when it has been proved that the *True Tragedy* is merely a bad quarto of *3 Henry VI*. Yet it has had a vogue long enough to distort the whole conception of Shakespeare's early dramatic career. It became one of the accepted commonplaces that far from coming up to London from Stratford well provided with the literary experiments of prolific youthful genius, he only discovered his bent by mending the works of others or by serving as a humble member of a team.

Smart has corrected the false notion not only by exploding a false interpretation but by substituting a more positive picture. He has shown that the note in Aubrey's *Brief Lives* that Shakespeare was a schoolmaster in the country is far better substantiated than the run of Shakespeare mythology, and he has thus done something to restore Shakespeare to the level of education we expect major poets to attain.

Alexander's proof that the *Contention of the two famous houses of York and Lancaster* and the *True Tragedy of Richard Duke of York* are bad quartos of *2* and *3 Henry VI*, accepted now by two *senes severiores* of Shakespearean criticism E. K. Chambers and W. W. Greg, has encouraged many readers to accept as authentic *1 Henry VI* and *Titus Andronicus* in addition. The bulk of authentic Shakespeare of undoubtedly early date becomes thus impressive. We cannot refuse to admit that by 1592 Shakespeare was a considerable poet: a *Johannes Factotum* who could legitimately excite the envy of a dissolute and disappointed minor dramatist.

It must in justice be added that Malone's theories on the above matters, though generally accepted, have always had their opponents. Grant White accused Malone of attributing to Shakespeare a degree of plagiarism without parallel in literary history. Thomas Kenny in his *Life and Genius of Shakespeare*, published in 1864, answered Malone very much as Alexander did many years later; but no one listened to him, and his work was forgotten. Later, Courthope renewed the conflict in his *History of English Poetry*: and more especially in his essay *On the authority of some of the early plays assigned to Shakespeare and their relationship to the development of his dramatic genius*, printed as an appendix to his fourth volume. Granted the date when he wrote, a date before the recent advances in the textual criticism of Shakespeare, Courthope is a most enlightened interpreter of the early Shakespeare. He perceives how initially improbable are the theories of the disintegrators: theories based on the stylistic resemblances of lines in the early Shakespeare to contemporary plays:

> On Malone's principle of criticism, it is certain that (internal evidence being alone considered) a person judging of Tennyson's style by *In Memoriam* or *The Idylls of the King*, without any historical study of the development of his genius, would deny that he could have had any share in the authorship of *Poems by Two Brothers*, published in 1827, and evidently written in imitation of Byron.

Courthope insisted on taking into account the larger matter of construction and concluded that only Shakespeare could have written the *Contention* and the *True Tragedy*:

> Looking at their structure and character, which are of much more importance than their verbal detail, I venture to say that no dispassionate reader can peruse *The Contention* and *The True Tragedy* without perceiving that . . . these plays are the work of a single mind. That was not the mind of Greene, Peele, or Marlowe. We may say with absolute certainty that it would have been impossible for the author of *Edward I* or the author of *James IV* to have conceived the combination of events and the contrast of characters which give a certain tragic unity to *The Contention* and

The True Tragedy . . . Shakespeare was the one dramatist alive capable of imagining the vast conflict of powerful wills, selfish purposes, and struggling ambitions, presented by the annals of the Wars of the Roses—the only one who had sufficient grasp of mind to imagine that historic drama as a consistent whole.

And though Courthope went wrong in thinking these two plays genuine early drafts of *2* and *3 Henry VI* he did not thereby impair the justice of judging Shakespeare by his large qualities.

In dealing with Shakespeare's earliest historical drama I cannot well avoid trying to place it among his other works. And in doing that I am forced, like anyone else, to resort to conjecture, to construct what seems the most probable hypothesis.

On grounds of style I would call the *Comedy of Errors* and *Titus Andronicus* two of the earliest, if not the earliest, plays of Shakespeare. Nor is this mere guessing. Smart perceived that an allusion commonly held to date the *Comedy of Errors* after 1589 actually points to a date before 1589. In Act II Scene 3 Antipholus and Dromio (both of Syracuse) discuss the anatomy of the kitchen-wench. Her shape is spherical (microcosm and macrocosm) and, says Dromio, "I could find out countries in her." Ireland and Scotland are located. Then to Antipholus's question of "Where France" Dromio answers "In her forehead: armed and reverted, making war against her heir." The pun may not be very good, for it would be more natural to think of the towzled hair invading the forehead than the other way round, but it served to introduce the topical allusion to France, "reverted" or in revolt against her rightful successor. Commentators have referred the allusion to the war between the Catholic League and Henry of Navarre, when by the death of Henry III in 1589, he succeeded to the throne. But, Smart points out, at that date he was no longer heir but actual king. Henry of Navarre became heir in 1584 on the death of the Duke of Anjou, and his war with the League began in 1585. Henry appealed to Elizabeth and in 1587 defeated the League at Coutras. A date before 1589 would leave the allusion just as pointed and more correct.

Titus Andronicus is in its violence akin to the *Spanish Tragedy* and *Locrine*. When Henslowe records its performance in 1594 as a new play, he cannot mean more than that it was performed (perhaps after a little touching up) for the first time at his theatre, the Rose. There is no reason why Ben Jonson should have made a mistake, when, in the Induction to *Bartholomew Fair* (1614) he wrote:

> He that will swear *Jeronimo* or *Andronicus* are the best plays yet, shall pass unexpected at here, as a man whose judgement shows it is constant and hath stood still these five-and-twenty or thirty years.

Jonson then thought that *Titus Andronicus* was written between 1584 and 1589.

This is not the place to talk at length about the above two plays; yet to consider, not their success, but the kind of plays they are may help us with the early History Plays.

Whatever the defects of the *Comedy of Errors* in its execution, it has certain large qualities. It is academic, ambitious, and masterfully plotted. It is academic not only in being derived from the models of classical comedy but in its references to current commonplaces. For instance, Luciana seeks to persuade Adriana of the male's authority in a very academic style:

> There's nothing situate under heaven's eye
> But hath his bound, in earth, in sea, in sky.
> The beasts, the fishes, and the winged fowls
> Are their males' subjects and at their controls.
> Men, more divine, the masters of all these,
> Lords of the wide world and wild watery seas,
> Indued with intellectual sense and souls,
> Of more pre-eminence than fish and fowls,
> Are masters of their females, and their lords.
> Then let your will attend on their accords.

The play is ambitious in going beyond the bounds of its original, the *Menaechmi* of Plautus. Shakespeare doubles the pair of indistinguishable twins by giving them servants of the same kind. This means a vast complication of detail. He also adds a different kind of writing, something beyond the comic, by inventing the character of Aegeon, father of the twins, and recounting his troubles with the Duke's laws at Ephesus. Shakespeare must needs outdo Plautus, as, according to Gabriel Harvey, Spenser sought to outdo the *Orlando Furioso*. But though Shakespeare complicated his plot he is serenely in command: he is easy master of the whole material.

Besides these general qualities, there is of course, as always in Shakespeare, the recurrent human touch: not very frequent but unmistakable. But more to our purpose, for critics have heeded the human touch sufficiently (and often to the exclusion of much else), is the touch of political interest, surprising in the comic context. The Duke, pronouncing Aegeon's doom for breaking the laws of Ephesus at the opening of the play, is not just the conventional ruler useful in getting the plot in motion; he is a human being, in a great office, subjected, as all such people must be, to the conflict between personal feelings and political duty. He pities Aegeon but cannot allow his pity to stop the course of justice.

> Merchant of Syracusa, plead no more;
> I am not partial to infringe our laws.
> The enmity and discord which of late
> Sprung from the rancorous outrage of your duke
> To merchants, our well-dealing countrymen,
> Who, wanting guilders to redeem their lives,
> Have seal'd his rigorous statutes with their bloods,
> Excludes all pity from our threatening looks.
> For, since the mortal and intestine jars
> 'Twixt thy seditious countrymen and us,
> It hath in solemn synods been decreed,
> Both by the Syracusians and ourselves
> To admit no traffic to our adverse towns.

It is solemn verse, while the very phrases, *mortal and intestine jars* and *seditious countrymen* suggest a context very remote from Plautine comedy. *Jars* is the word constantly used for the wars between the houses of Lancaster and York.

That so profound a student of the artificial mode of the detective story as T. S. Eliot should have gone completely wrong over *Titus Andronicus* is surprising. He calls it "one of the stupidest and most uninspired plays ever written, a play in which it is incredible that Shakespeare had any hand at all." Actually this play has exactly the same large qualities as the *Comedy of Errors*: it is academic, ambitious, and masterfully plotted. Miss Bradbrook sees the academicism very plainly:

> *Titus Andronicus* is a Senecal exercise; the horrors are all classical and quite unfelt, so that the violent tragedy is contradicted by the decorous imagery. The tone is cool and cultured in its effect.

Actually, there is just as much Ovid in the play as there is Seneca. The rape and mutilation of Lavinia comes from Ovid's

story of Procne and Philomela, though the culminating scene of
Tamora eating her son's flesh in a pasty comes from Seneca's
most popular play, the *Thyestes*. Classical tags litter the pages
thickly. This strengthening of Seneca by Ovid duplicates the
complication of plot in the *Comedy of Errors*. Shakespeare in his
youthful ambition must needs outdo Seneca. So he brings in
Ovid and much else besides. Although there is a little confusion at the beginning with the rapid courtship of Tamora by
Saturninus, Bassianus's abduction of Lavinia and the quarrels
among the Andronici, the plotting of the whole is masterly.
The author holds everything in his head, and event follows
event with measured precision. The very violences are exquisitely proportioned. The culminating horror of Tamora eating
her own son is made necessary, for nothing less violent would
have had any emphasis after the many violences already
transacted.

Apart from these general qualities, duplicating the *Comedy of
Errors*, there are many things added. *Titus Andronicus* is indeed
an abounding play which, though academic, breaks out on
many sides beyond its prescribed classical limits. There are
beautiful lyrical passages, fresh descriptions of nature, while
Aaron is a magnificent comic villain. Aaron is also related to
other Shakespearean characters. He is bluff and hearty, as
well as villainous. He looks forward to the hearty effrontery of
Richard III and is the evil counterpart of the plain good characters such as Humphrey of Gloucester and the Bastard
Falconbridge. The scene where he defends his blackamoor
baby from Chiron and Demetrius is brilliant. His words are
forceful and sardonically humorous:

> Stay, murderous villains! will you kill your brother?
> Now, by the burning tapers of the sky,
> That shone so brightly when this boy was got,
> He dies upon my scimitar's sharp point
> That touches this my first-born son and heir.
> I tell you, younglings, not Enceladus,
> With all his threatening band of Typhon's brood,
> Nor great Alcides, nor the god of war,
> Shall seize this prey out of his father's hands.
> What, what, ye sanguine, shallow-hearted boys,
> Ye white-lim'd walls, ye alehouse painted signs,
> Coal-black is better than another hue,

In that it scorns to bear another hue;
For all the water in the ocean
Can never turn the swan's black legs to white,
Although she lave them hourly in the flood.
Tell the emperess from me I am of age
To keep my own, excuse it how she can.

It is an astonishing speech, because it is so rich, so bursting with
promise. In another sense it is the very reverse of astonishing,
because it is precisely the kind of writing that common sense
would expect from the young Shakespeare.

But for my present purpose the most interesting incidental
quality is the strong political trend of parts of the play. In the
Comedy of Errors there was a single instance of this; but *Titus* is
rich in political doctrine. Questions of title and succession were
crucial in Elizabethan thought, and their importance had been
tragically set forth in the acts of the Wars of the Roses. *Titus
Andronicus* begins with a dispute about the succession: Saturninus,
the elder son of the late king, claiming the throne by primogeni-
ture; Bassianus, the younger, on the plea of merit, to be backed
by a free election. Marcus Andronicus, the tribune, tells the two
princes that the Roman people have already elected his brother,
Titus Andronicus, king. The princes consent to disband their
followers and await the return of Titus and the verdict of the
people. Titus returns with Gothic captives and followed by the
populace. His brother offers him the crown, but he refuses as
too old to sustain it. But the tribunes and the people will
accept anyone he chooses. Titus, with Elizabethan correctness,
chooses Saturninus, the late king's elder son. Poetically the
scene is stiff, the work of a young man being solemn beyond the
capacity of his years, but of a young man *interested* in his theme,
and minding about his politics, not dragging them in to satisfy
convention. Titus, now the servant of the new emperor, proceeds to behave with the correctness of a loyal subordinate and
lays all his martial trophies at his master's feet. Saturninus
promises never to forget his fealty. Later, before the main
melodrama of the play begins (II. 3) Titus tells his sons "to
attend," as he will, "the emperor's person carefully."

The high political theme, that of the wounds of civil war and
their cure, recurs at the end of the play. Rome has been in an
uproar; Lucius Andronicus, Titus's son, having fled for safety
to the Goths, returns with an army (not unlike the Earl of

Richmond from Brittany) and survives, the sole possible successor to the throne.   These are the words Marcus Andronicus
addresses to the people to introduce to them his nephew,
Lucius, the future king.

> You sad-fac'd men, people and sons of Rome,
> By uproar sever'd like a flight of fowl
> Scatter'd by winds and high tempestuous gusts,
> O, let me teach you how to knit again
> This scatter'd corn into one mutual sheaf,
> These broken limbs again into one body;
> Lest Rome herself be bane unto herself,
> And she whom mighty kingdoms court'sy to,
> Like a forlorn and desperate castaway,
> Do shameful execution on herself.

And Lucius, chosen emperor, says,

> May I govern so,
> To heal Rome's harms and wipe away her woe.

Marcus's speech is in the high political vein, permeated with
the cosmic consciousness described in my first chapter and the
horror of civil discord described in my second.   The tempests
of the air duplicate the commotions of the commonwealth, and
the commonwealth is figured in the anatomy of a man.   Rome
must cease to be a bane to herself, as England is later to be told
it will never fear a foreign foe, if it "to itself do rest but true."

From the political theme of *Titus* it is a natural step to my
next concern: the likenesses between that play and *1 Henry VI*.
First, let me revert to the place (I. 1. 244) where Titus does
homage to the newly created emperor.   This scene is followed,
ironically, by the complicated brawl after Bassianus's seizure of
Lavinia.   The pattern recurs at the end of Act 3 of *1 Henry VI*.
Here Talbot does homage to Henry VI, just crowned in Paris,
and lays his conquest at his king's feet in precisely the same
manner; and this scene is followed by a brawl between par-
tisans of York and Lancaster.   Titus and Talbot are indeed the
same character, the disinterested and utterly brave warrior,
unswerving servant of his royal master, though Titus is pictured
the elder by many years.   In his madness, of course, Titus
comes close to Kyd's Hieronymo, but none the less in his sanity
he is an elderly Talbot.   Again it is a woman who, by fascinating the king or prince, defeats the good designs of the warrior-

hero in each play. Tamora is indeed not at all the same character as Joan, but she is a bad woman, a foreigner, and she is
the prime enemy of Titus. Joan, too, is Talbot's evil genius.
Tamora works evil by seducing Saturninus, yet being unfaithful
to him. Joan fascinates Charles the Dauphin but confesses to
adultery before her execution. I think the two plays must have
been written about the same time.

The *Comedy of Errors* and *Titus Andronicus* revealed their
author as ambitious. If he wrote *1 Henry VI* about the same
time, the extent of his ambitions is enlarged. Here we have a
young man trying his hand in three great literary modes, classical comedy, Senecan tragedy, and, in keeping with the political proclivities of his age, a highly serious historical play. We
find, not the brilliant apprentice and tinker of others' matter,
but an original poet, educated, confident of himself, already
dedicated to poetry; a man passing through the states common
to any very great artist, akin to Dante and Milton not only
through mature achievement but in the manner in which he
began his life-work.

It is plain enough that much of the substance of Shakespeare's
more serious thoughts in his early years must have been political: otherwise he would not have spent himself on his great
historical tetralogy, the three parts of *Henry VI* and *Richard III*.
But the intrusion of politics in the *Comedy of Errors* and *Titus
Andronicus*, where there was no need for them, shows how
strongly they gripped his mind. Was this surprising at such a
time, and what were the likely alternatives?

A young man, however gifted with originality, can, for his
chief interests, do no more than select from among the matters
current in his age. What were the options in Shakespeare's
formative years likely to appeal to an intelligent and well-
educated young man? There was, for instance, an interest in
law. Mulcaster had translated Fortescue's *De Laudibus Legum
Angliae* in 1567 and Sir Thomas Smith's *De Republica Anglorum*
was published in 1583. Hooker, though his great work was
not published till after 1590, was about ten years Shakespeare's
senior. The age in which Shakespeare grew up was propitious
to meditations on the nature of law. Then it was an age of
mathematicians, of Baker, Dee, Harriot, and Bruno's visit to
England. There were the voyages of discovery with Sir John
Hawkins's *True Declaration of his Voyage* published in 1569 and
Sir Humphrey Gilbert's *Discourse of a new Passage to Cataia* pub-

lished in 1576. The temper of the age was not averse to an English equivalent of the *Lusiads* of Camoens. There was theological controversy. There was the new Italianate Platonism. None of these interests, however, was so powerful as the steadily rising pride in political accomplishment, in the growing awareness of having made good nationally, in having emerged against all odds from the hazards which had so beset the rest of Europe. England was in process of escaping the equivalent of the Peasants' Revolt in Germany and of the wars of religion in France; and the gradual transformation of hope into certainty during the time of Shakespeare's youth must have been one of the obsessing experiences of a sensitive mind.

The less inquiring spirits turned these ways of thinking into a simple detestation of rebellion and civil war and Elizabeth into a symbol of the good state of affairs to which the country was attaining. The more thoughtful joined in turning Elizabeth into a symbol but prolonged their excitement over a current historical process by dwelling on these processes in the past and on the moral principles that governed historical events. To feed this appetite there were the political works of literature belonging to an earlier age: the Church Homilies, the early Protestant denunciations of sedition like Cheke's, Hall's chronicle, the *Mirror for Magistrates*, and *Gorboduc*. But the great imaginative writers of Shakespeare's youth are also permeated with political thought. Sidney's *Arcadia* is in one aspect a tract against civil war and a repertory of political wisdom; a whole layer of the meaning of Spenser's *Fairy Queen* is political; Lyly's *Euphues* issues into a panegyric on the political felicity of England and of the glories of her ruler.

The occurrence of these things in Lyly is peculiarly striking, because they are the last things with which popular opinion associates him, and particularly apt, because it is agreed that Shakespeare knew Lyly very well. Near the end of the second part, *Euphues and his England*, occurs the section called *Euphues's Glass for Europe*, addressed to the ladies and gentlewomen of Italy. It is largely borrowed from Harrison's *Description of Britain*, and in it occur these political passages, which sum up both the Tudor myth and the contemporary thankfulness and pride at having made good as a nation.

There were for a long time civil wars in this country by reason of several claims to the crown between the two famous and noble houses of Lancaster and York, either of them pretending to be of the royal blood, which caused them both to spend their vital blood. These jars continued long, not without great loss both to the nobility and commonalty, who, joining not in one but in divers parts, turned the realm to great ruin, having almost destroyed their country before they could anoint a king. But the living God, who was loath to oppress England, at last began to repress injuries and to give an end by mercy to those that could find no end of malice nor look for any end of mischief. So tender a care hath he always had of that England, as of a new Israel, his chosen and peculiar people. This peace began by a marriage solemnised by God's special providence between Henry Earl of Richmond, heir to the house of Lancaster, and Elizabeth daughter of Edward IV, the undoubted issue and heir of the house of York, whereby, as they term it, the red rose and the white were united and joined together.

There follows a gorgeous panegyric of Elizabeth, whose symbolising the marvellous fortune of England over continental countries Lyly renders as follows:

This is the only miracle that virginity ever wrought: for a little island, environed round about with wars, to stand in peace; for the walls of France to burn, and the houses of England to freeze; for all other nations either with civil sword to be divided or with foreign foes to be invaded, and that country neither to be molested with broils in their own bosoms nor threatened with blasts of other borderers but always, though not laughing, yet looking through an emerald at others' jars.

This peace hath the Lord continued with great and unspeakable goodness among his chosen people of England. How much is that nation bound to such a prince, by whom they enjoy äll benefits of peace; having their barns full when others famish, their coffers stuffed with gold when others have no silver; their wives without danger when others are defamed, their daughters chaste when others are deflowered, their houses furnished when others are fired, where they have all things for superfluity others nothing to sustain their need. This peace hath God given for her virtues pity moderation virginity; which peace the same God of peace continue for his name's sake.

Lyly's instincts did not draw him to politics, but he had a receptive sensitive nature. The present stream of opinion overwhelms him and makes him eloquent on the twin themes of the mission of the Tudors and of gratitude at escaping the miseries of civil war.

This same stream of opinion affected Shakespeare more fully than it did Lyly. Recent history and its lessons were to him what the French Revolution and the doctrines that accompanied it were to Wordsworth, or Godwinism to Shelley. They were the chief things, external to himself, that battered at him and captured him. They became as it were his official interest, the interest that his adolescent conscience took most seriously. That the business began with his hearing the Homilies in Stratford Church at the time of the rebellion in the north, according to Hart's supposition, is highly probable. His neglect of the Arthurian side of the Tudor myth and his main concentration on history from Richard II to Henry VIII make it likely that he derived his more special interests in history from Hall and the *Mirror for Magistrates* and not from Spenser and Warner. I have no doubt that Shakespeare had read Hall in his youth, though this cannot be proved. The edition of Holinshed he used was not published till 1587, when he became 23. I cannot believe he had not read the chronicles till that age; and Hall, his other chief chronicle source, had always been available. It is in the early Histories that he borrows most from Hall: in the later group the specific borrowings are scarcer. It looks as if he had assimilated Hall so well that he did not need to refer to him any more. Hall's ideas had by this time become a part of his mind. Added to this was the vogue and the influence of the *Mirror for Magistrates*. Finally, the occurrence in Lyly of what is much like an abstract of Hall's opinions on English history leading to the Tudors suggests that these opinions were the property of the select educated class to which Lyly belonged. Whether in Shakespeare's very early years as a dramatist he had social access to this class we do not know. But at least he probably knew their opinions. All these things—early impressions, youthful reading, ambition to share the best intellectual life of the time—would account for his dedicating himself to the historical theme.

However, the most powerful external dominations of a young man's mind are not always the most steadily influential. And while the main concern of this book must be the way Shakespeare turned high politics into poetry and drama, a subsidiary and intrinsically more important theme must be the way in which Shakespeare either freed himself from or transmuted the mainly political motive. A man will learn that his official self, the self that presented a façade both to him and the outside world, may not be the true self after all. He may discover more about his own nature, thereby changing his main interests; or he may revise the sc.. of estimates he applied to the different external matters that had filled men's minds in his early years. I mentioned law, mathematics, and travel as matters of this kind. A matter more powerful and with a nearer bearing on Shakespeare I purposely omitted till I had finished writing generally of the political theme. It is the idea of education or "nurture." The political theme, in the form adopted by Shakespeare, was peculiarly English: a set of generalisations given special vitality through the favoured position in which by good luck England found herself. The idea of education was the great Renaissance motive, applicable equally to Christian and Stoic, Protestant and Catholic, translatable into terms as well of knowing yourself as of losing your life to gain it. And along with the political theme it had figured largely if not principally in the works of the three great imaginative artists of Shakespeare's formative years: Sidney, Spenser, and Lyly. Sidney's *Astrophel and Stella* is in the main the story of a deliberate act of self-education through the stormy experience of love. The object of the *Fairy Queen* was educative: the fashioning of a gentleman. Lyly's *Euphues* has far more obviously the theme of *Astrophel and Stella*; *Campaspe* (like *Edward III* later) shows a great king educated out of his lusts.

Now though the political interest was the most obvious one in Shakespeare's early work and though he pursues it with the greatest surface solemnity, the theme of education occurs more than once. In the *Taming of the Shrew* a man educates a woman, and in *Love's Labour's Lost* four women educate four men. In both plays the process is gone through lightly and comically. But in course of time Shakespeare allowed the theme of education first to rank with the political theme and finally to rank before it. In *Henry IV* the education of the Prince is a major theme; in *King Lear* the education of Lear in the knowledge both of himself and of other human beings is paramount.

Finally, there is quite another side of the early Shakespeare: one that has nothing to do with the great themes either of politics or of education. It is indeed true that for the young Shakespeare the political theme of England, her past history and her present glory, was the theme which had the greatest surface solemnity and which he thought he minded most about. But it could be hazarded that in another sense Shakespeare is also being quite serious when, disregarding the external pressure of contemporary ideas on politics and education, he sets alongside Armado's exquisitely stilted prose—

> This side is Hiems, Winter; this Ver, the Spring; the one maintained by the owl, the other by the cuckoo—

the timeless lyricism of

> When daisies pied and violets blue,

and

> When icicles hang by the wall.

The political doctrines of the History Plays fascinate partly because they are remote and queer. The theme of education, though of perennial interest, is a little remote from us because we are more disillusioned about it than were the men of the Renaissance. But when, after the fantastic medley of courtly affectations, Shakespeare suddenly shows us his maidens bleaching their summer frocks and Tom bearing logs into the hall, we make no reservations but merely think: that is life; then, and now. For the moment Shakespeare has discarded his official self.

Not that this official self was not a very grand affair.

CHAPTER II

The First Tetralogy

1. INTRODUCTORY

TEN plays of the First Folio have English history as their theme. They are distributed in a curious regularity. First there is a sequence of four closely linked plays: the three parts of *Henry VI* and *Richard III*. There follows an isolated play, *King John*. Then comes a second sequence of four: *Richard II*, the two parts of *Henry IV*, and *Henry V*. And there is a second isolated play, *Henry VIII*. Disregarding the two isolated plays, we can say further that the two tetralogies make a single unit. Throughout the *Henry VI's* and *Richard III* Shakespeare links the present happenings with the past. We are never allowed to forget that, as Hall said in his preface, "King Henry the Fourth was the beginning and root of the great discord and division." For instance, in *1 Henry VI* the dying Mortimer says to his nephew, the future Duke of York:

> Henry the Fourth, grandfather to this king,
> Depos'd his nephew Richard, Edward's son,
> The first-begotten and the lawful heir
> Of Edward King, the third of that descent;
> During whose reign the Percies of the north,
> Finding his usurpation most unjust,
> Endeavour'd my advancement to the throne.

In *2 Henry VI* York, explaining his titles to Salisbury and Warwick, goes back to Edward III and his sons to the lucky number of seven, whom he solemnly enumerates, and fixes the mainspring of subsequent English history in the murder of Richard II:

> Edward the Black Prince died before his father
> And left behind him Richard, his only son:
> Who after Edward the Third's death reign'd as king,
> Till Henry Bolingbroke, Duke of Lancaster,
> The eldest son and heir of John of Gaunt,
> Crown'd by the name of Henry the Fourth,

> Seiz'd on the realm, depos'd the rightful king,
> Sent his poor queen to France, from whence she came,
> And him to Pomfret; where, as all you know,
> Harmless Richard was murder'd traiterously.

In *Richard III* Earl Rivers, awaiting execution in Pomfret
Castle, links present with past by recalling the murder of
Richard II:

> O Pomfret, Pomfret, O thou bloody prison,
> Fatal and ominous to noble peers!
> Within the guilty closure of thy walls
> Richard the Second here was hack'd to death.
> And for more slander of thy dismal seat
> We give thee up our guiltless blood to drink.

These are precisely the themes which Shakespeare repeated
when he makes Henry V before Agincourt pray to God,

> Not to-day, O Lord,
> O not to-day, think not upon the fault
> My father made in compassing the crown.
> I Richard's body have interred new,
> And on it have bestow'd more contrite tears
> Than from it issued forced drops of blood.

Further, Shakespeare seems himself to declare the continuity of
the two tetralogies when the Chorus at the end of *Henry V*
makes a link with the next reign and refers back to the earlier
written sequence.

> Henry the Sixth, in infant bands crown'd king
> Of France and England, did this king succeed;
> Whose state so many had the managing,
> That they lost France and made his England bleed:
> Which oft our stage hath shown; and for their sake
> In your fair minds let this acceptance take.

The last line and a half mean: let the good success of my plays
about *Henry VI* influence you in favour of the play you have just
witnessed, *Henry V*. Shakespeare not only implies the continuity of the two tetralogies but expresses satisfaction with the
one he had written in his youth. That he should, as it were,
accept responsibility for all eight plays at the end of the last
written one is important because it helps to confirm what even

without this confirmation should be evident: that Shakespeare
had in his early years disposed what for the Elizabethans was
the most exciting and significant stretch of English history into
a pattern; a pattern of such magnitude that it needed the space
of eight plays and about ten years in the execution. The outlines of the pattern he derived from Hall, but the sustained
energy of mind needed to develop them he got from his own
ambitions and the example of other works, particularly of the
Mirror for Magistrates.

There is no need to give details of Shakespeare's debt to Hall,
as these can be found in articles by Edleen Begg and W. Gordon
Zeeveld. But it is likely that Shakespeare got the hint of organi-
sing Hall's material into two tetralogies by taking for his
culminating points the two reigns to which Hall had stuck
specifically dramatic labels (the *Victorious acts of Henry V* and
the *Tragical doings of Richard III*) and which he had treated in a
heightened way exceptional to the rest of his chronicle (see
above pp. 43, 48-9). Shakespeare can end with the reign of
Richard III because Richard's death both resolves the plot and
fulfils the title of Hall's history: *The Union of the two noble and
illustre Families of Lancaster and York.*

Why Shakespeare wrote the second half first we can only
guess. Perhaps, like others, he thought that vice was easier to
picture than virtue, hell than paradise, and that it would be
safer to spend his present energies on pictures of chaos and a
great villain, leaving the more difficult picture of princely perfection to his maturity. But there is a very different explanation of
what is after all a curious procedure. That it is hazardous and
revolutionary should not preclude its being seriously considered.
In the nature of things so fluent an author as Shakespeare
probably wrote in his youth much that has perished. He
may well have written early versions of the plays of the second
tetralogy, *Richard II*, *Henry IV*, and *Henry V*, now lost but recast
in the plays we have. Further, the *Famous Victories of Henry V*
may well be an abridgement—a kind of dramatic Lamb's Tale
—of Shakespeare's early plays on the reigns of Henry IV and
Henry V. With the first version of the plays dealing with history from Henry VI onwards Shakespeare would have been
sufficiently content to forbear revision. And he is not ashamed
to refer to them in his epilogue to *Henry V.*

Shakespeare's first debt then in his earlier tetralogy is to
Hall; but this must not cause us to overlook the many different

strains Shakespeare here unites. It is indeed this masterly inclusiveness that raises to greatness a series of plays which in the execution are sometimes immature and ineffective. I will recapitulate these strains and illustrate them from the actual plays.

First, this tetralogy to an equal extent with the later tetralogy and more powerfully than the most civilised of the Chronicle Plays shows Shakespeare aware of order or degree. Behind all the confusion of civil war, and the more precious and emphatic because of the confusion, is the belief that the world is a part of the eternal law and that earthly mutability, as in Spenser's last cantos, is itself a part of a greater and permanent pattern. Further, human events as well as being subject to the eternal law are part of an elaborate system of correspondences and hence the more firmly woven into the total web of things. The very first words of the first of the four plays will illustrate. They are spoken by the Duke of Bedford at the funeral procession of his brother Henry V.

> Hung be the heavens with black, yield day to night,
> Comets, importing change of times and states,
> Brandish your crystal tresses in the sky
> And with them scourge the bad revolting stars
> That have consented unto Henry's death!

Here the stars that have "consented unto," which means "conspired to procure," the death of Henry are intended to be the counterpart in the heavens of the English nobility who have already fallen into discord. The universe, in fact, was so much of a unity that the skies had to re-enact the things that happened in the human polity. It is the same correspondence that occurs in the speech on "degree" in *Troilus and Cressida*.

> But when the planets
> In evil mixture to disorder wander,
> What plagues and what portents, what mutiny,
> What raging of the sea, shaking of earth,
> Commotion in the winds, frights changes horrors,
> Divert and crack, rend and deracinate
> The unity and married calm of states
> Quite from their fixure!

In *Troilus and Cressida* Ulysses is maintaining the need for degree, and in *Henry VI* Bedford assumes as the righteous norm his brother Henry V, the strong upholder of order in his own kingdom.

The same play, though like the rest mainly occupied with revolt and disorder and misfortune, finds place for a positive example of the virtue of degree. It is where Henry VI, now in Paris for his coronation, accepts the homage of Talbot and rewards him with an earldom.

> *Tal.* My gracious prince and honourable peers,
> Hearing of your arrival in this realm,
> I have awhile given truce unto my wars,
> To do my duty to my sovereign:
> In sign whereof this arm, that hath reclaim'd
> To your obedience fifty fortresses,
> Twelve cities and seven wall'd towns of strength,
> Besides five hundred prisoners of esteem,
> Lets fall his sword before your highness' feet,
> And with submissive loyalty of heart
> Ascribes the glory of his conquest got
> First to my God and then unto your grace.
> *Hen.* Welcome, brave captain and victorious lord!
> When I was young, as yet I am not old,
> I do remember how my father said
> A stouter champion never handled sword.
> Long since we were resolved of your truth,
> Your faithful service and your toil in war;
> Yet never have you tasted our reward
> Or been reguerdon'd with so much as thanks,
> Because till now we never saw your face.
> Therefore, stand up, and for these good deserts
> We here create you Earl of Shrewsbury;
> And in our coronation take your place.

Any Elizabethan would have perceived that the scene was a deliberate setting up of an ideal norm. Every detail suggests an exact and orderly disposition. God, the king, the peers, the captives are ranged in their degrees. Talbot, the last created earl, will take his proper place in the coronation. The very numbers of the things or persons captured suggest precise significances. Henry, in contrast to his usual practice, does exactly the right thing; and, in violent contrast to the facts of history (for he was only nine months old when Henry V died) is momentarily animated by the judgements of the perfect king, his father.

But the most effective statement of the principle of order occurs in the passage which largely by accident is the most famous of all three Henry VI plays, Henry's pathetic soliloquy where he regrets that he was born a king and not a shepherd.

> O God! methinks it were a happy life
> To be no better than a homely swain;
> To sit upon a hill, as I do now,
> To carve out dials quaintly, point by point,
> Thereby to see the minutes how they run,
> How many make the hour full complete;
> How many hours bring about the day;
> How many days will finish up the year;
> How many years a mortal man may live.
> When this is known, then to divide the times:
> So many hours must I tend my flock;
> So many hours must I take my rest;
> So many hours must I contemplate;
> So many hours must I sport myself;
> So many days my ewes have been with young;
> So many weeks ere the poor fools will ean;
> So many years ere I shall shear the fleece:
> So minutes hours days months and years,
> Pass'd over to the end they were created,
> Would bring white hairs unto a quiet grave.
> Ah, what a life were this, how sweet, how lovely!

It is a beautiful passage, justly famous. But it is famous partly because it is so easily anthologised and partly because it is almost omitted from the *True Tragedy of Richard Duke of York*, once thought to be the play on which Shakespeare founded the third part of *Henry VI* and now proved to be a pirated version of it. The passage thus appeared to be a clear addition to the old play, hence genuine Shakespeare, hence to be read without embarrassment. Actually its full meaning, its full pathos and irony, are quite hidden when it is taken as a mere Shakespearean afterthought, fit for a volume of beauties. The context is the Battle of Towton, where the Lancastrians suffered their bloodiest defeat and which Shakespeare selects from all the battles as most emphatically illustrating the full horrors of civil war. Henry has been "chidden from the field" by his terrible queen and the fierce Clifford, because he brings bad luck; but immediately after his soliloquy he witnesses two spectacles of the utmost horror, first a son discovering that he has killed his father and then a father discovering that he has killed his son. Henry's speech must be judged before this background of chaos. It signifies not, as naturally thought of out of its context, a little bit of lyrical escapism but Henry's yearning for an ordered life. This ordered life of the shepherd is a pitifully small thing compared with the majestic order he as a king should have been able to impose. Yet it stands for the great principle of degree, while bringing out Henry's personal tragedy: his admirable intentions and his utter inability to carry them out.

Another most explicit version of the same thing is the contrast between the lawlessness of Jack Cade and the impeccable moderation and discipline of the Kentish squire Iden, in *2 Henry VI*. Cade openly boasts, "But then we are in order when we are most out of order." All degree is to be levelled away:

> There shall be in England seven halfpenny loaves sold for a penny; the three-hooped pot shall have ten hoops; and I will make it a felony to drink small beer: all the realm shall be in common; and in Cheapside shall my palfry go to grass . . . there shall be no money; all shall eat and drink on my score; and I will apparel them all in one livery that they may agree like brothers and worship me their lord.

Iden, who catches the fugitive Jack Cade in his garden and kills him, is a flat symbolic character, beautifully contrasted with the realism of the rebels. He is entirely content with his own station in the social hierarchy, as smug as any eighteenth century moralist over the virtues of the middle station of life. He introduces himself to us by this soliloquy in his garden:

> Lord, who would live turmoiled in the court,
> Who may enjoy such quiet walks as these?
> This small inheritance my father left me
> Contenteth me, and worth a monarchy.
> I seek not to wax great by others' waning;
> Or gather wealth I care not, with what envy:
> Sufficeth that I have maintains my state
> And sends the poor well pleased from my gate.

This speech for all its smugness is perfectly serious in giving the norm of order, upset by Cade.

As powerful as the theme of order in the tetralogy is the continual insistence on cause and effect in the unfolding of history. Shakespeare adopts the whole teaching of Hall and of the *Mirror for Magistrates*. The passages about the death of Richard II quoted above serve to illustrate this just as well as to illustrate the conceptual continuity of the two tetralogies. But again and again, at any great happening, Shakespeare seeks to bring out the concatenation of events. Thus in *2 Henry VI* Gloucester, about to be murdered, sees his death the cause of great misery to the land and of ruin to his king. He says to Henry:

> I know their complot is to have my life,
> And if my death might make this island happy
> And prove the period of their tyranny,
> I would expend it with all willingness.
> But mine is made the prologue to their play;
> For thousands more, that yet suspect no peril,
> Will not conclude their plotted tragedy.

And, referring to his own services as Protector of the realm in Henry's minority, he adds:

> Ah, thus King Henry throws away his crutch
> Before his legs be firm to bear his body.
> Thus is the shepherd beaten from thy side
> And wolves are gnarling who shall gnaw thee first.
> Ah, that my fear were false, ah, that it were!
> For, good King Henry, thy decay I fear.

Again Margaret of Anjou is not merely a strong-minded and troublesome woman who prolongs the civil wars by her tenacity and fulfils the dramatic part of avenging fury; she has her precise place in the chain of events. Her marriage with Henry VI was from the first a disaster and brought to a head the troubles between Lancaster and York which otherwise would have lain quiet. Edward IV, in front of York, addresses these words to her about Henry's marriage:

> And had he match'd according to his state,
> He might have kept that glory to this day;
> But when he took a beggar to his bed
> And grac'd thy poor sire with his bridal day,
> Even then that sunshine brew'd a shower for him,

That wash'd his father's fortunes forth of France
And heap'd sedition on his crown at home.
For what has broach'd this tumult but thy pride?
Hadst thou been meek, our title still had slept;
And we, in pity for the gentle king,
Had slipp'd our claim until another age.

Many examples, and there are a great many, would be
tedious. It is enough to mention the most elaborate of all.
The ghosts that terrify and comfort the sleeps of Richard and
Richmond on the night before Bosworth are not just enemies or
friends but a convergence of causes leading to the defeat of
Richard and to the issue of England's fortunes into prosperity
through the union of the red rose and the white.

Shakespeare is more interested in the chain of cause and
effect than in the ideas that history repeats itself and hence that
we may apply to the present the exemplary lessons of the past.
But these motives are not absent. For instance when in
Richard III Queen Margaret breaks in on Richard making
trouble with Queen Elizabeth's kindred she calls down curses
on her enemies to correspond with the troubles she has had
herself, as if this repetition of history were a probability. Addressing herself to Elizabeth, wife of Edward IV, she says:

Edward thy son, which now is Prince of Wales,
For Edward my son, which was Prince of Wales
Die in his youth by like untimely violence;
Thyself a queen, for me that was a queen,
Outlive thy glory like my wretched self;
Long mayst thou live to wail thy children's loss,
And see another, as I see thee now,
Deck'd in thy rights, as thou art stall'd in mine!

And behind all the unfolding of civil war there is the great
lesson (implied always and rarely stated) that the present time
must take warning from the past and utterly renounce all civil
dissension. Here for instance is Sir William Lucy's comment
on York's refusal to help Talbot on account of his jealousy of
Somerset:

Thus while the vulture of sedition
Feeds in the bosom of such great commanders,
Sleeping neglection doth betray to loss
The conquest of our scarce cold conqueror,

That ever living man of memory,
Henry the Fifth. Whiles they each other cross,
Lives, honours, lands, and all hurry to loss.

There is a short scene (II. 3) in *Richard III*, the kind of scene that is omitted from modern performance because it does not advance the plot and apparently can be spared, which in a brief space epitomises a number of Tudor commonplaces on history. It is a choric comment by three citizens on the death of Edward IV. The third citizen is a pessimist, who "looks to see a troublous world" and quotes the adage,

Woe to that land that's govern'd by a child!

The other two are more optimistic, and the first citizen hopes that history will repeat itself in making the early years of Edward V prosperous like those of Henry VI when his uncles Bedford and Gloucester "enrich'd the land with politic grave counsel." But the third citizen denies the analogy: Edward's uncles are not at all like Henry VI's. He fears the worst, but adds

All may be well. But if God sort it so,
'Tis more than we deserve or I expect.

In other words, the troubles of a country are God's punishment for its sins. His mixed sentiments are prophetic: God both punished the land and caused all to be well through the Earl of Richmond. Shakespeare is perfectly clear in making Richmond the emissary of God.

It is in the last two plays of the tetralogy that the prevalent high theme of the *Mirror for Magistrates*, the fall of an eminent and erring statesman, is most evident. In the first two plays Talbot and Humphrey of Gloucester are too individual and too virtuous to fit into the norm of that poem. But in the third play the tragedy of Richard Duke of York is solemnly enacted, and in *Richard III* the motive of the *Mirror* occurs with great power. Clarence perishes for his false oath, and in the fate of Buckingham Shakespeare may actually allude to the most famous portions of the *Mirror*: the contributions of Sackville. At the beginning of the fourth scene of the fourth act Queen Margaret says:

So, now prosperity begins to mellow
And drop into the rotten mouth of death.
Here in these confines slily have I lurk'd

To watch the warring of mine adversaries.
A dire induction am I witness to,
And will to France, hoping the consequence
Will prove as bitter, black, and tragical.

The use of the words *induction* and *tragical* may well contain a
hint of Sackville's *Induction* and his *Tragedy of Buckingham*;
especially as Buckingham's fall is the theme of the next scene.
And Buckingham confesses to his sin of treachery and to a false
oath and admits the justice of his fate—

Wrong hath but wrong, and blame the due of blame—

in a spirit entirely in accord with the morality of the *Mirror for
Magistrates*.

So much for Shakespeare's use in his tetralogy of the conceptions of world order and the processes of history: the ideas that
appear so little in the Chronicle Plays and seem to have been
the property of a select and educated class, that ally Shakespeare with Chapman and Daniel and Sir John Hayward. His
use of them illustrates the academic side of himself that was so
prominent in his early years. It is to his History Plays what the
Plautine form is to the *Comedy of Errors* and the Senecan and
Ovidian elements and conventions to *Titus Andronicus*.

But Shakespeare was not only academic in his first historical
tetralogy: he was a popular dramatist too. Not that the
populace would have objected to his superior opinions on history; they would have been willing to be impressed if they also
got the things they expected: which they most certainly did.
And first, for this popular material, there is what I have called
sometimes Higden and sometimes Holinshed: the mediation
of sheer fact. For though Shakespeare did see history in an
intelligible pattern he compressed into a popular and lively
form an astonishing quantity of sheer historical fact. He can
indeed be nearly as informative as the author of the *True
Tragedy of Richard III*, from which extracts were quoted above
(p. 100). This, for instance, is how York begins the genealogical statement on which he claims his title to the throne in
2 Henry VI:

Edward the Third, my lords, had seven sons:
The first, Edward the Black Prince, Prince of Wales;
The second, William of Hatfield, and the third,

Lionel Duke of Clarence; next to whom
Was John of Gaunt, the Duke of Lancaster;
The fifth was Edmund Langley, Duke of York;
The sixth was Thomas of Woodstock, Duke of Gloucester;
William of Windsor was the seventh and last.

There seems to have been a genuine popular demand for this sheer information. And beyond presenting this unmitigated fact Shakespeare succeeded conspicuously in making palatable to his public a greater bulk of chronicle material than other dramatists were able to do.

Shakespeare also satisfied the popular taste in setting forth the great popular political theme, the horror of civil war, and in giving his plays the required chauvinist tone. Joan of Arc is a bad enough woman, Margaret of Anjou an intriguing enough queen; an Englishman is worth a sufficient number of Frenchmen; Frenchmen are sufficiently boastful and fickle, to satisfy every popular requirement.

Finally, Shakespeare occasionally satisfies the taste for the startling but irrelevant anecdote; the pieces of sensation that pleased the people but could be spared from the play. There is for example the scene in *1 Henry VI* (II. 3) where the Countess of Auvergne plots Talbot's death by inviting him to her house and he prevents her by summoning his men by a blast from his horn; and the scene in *2 Henry VI* (I. 4) where Bolingbroke the conjurer calls up spirits at the command of the Duchess of Gloucester.

In sum Shakespeare in his first effort could beat the writers of Chronicle Plays on their own ground.

Among the strains found in Tudor history was that akin to Froissart and shown in the work of More and Cavendish: a dramatic liveliness and a closeness to the event. This strain appears in Shakespeare's first historical tetralogy; but how much he owed to Berners's Froissart and to the lives of Richard III and Wolsey, and how much to his own dramatic inclinations, it is impossible to assess. However, it matters little whence he got the strain, but much more that it should be there. It is of course precisely this strain that the disintegrators have been after whenever they have wished to fish out any fragments of true Shakespeare from the general wreckage; and they have found it, for instance, in the first declaration of the feud between red and white rose in *1 Henry VI* and in the Jack

Cade scenes in *2 Henry VI*. There is nothing wrong in praising these scenes and calling them typical of Shakespeare. But it is very wrong indeed to emphasise them and to make them the norm by which to judge the whole tetralogy. They enrich the tetralogy but on a balance they are exceptional to it.

To redress this wrong emphasis we must think of yet another strain in this tetralogy: that of formalism and stylisation. It is something archaic, inherited from the Morality Play. But it is the very feature through which the essential life of the poetry is expressed. When we encounter an unnatural and stylised balance of incident or an artificial pattern of speech we must not think that here is merely an archaic survival: we must accept them as things having contemporary vitality and must make them the norm of the play. We must in fact be good Aristotelians, for the moment, and believe that the soul of the play is in plot rather than in character. The realism of the Jack Cade scenes is not their main point but a subsidiary enrichment. Their main point is to make half a pattern, the other half being implied by the blameless orderliness of Iden. We are apt to praise the Cade scenes for being realistic and jeer at Iden for being a dummy, when we should merge praise and blame into the appreciation of a piece of stylisation which includes the whole. Similarly Henry VI's pathetic piece of nostalgia as he sits on the molehill watching the Battle of Towton has been isolated into a piece of poetic and "human" writing in a boring and inhuman context. Actually it loses most of its virtue apart from the context; apart from the terrible scene of the father killing his son and the son killing his father. That scene embodies a traditional motive; for these acts had been chosen by the authors of the Homilies, by Hall, and by the authors of the *Mirror for Magistrates* as the clearest symbol of the horrors of civil war. Shakespeare's fathers and sons here are as flat characters as Iden; and they have no business to be anything else. They stand as great traditional types, in whom realism would be impious. They enact a tableau; though they speak they are not far off a dumb-show: and their flatness adds enormous point to the ineffective humanity of the weak king. The most moving of all the scenes in the tetralogy, the ghosts visiting the sleeps of Richard III and Richmond in *Richard III*, is perhaps the most rigidly patterned and most grossly unrealistic of any. What could be remoter from actuality than the juxtaposition of the two tents and the liturgical chantings of each ghost as it passes? But to object to this scene on these grounds is as stupid as to blame the *Eumenides* of Aeschylus for being deficient in the realistic psychology of the *Electra* of Euripides. When this principle has been grasped and accepted the tetralogy comes out a much more assured and solid affair than it is generally thought to be.

But if the Morality Play prompted the formality of Shakespeare's first tetralogy it also supplied a single pervasive theme; one which overrides but in no way interferes with the theme he derived from Hall. In none of the plays is there a hero: and one of the reasons is that there is an unnamed protagonist dominating all four. It is England, or in Morality terms Respublica. Just as London, which appears only in the prologue, is the hero of Wilson's *Three Lords and three Ladies of London* (itself more a Morality Play than a developed Elizabethan drama), so England, though she is now quite excluded as a character, is the true hero of Shakespeare's first tetralogy. She is brought near ruin through not being true to herself; yielding to French witchcraft and being divided in mind. But God, though he punishes her, pities her and in the end through his grace allows the suppressed good in her to assert itself and restore her to health. I reserve the details of this scheme till the sections on the separate plays. How in the first three plays of his second tetralogy Shakespeare developed and enriched the Respublica theme will be described in due course.

Finally Shakespeare reinforces the structural unity which the themes of the Morality and of Hall create, by sowing in one play the seeds that are to germinate in the next and by constant references back from a later play to an earlier. In *1 Henry VI* he gives us modestly but with sufficient emphasis the first clash of York and Lancaster and the rivalry of Cardinal Beaufort with the good Protector, Humphrey Duke of Gloucester, which are to be a prevailing theme of the second play. In *2 Henry VI* Margaret of Anjou is important, yet she is kept subordinate to other characters in readiness to develop into a major character in the third play. Again, York begins faintly in the first play, gathers force in the second, and is cut off in the third, while the ruthlessness and hypocrisy of Richard Crookback begin faintly in the second play, grow big in the third, and overreach themselves to destruction in the last.

For all the inequality of execution, the vast crowding in of historical incident (some of it inorganic), Shakespeare planned his first historical tetralogy greatly, reminding one of Hardy in the *Dynasts*. When we consider how deficient his fellow-dramatists were in the architectonic power, we can only conclude that this was one of the things with which he was conspicuously endowed by nature. Far from being the untidy genius, Shakespeare was in one respect a born classicist.

I will treat the details of structure along with the other qualities of the separate plays.

2. THE FIRST PART OF HENRY VI

I am fully in accord with a growing trend of belief that Shakespeare wrote this play. It is not in the least surprising if the style is hesitant and varied. If a young man attempts a big thing, a thing beyond his years, he will imitate others when his own invention flags. Some of the verse in this play, as in the rest of the tetralogy, is in the common, little differentiated dramatic idiom of the age: it is the sort of thing that just was being written. That Shakespeare should have had recourse to it was perfectly natural. Why should he, more than another poet, be expected to find himself instantaneously? No one disputes the authorship of Pope's *Pastorals* because they do not show the author's achieved and unmistakable genius throughout, or collects the truly Popean lines and conjectures that he added just these to a lost original. Such treatment is kept for Shakespeare. One cannot of course be sure that a manuscript which waited over thirty years for publication remained in every word or sentence as the poet penned it. But the editors of the First Folio thought the play to be Shakespeare's; and this is evidence that only something very solid on the other side should be allowed to gainsay. The evidence, apart from the First Folio, that is overwhelmingly on the side of Shakespeare's being the author is the masterly structure. None of his contemporary dramatists was capable of this. The steady political earnestness is further proof.

I cannot believe either that this part was written after the other two parts of *Henry VI*. The evidence for a later date is the entry in Henslowe's Diary for 3 March 1591-2 of *Henry VI* as "ne" or new. Alexander has argued that the entry probably refers to another play altogether. Quite apart from the greater immaturity of its style, in itself a strong argument for earlier date, the first part is a portion of a larger organism. The very difference of its structure from that of the second part is an essential and deliberate contrast within a total scheme, while characters, embryonic in the first part, develop in the second in full congruity with their embryonic character.

Nor can I agree with Alexander that the scenes at the end of the play of Suffolk fetching Margaret of Anjou are an after-thought designed to link the play closely with the next. They have the same function as the last scenes in the next two plays, which suggest the opening scenes of their successors. They *all* argue the organic nature of the whole tetralogy.

Apart from the queer reluctance to allow Shakespeare to have written ill or like other dramatists when he was immature, the chief reason why people have been hostile to Shakespeare's authorship is the way he treats Joan of Arc. That the gentle Shakespeare could have been so ungentlemanly as to make his Joan other than a saint was intolerable. This is precisely like arguing that Shakespeare could not have written *King John* because he does not mention Magna Carta. That England adopted the French opinion of Joan of Arc and saw the begin-nings of our liberties in Magna Carta may have been excellent things; but these acts are comparatively recent, belonging to the "1066 and All That" phase of history, about which the Elizabethans knew nothing. To an Elizabethan, France did not mean saints, but instability, wars of religion, political in-trigue, with the Massacre of St. Bartholomew the outstanding event. Not that moderns can enjoy the way Shakespeare treats the French, Joan of Arc included. But he is just as bad (and with less excuse because older) in *Henry V*; and any argument, based on Joan of Arc, against the Shakespearean authorship of *1 Henry VI* is just as pertinent to the later play. It is some comfort to reflect that in his contribution to *Sir Thomas More* Shakespeare treated the alien like an ordinary human being. George Betts has said that expelling the London aliens will be good for trade, and More replies:

> Grant them remov'd and grant that this your noise
> Had chid down all the majesty of England.
> Imagine that you see the wretched strangers,
> Their babies at their backs and their poor luggage,
> Plodding to th' ports and coasts for transportation—

But these were aliens who could be seen and heard, and taken as individuals. Frenchmen in the mass were judged by other standards.

The *First Part of Henry VI* is the work of an ambitious and reflective young man who has the power to plan but not worthily to execute something great. His style of writing lags behind the powerful imagination that arranged the inchoate mass of historical material into a highly significant order. The characters are well thought out and consistent but they are the correct pieces in a game moved by an external hand rather than self-moving. Yet they come to life now and then and, in promise, are quite up to what we have any right to expect from Shakespeare in his youth.

If this play had been called the *Tragedy of Talbot* it would stand a much better chance of being heeded by a public which very naturally finds it hard to remember which part of *Henry VI* is which, and where Joan of Arc or Jack Cade, or Margaret crowning York with a paper crown, occur. And if we want something by which to distinguish the play, let us by all means give it that title. It is one that contains much truth, but not all. The whole truth in this matter is that though the action revolves round Talbot, though he stands pre-eminently for loyalty and order in a world threatened by chaos, he is not the hero. For there is no regular hero either in this or in any of the other three plays; its true hero being England or Respublica after the fashion of the Morality Play, as pointed out in the last section. It is therefore truer to the nature of the separate plays that they should be given colourless regal titles than that they should be named after the seemingly most important characters or events.

Along with the Morality hero goes the assumption of divine interference. The theme of the play is the testing of England, already guilty and under a sort of curse, by French witchcraft. England is championed by a great and pious soldier, Talbot, and the witchcraft is directed principally at him. If the other chief men of England had all been like him, he could have resisted and saved England. But they are divided against each other, and through this division Talbot dies and the first stage in England's ruin and of the fulfilment of the curse is accomplished. Respublica has suffered the first terrible wound.

As so often happens in literature the things which initially are the most troublesome prove to be the most enlightening. The Joan episodes, unpleasant and hence denied Shakespeare,

are the clue to the whole plot.   They are hinted at right in the
front of the play.   In the first scene Exeter, commenting on the
funeral of Henry V, says:

> What! shall we curse the planets of mishap
> That plotted thus our glory's overthrow?
> Or shall we think the subtle-witted French
> Conjurers and sorcerers, that afraid of him
> By magic verses have contriv'd his end?

One cannot understand the bearing of these lines on the play
without remembering how the influence of the stars and witchcraft fitted into the total Elizabethan conception of the universe.
Though these two things were thought to be powerful in their
effects and were dreaded, they did not work undirected.   God
was ultimately in control, and the divine part of man, his
reason and the freedom of his will, need not yield to them.
Further, God used both stars and evil spirits to forward his own
ends.   Joan, then, is not a mere piece of fortuitous witchcraft,
not a mere freakish emissary of Satan, but a tool of the Almighty, as she herself (though unconsciously) declares in her
words to Charles after her first appearance,

> Assign'd am I to be the English scourge.

Who but God has assigned her this duty?   True, if this line
were unsupported, we might hesitate to make this full inference.
But combined with the various cosmic references and the piety
of Talbot, it is certain.   For not only the first scene of the play,
but the second scene (where Joan first appears) begins with a
reference to the heavens.   The first passage was quoted above;
the Dauphin Charles begins the second scene:

> Mars his true moving, even as in the heavens
> So in the earth, to this day is not known:
> Late did he shine upon the English side;
> Now we are victors; upon us he smiles.

Not only do these words contrast significantly with Bedford's
opening speech about the "bad revolted stars"; they combine
with it in presenting the whole world order with God, the unmoved mover, directing it.   And the full context of witchcraft
is implied when Talbot before Orleans, already harassed by
Joan's supernatural power, exclaims of the French:

> Well, let them practise and converse with spirits:
> God is our fortress, in whose conquering name
> Let us resolve to scale their flinty bulwarks.

A modern, who needs much working up to pay any real heed to witchcraft, is apt not to notice such a passage and to pass on faintly disgusted with Talbot for being not only a butcher but a prig: an Elizabethan, granted a generally serious context, would find Talbot's defiance apt and noble.

What were the sins God sought to punish? There had been a number, but the pre-eminent one was the murder of Richard II, the shedding of the blood of God's deputy on earth. Henry IV had been punished by an uneasy reign but had not fully expiated the crime; Henry V, for his piety, had been allowed a brilliant reign. But the curse was there; and first England suffers through Henry V's early death and secondly she is tried by the witchcraft of Joan.

Into the struggle between Talbot and Joan, which is the main motive of the play, is introduced the theme of order and dissension. The first scene presents the funeral of Henry V and declares the disaster of his death. Dissension appears through the high words between the bad ambitious Beaufort, Bishop of Winchester, and Humphrey Duke of Gloucester, honest but hot-tempered, the regent of England. Bad news from France follows. But the case of England is not hopeless. Bedford sets off at once for France, Gloucester takes charge at home.

The next scene is before Orleans. The French are in a mood of facile triumph. They will relieve the town, still besieged by Salisbury and the English. Though ten to one they are beaten back with loss and confusion. That, the poet makes us feel, is the natural order, God's order, provided England is true to herself. Then Joan enters, a dazzling blonde, claiming her beauty to be from the Virgin—

> And, whereas I was black and swart before,
> With those clear rays which she infus'd on me
> That beauty am I bless'd with which you see—

but of course owing it to the Devil. She fascinates Charles and ends by imposing on the French a discipline and an order which by nature is not theirs. That this order is bogus, a devilish not a divine one, is evident by the single combat Charles the Dauphin has with Joan to test her pretensions. He is beaten;

and for a man to yield to a woman was a fundamental upsetting of degree.

Then, before a background of dissension in England, the struggle between Talbot and Joan is worked out. There are three episodes: Orleans, Rouen, Bordeaux. Before Orleans Talbot's men melt before Joan's attack, and, though he is dauntless, she relieves the town. The French triumph. But now Bedford has arrived with Burgundian allies: there is a new union on the English side, and the town (quite unhistorically) is captured. Talbot has kept up his heart and with united supporters he triumphs. The pattern is repeated at Rouen. Through a trick Joan wins the town for the French. Again Talbot does not lose heart. He gets Burgundy to swear to capture the town or die. Bedford, brought in on a litter and near his death, insists on taking his share:

> Here will I sit before the walls of Roan [1]
> And will be partner of your weal or woe.

Union once more and it succeeds. The town is captured, and Talbot emerges more strongly than ever the symbol of true and virtuous order:

> Now will we take some order in the town,
> Placing therein some expert officers,
> And then depart to Paris to the king,
> For there young Henry with his nobles lie.

To which Burgundy, again showing the natural relation of French to English, replies,

> What wills Lord Talbot pleaseth Burgundy.

Talbot then goes on to more proprieties:

> But yet, before we go, let's not forget
> The noble Duke of Bedford late deceas'd
> But see his exequies fulfill'd in Roan.

But Joan had not yet ceased to be the English scourge, and Talbot was wrong in saying just before the above lines,

> I think her old familiar is asleep.

In the next scene, outside Rouen, Joan cheers the dispirited

---

[1] A monosyllable: the Elizabethan form of Rouen (now, alas, given up).

French leaders and says she has another plan: she will detach
Burgundy from the English alliance.   Then, in what must have
been a most effective scene on the Elizabethan stage, the English
forces pass across in triumph with colours spread, headed
by Talbot, on their way to Paris.   The Burgundians follow and
Joan waylays them.   She addresses to their Duke those commonplaces about avoiding civil war of which, ironically, England
was even then in such desperate need, for between the episodes
of Orleans and Rouen had come the quarrel between Lancastrians and Yorkists in the Temple Garden and Richard Plantagenet's resolve to claim the Duchy of York:

> See, see the pining malady of France;
> Behold the wounds, the most unnatural wounds,
> Which thou thyself hast given her woeful breast.
> O, turn thy edged sword another way;
> Strike those that hurt and hurt not those that help.
> One drop of blood drawn from thy country's bosom
> Should grieve thee more than streams of foreign gore.

Excellent advice when applied to England; but to France,
where Massacres of St. Bartholomew were endemic, quite perverse.   With a speed, familiar to readers of contemporary
Elizabethan drama or of *Savonarola Brown*, Burgundy acquiesces
and joins with the French.   Joan, with a cynicism that anticipates the Bastard Falconbridge, exclaims:

> Done like a Frenchman: turn, and turn again!

Meanwhile Talbot, ignorant of Burgundy's defection, arrives
in Paris and does homage to Henry in the scene I have already
pointed to (p. 151) as epitomising the principle of degree and
the way a kingdom should be ordered.   Henry is crowned, and
immediately after comes the news of Burgundy's defection.
Talbot leaves at once to renew the wars.   But the court he
leaves, that should have been his base and his certainty, shows
itself divided and weak.   Yorkist and Lancastrian refer their
quarrels to the king, who quite fails to grasp the ugliness of the
situation, frivolously chooses a red rose for himself with the
words,

> I see no reason, if I wear this rose,
> That anyone should therefore be suspicious
> I more incline to Somerset than York,

and sets out to return to England, leaving Somerset and York
in divided command of all the forces except the few that accom-
pany Talbot. English division is now acutely contrasted with
French reconciliation. Exeter pronounces the choric comment
that prepares for the culminating catastrophe:

> No simple man that sees
> This jarring discord of nobility,
> This shouldering of each other in the court,
> This factious bandying of their favourites,
> But that it doth presage some ill event.
> 'Tis much when sceptres are in children's hands,
> But more when envy breeds unkind division:
> There comes the ruin, there begins confusion.

From this there follows inevitably the final tragedy of Talbot
near Bordeaux. Twice he had resisted the machinations of
Joan and triumphed; but then he was supported by his own
people. The third time, though he does all he can, he perishes;
for York and Somerset, to whom he had sent for help, each
refuses it for envy of the other. Joan is not allowed to kill
Talbot; that would be unseemly: he must die on heaps of
French dead. After his death she reports how his son had
refused to fight her ("to be the pillage of a giglot wench")
and insults over his body. Lucy, who has come to learn the
news, recites the full list of Talbot's great titles; at which Joan
exclaims:

> Here is a silly stately style indeed!
> The Turk, who two and fifty kingdoms hath,
> Writes not so tedious a style as this.
> Him that thou magnifi'st with all these titles
> Stinking and fly-blown lies here at our feet.

Joan, by God's permission and through the general collapse of
order among the English nobility, has dealt England a great
blow. Having dealt it, and ceasing to be God's tool, she loses
her power. Her evil spirits desert her, and she is captured and
burnt for the wicked woman she is. It is possible that we are
meant to think that her evil spells are transferred to another
Frenchwoman, Margaret of Anjou, who, at the end of the
play, is allowed through the machinations of her would-be
paramour, the unscrupulous Suffolk, to supplant the daughter

of the Earl of Armagnac, already affianced, in the affections
of Henry VI. On the ominous note of this royal perjury
the play ends.

Such is the play's outline. There is no scene or episode not
mentioned above that does not reinforce one or other of the
main themes. Even the episode of Talbot and the Countess of
Auvergne serves to exalt the hero as well as creating a legitimate
diversion at a pause in the action.

Shakespeare took great trouble over his plot, but his emo-
tions too were deeply stirred in his task. The gradual but sure
stages in Talbot's destruction express the painful seriousness
with which Shakespeare took the historical theme. He also
took trouble over the characters, but he felt far less strongly
about them. At least he made them consistent, even if he did
not give them a great deal of life. For instance, Suffolk at his
first appearance in the Temple Garden (II. 4) shows himself
both diplomatic and unscrupulous. It is he who has brought
the dispute between Somerset and York from the hall into the
privacy of the garden:

> Within the Temple Hall we were too loud;
> The garden here is more convenient.

And, when asked his opinion on the legal point, he coolly
says,

> Faith, I have been a truant in the law
> And never yet could frame my will to it;
> And therefore frame the law unto my will.

York is the true anticipation of the

> dogged York, that reaches at the moon

of the second part. He is violently ambitious, yet not rashly
but obstinately and persistently: strong in all the regal qualities but goodness of heart. Gloucester is simply but sufficiently
shown as the opposite of York: good-hearted but free-spoken
to a fault. The contrast of their characters already prepares
for the main motive of the next play.

Talbot and Joan are the most alive, for they both have a
touch of breeziness, or hearty coarseness with which Shakespeare liked to furnish his most successfully practical characters.
Joan's remarks on Burgundy's change of mind and on Talbot's

dead body, quoted above, are examples. And this is Talbot's comment on Salisbury's dying wounds received before Orleans:

> Hear, hear how dying Salisbury doth groan!
> It irks his heart he cannot be reveng'd.
> Frenchmen, I'll be a Salisbury to you:
> Pucelle or puzzle, Dolphin or dogfish,
> Your hearts I'll stamp out with my horse's heels
> And make a quagmire of your mingled brains.
> Convey me Salisbury into his tent.

In Henry VI's character Shakespeare shows little interest. There is a strong religious feeling throughout the tetralogy that culminates in *Richard III*, but it is religion applied to the workings of history not the religious feelings in the mind of a poor king and a saint. Shakespeare stops short at the poor king, who is also pathetic; he omits the more interesting self-questionings of the same character in the *Mirror for Magistrates*.

For style, much of the play is a competent example of the dramatic norm of the period. As this:

> Crossing the sea from England into France,
> This fellow here with envious carping tongue
> Upbraided me about the rose I wear;
> Saying, the sanguine colour of the leaves
> Did represent my master's blushing cheeks,
> When stubbornly he did repugn the truth
> About a certain question in the law
> Argu'd betwixt the Duke of York and him,
> With other vile and ignominious terms.
> In confutation of which rude reproach
> And in defence of my lord's worthiness
> I crave the benefit of law of arms.

But this is not the only way of writing. Once or twice the rhythm is unpleasantly lame, as when Joan says to Charles, about to try her in single combat,

> I am prepar'd. Here is my keen-edg'd sword,
> Deck'd with five flower-de-luces on each side,
> The which at Touraine, in Saint Katharine's churchyard,
> Out of a great deal of old iron I chose forth.

Such lameness is not so surprising when we refer the passage to its original in Holinshed:

Then at the Dolphin's sending, by her assignment, from Saint Katharine's Church of Fierbois in Touraine (where she never had been and knew not) in a secret place there, among old iron, appointed she her sword to be sought out and brought her, that with five flower-delices was graven on both sides.

Shakespeare much later in his career was apt to be careless of rhythms when he paraphrased Holinshed. Besides, Holinshed is here reporting the French version of Joan's inspiration, and Shakespeare may be deliberately making it ridiculous; just as, in general, he made the French talk foolishly. Then sometimes there are outbursts of the turgid or dulcet writing dear to the University Wits, to vary the more sober norm of the play. The classical references, profuse for a play on a historical theme, are in keeping with these and form yet another link with *Titus Andronicus*. Here is Talbot's account of how the French treated him in captivity:

> In open market-place produc'd they me,
> To be a public spectacle to all.
> Here, said they, is the terror of the French,
> The scarecrow that affrights our children so.
> Then broke I from the officers that led me
> And with my nails digg'd stones out of the ground
> To hurl at the beholders of my shame.
> My grisly countenance made others fly;
> None durst come near for fear of sudden death.
> In iron walls they deem'd me not secure.
> So great fear of my name 'mongst them was spread
> That they suppos'd I could rend bars of steel
> And spurn in pieces posts of adamant.

And for the dulcet style Suffolk's words to Margaret of Anjou when he has captured her will do as illustration:

> Be not offended, nature's miracle,
> Thou art allotted to be ta'en by me:
> So doth the swan her downy cygnets save,
> Keeping them prisoner underneath her wings.
> Yet, if this servile usage once offend,
> Go and be free again as Suffolk's friend.
> O, stay! I have no power to let her pass;
> My hand would free her, but my heart says no.
> As plays the sun upon the glassy streams,

Twinkling another counterfeited beam,
So seems this gorgeous beauty to mine eyes.

When Shakespeare has to deal with his climax, the death of
Talbot, he wisely adds the formality of rhyme to the heightened
style of the University Wits. This is how Talbot describes his
son's death:

Triumphant Death, smear'd with captivity,
Young Talbot's valour makes me smile at thee.
When he perceiv'd me shrink and on my knee,
His bloody sword he brandish'd over me,
And like a hungry lion did commence
Rough deeds of rage and stern impatience:
But when my angry guardant stood alone,
Tendering my ruin and assail'd of none,
Dizzy-eyed fury and great rage of heart
Suddenly made him from my side to start
Into the clustering battle of the French;
And in that sea of blood my boy did drench
His over-mounting spirit and there died,
My Icarus, my blossom, in his pride.

Shakespeare seems to have known that his power over words
did not match the grandeur of conception contained in Talbot's
death. So he resorted to the conventional, the formal, the
stylised, as the best way out.

But in compensation, bits of imaginative writing show themselves at intervals throughout the play; and as much in the less
dignified scenes as in the rest. That they are thus scattered is
a strong argument for the whole play being Shakespeare's.
Thus Reignier, commenting on English valour, uses the metaphor of the artificial figure of a man striking the hours of a clock
with a hammer, as Shakespeare was to use it again with superb
effect in *Richard III*:

I think by some odd gimmers or device
Their arms are set like clocks, still to strike on;
Else ne'er could they hold out so as they do.

Again, Talbot, deserted by his men in front of Orleans,
exclaims,

My thoughts are whirled like a potter's wheel.

Shakespeare knows exactly what to make the servingmen of Gloucester and Winchester say, when they quarrel:

> *First Serv.* Nay, if we be forbidden stones, we'll fall to it with our teeth.
> *Second Serv.* Do what ye dare, we are as resolute.

Talbot, offering terms to the French commanders in Bordeaux, gets beyond good melodrama and touches true grandeur:

> But, if you frown upon this proffer'd peace,
> You tempt the fury of my three attendants,
> Lean famine, quartering steel, and climbing fire;
> Who in a moment even with the earth
> Shall lay your stately and air-braving towers,
> If you forsake the offer of their love.

But it is rare for Shakespeare's execution to be thus equal to his theme; and the chief virtue of the play must reside in the vehement energy with which Shakespeare both shaped this single play and conceived it as an organic part of a vast design.

3. THE SECOND PART OF HENRY VI

In the first part there had been disaster abroad. Respublica had lost most of her foreign possessions, and with the death of her greatest captain, Talbot, and of her soldier-administrator, Bedford, had no chance of regaining them. There had also been dissensions among the English, but though these had ruined Talbot they had not ruined the actual land of England. Here the good Duke Humphrey of Gloucester is in charge and has kept going the due administration of justice. In the second part the dissensions, which in the first part had been the background, are developed at home as the main theme, with the Duke of York the emergent figure. They cause Duke Humphrey's fall and at the end bring the country to the edge of chaos. The play pictures the second stage in the country's ruin, in the working out of the inherited curse.

In many ways the second part is contrasted with the first. The plot-pattern is the main thing in the first part, and with this emphasis goes a pageantlike, stylised execution. One happening is contrasted ironically with another, the irony being more important than the richness of either happening. Characters may have much abstract meaning but as persons have little depth. Talbot is a grand symbol of loyalty and order; his touch of coarse humour goes a little way and only a little way towards making him interesting. The second part is very well plotted, yet with another emphasis. Events, as befits the domestic setting, matter more in themselves. They are richly and elaborately developed. And they concern a wider section of the community. We are shown dissension affecting not only the prime movers of it, the nobles, but the common people and the middle classes. The whole frame of Respublica is beginning to suffer. Thus it is that the scenes of Horner the armourer and his man Peter, of the pirates who capture Suffolk, and of Jack Cade and Iden, at first sight episodic, are greatly to the point. Lastly there is a vastly heightened interest in personality. Shakespeare is wonderfully alive to the fascination of the mere force of character. The main English nobles are bad and they ruin the country, but they are all positive characters, characters who start trains of events, who are at the centre of living. Gloucester's description of the men who are plotting against him brings out to perfection this side of the play:

> I know their complot is to have my life,
> And if my death might make this island happy
> And prove the period of their tyranny,
> I would expend it with all willingness.
> But mine is made the prologue to their play;
> For thousands more, that yet suspect no peril,
> Will not conclude their plotted tragedy.
> Beaufort's red sparkling eyes blab his heart's malice,
> And Suffolk's cloudy brow his stormy hate;
> Sharp Buckingham unburthens with his tongue
> The envious load that lies upon his heart;
> And dogged York, that reaches at the moon,
> Whose overweening arm I have pluck'd back,
> By false accuse doth level at my life;
> And you, my sovereign lady, with the rest
> Causeless have laid disgraces on my head
> And with your best endeavour have stirr'd up
> My liefest liege to be mine enemy.

In presupposing the background of degree and of God's order the second part is like the first, but it allows that background to

be dimmer. Gloucester is more the honest statesman than the
pure symbol of degree. And it is Iden, the virtuous Kentish
squire, who in a far smaller way than Talbot fulfils this symbolic
function. But there are enough incidental touches to remind us
of the whole cosmic context, as when in the hawking scene near
St. Albans Henry thus comments, as the nobles begin to bicker:

> The winds grow high; so do your stomachs, lords.
> How irksome is this music to my heart!
> When such strings jar, what hope of harmony?

Here we have the duplication of uproar in macrocosm and
microcosm, and the cosmos as a harmonious dance or a piece
of music.

Not only does Iden stand as the symbol of degree; he also
indicates the design of the play when he says of himself,

> I seek not to wax great by others' waning.

These words are a comment by implication on the rise of York
at the expense of Gloucester, and should recall to us York's own
policy as revealed at the end of Act II Scene 2 to Salisbury and
Warwick:

> Do you as I do in these dangerous days:
> Wink at the Duke of Suffolk's insolence,
> At Beaufort's pride, at Somerset's ambition,
> At Buckingham and all the crew of them,
> Till they have snar'd the shepherd of the flock,
> That virtuous prince, the good Duke Humphrey.

In contrast to the first part, where the main theme was the fate
of a single man, we have here simultaneously the fall of one
man and the rise of another, the pattern of the two buckets on
one chain, repeated in *Richard II*. However much other business there is, it does not obscure the central theme.

The central theme then is political intrigue, which of itself
dictates that greater stress on events and smaller emphasis on
symbol and principle, already noted. Shakespeare may have
made this change for the sake of variety, but it also corresponds
to his growing power; for in this play he shows to the full, as he
hardly did in the first part, his wonderful faculty of animating
a heavy mass of material: a repetition, on the serious historical
side, of his masterly manipulation of a complicated comic situation in the *Comedy of Errors*. Reviewing the opening scenes of

1 and 2 Henry VI, which both get through a great deal of business
and succeed in setting forth the whole situation, one must contrast the staccato presentation of events in the first part with the
melting of one event into another of the second part; and
wherever there is a large, exciting, and quickly moving political
theme, as the events round Gloucester's murder and the final
alignment of Yorkists against Lancastrians before the battle of
St. Albans, Shakespeare is no longer the compiler but the con-
troller of his material.

It has not been the practice to consider *2 Henry VI* as a whole.
But it is pre-eminently as such, as a fine piece of construction,
that it is to be enjoyed. Thus I cannot avoid going into the
details of its ordering. Unluckily, such details are boring to
anyone who does not hold the subject in his head. The following pages, indeed, are not likely to mean much unless applied
to an actual reading of the play. But I do not see how I can
omit them, for I must seek to establish my assertion that the
play is a fine whole. I can but advise the reader to skip them,
if he is not in a position to find them intelligible.

The play opens with Suffolk's return from France with
Margaret of Anjou. And we must remember Henry's broken
betrothal from the previous play and the beginnings of guilty
love between Suffolk and Margaret. The omens are bad.
Henry is unmoved by the disgraceful terms of the match: no
dowry and the surrender of Anjou and Maine. In the first part
Talbot had presented him with many captives and "fifty for-
tresses, twelve cities and seven wall'd towns of strength," and
been rewarded with the earldom of Shrewsbury; in this scene,
in ironic contrast, Suffolk presents him with a doubtful French
bride and the surrender of Anjou and Maine, and is rewarded
with the dukedom of Suffolk. We must also remember from
the last play first the pride and ambition of Bishop (now Cardinal) Beaufort and his hatred of Duke Humphrey; and second
the quarrel between Richard Plantagenet, Duke of York, and
Edmund Beaufort, Duke of Somerset. The quarrel in the
Temple Garden in the first part was not over the succession to
the throne but over Richard's right to inherit the title of York.
Somerset had opposed this right on the ground that Richard's
father, Earl of Cambridge, had forfeited his patrimony because
he had been executed for treason under Henry V. The red
and the white rose are at present the emblems of factions
within the kingdom not of rival claimants to the throne.

Mortimer, York's uncle, had recommended discretion, on his deathbed:

> With silence, nephew, be thou politic:
> Strong-fixed is the house of Lancaster
> And like a mountain not to be removed.

And though we know York to be ambitious he has not opened his mind to anyone. After Henry has retired with Margaret and Suffolk—significant trio—the peers remain and reveal their motives in a splendidly marshalled scene. Duke Humphrey appeals to them *all* to resent the terms of the new match: he tries to unite the peers and their differences in this common feeling, naming each in turn. England has still one great champion of order; the condition of Respublica is not yet quite desperate. Cardinal Beaufort at once opposes him: for him hatred of Duke Humphrey is stronger than the welfare of England; he is unmitigatedly bad. Then Salisbury (son-in-law of the Salisbury who died at Orleans), Warwick his son and York, with whom Warwick had been associated in the first part, support Duke Humphrey, who, however, is so stung by the Cardinal's rudeness that he goes out for fear of renewing their habitual quarrels. Humphrey thus allows himself to be isolated. Then the Cardinal maligns Humphrey, and Buckingham and Somerset agree to combine with Suffolk to get Humphrey out of the protectorship. The Cardinal goes out to find Suffolk. Somerset tells his cousin Buckingham to watch the Cardinal and his ambitions, and we think that the plot against Humphrey may not be too dangerous if its promoters thus distrust one another. Buckingham and Somerset go out, and Salisbury, watching them go, makes a speech to York and Warwick that explains much of the play's design:

> Pride went before, Ambition follows him.
> While these do labour for their own preferment,
> Behoves it us to labour for the realm.
> I never saw but Humphrey Duke of Gloucester
> Did bear him like a noble gentleman.
> Oft have I seen the haughty cardinal,
> More like a soldier than a man o' the church,
> As stout and proud as he were lord of all,
> Swear like a ruffian and demean himself
> Unlike the ruler of a commonweal.

Warwick, my son, the comfort of my age,
Thy deeds thy plainness and thy housekeeping
Hath won the greatest favour of the commons,
Excepting none but good Duke Humphrey.
And, brother York, thy acts in Ireland
In bringing them to civil discipline,
Thy late exploits done in the heart of France,
When thou wert regent for our sovereign,
Have made thee fear'd and honour'd of the people.
Join we together for the public good,
In what we can to bridle and suppress
The pride of Suffolk and the Cardinal,
With Somerset's and Buckingham's ambition;
And, as we may, cherish Duke Humphrey's deeds,
While they do tend the profit of the land.

First, the opening of this speech should remind us of the Morality theme. It is the Realm, Respublica, that is the main concern; and for the moment Buckingham and Somerset have turned into two allegorical characters, Pride and Ambition, the bane of the realm. Second, we see that if Salisbury with his disinterestedness, Warwick with his liberal living that had endeared him to the people, and York with his political authority back Humphrey up, the state may be saved. Even the two Nevils, Salisbury and Warwick (who go out together) might suffice. York remains, and though he has made a show of uniting with Salisbury and Warwick he reveals in a splendid soliloquy (anticipating the eminence of his son, Richard III, in that art) that he means to double-cross them. Here is the part of the speech that explains his plans and the course of the play:

A day will come when York shall claim his own;
And therefore I will take the Nevils' part
And make a show of love to proud Duke Humphrey,
And, when I spy advantage, claim the crown,
For that's the golden mark I seek to hit.
Nor shall proud Lancaster usurp my right,
Nor hold the sceptre in his childish fist,
Nor wear the diadem upon his head,
Whose churchlike humours fits not for a crown.
Then, York, be still awhile, till time do serve.
Watch thou, and wake when others be asleep,
To pry into the secrets of the state;

Till Henry, surfeiting in joys of love,
With his new bride and England's dear-bought queen,
And Humphrey with the peers, be fall'n at jars.
Then will I raise aloft the milk-white rose,
With whose sweet smell the air shall be perfum'd,
And in my standard bear the arms of York
To grapple with the house of Lancaster;
And, force perforce, I'll make him yield the crown
Whose bookish rule hath pull'd fair England down.

The next solemn scene that greatly advances the plot is
Act II Scene 2, where York unfolds his plans to Salisbury and
Warwick. In between, the fortunes of Humphrey and the
growing insolence of Queen Margaret are the main theme.
Humphrey resists the temptations of his wife to aim at the
crown, but she persists in her ambition, saying,

> I will not be slack
> To play my part in fortune's pageant.

(as she had played it already among the tragedies of *A Mirror
for Magistrates*) and proceeds to have spirits raised for her, to
foretell the future and get encouragement for her ambition.
These doubtful doings, reported by spies to the Cardinal, help
the downfall of her husband. Meanwhile Humphrey shows how
efficiently he administers justice in his arranging the dispute
between Thomas Horner the armourer and his apprentice
Peter, and in showing up the bogus miracle at St. Albans.
Queen Margaret and Suffolk, in a scene which is related to
Isabel and young Mortimer in Marlowe's *Edward II*, appear in
league, hostile to the whole court and contemptuous of the king.
Suffolk warns Margaret of the power of the Nevils:

> Salisbury and Warwick are no simple peers,

and again we reflect that these two men hold the balance of
power. Finally, Margaret and Suffolk reveal themselves as the
Lancastrian counterpart of York: willing to use others for their
own ends but aiming ultimately at sole power; as Suffolk says,

> Although we fancy not the cardinal,
> Yet must we join with him and with the lords,
> Till we have brought Duke Humphrey in disgrace.
> So, one by one, we'll weed them all at last,
> And you yourself shall steer the happy helm.

Humphrey's downfall is hastened by his unfortunate but strictly just advice about the regency of France. York and Somerset are the claimants. Humphrey and the Nevils back York, the Cardinal and Buckingham back Somerset. Then, when the dispute between Horner and Peter brings in question the loyalty of York, Humphrey changes sides and without consulting the Nevils, abruptly, as protector of the realm, pronounces his verdict:

> Let Somerset be regent o'er the French,
> Because in York this breeds suspicion.

Remembering this episode, we should not find Act II Scene 2 insufficiently motivated.

This scene is one of those stiff, factual expositions, full of resounding names, that must have been listened to breathlessly by an audience for whom the questions of titles and successions were a living issue, and the Wars of the Roses a terrible spectacle of what could so easily happen again. The bare exposition, granted a solemn versification, was enough; the bare facts had their own momentum: realism would be inappropriate, almost impious. York, in keeping with the secretiveness of his methods, chooses

> In this close walk to satisfy myself
> In craving your opinion of my title,
> Which is infallible, to England's crown,

and going back in history to the great days of Edward III, proceeds to enumerate, with all the solemnity inherited from Hall and his principles of history, this king's seven sons. Then he turns to the usurpation of Henry IV, the murder of Richard II, and finally to his own descent from Edward's third son, Duke of Clarence, as against the descent of the Henrys from John of Gaunt, the fourth son. Salisbury and Warwick, acting by dramatic convention and not by human probability, appear to have heard all this for the first time: an astonishing piece of news to which they offer not the slightest resistance. Overcome, they exclaim in unison:

> Long live our sovereign Richard, England's king!

But these gross offences against probability, this calm acquiescence in a convention ridiculous by later standards, do not mean that Shakespeare had really abandoned all motivation.

He did not want to complicate the momentous happening by the accidents of personality, to take the attention off the tremendous workings of events just at this place. Yet he had prepared us for a change of heart in Salisbury and Warwick in the scene referred to above where Humphrey without consulting them had ended in supporting Somerset against York as Regent of France. That had been an insult the Nevils could not tolerate. And so it is that they do not protest when York advises them to sacrifice the good Duke:

> Do you as I do in these dangerous days:
> Wink at the Duke of Suffolk's insolence,
> At Beaufort's pride, at Somerset's ambition,
> At Buckingham and all the crew of them,
> Till they have snar'd the shepherd of the flock,
> That virtuous prince, the good Duke Humphrey.
> 'Tis that they seek, and they in seeking that
> Shall find their deaths, if York can prophesy.

This is the turning-point of the play. Deserted by the Nevils, Duke Humphrey cannot remain protector. Once he ceases to be protector, the way is open for the strongest and most cunning man to emerge on top.

Subsequent scenes show, as they are bound to do, the stages of Humphrey's fall and the extent and character of York's designs. First, the Duchess of Gloucester is condemned to penance and banishment for her dealings with witchcraft, and Humphrey surrenders his office. Peter kills his master, Horner, in the judicial duel; and Horner, dying, confesses to treason, to his talk about York being the rightful king. We thus see the question of the title to the throne spread from the nobility to the people. Then comes another large scene where Shakespeare marshals a great mass of material: the parliament at Bury St. Edmunds. It is here that the full force of York's policy shows itself, for here, with Salisbury and Warwick watching but taking no part, York joins with the queen, Suffolk, and the Somerset faction in demanding of Henry the arrest and trial of Humphrey. Henry of course cannot resist, though convinced of Humphrey's innocence; and Humphrey foretells the havoc the plotting lords will work, in lines already quoted (p. 174). Humphrey is taken off under arrest and Henry follows shortly. Perhaps Salisbury and Warwick go with him. Anyhow they say nothing during the entire scene, and for a good reason,

which appears later.   The queen, Suffolk, York, and the Cardinal agree to have Humphrey murdered: the curse incurred
by the family of Henry IV from the murder of Richard II
begins to work in earnest.   Then news comes of a revolt in
Ireland, and after some bickering between York and Somerset
it is agreed that ·York should go there as regent with troops
raised by Suffolk.   York remains behind and in another fine
soliloquy unfolds the plans which he has quickly and brilliantly
conceived.   He will use Suffolk's men to forward his own ends,
raise more in Ireland and get things well stirred up for revolution in England by egging on Jack Cade and the men of Kent
to riot.   When things are well prepared, he will return and reap
the harvest.

In the next scene, another of the great ones, Humphrey is
murdered and Suffolk brings the news to the court.   Henry
swoons, and, reviving, guesses that Suffolk is the murderer.
The queen, acting the hysterically selfish woman, tries to attract
Henry's attention to herself and to screen her lover Suffolk.
Warwick and some of the commons break in with the news that
the people are in an uproar over Humphrey's death and suspect
Suffolk and the cardinal.   Henry sends Warwick to view the
corpse, and, in words that go beyond the personal horror of a
pious man, prays to God:

> O thou that judgest all things, stay my thoughts,
> My thoughts that labour to persuade my soul
> Some violent hands were laid on Humphrey's life.
> If my suspect be false, forgive me, God,
> For judgement only doth belong to thee.

We are in fact invited to watch out for the judgement of God
on the murder of Duke Humphrey.   Warwick returns with
the duke's body on a bed and in a superb heightened description
of the corpse pronounces that a certain murder has been committed.   He throws the suspicion on Suffolk and the cardinal.
Suffolk and he are in the middle of a quarrel, when Salisbury
enters with the news that the commons will tear Suffolk from
the palace unless he is banished.   Henry yields and banishes
Suffolk, who remains behind with the queen to take a long and
lyrical farewell.   What are we to make of Warwick's behaviour?
A Bradley could find a motive for him without difficulty.   He
could assume an arrangement between York, Salisbury, and
Warwick, by which York would actively accuse Duke Hum-

phrey while the other two would remain in the background till after the murder, express surprise and horror at it, and cast the blame on Suffolk and the Somersets. Warwick then would be acting a part when he comes in with Duke Humphrey's body. All this would be in keeping with the reticence of Salisbury and Warwick in the scene when Humphrey is accused. But what are we to make of these lines, spoken by Warwick just after the body has been brought in?

> As surely as my soul intends to live
> With that dread King that took our state upon him
> To free us from his Father's dreadful curse,
> I do believe that violent hands were laid
> Upon the life of this thrice-famed duke.

If Warwick is acting a part when he says this he must be an abandoned sinner indeed. But that is not his character. He is a man on the whole good, but, like most men of powerful character in his position, ambitious. Warwick's words are better understood through one of the common conventions of the Elizabethan stage by which a person may temporarily shed his proper character and become a choric commentator. Salisbury and Warwick have indeed been kept in the background in order that they may fulfil this function without undue strain. They are for the moment English Peers, any English Peers, showing the conventionally correct reaction to a frightful crime. When they next appear it is at the Battle of St. Albans, where they have reverted to being ordinarily human noblemen and York's chief supporters.

The judgement of God, invoked by Henry, is quick in striking two of Gloucester's murderers. Cardinal Beaufort dies in an agony of evil conscience, Suffolk is captured by a warship off the coast of Kent and put to death after the ship's captain has recited a list of his crimes. The two other plotters of Gloucester's death, York and Queen Margaret, get their punishment in the next play.

The captain of the warship had given the news that the commons of Kent were up in arms, thus preparing for Cade's rebellion in the next scene. The rebellion serves to forward York's plot, to extend the scope of the action to all sections of the community, and to offer the impious spectacle of the proper order reversed. Cade will make literacy a crime; he orders the rebels to burn all the records of the realm. All things henceforward are to be in common and "My mouth shall be the parliament of England." The climax of horror is when the heads of Lord Saye and Sir James Cromer are put on poles and made to kiss at every street corner. But disorder does not yet triumph. The rebellion is suppressed, and through the efforts of the Lancastrian party, who are now in control of the court. In this suppression a new character is active: Lord Clifford, who with his son figures prominently at the end of this play and the beginning of the next. Thus Shakespeare prepares his transitions. York now returns in force from Ireland, keeping his army on the pretext of Cade's rebellion and his enmity towards Somerset, whom he accuses of treason. York feigns submission when Somerset is imprisoned in the Tower, but the queen procures his liberty, and York at last comes into the open.

> How now, is Somerset at liberty?
> Then, York, unloose thy long-imprison'd thoughts
> And let thy tongue be equal with thy heart.
> Shall I endure the sight of Somerset?
> False King, why hast thou broken faith with me,
> Knowing how hardly I can brook abuse?
> King did I call thee? no, thou art not king,
> Not fit to govern and rule multitudes,
> Which dar'st not, no, nor canst not rule a traitor.
> That head of thine doth not become a crown;
> Thy hand is made to grasp a palmer's staff
> And not to grace an awful princely sceptre.
> That gold must round engirt these brows of mine,
> Whose smile and frown, like to Achilles' spear,
> Is able with the change to kill and cure.
> Here is a hand to hold a sceptre up
> And with the same to act controlling laws.
> Give place! by heaven thou shalt rule no more
> O'er him whom heaven created for thy ruler.

There follows the definitive alignment of Lancastrian and Yorkist. Two of York's sons, Edward and Richard, and the two Nevils, Salisbury and Warwick, come in to fill the Yorkist complement. A link with the two next plays is created when Clifford says to Richard:

> Hence, heap of wrath, foul indigested lump,
> As crooked in thy manners as thy shape.

The working out of the motives is now complete. The battle of St. Albans, where York triumphs, is the physical ratification of the process and ends the play. Richard kills Somerset, but Queen Margaret escapes, now York's chief rival. The two surviving contrivers of Duke Humphrey's murder are set one against the other.

I have already noted the heightened interest of the characters in this play. We get instead of simple juxtapositions the crossing of currents, of which the above account of the plot should have given sufficient illustration. There is also more life starting up in the separate characters than in the first part. For instance, Gloucester's efforts to deal with his own hot temper are memorable and amusing. In the third scene of the play, when the Suffolk faction bait him, he goes out and after a little returns, saying,

> Now, lords, my choler being over-blown
> With walking once about the quadrangle,
> I come to talk of commonwealth affairs.

It is not surprising that the author of *Woodstock* made him the model of his hero. The St. Albans impostors, Simpcox and his wife, are slightly but brilliantly drawn, and the wife's plea when they are found out, "Alas, sir, we did it for pure need," breaks effectively into the general hearty brutality. Jack Cade's fellows are admirable studies of simple people. On the whole, however, the force of the characters is in their bearing rather than in their minds.

But though Shakespeare has extended the range of his characters and gone farther towards making them lifelike and in entering their minds, the problem of character to which he applies himself most steadily is that of the right kind of king. In fact this is the first play in which he set forth a problem that was to maintain its interest for him all through his working career. There are three regal figures: Henry the actual king, Gloucester the regent, and York the claimant of the throne. In their joint characters they possess the requirements for a good king, and in their relations they make a set of character-patterns that gives coherence to the play. Of the three York is the dominant character and he is contrasted with Gloucester at the beginning and with Henry at the end of the play. York has eminent kingly qualities: he is strong both in character and in his title to the throne. He speaks the truth when he says of himself:

> I am far better born than is the king,
> More like a king, more kingly in my thoughts.

He is also an excellent diplomat. In fact he combines the two great qualities of lion and fox. He would have been a great king if he had reigned; and his repeated assurances that he would win back France if he had the chance are not hollow. But Shakespeare did not think that lion and fox alone made a good king. A third quality, disinterestedness, the attribute of the pelican, was needed; and this York did not possess. Gloucester had the qualities of lion and pelican but not of fox. Henry had those of the pelican alone. That is the formal pattern of the three regal characters. Dramatically, York stands out. Shakespeare in no way complicates him. He is hardly human, and is more the simple embodiment of personal ambition. But the concentration of purpose in him is tremendous. He is a character that makes one think of the creations of Aeschylus, just as the stages by which the curse on the land is worked out suggest the movement of the *Oresteia*.

The style has filled out. The stretches of verse in the period's undifferentiated norm are fewer, and while the bulk of the play is in the massive, rather clotted grandeur of the young man whose subtlety has not kept pace with his force and energy, there are many brilliant touches. Here are one or two of the outstanding things. This is York in his first soliloquy comparing himself to the owner of a ship watching the pirates making free with his goods:

> Anjou and Maine are given to the French;
> Paris is lost; the state of Normandy
> Stands on a tickle point, now they are gone.
> Suffolk concluded on the articles,
> The peers agreed, and Henry was well pleased
> To change two dukedoms for a duke's fair daughter.
> I cannot blame them all: what is't to them?
> 'Tis thine [1] to give away, and not their own.
> Pirates may make cheap penn'orths of their pillage
> And purchase friends and give to courtezans,
> Still revelling like lords till all be gone;

---

[1] Meaning *mine*, for York is here addressing himself.

> Whileas the silly owner of the goods
> Weeps over them and wrings his hapless hands
> And shakes his head and trembling stands aloof,
> While all is shar'd and all is borne away,
> Ready to starve, and dare not touch his own;
> So York must sit and fret and bite his tongue,
> While his own lands are bargain'd for and sold.

Young Clifford, commenting at the battle of St. Albans on the Lancastrian defeat and then on his father's death, gets beyond youthful rhetoric to verse that would not discredit Shakespeare in his maturity:

> Shame and confusion! all is on the rout;
> Fear frames disorder, and disorder wounds
> Where it should guard.   O war, thou son of hell,
> Whom angry heavens do make their minister,
> Throw in the frozen bosoms of our part
> Hot coals of vengeance.   Let no soldier fly.
> He that is truly dedicate to war
> Hath no self-love, nor he that loves himself
> Hath not essentially but by circumstance
> The name of valour.

Then he sees his dead father and goes on,

> O let the vile world end,
> And the premised flames of the last day
> Knit earth and heaven together.
> Now let the general trumpet blow his blast,
> Particularities and petty sounds
> To cease.

Here is that mixture of the pompously latinised and the homely which Shakespeare all through his career could put to such good effect.   Lastly here are Suffolk's words as he parts from Margaret, again looking forward to Shakespeare's maturity:

> If I depart from thee, I cannot live;
> And in thy sight to die, what were it else
> But like a pleasant slumber in thy lap?
> Here could I breathe my soul into the air
> As mild and gentle as the cradle-babe
> Dying with mother's dug between its lips;
> Where, from thy sight, I should be raging mad

And cry out for thee to close up mine eyes,
To have thee with thy lips to stop my mouth.
So should thou either turn my flying soul;
Or I should breathe it so into thy body,
And then it liv'd in sweet Elysium.

Though not the best play of the tetralogy, *2 Henry VI* is perhaps the most harmonious. Shakespeare was able to concen-
trate on the business in hand. He was interested in what he
was doing, for he had acquired new powers and was able to
occupy them fully in coping with the sort of material that
previously had been rather too much for him. He achieved a
happy adjustment of material and means of expression that was
to be upset in his next play, better though that play was in some
ways to be.

4. THE THIRD PART OF HENRY VI

The second part had showed us the murder of Duke Humphrey of Gloucester, the rise of York, the destruction of two of
Humphrey's murderers and the enmity of the two survivors,
York and Queen Margaret. Through these happenings the
country had been brought to the edge of chaos. In the third
part Shakespeare shows us chaos itself, the full prevalence of
civil war, the perpetration of one horrible deed after another.
In the second part there had remained some chivalric feeling.
At the battle of St. Albans York says to Clifford,

> With thy brave bearing should I be in love,
> But that thou art so fast mine enemy.

And Clifford answers,

> Nor should thy prowess want praise and esteem,
> But that 'tis shown ignobly and in treason.

But in the third part all the decencies of chivalric warfare are
abandoned. Young Clifford kills the twelve-year-old Rutland
at Wakefield. The three sons of York successively stab Prince
Edward, son of Henry VI, taken prisoner at Tewkesbury. At
Towton is displayed the supreme and traditional picture of
chaos, the denial of all chivalric pieties, a father killing and
robbing a son and a son killing and robbing a father. Here is

the culminating expression of the horrors and wickedness of
civil war.

In such a welter of crime the part of heaven is mainly to
avenge. And Shakespeare is extremely punctilious in furnish-
ing a crime to justify every disaster. Indeed his lavishness tends
to monotony. Edward IV, for instance, commits three major
crimes, any one of which was enough to imperil himself and his
posterity. He encouraged his father, York, to go back on his
oath of loyalty to Henry VI in return for the reversion of the
crown; he promised the Mayor of York that he had returned
to England to claim his dukedom and not the crown; and he
stabbed his prisoner the young prince Edward. There is, however, sufficient reference to the positive principles of order for
us not to forget the less immediate and more beneficent workings of heaven. It is Henry VI who is the chief instrument of
their expression. Whereas in the second part he was conspicuous for his weakness, he is now more conspicuous by his high
principles and his humanity. At Towton, as described above,
he set up the miniature order of the shepherd's life against the
major chaos of battle. In front of York he protests against the
brutality of the head of his dead enemy York being set up on the
walls. And it is he and no one else who blesses the boy Richmond and, as if divinely inspired, prophesies a rescue through
him from the present ills:

> Come hither, England's hope. If secret powers
> Suggest but truth to my divining thoughts,
> This pretty lad will prove our country's bliss.
> His looks are full of peaceful majesty,
> His head by nature fram'd to wear a crown,
> His hand to wield a sceptre, and himself
> Likely in time to bless a regal throne.
> Make much of him, my lords, for this is he
> Must help you more than you are hurt by me.

Warwick's dying soliloquy at Barnet is full of the traditional
commonplaces associated with degree. Speaking of himself he
says:

> Thus yields the cedar to the axe's edge,
> Whose arms gave shelter to the princely eagle,
> Under whose shade the ramping lion slept,
> Whose top branch overpeer'd Jove's spreading tree
> And kept low shrubs from winter's powerful wind.

Warwick is thinking of his own power in making and unmaking kings. He is not the oak, the king of trees, but a cedar over-topping the oak; and he refers to a whole sequence of primates in the chain of being : God or Jove in heaven, the king on earth, the lion among beasts, the eagle among birds, and the oak among plants.

With chaos as his theme it was not likely that Shakespeare would wish to cast this play into the clear patterns of the first and second parts. Indeed, formlessness of a sort was as neces-sary to his purposes here as the wide scattered geography of *Antony and Cleopatra* was to the imperial setting of that play. But unfortunately with the relaxation of form goes a decline of vitality. Shakespeare had a great mass of chronicle matter to deal with and he failed to control it; or rather in paring it to manageable length he fails to make it significant. The third part of *Henry VI* is Shakespeare's nearest approach to the Chronicle Play. There are indeed splendid things in it, but they are rather islands sticking out of a sea of mediocrity than hills arising from the valleys or undulations of an organic landscape. In the intermediate passages Shakespeare is either tired or bored : or perhaps both. He may have been tired because he had already sustained his theme of civil dissension so long; he may have been bored because he was even then absorbed in the character of Richard and anxious to write the play to which he gave his name. He may too have disliked repeating himself; yet felt too much committed to a certain kind of play to be able to fashion something quite new. Thus he entirely omits one of his master-themes in the previous play : the character of the good king. But he cannot escape giving more examples of fierce noblemen exchanging high words. And in plotting out cause and effect, in consonance with his loyalty to Hall and the *Mirror for Magistrates*, whereas in the other two plays he worked freely and with enthusiasm, he now repeats himself from a sense of duty. In the second scene of the play, which as a whole is a good example of this routine repetition, there is something factitious in the way York and his sons incriminate themselves by deciding to go back on York's oath to allow Henry the throne during his lifetime; as if Shakespeare were deliberately fashion-ing the moral justification of York's terrible punishment at Wakefield immediately after. Another sign that Shakespeare's interest in cause and effect had worn a little thin is that he misses one of the big things in Hall. Act IV Scene 7, where

Edward IV returning from France after his deposition tries to obtain entry into the town of York, is not very emphatic. The Mayor of York from the ramparts says he cannot let him in because he now owes allegiance to Henry. Edward says that he is claiming only his dukedom not his crown:

> Why, and I challenge nothing but my dukedom,
> As being well content with that alone.

In Hall Edward takes an oath; and the breaking of this oath is one of the major motives of the disasters that happened to England. Through his perjury Edward settled the fate of his two sons. Shakespeare takes care to incriminate Edward, but through several crimes, none of them particularly emphatic. In his sense of drama he here falls far behind Hall.

It would be tedious and fruitless to recount the vast course of the plot covering almost the whole of the Wars of the Roses, but I will describe the matters that Shakespeare really had at heart, and conjecture how he put the play together.

Shakespeare wanted to give his picture of civil chaos and to prepare for his next play. But he was committed, as a dramatic chronicler of history, to including a very big body of material. In his two first plays, not having included more matter than suited him, he was able to organise it into two well-proportioned wholes. But he paid for it by being left with a large and scarcely manageable residue. He spent himself on two great scenes of civil war, the battles of Wakefield and Towton, and on building up the character of Richard in the second half of his play. Into the gaps he fitted the bulk of his stuff as best he could. It is possible, however, that he tried to give some vague shape to the play through a hierarchy in the characters. Though the pirated version named the play after the Duke of York, he is not the chief character, for he is killed in the first act; nor are his sons, Edward and Richard, though all necessary preparations are made for Richard to become so in the next play. The chief characters are the instigators of the two kings who figure in the play, Margaret wife of Henry VI and Warwick on whose backing the sons of York rely. Such plot as there is (mere chronicling apart) consists in the emergence of these two as the truly dominant persons in the civil war, their opposition and varying fortunes, their unexpected reconciliation, and their final defeat largely through the expanding genius of Richard Duke of Gloucester. If these two characters were sufficiently emphasised, the play as a whole might not act too badly.

The two early battle scenes are greater affairs than anything in the earlier parts. The first, Wakefield, where York is captured, crowned with a paper crown by Queen Margaret, and murdered, enjoyed contemporary fame. Against the general trend of the play the printer of the pirated version of 1595 called it the *True Tragedy of Richard Duke of York*, plainly wishing to advertise his book through a famous scene. And secondly there is Greene's parody of a line from it. To have any effect a parody must take off something well known. Furthermore Greene is jealous; and he betrays his jealousy by parodying something that must have been not only well known but admired. The scene itself shows the very height of wilful cruelty perpetrated by those who should have been the most civilised, the high aristocracy. It begins with Clifford, still ferocious from the loss of his father at St. Albans, as described at the end of the previous play, murdering York's son, Rutland, aged but twelve and still under the charge of a tutor. Then York is captured by Queen Margaret, Clifford, and Northumberland. Clifford is for killing him at once, but Margaret will not let him off so lightly. She makes him stand upon a molehill, gives him a napkin stained in Rutland's blood to wipe his tears, and crowns him with a paper crown, accompanying her acts with words of such coarse contempt for himself and his sons as make her one of the vituperators of genius:

> Brave warriors, Clifford and Northumberland,
> Come, make him stand upon this molehill here,
> That raught at mountains with outstretched arms,
> Yet parted but the shadow with his hand.
> What, was it you that would be England's king?
> Was't you that revell'd in our parliament
> And made a preachment of your high descent?
> Where are your mess of sons to back you now?
> The wanton Edward and the lusty George?
> And where's that valiant crook-back prodigy,
> Dicky your boy, that with his grumbling voice
> Was wont to cheer his dad in mutinies?
> Or, with the rest, where is your darling Rutland?
> Look, York: I stain'd this napkin with the blood
> That valiant Clifford with his rapier's point

Made issue from the bosom of the boy;
And if thine eyes can water for his death
I'll give thee this to dry thy cheeks withal.

When she has done she again prevents Clifford from killing
York because she wishes to "hear the orisons he makes." York
rises to it in the speech from which Greene got his quotation.
It is far from mere bombast. York thinks of all the things that
are likely to make Margaret most furious. He goes to his death
undefeated, in bitter contempt:

> She-wolf of France, but worse than wolves of France,
> Whose tongue more poisons than the adder's tooth,
> How ill-beseeming is it in thy sex
> To triumph, like an Amazonian trull,
> Upon their woes whom fortune captivates!
> But that thy face is visard-like, unchanging,
> Made impudent with use of evil deeds,
> I would assay, proud queen, to make thee blush.
> To tell thee whence thou cam'st, of whom deriv'd,
> Were shame enough to shame thee, wert thou not shameless.
> Thy father bears the type of King of Naples,
> Of both the Sicils and Jerusalem;
> Yet not so wealthy as an English yeoman.
> Hath that poor monarch taught thee to insult?
> It needs not, nor it boots not thee, proud queen,
> Unless the adage must be verified,
> That beggars mounted run their horse to death.
> 'Tis beauty that doth oft make women proud;
> But, God he knows, thy share thereof is small:
> 'Tis virtue that doth make them most admir'd;
> The contrary doth make thee wonder'd at:
> 'Tis government that makes them seem divine;
> The want thereof makes thee abominable.
> Thou art as opposite to every good
> As the Antipodes are unto us,
> Or as the south to the septentrion.
> O tiger's heart wrapt in a woman's hide,
> How couldst thou drain the life-blood of the child,
> To bid the father wipe his eyes withal,
> And yet be seen to bear a woman's face?
> Women are soft, mild, pitiful and flexible;
> Thou stern, obdurate, flinty, rough, remorseless.

The episode gains much when set alongside the battle of Towton, with which it is so carefully compared and contrasted that the two make a beautiful pattern. While at Wakefield we see the cruel authors of all this discord, who ought to have known better, at Towton we see the unhappy victims, who hate the part they are forced to play. Henry has been led into the war by the fury of his queen, the son who has killed his father records how

> From London by the king I was press'd forth;
> My father, being the Earl of Warwick's man,
> Came on the part of York, press'd by his master.

And instead of glorying in their cruel deeds the surviving father and son are broken with remorse. In both battles the molehill figures, and with obvious intention. At Wakefield York *stands* on his molehill and instead of the real crown he had hoped for is given one of paper. At Towton Henry, the actual King, *sits* humbly on his molehill and wishes he could abandon his authentic golden crown and become a shepherd. Fate is impartial in denying to each his different and contrasted aspiration. In style too the episodes are contrasted. The first is written in a heightened version of the usual forthright powerful rhetorical norm of Shakespeare's early blank verse. It is realistically rhetorical rather than stylised: the language of lawcourt, market-place, or house of parliament. The second, though it contains touches of realism more genuine than the first, is mainly ritual not rhetorical. It is slow-moving, full of repetitions within the speeches, and antiphonic in the way many of the speeches are arranged.

> So many hours must I tend my flock;
> So many hours must I take my rest;
> So many hours must I contemplate;
> So many hours must I sport myself.

That is Henry soliloquising, but he bears his part later in the antiphony of the surviving father and son.

> *Son.* How will my mother for a father's death
>   Take on with me and ne'er be satisfied!
> *Fath.* How will my wife for slaughter of my son
>   Shed seas of tears and ne'er be satisfied!
> *Hen.* How will the country for these woeful chances
>   Misthink the king and not be satisfied!

It is unfair to isolate this piece of stylised ritual writing and to call it dull, primitive, and ingenuous. It forms part of the great whole composed of the two battle scenes of Wakefield and Towton. Coming after all the pomp and rhetoric and forthright horror, it expresses worthily the breakdown of violent human action into something humiliated and de-vitalised. Life in these extremes falls back on habit and routine; and the ritual repetitions together with the utter artlessness of the language express these straits into which life has come.

After the scene at Towton Shakespeare does not regain his full vitality till Richard's soliloquy in Act III Scene 2. But here he not only regains his vitality but shows us his genius suddenly enlarged. One has to compare this speech with York's two soliloquies in part two (at the end of I. 1 and III. 1) to see what has happened. York simply voices the motives Shakespeare has from outside put into his mouth; Richard appears to speak from within. And not only that, but to have grown then and there into the state of mind he expresses. He has just been witnessing Edward's courtship of Lady Grey, and it is the ecstasy of jealousy thereby aroused that both sharpens his malignity towards his brother and strengthens, in compensa-tion for his own deficiencies in amorous scope, his already ex-cessive ambitions. Such a change in presenting character implies of course a change in language; and here Shakespeare has indeed fully emerged from the κοινή of the period. He no longer adopts and embellishes the stereotyped phrases of the time, but, while strictly contemporary, fashions his speech anew. It is the old metal, the common stock of his time, but quite broken down and dissolved and then re-created after his own fashion, fresh with his own predominant interests, his own authentically experienced imagery, his own sense of how the lines ought to run and to be spoken. His very first image is both apt to himself and authentically Shakespeare's:

> Ay, Edward will use women honourably.
> Would he were wasted, marrow, bones, and all,
> That from his loins no hopeful branch may spring,
> To cross me from the golden time I look for.

Richard, as befits a diabolic character, is consistently well-informed on religious matters, sufficiently furnished with theo-logical information to be efficiently profane. Near the end of

part two, before the battle of St. Albans, he counters Young
Clifford's defiance with

> Fie, charity, for shame! speak not in spite,
> For you shall sup with Jesu Christ to-night,

and this gratuitous religious reference is typical. Thus it is
likely that the hopeful branch springing from Edward's loins
should also suggest a religious reference: the tree of Jesse. I
have no doubt that Shakespeare was here drawing on his
memory of such pictures; and that the word *cross* is a physical
image suggested by the efficient massiveness of the stem that
springs in the works of art from the loins of the recumbent
Jesse. Similarly the image of the man lost in a wilderness of
thorn-bushes (repeated at a culminating point in *King John*) has
its origin in something that Shakespeare had experienced either
himself or by report:

> And I, like one lost in a thorny wood,
> That rends the thorns and is rent with the thorns,
> Seeking the way and straying from the way,
> Not knowing how to find the open air
> But toiling desperately to find it out,
> Torment myself to catch the English crown.

A single line will suffice to illustrate the newly won sense of just
how the line should run dramatically:

> Flattering me with impossibilities.

Vague in rhythm at first reading, it soon falls into its definitive
shape:

> Flatt'ring me with—impossibilities.

The pause between preposition and noun both defines the
rhythm and adds a wealth of implication to the noun.

That the next scene (Queen Margaret and Warwick at the
court of the French King) should be a dull, routine affair shows
that Shakespeare's inclinations were at odds with his will and
duty. It is only in the last act, and as Richard begins to emerge
as the chief character, that Shakespeare revives again. Clarence's shameless perjury in forsaking Warwick and rejoining his
brothers before Coventry in the first scene is brought out
strongly. Shakespeare was preparing for his next play and
Clarence's punishment there.

Few readers would deny that Richard's soliloquy both prepares for the next play and shows a treatment of character new
in Shakespeare's History Plays.   There remains yet another
possible innovation, less likely to find universal acceptance.
A. P. Rossiter has noticed that the elaborately patterned writing, used for the battle of Towton and illustrated above, occurs
there for the first time, to be repeated several times through the
rest of the play and become frequent and very important in
Richard III.   He thinks that this is a new departure, a reaction
from a "documentary" to a "ritual" method of presenting historical material, creating a rift in the continuity of the tetralogy.
Though I disagree about the importance of this rift and may
interpret this ritual type of writing not quite as Rossiter does, I
am greatly indebted to his observation and admire his detailed
analysis of some of the main "ritual" passages.   I fully agree
with his associating the ritual technique with the Morality Play,
but I think he is wrong in confining the Morality strain too
closely to this single matter of style.   There are other acts of
ritual than verbal repetition and antiphony.

Generally, the Chronicle Play had substituted fact and direct
statement for the rigidly contrasted and unrealistic presentation
of good and evil used in the Morality Play.   Shakespeare had
accepted the substitution up to a point.   But he impressed on
his facts an interpretation of history that he derived neither
from the Higden-Holinshed tradition followed by the Chronicle
Plays nor from the now superannuated Morality but from Hall
and the most intelligent creative writers current in his youth.
Further, throughout the tetralogy he owed something to the
Morality Play technique, the ritual method, though he used it
in different degrees of frequency and obviousness.   Rossiter
admits some slight element of ritual in *1 Henry VI*, but he under-
estimates.   Far from being mainly documentary, the three
attempts made by Joan of Arc to ruin Talbot, worked out before
Orleans, Rouen, and Bordeaux, are both violently untrue to
history and make a regular pattern akin to ritual.   The rhyme
used in the culminating scene of the Talbots' death is not indeed
as strongly patterned as some of the antiphonic writing in
3 Henry VI and *Richard III* but it is the vehicle of a very unrealistic catastrophe.   In *2 Henry VI*, where Rossiter finds no ritual
element whatever, the characters are grouped at the opening in
a severe balance that resembles the balancing of Virtues and
Vices in a Morality.   True, the groups are later broken and re-

formed, but this does not destroy the established formality. The scene where York unfolds his title to the throne to Salisbury and Warwick is incantatory in its enunciation of many great names: not unlike a ritual invocation of a god under many different titles or an enunciation of many divine attributes. And by standards of realism it is ridiculous. Thus though in the third part Shakespeare introduces (or borrows) a type of ritual he had not exploited before, he does not make the violent innovation of substituting a ritual style for something that had been almost entirely documentary; rather he develops in a different way a ritual method that had always been important.

Rossiter's observation confirms my opinion that Shakespeare was bored with the sheer documentation to which he was committed, and that, while unable to escape from it, he was impelled to develop independently of it, in other ways. One way was through Richard's character (which was already there in embryo), another was through developing the archaic Morality strain of historical presentation (already employed in the two earlier plays).

Finally, Rossiter points out how the most elaborate piece of stylistic ritual occurs in the scene immediately before Richard's first great soliloquy, Edward's courtship of Lady Grey with Clarence and Richard making ironic and indecent remarks in the background. Plainly Shakespeare wants it to carry much weight. Here is yet another indication that Shakespeare was growing restless and beginning to find new outlets for his powers. Tired by his grim and long fidelity to Hall's pattern of cause and effect in history, he temporarily departs from it by minimising Edward IV's false oath before the walls of York (as described above) and erecting as the main cause of his downfall the less edifying but psychologically more interesting motive of his weakness for the female sex.

Temporarily, for in *Richard III* Hall's pattern of history is there in full seriousness.

5. RICHARD III

If in *3 Henry VI* Shakespeare was at times hesitant, impatient, bored, and explanatory, he did in compensation succeed in putting his whole heart into *Richard III*. He was to do better when he matured, but in *Richard III* he delivered himself of what he was good for at that time. Not being the fully accomplished artist he had to labour prodigiously and could not conceal the effort. But of the sheer accomplishment there can be no doubt.

If *Titus Andronicus*, the *Comedy of Errors*, and *1 Henry VI* show the full scope of his earliest powers, *Love's Labour's Lost* joins with *Richard III*, which unites the strains of tragedy and history, to do the same thing later. This comedy is a splendid laboured affair, massive like *Richard III*, though in its own different way. The two plays have other things too in common. They abound in formal balance; they are both strong in the ritual element described in the last chapter. The scenes of formal wit in *Love's Labour's Lost* are strongly and powerfully worked out like the complicated political scenes in *Richard III*. And in both plays Shakespeare is constantly starting out of the easier security of an accepted norm (easier, however much heightened and embellished beyond the capacities of any of his contemporaries) into his own unique utterance. Thus the discourse of Clarence's Second Murderer on conscience is in its freshness like the spring and winter songs at the end of *Love's Labour's Lost*:

> I'll not meddle with it. It is a dangerous thing. It makes a man a coward: a man cannot steal but it accuseth him; he cannot swear but it checks him; he cannot lie with his neighbour's wife but it detects him. 'Tis a blushing shamefast spirit that mutinies in a man's bosom. It fills one full of obstacles. It made me once restore a purse full of gold that I found: it beggars any man that keeps it. It is turned out of all towns and cities for a dangerous thing; and every man that means to live well endeavours to trust to himself and to live without it.

This is prose as easy and exquisite in its way as the lyrics in the comedy.

In spite of the eminence of Richard's character the main business of the play is to complete the national tetralogy and to display the working out of God's plan to restore England to prosperity.

In its function of summing up and completing what has gone before, *Richard III* inevitably suffers as a detached unit. Indeed it is a confused affair without the memory of Clarence's perjury to Warwick before Coventry, of Queen Margaret's crowning York with a paper crown before stabbing him at Wakefield, and of the triple murder of Prince Edward at Tewkesbury. The

play can never come into its own till acted as a sequel to the
other three plays and with the solemnity that we associate rather
with the Dionysia at Athens and the Wagner Festival at Bayreuth
than with the Shakespeare Festival at Stratford.   I advisedly
include all four plays, because, though for immediate understanding of incident a memory of *3 Henry VI* is sufficient, there
are many links with the other two parts.   Thus *Richard III*, after
the temporary boredom of *3 Henry VI*, regains the interest, so
powerful in *2 Henry VI*, in the massive scene of political intrigue:
for instance in Act I Scene 3, where Richard makes trouble with
the queen and her relations and Queen Margaret appears, to
curse all; or in Act III Scene 7, where Richard is jockeyed into
the throne.   In the first of these there is even a direct reference
back to *2 Henry VI*.   Margaret, advancing to the front of the
stage where Richard and Queen Elizabeth's kindred have been
quarrelling, says:

> Hear me, you wrangling pirates, that fall out
> In sharing that which you have pill'd from me.

This is the metaphor York had used in his first soliloquy in
2 Henry VI, quoted above, pp. 186-7.   Only now the position has
changed, and it is the house of Lancaster that watches the Yorkists fighting over the spoil.   With *1 Henry VI* the resemblances
are closer and different, and they have to do with the plot.
Both *1 Henry VI* and *Richard III*, unlike the other plays, have a
clear-marked hero, and both heroes have a Frenchwoman as
their chief opponent.   Talbot stands for order and Richard for
its contrary, chaos, and whereas Joan prospers in her efforts to
humiliate England, Margaret through her curses unwittingly
creates the unity of the land she has so terribly injured.   Again,
in *1 Henry VI* the nobles are wantonly disunited, while in *Richard
III* they are schooled by their sufferings into a unity otherwise
unattainable.   When there is already so much evidence that
Shakespeare wrote his tetralogy deliberately and academically
and that he was deeply influenced by the Morality tradition
with its medieval passion for equivalences, it is not pressing
things to assert that Shakespeare fully intended the above
cross-references between the first and last plays of his
series.

However, the greatest bond uniting all four plays is the steady
political theme: the theme of order and chaos, of proper political degree and civil war, of crime and punishment, of God's

mercy finally tempering his justice, of the belief that such had been God's way with England.

I noticed that in each part of *Henry VI* there was some positive, usually very formal or stylised reference to the principle of order. In *1 Henry VI* there was the scene of Talbot doing homage to his king, in *2 Henry VI* the blameless conduct of Iden and his perfect contentment with his own station in life, in *3 Henry VI* Henry's pathetic longing for the precisely ordered life of a shepherd. In *Richard III* Shakespeare both continues this technique by inserting the choric scene of the three citizens, mentioned above, p. 156, and at the end of the play comes out with his full declaration of the principle of order, thus giving final and unmistakable shape to what, though largely implicit, had been all along the animating principle of the tetralogy. His instrument, obviously and inevitably, is Richmond; and that this instrument should be largely passive, truly an instrument (hence likely to be overlooked or made little of by the modern reader) was also inevitable in the sort of drama Shakespeare was writing. In the tremendous evolution of God's plans the accidents of character must not be obtruded. Every sentence of Richmond's last speech, today regarded as a competent piece of formality, would have raised the Elizabethans to an ecstasy of feeling. Richmond gets everything right and refers to all the things they minded about. He is conventionally pious, his first words after the victory being, "God and your arms be prais'd, victorious friends"; just as Talbot after his capture of Rouen had said "Yet heavens have glory for this victory." Then he thinks of the immediate problems and asks about the dead. Hearing of them, he begins his last speech,

> Inter their bodies as becomes their birth,

and thereby implies: after thanks to God, the keeping of due degree on earth. And again he duplicates Talbot, who in the same scene, after thanking God, said

> let's not forget
> The noble Duke of Bedford late deceas'd,
> But see his exequies fulfill'd in Roan.

Then, after degree, mercy:

> Proclaim a pardon to the soldiers fled
> That in submission will return to us.

And lastly an oath, taken with full religious solemnity and duly observed, and the healing of the wounds of civil war, with an insensible and indeed very subtle transfer of reference from the epoch of Bosworth to the very hour of the play's performance, from the supposed feelings of Richmond's supporters to what Shakespeare's own audience felt so ardently about the health of their country. The reference to father killing son and son killing father served at a single stroke both to recall the battle of Towton and to take the audience out of the Wars of the Roses to the wider context of civil wars in general: to Israel, France, and Germany; to the writers of chronicles and the Homilies; to what they had heard endlessly repeated on the subject by fireside or in tavern.

> And then, as we have ta'en the sacrament,
> We will unite the White Rose and the Red.
> Smile heaven upon this fair conjunction,
> That long have frown'd upon their enmity!
> What traitor hears me and says not amen?
> England hath long been mad and scarr'd herself:
> The brother blindly shed the brother's blood;
> The father rashly slaughter'd his own son;
> The son, compell'd, been butcher to the sire.
> All this divided York and Lancaster,
> Divided in their dire division,
> O now let Richmond and Elizabeth,
> The true succeeders of each royal house,
> By God's fair ordinance conjoin together;
> And let their heirs, God, if thy will be so,
> Enrich the time to come with smooth-fac'd peace,
> With smiling plenty and fair prosperous days.
> Abate the edge of traitors, gracious Lord,
> That would reduce these bloody days again,
> And make poor England weep in streams of blood.
> Let them not live to taste this land's increase
> That would with treason wound this fair land's peace.
> Now civil wars are stopp'd, peace lives again:
> That she may long live here God say amen.

An Elizabethan audience would take the dramatist's final amen with a transport of affirmation.

But Richmond's final speech not only voiced popular opinion, it showed Shakespeare fulfilling his old debt to Hall, when he

invested the very practical and politic match between Richmond and Elizabeth with a mysterious and religious significance. True, Shakespeare quite omits the Tudors' ancient British
ancestry; but his references to the marriage are in the very
spirit of Hall's title, *The Union of the two noble and illustre Families
of Lancaster and York* and his statement in his preface of the
"godly matrimony" being "the final end of all dissensions
titles and debates." Nor is this the only place in the play
that sends us back to Hall and Tudor conceptions of history.
There are some rather queer lines in III. 1, where Edward V,
Richard, and Buckingham talk about oral and written tradition.
They serve to bring out Edward's precociousness but they
also take us into the centre of contemporary opinions on
history. Edward, before the Tower, asks if Julius Caesar
built it. Buckingham tells him that Julius Caesar began
it; and Edward asks:

> Is it upon record, or else reported
> Successively from age to age, he built it?

Buckingham answers it is "upon record," and Edward goes on:

> But say, my lord, it were not register'd,
> Methinks the truth should live from age to age,
> As 'twere retail'd to all posterity,
> Even to the general all-ending day.

His words take us to the familiar medieval and renaissance context of fame: its capriciousness, its relation to all history and to
all time. And he goes on to a more specifically historical
commonplace:

> That Julius Caesar was a famous man.
> With what his valour did enrich his wit,
> His wit set down to make his valour live.
> Death makes no conquest of this conqueror,
> For now he lives in fame though not in life.

It was a stock saying in discussions on history that Caesar provided both the material of history and its memorial. Shakespeare was telling his audience that they must put his tetralogy
among other solemn documents of history, that he is striving to
continue the high tradition of Polydore and Hall.

Above, I put the theme of *Richard III* partly in terms of God's intentions. As it is usual to put it in terms of Richard's character, I had better expand my thesis. But it is a delicate matter. People are so fond of Shakespeare that they are desperately anxious to have him of their own way of thinking. A reviewer in the *New Statesman* was greatly upset when I quoted a passage in *Measure for Measure* as evidence that Shakespeare was familiar with the doctrine of the Atonement: he at once assumed I meant that Shakespeare believed the doctrine personally. And if one were to say that in *Richard III* Shakespeare pictures England restored to order through God's grace, one gravely risks being lauded or execrated for attributing to Shakespeare personally the full doctrine of prevenient Grace according to Calvin. When therefore I say that *Richard III* is a very religious play, I want to be understood as speaking of the play and not of Shakespeare. For the purposes of the tetralogy and most obviously for this play Shakespeare accepted the prevalent belief that God had guided England into her haven of Tudor prosperity. And he had accepted it with his whole heart, as later he did not accept the supposed siding of God with the English against the French he so loudly proclaimed in *Henry V*. There is no atom of doubt in Richmond's prayer before he falls asleep in his tent at Bosworth. He is utterly God's minister, as he claims to be:

> O Thou, whose captain I account myself,
> Look on my forces with a gracious eye;
> Put in their hands thy bruising irons of wrath,
> That they may crush down with a heavy fall
> The usurping helmets of our adversaries.
> Make us thy ministers of chastisement,
> That we may praise thee in the victory.
> To thee I do commend my watchful soul,
> Ere I let fall the windows of mine eyes.
> Sleeping and waking, O, defend me still.

In the same spirit Shakespeare drops hints of a divine purpose in the mass of vengeance that forms the substance of the play, of a direction in the seemingly endless concatenation of crime and punishment. In *3 Henry VI*, York at Wakefield, Young Clifford at Towton, Warwick at Barnet, and Prince Edward at Tewkesbury die defiantly without remorse. In *Richard III* the great men die acknowledging their guilt and thinking of others. Clarence, before his murderers enter, says:

> O God, if my deep prayers cannot appease thee,
> But thou wilt be aveng'd on my misdeeds,
> Yet execute thy wrath in me alone:
> O spare my guiltless wife and my poor children.

Edward IV, near his death, repents his having signed a warrant for Clarence's death and while blaming others for not having restrained him blames himself the most:

> But for my brother not a man would speak,
> Nor I, ungracious, speak unto myself
> For him, poor soul.   The proudest of you all
> Have been beholding to him in his life;
> Yet none of you would once plead for his life.
> O God, I fear thy justice will take hold
> On me and you and mine and yours for this.

The Duchess of York, who once rejoiced when her family prospered, now in humility acknowledges the futility of ambitious strife.

> Accursed and unquiet wrangling days,
> How many of you have mine eyes beheld.
> My husband lost his life to get the crown,
> And often up and down my sons were toss'd,
> For me to joy and weep their gain and loss.
> And, being seated and domestic broils
> Clean overblown, themselves, the conquerors,
> Make war upon themselves: blood against blood,
> Self against self.   O, preposterous
> And frantic outrage, end thy damned spleen.

All this penitence cannot be fortuitous; and it is the prelude to forgiveness and regeneration.   But the full religious temper of the play only comes out in the two great scenes in the last third of the play: the lamentations of the three queens after Richard has murdered the princes in the Tower, and the ghosts appearing to Richard and Richmond before Bosworth.   These are both extreme and splendid examples of the formal style which I suggested above (p. 197) should be considered the norm rather than the exception in the tetralogy.   Both scenes are ritual and incantatory to a high degree, suggesting an ecclesiastical context; both are implicitly or explicitly pious; and both are archaic, suggesting the prevalent piety of the Middle

Ages. The incantation takes the form not only of an obvious antiphony like Queen Margaret's balancing of her own woes with Queen Elizabeth's—

> I had an Edward, till a Richard kill'd him;
> I had a Harry, till a Richard kill'd him;
> Thou hadst an Edward, till a Richard kill'd him;
> Thou hadst a Richard, till a Richard kill'd him—

but of a more complicated balance of rhythmic phrases and of varied repetitions, as in the Duchess of York's self-address:

> Blind sight, dead life, poor mortal living ghost,
> Woe's scene, world's shame, grave's due by life usurp'd,
> Brief abstract and record of tedious days,
> Rest thy unrest on England's lawful earth,
> Unlawfully made drunk with innocents' blood.

The piety in this scene is implicit rather than explicit, and the two passages just quoted will illustrate it. Queen Margaret is thinking of Richard's crimes and the vengeance he will incur, yet by repeating a phrase in four successive lines she expresses unconsciously the new and fruitful unity that God is to construct out of Richard's impartial wickedness. The Duchess's mention of England's *lawful* earth is in itself an assertion of the principle of order and an implicit prayer for a juster age. The medievalism and its accompanying suggestion of piety comes out in Margaret's great speech to Elizabeth, itself an example of incantation and antiphony. She refers to her prophecies made earlier in the play and now fulfilled.

> I call'd thee then vain flourish of my fortune.
> I call'd thee then poor shadow, painted queen;
> The presentation of but what I was;
> The flattering index of a direful pageant;
> One heav'd a-high, to be hurl'd down below;
> A mother only mock'd with two sweet babes;
> A dream of what thou wert, a breath, a bubble,
> A sign of dignity, a garish flag,
> To be the aim of every dangerous shot;
> A queen in jest, only to fill the scene.
> Where is thy husband now? where be thy brothers?
> Where are thy children? wherein dost thou joy?
> Who sues to thee and cries 'God save the queen'?
> Where be the bending peers that flatter'd thee?

Where be the thronging troops that follow'd thee?—
Decline all this and see what now thou art:
For happy wife a most distressed widow;
For joyful mother one that wails the name;
For queen a very caitiff crown'd with care;
For one being sued to one that humbly sues;
For one that scorn'd at me now scorn'd of me;
For one being fear'd of all now fearing one;
For one commanding all obey'd of none.
Thus hath the course of justice wheel'd about
And left thee but a very prey to time;
Having no more but thought of what thou wert
To torture thee the more being what thou art.

The speech takes us back to the Middle Ages; to the laments of the fickleness of fortune, to the constant burden of *Ubi sunt*, and to the consequent contempt of the world. It contains the same matter as the verses attributed to St. Bernard, of which the following is a specimen in Elizabethan translation:

Where is that Caesar now, whose high renowmed fame
Of sundry conquests won throughout the world did sound?
Or Dives rich in store and rich in richly name,
Whose chest with gold and dish with dainties did abound?
Where is the passing grace of Tully's pleading skill?
Or Aristotle's vein, whose pen had wit and will?

Or still more apt, because narrowing the general passing of the great to the loss of a single person's treasures, is the complaint of Henryson's Cressida:

Quhair is thy garding with thir greissis gay
And fress flouris,.quhilk the quene Floray
      Had paintit plesandly in every pane,
Quhair thou was wont full merily in May
To walk and tak the dew be it was day
      And heir the merle and mavis mony ane;
      With ladyis fair in carrolling to gane
And see the royal rinkis in thair array
      In garmentis gay garnishit on every grane? [1]

---

[1] " Where is your garden with its gay lawn and fresh flowers, which Queen Flora has painted delightfully in every bed ; where you used to walk so merrily in May and take the dew before daylight, and hear all the blackbirds and thrushes ; where you used to go singing with fair ladies and see the throng of courtiers dressed in gay clothes of all colours ? "

The scene of the ghosts of those Richard has murdered
follows immediately on Richmond's solemn prayer, quoted
above. It is essentially of the Morality pattern. Respublica or
England is the hero, invisible yet present, contended for by the
forces of heaven represented by Richmond and of hell represented by Richard. Each ghost as it were gives his vote for
heaven, Lancaster and York being at last unanimous. And
God is above, surveying the event. The medieval strain is continued when Richard, awaking in terror, rants like Judas in the
Miracle Plays about to hang himself. The scene, like Richmond's prayer and his last speech, is very moving. It may have
issued from Shakespeare's official self, from Shakespeare identifying himself with an obvious and simple phase of public
opinion. But the identification is entirely sincere, and the
opinion strong and right, to be shared alike by the most
sophisticated and the humblest. The scene becomes almost an
act of common worship, ending with Buckingham's assertion:

> God and good angels fight on Richmond's side;
> And Richard falls in height of all his pride.

And just because he participates so fully, because he holds
nothing of himself back, Shakespeare can be at his best, can give
to his language the maximum of personal differentiation of
which he was at the time capable. This differentiation he
achieves, not as in some of the other great places in the play by
surprising conjunctions of words or new imagery but by subtle
musical variations within a context of incantation. He seems
indeed to have learnt and applied the lessons of Spenser. At
the same time the substance of what each ghost says is entirely
appropriate to the speaker and by referring back to past events
in the tetralogy serves to reinforce the structure of the plot.
There may be better scenes in Shakespeare, but of these none
is like this one. Of its kind it is the best.

That the play's main end is to show the working out of God's
will in English history does not detract from the importance of
Richard in the process and from his dominance as a character.
And it is through his dominance that he is able to be the instrument of God's ends. Whereas the sins of other men had merely
bred more sins, Richard's are so vast that they are absorptive,
not contagious. He is the great ulcer of the body politic into
which all its impurity is drained and against which all the
members of the body politic are united. It is no longer a case

of limb fighting limb but of the war of the whole organism against an ill which has now ceased to be organic. The metaphor of poison is constantly applied to Richard, and that of beast, as if here were something to be excluded from the human norm. Queen Margaret unites the two metaphors when she calls him "that poisonous bunch-back'd toad" and that "bottled spider," the spider being proverbially venomous.

In making Richard thus subservient to a greater scheme I do not deny that for many years now the main attraction of the play has actually been Richard's character in itself, like Satan's in *Paradise Lost*. Nor was this attraction lacking from the first. Indeed it antedates the play, going back to More's *History of Richard III*, which was inserted with trifling modifications into Hall's chronicle and repeated thence by Holinshed. Shakespeare in singling out Richard III and later Henry V for special treatment as characters is not therefore departing from tradition but following closely his own main teacher of the philosophy of history, Hall.

One would like to think of Shakespeare hailing More (through Hall) as a kindred spirit and using his charm as an inspiration. Actually, though Shakespeare accepts More's heightened picture of Richard as an arch-villain, he can very coolly reject the episodes of which More made much. He quite omits Edward's wonderful speech on his deathbed and the most moving scene of all, the Archbishop persuading Queen Elizabeth to give up her younger son out of sanctuary. It may be however that More's abundant sense of humour encouraged Shakespeare to add to Richard that touch of comedy that makes him so distinguished a villain.. His aside after he has gone on his knees to ask his mother's blessing is very much in More's spirit:

> *Duch.* God bless thee, and put meekness in thy mind,
>   Love, charity, obedience, and true duty.
> *Rich.* Amen; and make me die a good old man.
>   That is the butt-end of a mother's blessing:
>   I marvel why her grace did leave it out.

A number of people have written well on the character of Richard: in one place or another all has been said that need be said. It remains now to think less in terms of alternatives and to include more than is usually done in Richard's character, even at the sacrifice of consistency. Lamb, for instance, who in his brief references raised most of the pertinent questions, wants to exclude the melodramatic side:

> Shakespeare has not made Richard so black a monster as is supposed. Wherever he is monstrous, it was to conform to vulgar opinion. But he is generally a Man.

Actually Shakespeare was already at one with vulgar opinion and willingly makes him a monster. But only in some places; in others he keeps him human. Similarly we need not choose between Richard the psychological study in compensation for physical disability and Richard the embodiment of sheer demonic will, for he is both. It *is* true that, as Lamb notes, Richard in the allusions to his deformity

> mingles . . . a perpetual reference to his own powers and capacities, by which he is enabled to surmount these petty objections; and the joy of a defect *conquered*, or *turned* into an advantage, is one cause of these very allusions, and of the satisfaction, with which his mind recurs to them.

But Dowden also is right when he says of Richard that

> his dominant characteristic is not intellectual; it is rather a daemonic energy of will. . . . He is of the diabolical class. . . . He is single-hearted in his devotion to evil. . . . He has a fierce joy, and he is an intense believer,—in the creed of hell. And therefore he is strong. He inverts the moral order of things, and tries to live in this inverted system. He does not succeed; he dashes himself to pieces against the laws of the world which he has outraged.

It might be retorted that the above distinction is superfluous, because an extreme manifestation of demonic will can only arise from the additional drive set in motion by an unusual need to compensate for a defect. But the point is that Shakespeare does actually make the distinction and that Richard, within the limits of the play, is psychologically both possible and impossible. He ranges from credibly motivated villain to a symbol, psychologically absurd however useful dramatically, of the diabolic.

This shift, however, is not irregular. In the first two scenes, containing his opening soliloquy, his dealings with Clarence, his interruption of the funeral of Henry VI with his courtship of Ann Nevil, he is predominantly the psychological study.

Shakespeare here builds up his private character. And he is credible; with his humour, his irony, and his artistry in crime acting as differentiating agents, creating a sense of the individual. After this he carries his established private character into the public arena, where he is more than a match for anyone except Queen Margaret. Of her alone he is afraid; and her curse establishes, along with the psychologically probable picture just created, the competing and ultimately victorious picture of the monstrosity, the country's scapegoat, the vast impostume of the commonwealth. She makes him both a cosmic symbol, the "troubler of the poor world's peace," and sub-human, a "rooting hog," "the slave of nature and the son of hell." She calls on him the curse of insomnia, which later we find to have been fulfilled. Clearly this does not apply to the exulting ironic Richard: *he* must always have slept with infant tranquillity. Thus Margaret's curse is prospective, and though he continues to pile up the materials for the construction of his monstrosity, it is the credible Richard, glorying in his will and his success in compensating his disabilities, who persists till the end of the third act and the attainment of the throne. Thenceforward, apart from his outburst of energy in courting Queen Elizabeth for her daughter's hand, he melts from credible character into a combination of sheer melodrama villain and symbol of diabolism. His irony forsakes him; he is unguarded not secretive in making his plans; he is no longer cool but confused in his energy, giving and retracting orders; he *really* does not sleep; and, when on the eve of Bosworth he calls for a bowl of wine because he has not "that alacrity of spirit nor cheer of mind that I was wont to have," he is the genuine ancestor of the villain in a nineteenth century melodrama calling for whiskey when things look black. Then, with the ghosts and his awakening into his Judas-like monologue, psychological probability and melodramatic villainy alike melt into the symbol of sheer denial and diabolism. Nor does his momentary resurrection at Bosworth with his memorable shout for a horse destroy that abiding impression. That a character should shift from credible human being to symbol would not have troubled a generation nurtured on Spenser. Richard in this respect resembles one of Spenser's masterpieces, Malbecco, who from a realistic old cuckold is actually transformed into an allegorical figure called Jealousy.

Finally we must not forget that Richard is the vehicle of an orthodox doctrine about kingship. It was a terrible thing to fight the ruling monarch, and Richard had been crowned. However, he was so clearly both a usurper and a murderer that he had qualified as a tyrant; and against an authentic tyrant it was lawful to rebel. Richmond, addressing his army before Bosworth, makes the point absolutely clear:

> Richard except, those whom we fight against
> Had rather have us win than him they follow.
> For what is he they follow? truly, gentlemen,
> A bloody tyrant and a homicide;
> One rais'd in blood and one in blood establish'd;
> One that made means to come by what he hath
> And slaughter'd those that were the means to help him;
> One that hath ever been God's enemy.
> Then if you fight against God's enemy,
> God will in justice ward you as his soldiers;
> If you do sweat to put a tyrant down,
> You sleep in peace, the tyrant being slain.

And Derby, handing Henry the crown after the battle, calls it "this long-usurped royalty."

I have indicated in outline the course of the play: the emerging of unity from and through discord, the simultaneous change in Richard from accomplished villain to the despairing embodiment of evil. Shakespeare gives it coherence through the dominant and now scarcely human figure of Queen Margaret: the one character who appears in every play. Being thus a connecting thread, it is fitting that she give structural coherence to the crowning drama. As Richard's downfall goes back to her curse, so do the fates of most of the characters who perish in the play go back to her curses or prophecies in the same scene, I. 3. Nor are her curses mere explosions of personal spite; they agree with the tit-for-tat scheme of crime and punishment that has so far prevailed in the tetralogy. She begins by recalling York's curse on her at Wakefield for the cruelty of her party to Rutland and the penalty she has paid; and then enumerates the precisely balanced scheme of retribution appointed for the house of York:

> If not by war, by surfeit die your king,
> As ours by murder, to make him a king.
> Edward thy son, which now is Prince of Wales,

For Edward my son, which was Prince of Wales,
Die in his youth by like untimely violence.
Thyself a queen, for me that was a queen,
Outlive thy glory like my wretched self.

Curses on minor characters follow, but Richard, as befits, has a speech to himself. His peculiar curse is the gnawing of conscience, sleeplessness, and the mistake of taking friends for enemies and enemies for friends. I have spoken of the sleeplessness above, how it could not apply to the Richard of the first three acts. Similarly it is not till Bosworth that the curse of thinking his enemies friends comes true. We are meant to think of it when Richmond says in lines quoted above that "those whom we fight against had rather have us win than him they follow." The man with the best brain in the play ends by being the most pitifully deceived. For a detailed working out of the different curses I refer the reader to A. P. Rossiter's study of the play. But it is worth recording that Margaret in her last lines before she goes out unconsciously forecasts the larger theme of the plays. Talking of Richard she says:

Let each of you be subject to his hate,
And he to yours, and all of you to God's.

Margaret does not realise that this grouping of Yorkists against Richard will unite them to the Lancastrians similarly opposed, and that the just vengeance of God had even then given way to his mercy.

In style the play is better sustained than its predecessor. There is less undifferentiated stuff, and the finest pieces of writing (as distinguished from the finest scenes) are more dramatic. The quiet concentration of the Duchess of York's last words to Richard is beyond anything in the other three plays:

Either thou wilt die, by God's just ordinance,
Ere from this war thou turn a conqueror,
Or I with grief and extreme age shall perish
And never look upon thy face again.
Therefore take with thee my most heavy curse;
Which, in the day of battle, tire thee more
Than all the complete armour that thou wear'st!
My prayers on the adverse party fight;
And there the little souls of Edward's children
Whisper the spirits of thine enemies

And promise them success and victory.
Bloody thou art, bloody will be thy end;
Shame serves thy life and doth thy death attend.

Richard's plotting with Buckingham and his acquisition of the throne though strongly organised must have tired Shakespeare. There are even signs of strain in the last stage of the process when Richard appears between the two bishops; the verse droops somewhat. After this (and it is here that Richard begins his change of nature) the vitality flags, except in patches, till the great scene when the three queens get together to join in lamentation. The courting of Elizabeth for her daughter is a prodigious affair, but not at all apt at this point. It leads nowhere; for in the very next scene (IV. 5) Elizabeth is reported to have consented to her daughter's union with Richmond. Are we to think, with E. K. Chambers, that Elizabeth had outwitted Richard and had consented, only to deceive? This is so contrary to the simple, almost negative character of Elizabeth and so heavily ironical at Richard's expense that I cannot believe it. A better explanation is that Elizabeth was merely weak and changeable and that Richard's comment on her as she goes from him, having consented,

Relenting fool and shallow, changing woman,

was truer than he thought, forecasting the second change. It is fitting that Richard, having been so often ironical at the expense of others, should himself be the occasional victim of the irony of events. Even so, the scene is far too elaborate and weighty for its effect on the action. Indeed I suspect an afterthought, a mistaken undertaking to repeat the success of the earlier scene of courtship. It would have been better to have gone quickly on to the great finale of the ghosts and of Bosworth, to that consummate expression, achieved here once and for all, of what I have ventured to call Shakespeare's official self.

CHAPTER III

King John

THE study (and perhaps the appreciation) of *King John* is complicated by the survival of a play clearly related to it, the *Troublesome Reign of King John*, published in two parts in the year 1591. The two plays are very close in construction, but their intentions are quite different. Nor are the verbal likenesses very many. The *Troublesome Reign* is a Chronicle Play exploiting the frivolity and the treachery of the French and picturing John as a king more good than bad, the righteous champion of Protestantism against papal tyranny yet not virtuous enough to be God's agent of definitive reformation. It derives from Holinshed, who admits that John's contemporaries thought very ill of him but who puts down that ill opinion to clerical prejudice. Holinshed sums up by saying:

> The man had a princely heart in him and wanted nothing but faithful subjects to have assisted him in revenging such wrongs as were done and offered by the French king and others.

Shakespeare's play is but mildly Protestant in tone and shows no extreme hostility to the French. On the political side it treats of the character of the true king but goes against Holinshed in quite denying John a princely heart; it also treats of the theory of loyalty and when it is lawful to rebel against the reigning king. On the dramatic side it shows Shakespeare bursting out in a kind of creative energy new and unconnected with the History Play. In construction the *Troublesome Reign* is better balanced than *King John*. Shakespeare huddles together and fails to motivate properly the events of the last third of his play. In the *Troublesome Reign* things happen evenly and in good proportion. It is interesting that the first part of the *Troublesome Reign* corresponds to two-thirds of Shakespeare's play and the whole of the second part to only the last third. Thus a massive scene in the *Troublesome Reign* (II. 3) of nearly three hundred lines, showing the solemn banding of the English nobles against John at Bury St. Edmunds, is, as a scene, quite omitted in Shakespeare. Finely as the *Troublesome Reign* is

215

plotted, its language is queer and fitful. There is a good deal of competently dignified verse, some amazing pieces of rant, prose passages suggesting garbled and abbreviated verse, pieces of really imaginative writing, a competent scene of knockabout in a monastery alien in tone to the rest of the play, and again and again solid and sensible writing dropping into verse that does not sound too bad and yet which does not quite make full sense.

The common opinion is that Shakespeare took the disposition of his material from the old play and rewrote it in his own language, with a different intention, and with transformed characters. Alexander sought to put the debt the other way round, but Dover Wilson has quite disposed of this endeavour. Nevertheless as an authentic, consistent, and self-supporting composition the *Troublesome Reign* cannot pass. The masterly construction is quite at odds with the heterogeneous execution. It is worth considering a third alternative.

Courthope in his essay mentioned above (p. 134) may be nearer the truth when he made Shakespeare the author of both plays. Relying on the principle (too often ignored) that structure and character matter more than verbal detail, he joins the *Troublesome Reign* to the *Contention of the two famous Houses of York and Lancaster* and the *True Tragedy of Richard Duke of York* and accounts for them all as the original Shakespearean versions of the accepted Shakespearean plays to which they are related. No dramatist but Shakespeare, he thought, had the power to marshal his material as it is marshalled in the *Troublesome Reign*:

> In the energy and dignity of the State debates, the life of the incidents, the variety and contrast of the characters, and the power of conceiving the onward movement of a great historical action, there is a quality of dramatic workmanship exhibited in the play quite above the genius of Peele, Greene, or even Marlowe. . . . The representation of mental conflict is a marked feature of *The Troublesome Raigne*. . . . If we assume Shakespeare to have been the sole author of *The Troublesome Raigne*, we credit him with a drama doubtless crude, ill-constructed, full of obvious imitation, such as might be expected from a dramatist of small experience, but yet containing more of the elements of greatness than any historic play which had yet been produced on the English stage.

Courthope, as was pointed out above, was nearer the truth
about the *Contention* and the *True Tragedy* than almost all the
contemporary experts. He may well be nearer the truth, and
in a similar fashion, over the *Troublesome Reign*. In other words,
as the *Contention* and the *True Tragedy* have turned out to be bad
quartos of *2 and 3 Henry VI*, so may the *Troublesome Reign* turn
out to be a bad quarto (though perhaps in a different way bad)
not of *King John* as we have it but of an early play by Shakespeare on the same theme. This play would then be the original
both of the *Troublesome Reign* and of *King John*: the former
keeping on the whole the fine construction of the original but
garbling the execution and inserting an alien scene; the latter
following but impairing the construction and altering the intention and some of the characterisation of its original.

That Shakespeare wrote and revised an early *John* cannot be
proved; but I find the supposition best able to explain the
facts. If he wrote it, he probably did so near the time of
1 Henry VI, for there is much in *King John* that suggests this play.
Both plays deal with French deceit, both contain long scenes of
siege-warfare in France. I noted how like the Bastard's were
some of the remarks of Talbot and Joan. Shakespeare's first
picture of the Bastard would have been one of a much simpler
loyalty and would have been close to Talbot. The details of his
character are derived principally from the character of Dunois,
Bastard of Orleans, as described by Hall. Now Dunois occurs
in *1 Henry VI*, and Shakespeare used Hall as well as Holinshed
for that play. So his own Bastard Falconbridge is drawn from
the material of *1 Henry VI*. It looks too as if in *1 Henry VI*
Shakespeare had the material of *King John* in mind, for he
makes Talbot say before Rouen:

> And I, as sure as English Henry lives
> And as his father here was conqueror,
> As sure as in this late betrayed town
> Great Cordelion's heart was buried. . . .

Like *1 Henry VI* the *Troublesome Reign* abounds in classical reference,
while the norm of its verse in places which do not seem corrupt,
could well pass in *1 Henry VI*: for instance the lines that close the
play,

> Thus England's peace begins in Henry's reign
> And bloody wars are clos'd with happy league.
> Let England live but true within itself,

And all the world can never wrong her state.
Lewis, thou shalt be bravely shipt to France,
For never Frenchman got of English ground
The twentieth part that thou hast conquered.
Dauphin, thy hand! To Worcester we will march:
Lords all, lay hands to bear your sovereign
With obsequies of honour to his grave.
If England's peers and people join in one,
Not Pope, nor France, nor Spain can do them wrong.

It is usually thought that the *Troublesome Reign* was published in two parts by an unscrupulous publisher wishing to get double profits out of his buyers and using the precedent of the two parts of *Tamburlaine*. But it may well be that he was merely reproducing in abbreviated and garbled form the two genuine parts of Shakespeare's early play.

The matters thus far treated in this chapter are not such as I wish to include in a book of this kind, but they may really help us to understand why *King John* should be so badly proportioned. In rewriting old matter Shakespeare could not avoid expanding in certain ways. Thus the difficulty of effective compression of two parts of a play (each the length of a normal play) into a single unit would be very great. He coped with it initially, but even so was left with a great residue of matter which he had to compress so drastically as to leave scrappy, unemphatic, and poorly motivated.

I turn now to *King John*, as we have it, apart from its previous history; the play as Shakespeare left it, probably in 1594, to be printed for the first time in the first folio.

Though in earnestness and width of political interest *King John* cannot compete with the historical tetralogy it succeeded, it does dwell on certain specific political themes with powerful effect; and through wonderful innovations of character and language. Shakespeare troubles less with what I have called his official self but in redress allows the spontaneous powers of his imagination a freer, if fitful, effusion.

One sign of this diminished earnestness is that there is much less of the cosmic lore which had been abundant in the tetralogy, while the chief example of it is given a new, ironic, turn. True to the ordinary tradition are the references to the sun setting on the battle-field in Act Five, which duplicate King John's decline into sickness and death. Shortly after Pembroke has said that

"King John sore sick hath left the field," come these lines from
Melun:

> But even this night, whose black contagious breath
> Already smokes about the burning crest
> Of the old feeble and day-wearied sun . . .

where "contagious" (suggesting sickness) and the sun combine
to indicate the King's present sickness through poison. And in
the next scene Lewis unconsciously refers to the coming death-
struggle in John when he opens it with

> The sun of heaven methought was loth to set.

Early in the play, before Angiers, John develops the correspondence between the human body and the body politic by putting
the different parts of Angiers in anatomical terms with gates
standing for eyes, walls for waist, and the shaking of the walls
by the siege for a fever shaking the whole body. But none of
these references has the elaboration of the Bastard's account of
the god Commodity, or Self-Interest, and his interference in the
world's course. Commodity is a "sly devil" who upsets the
great and godlike principle of Order:

> Commodity, the bias of the world,
> The world, who of itself is peised well,
> Made to run even upon even ground,
> Till this advantage, this vile-drawing bias,
> This sway of motion, this Commodity,
> Makes it take head from all indifferency,
> From all direction, purpose, course, intent:
> And this same bias, this Commodity,
> This bawd, this broker, this all-changing Word . . .

Commodity has undone God's work by corrupting the world
created in the shape of a perfect sphere turning true into a bowl
with its bias running crooked. "Direction, purpose, course,
intent" are all the attributes of "Degree" and anticipate the
list in Ulysses's speech on Degree in *Troilus and Cressida*,

> Insisture course proportion season form
> Office and custom.

When Shakespeare calls Commodity "this all-changing Word"
he means what Pope meant at the end of the *Dunciad* when he

spoke of Dullness quenching light by her "uncreating word."
As God himself had created the world through the Word, the
second person of the Trinity, so Commodity is the evil "Word"
undoing the great act of creation. And this theological reference is clinched when the Bastard a few lines later brings in the
familiar ambiguity of the word *angel* as both coin and heavenly
ministrant:

> Not that I have the power to clutch my hand,
> When his fair angels would salute my palm.

Commodity used his angels or gold coins to corrupt the holy
ends which God's angels have been promoting. Hitherto
Shakespeare had used his cosmic lore with traditional and
official solemnity; now he has become more sophisticated and,
while remaining serious, can use it for subtle ends. The Bastard
ironically hails this dubious gospel so fitting on the surface to his
own dubious begetting. Yet all the time he is more kingly than
the real king, the true upholder of the great principle of Degree.

As there is little cosmic lore so is there little reflection on the
great motives of history. John's greatest crime, his inciting
Hubert to kill Arthur, seems to contribute much less to his
humiliations than does his own unstable character. This is a
great change from the earlier tetralogy, and especially *Richard
III*, where crime and punishment are so conscientiously connected. Thus in this play it comes as a slight shock when
Salisbury refers to the great processes of history. Knowing
John to be near death he says to Prince Henry,

> Be of good comfort, prince; for you are born
> To set a form upon that indigest [1]
> Which he hath left so shapeless and so rude.

The same is true when Constance uses the current doctrine of
the sins of the royal grandparent being visited on the grand-
child, to assail Eleanor. Speaking of Arthur she says:

> This is thy eld'st son's son,
> Infortunate in nothing but in thee:
> Thy sins are visited in this poor child;
> The canon of the law is laid on him
> Being but the second generation
> Removed from thy sin-conceiving womb.

---

[1] Meaning " confused mass."

The specific political problems the play deals with are, in ascending order of importance, the succession, the ethics of rebellion, and the kingly character.

The succession does not count for much, though it may well have provided the original motive for Shakespeare's single excursion into English history outside the limits of Hall. John is plainly weak in his title, as his mother bluntly tells him near the opening of the play:

> *John.* Our strong possession and our right for us.
> *Eleanor.* Your strong possession much more than your right,
> Or else it must go wrong with you and me:
> So much my conscience whispers in your ear,
> Which none but heaven and you and I shall hear.

But the theme of a guilty conscience over the title is but faintly pursued. True, John guiltily evades the question when attacked by Lewis, saying

> Doth not the crown of England prove the king?

But once again we conclude that it is John's defective character, not his defective title, that ruins him. After dealing at length with the titles of York and Lancaster Shakespeare may well have wearied of this theme.

It is otherwise with the theme of rebellion and strife, which must have had an uncommon hold on Shakespeare's imagination and which is one of the main means of giving the play a certain unity.

First, he gives it great prominence by putting it several times in terms of the same metaphor: that of a river bursting out of its banks. The metaphor was not Shakespeare's invention but public property. For instance, the author of the *True Tragedy of Richard III* compares the abuses of the commonwealth to the waters of the Nile overflowing their banks. It is interesting too that in the Shakespearean passage of *Sir Thomas More* More speaking of the mob says,

> Whiles they are o'er the bank of their obedience
> Thus will they bear down all things.

In *King John* the metaphor does not always stand for political rebellion. Standing for any kind of unbridled excess, it does finally narrow itself to the excess of sedition and with a power-

ful, culminating effect.   John, arguing with Philip before
Angiers, likens his legitimate course of action to a stream which,
if Philip interposes an unlawful obstacle, will cause floods and
havoc.   Later, the Citizen of Angiers, urging the two kings to a
league, gives the contrary picture comparing their prospective
unity to two rivers joined, flowing peaceably and glorifying the
banks by which they flow.   Constance, still incredulous of the
league and the end of her hopes for Arthur, asks Salisbury, who
has given the news,

> Why holds thine eye that lamentable rheum,
> Like a proud river peering o'er its bounds?

John begging Pandulph to quell the civil war he has raised
calls it

> This inundation of mistemper'd humour,

where the word *inundation* shows that as well as the humours of
the body Shakespeare is thinking of the waves of a flood.   Thus
it is that when the revolting lords through the mouth of Salisbury use the same metaphor to express their return to the king,
it comes with powerful effect, catching up and crowning what
has gone before:

> We will untread the steps of damned flight
> And like a bated and retired flood,
> Leaving our rankness and irregular course,
> Stoop low within those bounds we have o'erlook'd
> And calmly run on in obedience
> Even to our ocean, to our great King John.

But if Shakespeare conveys through this repeated metaphor
that sedition and repentance of it are main themes of the play,
he commits at first sight a gross inconsistency when he compares
John to an ocean and calls him a great king; for John had
been behaving very meanly indeed.   It will be best to explain
this inconsistency before saying more about the doctrine of
rebellion; and to do this means examining the character of
John.
   Dowden noted the "show of kingly strength and dignity in
which John is clothed in the earlier scenes of the play" and
interpreted it as "no more than a poor pretence of true regal
strength and honour."   But it is most unlikely that an Eliza-

bethan audience, hearing John defy the French king through
his ambassador Chatillon—

> Be thou as lightning in the eyes of France;
> For, ere thou canst report I will be there,
> The thunder of my cannon shall be heard—

or administer excellent justice to the brothers Falconbridge, or
oppose the alien interference of the Pope, thought of him as
hypocritically assuming a part. Instead they would have
treated him somewhat as they would have treated Enobarbus
when he described Anthony meeting Cleopatra on the Cydnus.
Far from being troubled that Enobarbus should utter an ecstatic
passage of verse quite alien to his nature, they would willingly
have turned him into a choric character capable of any sort of
utterance and have allowed him to resume his individual function when the speech was over. Similarly John is not strictly
himself when he is face to face with a Frenchman but An English
King, bound to behave with seemly defiance and not to let
down the dignity of the English crown. It is just so that
Cymbeline's wicked queen behaved to the Roman ambassadors;
speaking to them she ceased to be a wicked woman and a witch
from a fairytale and turned into A British Queen. I noted the
same thing happening to Queen Eleanor in Peele's *Edward I*
(p. 104). We need not therefore be surprised if John is sometimes a conventionally dignified monarch and at others a mean
and treacherous man, realistically portrayed. Thus, when
Pembroke repents of sedition, it is to the anointed King of
England, not to the bad King John that he vows allegiance.
The King of England was indeed the ocean, rightfully claiming
the tribute of all the rivers flowing into it.

I turn to the problem of when rebellion may be allowed.
This is the theme of the play's culminating and best scene: Act
Four Scene Three—where Arthur dies after jumping from the
battlements, and first the seditious nobles, next the Bastard, and
then Hubert find his body. The behaviour of the nobles and of
the Bastard is sharply contrasted. Finding Arthur dead, Pembroke Salisbury and Bigot conclude, on the mere fact of his
death, that John was guilty; and they betray the levity of their
reasoning by the extravagance of their sentiments.

> *Sal.* This is the very top,
> The height, the crest, or crest unto the crest,

Of murder's arms: this is the bloodiest shame,
The wildest savagery, the vilest stroke,
That ever wall-eyed wrath or staring rage
Presented to the tears of soft remorse.
Pem. All murders past do stand excus'd in this:
And this, so sole and so unmatchable,
Shall give a holiness, a purity,
To the yet unbegotten sin of times;
And prove a deadly bloodshed but a jest,
Exampled by this heinous spectacle.

To which, with a self-restraint and an effort of reason sharply opposed to the facile passions of the nobles, the Bastard adds:

It is a damned and a bloody work;
The graceless action of a heavy hand,
If that it be the work of any hand.

Here the single word *graceless*, meaning beyond the scope of Divine Grace, is a more tremendous indictment than all the nobles' hyperboles, but one which the speaker refuses to invoke till he knows the truth. Certain that John is guilty, the nobles decide that rebellion is the virtuous course of action; and when Hubert enters, it is only the Bastard's intervention that stops them killing him as John's agent. It is when the nobles have gone and the need to balance their levity has been removed that the struggle in the Bastard's mind begins, that the problem of rebellion is set forth in its acutest and most distracting form. Appearances are all against Hubert, and if against him against his master; and violent suspicion excites the Bastard to speak poetry the sincere violence of which contrasts superbly with Salisbury's and Pembroke's rhetorical extravagances quoted above:

If thou didst but consent
To this most cruel act, do but despair;
And if thou want'st a cord, the smallest thread
That ever spider twisted from her womb
Will serve to strangle thee; a rush will be a beam
To hang thee on; or wouldst thou drown thyself,
Put but a little water in a spoon
And it shall be as all the ocean,
Enough to stifle such a villain up.
I do suspect thee very grievously.

Hubert protests his innocence. But, still deeply suspicious, the
Bastard has forced on him the terrible choice between sedition
and serving a usurper or at least a discredited king. Speaking
to Hubert and pointing to Arthur's body, he says:

> Go, bear him in thine arms.
> I am amaz'd, methinks, and lose my way
> Among the thorns and dangers of this world.
> How easy dost thou take all England up!
> From forth this morsel of dead royalty
> The life, the right and truth of all this realm
> Is fled to heaven; and England now is left
> To tug and scamble and to part by the teeth
> The unow'd interest of proud-swelling state.
> Now for the bare-pick'd bone of majesty
> Doth dogged war bristle his angry crest
> And snarleth in the gentle eyes of peace:
> Now powers from home and discontents at home
> Meet in one line; and vast confusion waits,
> As doth a raven on a sick-fall'n beast,
> The imminent decay of wrested pomp.
> Now happy he whose cloak and ceinture can
> Hold out this tempest. Bear away that child
> And follow me with speed. I'll to the king.
> A thousand businesses are brief in hand,
> And heaven itself doth frown upon the land.

These doubts, afflicting a man who has a natural bent for
action, are very moving. Hitherto the Bastard has needed to
do no more than serve his master faithfully. Now he is forced
to consider the whole case of Arthur. He admits Arthur's right
to the throne; he suspects John of murder; he knows that the
credit of the land has fallen far. He has to decide between the
sin of sedition and the dishonour of serving a bad master. With
superb strength and swiftness he makes his choice once and for
all and turns from perplexities to the "thousand businesses"
of the king.

What the Bastard has actually decided is that, though bad,
John is not a tyrant as was Richard III. And he has decided
right. It was better to acquiesce in John's rule, bad though it
was, hoping that God would turn the king's heart to good and
knowing that the sin of sedition would merely cause God to
intensify the punishment, already merited, the country was in

process of enduring. By his firmness the Bastard prevents the country from collapsing before the French, and God showed his forgiveness by uniting it very shortly under Henry III.

It is typical of the play that in this high place of the action the Bastard uses no cosmic lore. He could so easily have compared the distractions in his own microcosm to those in the body politic, as Brutus did in *Julius Caesar*. He prefers the undignified metaphor of dogs quarrelling over a bone, and the homely one, easily understood in an England unenclosed and still widely overgrown with scrub, of a man gone astray in a wilderness of thorn-bushes.

And, last of the political themes, there is that of the true king. It seems that Shakespeare was apt to speculate on him all through his career. We have seen how in *2 Henry VI* he measured both Humphrey of Gloucester and York by an imagined ideal and found them wanting, while as late as *Cymbeline* he differentiates between Guiderius and Arviragus, Cymbeline's two sons, making Guiderius, the future king, the quick and firm man of action; and Arviragus, the younger, the more imaginative and finer spoken. In *King John* as in *2 Henry VI* we have three pretenders to royalty; Arthur, John, and the Bastard: and they all lack something. Arthur is the genuine heir, but he lacks years and probably character. When he tells Hubert

> So I were out of prison and kept sheep,
> I should be as merry as the day is long,

he may well reveal himself to be of the kidney of Henry VI, who had the same wish. John is kingly only in appearance and in the possession of the crown: in mind he is hasty and unstable. The Bastard is illegitimate in birth but in other ways he is one of Shakespeare's great versions of the regal type.

Masefield, swayed by his hatred of Shakespeare's Henry V and observing several clear examples in Shakespeare of the unsuccessful idealist contrasted with the coarse but successful worldling, decries the Bastard, whom he considers a prototype of Henry V, and contrasts his worldly efficiency with the refined idealist nature of John. This is to complicate John and to simplify the Bastard overmuch. John is a bad king, or only good when not himself. The Bastard is a fuller man than the Henry of *Henry V*, and probably just because Shakespeare was not yet critical enough of the efficient man of action and of his limitations to desire to set up an idealist by whom to measure

or even reprove him. Shakespeare's first picture of the true
king, slightly drawn, was to come a little later in Theseus.

Middleton Murry has written so well of the Bastard's character and of the new vein of creation that went to his making
that I need treat of him only as embodying Shakespeare's
political opinions. In writing about the kingly characters of
2 Henry VI I said that to the qualities of the lion and the fox that
of another animal, the pelican, had to be added to make the
character of the genuine king. The Bastard has all three
qualities. His masterful strength is obvious, and it comes out
most brilliantly in the speech quoted above over Arthur's body.
Only a man of the firmest character could have made up his
mind so quickly when beset by such terrible perplexities. It is
no accident that in the next scene John is shown weakly handing
over the crown of England to Pandulph. And thereafter John's
resolution hardens or falters as the Bastard is present or absent.
Joined to resolution is speed of action. His defence of Hubert
against Salisbury is instantaneous. As Salisbury draws, he
retorts:

> Your sword is bright, sir; put it up again.

And when at the end of the play he believes the dauphin to be
in pursuit of the king's forces, his counsel is:

> Straight let us seek, or straight we shall be sought.

As the fox he is cunning in a bluffer way than a more strictly
Machiavellian character like Bolingbroke, but as effectively.
Breaking in on the dauphin and the English rebels at Bury
St. Edmunds, he feigns for John a confident defiance which the
plight of the English forces was far from bearing out.

> Now hear our English king;
> For thus his royalty doth speak in me.
> He is prepar'd, and reason too he should.
> This apish and unmannerly approach,
> This harness'd masque and unadvised revel,
> This unhair'd sauciness and boyish troops,
> The king doth smile at; and is well prepar'd
> To whip this dwarfish war, these pigmy arms,
> From out the circle of his territories.

In his first soliloquy, at the end of the first act, he confesses
himself "a mounting spirit," who will study the weaknesses of

the age so that he may "strew" or make less slippery "the foot-
steps of my rising." Yet even here, where he is deliberately
making himself out as self-seeking as possible, he admits that he
will learn to humour the times not in order to practise duplicity
but to avoid being tricked himself:

> Which, though I will not practise to deceive,
> Yet, to avoid deceit, I mean to learn.

In his second soliloquy, on Commodity, at the end of the second
act, he again professes himself as bad as possible: only free
from the corruption of graft because never tempted.

> And why rail I on this Commodity,
> But for because he hath not woo'd me yet?
> Not that I have the power to clutch my hand,
> When his fair angels would salute my palm;
> But for my hand, as unattempted yet,
> Like a poor beggar, raileth on the rich.
> Well, whiles I am a beggar, I will rail
> And say there is no sin but to be rich;
> And being rich, my virtue then shall be
> To say there is no vice but beggary.
> Since kings break faith upon commodity,
> Gain, be my lord, for I will worship thee.

Actually the Bastard has the English fear of being too openly
serious and righteous; and this declaration is no more a sign of
his being really corrupt than his later interjection,

> If ever I remember to be holy

argues his lack of religion. In actual deed he has the fidelity
and the self-abnegation, or at least the conscientiousness, of the
pelican. There is no insincerity in his words over John's body:

> Art thou gone so? I do but stay behind
> To do the office for thee of revenge.
> And then my soul shall wait on thee to heaven
> As it on earth hath been thy servant still.

This is the same spirit which in the actual king takes the form
of a sense of obligation to his subjects; the spirit which Theseus
possesses, when, showing how persistently interested in politics
Shakespeare was even in the act of comic creation, he blames

himself for being "over-full of self-affairs": words which are not only the justification of Theseus as king, but the condemnation of a Richard II.

Analysed under the above three headings, the character of the Bastard appears frigid enough. It is because Shakespeare conceived him so passionately and gifted him with so unbreakable an individuality that all these kingly qualities take on a life that is quite lacking in the character that should have been finer still: the Henry V of the play which goes under that title. In the character of the Bastard Shakespeare achieves an astonishing break-away from his official self, and through it he develops two weighty political themes which give the play its proper and effective value as part of a great historical series.

Constance has been recognised as the second great character of the play: partly perhaps because Mrs. Siddons played her with enthusiastic devotion. Mark Van Doren rightly sees her as the last of the long series of mourning women who figure in the last three plays of the early tetralogy. But she is rather different. There is nothing ritual or symbolic about her complaints; and her grief is private not choric. Without astonishing as the Bastard does she yet marks an advance in Shakespeare's process of differentiating and individualising character. We must think of her as young, beautiful, and witty; her youthful vitality and charm tragically canalised into a torrent of excessive grief. Philip hints at her beauty when he speaks of "the fair multitude of those her hairs." Through her quickness of wit she overreaches her mother-in-law every time, as when she puns on the word *will* in their first encounter in France—

> *El.* Thou unadvised scold, I can produce
> A will that bars the title of thy son.
> *Con.* Ay, who doubts that? a will? a wicked will;
> A woman's will; a canker'd grandam's will—

and when she mimicks the language of the nursery:

> *El.* Come to thy grandam, child.
> *Con.* Do, child, go to it grandam, child:
> Give grandam kingdom, and it grandam will
> Give it a plum, a cherry, and a fig.
> There's a good grandam.

Even in the extremity of her grief she can be witty, as when she aims her invective at Austria, who had vowed so pompously to fight till Arthur was set on the English throne.   Referring to Austria's lion-skin she says:

> O Lymoges, O Austria, thou dost shame
> That bloody spoil: thou slave, thou wretch, thou coward;
> Thou little valiant, great in villainy;
> Thou ever strong upon the stronger side.
> Thou Fortune's champion, that dost never fight
> But when her humorous ladyship is by
> To teach thee safety, thou art perjur'd too
> And sooth'st up greatness.   What a fool art thou,
> A ramping fool, to brag and stamp and swear
> Upon my party.   Thou cold-blooded slave,
> Hast thou not sworn like thunder on my side,
> Been sworn my soldier, bidding me depend
> Upon thy stars thy fortune and thy strength,
> And dost thou now fall over to my foes?
> Thou wear a lion's hide! doff it for shame
> And hang a calf's-skin on those recreant limbs.

And when her grief threatens to dement her, she speaks with a rapid imagination akin to the feminine brilliance that Shakespeare was later to embody in Beatrice and Rosalind.

> Death, death, O amiable lovely death,
> Thou odoriferous stench, sound rottenness,
> Arise forth from the couch of lasting night,
> Thou hate and terror to prosperity;
> And I will kiss thy detestable bones
> And put my eyeballs in thy vaulty brows
> And ring these fingers with thy household worms
> And stop this gap of breath with fulsome dust
> And be a carrion monster like thyself.
> Come, grin on me, and I will think thou smilest,
> And buss thee as thy wife.

Mark Van Doren has written brilliantly on the prevailing style of the play. He takes for his text the famous passage about painting the lily and finds the excess of statement shown there to be typical of the play. But the excess, though uneconomical, is not null. It is the mark of a new burst of vitality; ust as the Bastard's criticism of the style of the play is a further burst, only in a contrary direction, surveying in high sophistication the journey just completed. Speaking of the proposed match between Lewis and Blanch, the Citizen of Angiers ends,

> for at this match
> With swifter spleen than powder can enforce
> The mouth of passage shall we fling wide ope
> And give you entrance: but without this match
> The sea enraged is not half so deaf,
> Lions more confident, mountains and rocks
> More free from motion, no, not Death himself
> In mortal fury half so peremptory,
> As we to keep this city.

However excessive, it is rousing rhetoric, but the Bastard (who can be rhetorical enough at times) is viciously critical of it:

> Here's a story
> That shakes the rotten carcass of old Death
> Out of his rags. Here's a large mouth indeed
> That spits forth death and mountains, rocks and seas,
> Talks as familiarly of roaring lions
> As maids of thirteen do of puppy-dogs.

Nor is such criticism confined to the Bastard. It is indeed but one part of a recurring proof that in this play Shakespeare faces (even if he does not solve) the problem of reconciling his private with his official self. Chatillon's account to King Philip early in Act Two of the English expedition is rhetorical enough, yet it provides its own self-criticism in the line describing the young English volunteers,

> With ladies' faces and fierce dragons' spleens.

Here we have a sudden flash of realism. Shakespeare is thinking of the bright young Elizabethan desperadoes who volunteered for voyages across the Atlantic or expeditions against the ports of Spain. This realism comes surprisingly in a description where Eleanor is called

> An Ate, stirring him to blood and strife.

Having taken so decided a turn towards the language of men it is not surprising that Shakespeare should have abandoned in *King John* the language of ritual. Though there is some rhetorical repetition, as in Constance's lines on death quoted

above, there is no antiphonal writing. Its lack corresponds to
the comparative lack of formal cosmic lore.

In construction the play lacks unity. The first three acts do
indeed give a well controlled account of complex political
action, of the shifting motives of self-seeking and ambitious men,
enlivened by the critical comments of the two most intelligent
of the participants, Constance and the Bastard. The second
act, containing all the business before Angiers, is the most lively
and varied and entertaining as well as the most massive of all
Shakespeare's war scenes. For a political scene, not an actual
scene of war, Pandulph's persuading the Dauphin to persist in
his plan of invading England (III. 4) is brilliant. The opening
lines of the play, where John defies Chatillon, are equally
brilliant in their swiftness of exposition and make a perfect
prelude to the amplitude of the business before Angiers. But
in the last two acts the political action loses its width or its
intensity: either narrowing to a more personal treatment as in
the scenes of Arthur threatened with blinding and of the Bastard
in perplexity over Arthur's body; or weakened and scamped
as in the scenes of John handing the crown to Pandulph and of
his death in the abbey orchard. And, even granted the altered
scale of the last two acts, the different scenes in them have no
organic relation. In itself the business over Arthur's body is
superb, but its energy and its new freedom of style are quite alien
to Arthur pleading with Hubert for his sight. This pleading
is usually praised as very pathetic or condemned as intolerably affected. It is indeed affected, but to an Elizabethan
audience would not have been intolerable. They probably
enjoyed it as an exhibition of rhetoric; and as such it is finely
built up, an elegant exercise in word-play, like many other
scenes in Shakespeare. It does not, however, square very well
with the more vigorous excesses of language noted earlier in
this chapter: in fact it does not fit naturally into the play at all.
The theme of rebellion may be prominent in the last two acts
and give some coherence of subject matter, yet it does not arise
naturally out of the peculiar virtues of the first three acts;
occurring rather as a personal problem than as the master
motive affecting the passions and fates of thousands of men.
Nor does it knit the two last acts with the great scenes early in
the play: it is simply not in our minds as we watch the armies
before Angiers.

Nor is there any Morality motive in the background to give

a felt though indefinable unity. The Bastard's personification, Commodity, does indeed recall such a figure as Cloaked Collusion in *Respublica*, but is no more than a detail. England or Respublica herself hardly figures. In his last speech over Arthur's body the Bastard likens her to a bone fought over by dogs and at the close of the play he pronounces the great doctrine of her inviolacy if she is united within herself. But the rest of the play does not greatly reinforce these sentiments. There is for instance very little display of the different grades of society, little to correspond to the humbler characters in *2 Henry VI*, who figure as part of a cross-section of England. Hubert's description of the common people hearing and spreading rumours of Arthur's death might seem to belie this:

> I saw a smith stand with his hammer, thus,
> The whilst his iron did on the anvil cool,
> With open mouth swallowing a tailor's news;
> Who, with his shears and measure in his hand,
> Standing on slippers, which his nimble haste
> Had falsely thrust upon contrary feet,
> Told of a many thousand warlike French
> That were embattailed and rank'd in Kent.
> Another lean unwash'd artificer
> Cuts off his tale and talks of Arthur's death.

But this we read more for itself, for its sheer descriptive poetry, for the delight it gives in showing Shakespeare's true (and in this play new) vein than for any large political motive it sets forth. We do not think of the artificers as members of the body politic.

In sum, though the play is a wonderful affair, full of promise and of new life, as a whole it is uncertain of itself. In his next efforts Shakespeare was both to fulfil the promise and achieve a new certainty.

CHAPTER IV

The Second Tetralogy

1. INTRODUCTORY

HOWEVER large the apparent differences in style between *Richard II* and *Henry IV*, these plays are connected with a network of cross-references. On the other hand, although *Richard II* may have been written not long after *King John*, the connections are fitful and unimportant. *Richard II* looks forward; and Shakespeare conceived his second tetralogy as one great unit.

The matter is important and calls for substantiation.

First and most important, Richard and Prince Hal are deliberately contrasted characters; Richard being the prince in appearance rather than in reality, Hal being the prince in reality whose appearance at first obscures the truth. Richard's emblem was the sun of royalty emerging from a cloud, a piece of symbolism to which Bolingbroke refers when Richard appears on the walls of Flint Castle:

> See, see, King Richard doth himself appear
> As doth the blushing discontented sun
> From out the fiery portal of the east,
> When he perceives the envious clouds are bent
> To dim his glory and to stain the track
> Of his bright passage to the occident.

But Richard did not live up to his emblem, for he allowed the clouds, his evil advisers, to obscure his proper glory. It is Prince Hal who adopts and justifies in himself the emblem, according to his own declaration at the end of the second scene of *1 Henry IV*:

> Yet herein will I imitate the sun,
> Who doth permit the base contagious clouds
> To smother up his beauty from the world,
> That, when he please again to be himself,
> Being wanted he may be more wonder'd at
> By breaking through the foul and ugly mists
> Of vapours that did seem to strangle him.

If this were the one possible cross-reference between *Richard II*
and *1 Henry IV* we might doubt its authenticity; being one of
many it can hardly not be intentional.

Secondly, the whole theme of insurrection and civil war as
developed in the plays is continuous, as if conceived as a whole.
Carlisle's speech in Westminster Hall, for instance, prophesying
civil war if Bolingbroke is crowned proclaims its sequel in future
plays:

> My Lord of Hereford here, whom you call king,
> Is a foul traitor to proud Hereford's king.
> And if you crown him, let me prophesy:
> The blood of English shall manure the ground,
> And future ages groan for this foul act;
> Peace shall go sleep with Turks and infidels,
> And in this seat of peace tumultuous wars
> Shall kin with kin and kind with kind confound;
> Disorder horror fear and mutiny
> Shall here inhabit, and this land be call'd
> The field of Golgotha and dead men's skulls.

If these lines in the first play of the tetralogy look forward,
Henry's prayer before Agincourt in the last one, that God
should not visit on him the death of Richard, looks right
back.

Thirdly, the Percies figure in *Richard II* in a way that suggests
that they will figure even more prominently in the future.
Northumberland is the main executant of Henry's rise; and
Richard, informed by Northumberland that he must go to
Pomfret Castle, warns him that one day he will think no reward
sufficient for his services:

> Northumberland, thou ladder wherewithal
> The mounting Bolingbroke ascends my throne,
> The time shall not be many hours of age
> More than it is, ere foul sin gathering head
> Shall break into corruption. Thou shalt think,
> Though he divide the realm and give thee half,
> It is too little, helping him to all;
> And he shall think that thou, which know'st the way
> To plant unrightful kings, will know again,
> Being ne'er so little urg'd, another way
> To pluck him headlong from the usurped throne.

When Hotspur is airing his grievances to Blunt before the battle of Shrewsbury he recalls Bolingbroke's promise that he had returned from exile for no further purpose than to claim the Duchy of Lancaster. This was the promise conveyed by Northumberland to Richard in Flint Castle in the previous play:

> His coming hither hath no further scope
> Than for his lineal royalties and to beg
> Enfranchisement immediate on his knees,
> Which on thy royal party granted once,
> His glittering arms he will commend to rust.

A casual remark made by Green to the queen that Worcester (Northumberland's brother, who does not figure in *Richard II* in person) has broken his staff of office and resigned his stewardship is caught up in *1 Henry IV*, when before Shrewsbury Worcester tells Henry IV

> For you my staff of office did I break
> In Richard's time.

Lastly, to cut short an argument that could easily be prolonged, King Henry in *2 Henry IV* actually quotes from *Richard II*. He reminds Warwick of the words Richard spoke to Northumberland when about to be taken to Pomfret, and proceeds to quote some of them:

> 'Northumberland, thou ladder by the which
> My cousin Bolingbroke ascends my throne,'
> (Though then, God knows, I had no such intent,
> But that necessity so bow'd the state
> That I and greatness were compell'd to kiss)
> 'The time shall come' thus did he follow it,
> 'The time will come, that foul sin gathering head
> Shall break into corruption'; so went on,
> Foretelling this same time's condition
> And the division of our amity.

Shakespeare would never have quoted from the History Play before last unless he had thought his sequence an organic whole. That he misquotes (as can be seen by comparing the original passage from *Richard II* just quoted) shows that he was more mindful of big than of little things.

If then the plays of the second tetralogy are so closely connected, we must treat them as a single organism. Confronted with different styles in *Richard II* and *Henry IV*, we shall have to refrain from calling the first archaic and the second suddenly and miraculously mature, but shall be forced to admit that Shakespeare knew what he was doing from the start and deliberately planned this stylistic contrast. Once we accept this compulsion we shall be the gainers, finding that the plays form a great symphonic scheme. The first three at least will become not only easier to understand but finer works of art. I will postpone further treatment of this subject till my chapters on the separate plays.

When he wrote his first tetralogy, Shakespeare went for intellectual support to past literature: to Hall, the Homilies, *Gorboduc*, and the *Mirror for Magistrates*. The literature of his own age was not so immediately useful; for the writers of the Chronicle Plays were his intellectual inferiors, while Spenser and Sidney and Lyly, though fully aware of the same intellectual concerns, expressed them through other means, remote from the Chronicle Play. But there are works belonging to the period of his second tetralogy which, quite apart from any influences one way or the other, have the closest intellectual kinship with Shakespeare. It is worth saying a little about these in order to show how sensitive Shakespeare was to the intellectual climate of his time, how truly he was the voice of his own age first and only through being that, the voice of humanity. Further, he may have been encouraged to a very great effort by the thought that others were trying to say the same sort of thing. The writers I refer to are Daniel and Sir John Hayward.

Before dealing with these I must point out that their historical writings, so similar to Shakespeare's History Plays, are not mere isolated works but express powerful, serious, and widely held opinions on how English history evolved: opinions which continued many years after the age of Elizabeth. A single example will make my point. Christopher Goodman in his epistle dedicatory to the *Fall of Man*, a theological work published in 1616, has a long account of the glories of Henry VII and their relation to the present happy state of the British monarchy. He recounts how God raised him up to end the tyranny of Richard III; how he united the virtues of Henry IV, Henry V, and Henry VI (or, in the terms I have used above, of fox, lion, and pelican); how he made loyal the unjustly oppressed Cambro-Britons, from whom he was descended; how he called his eldest son Arthur in token of his descent; how he healed the kingdom's divisions by his marriage with the York heiress; how wise he was in marrying his eldest daughter to a Scottish and not to a French prince, thereby providing the ultimate means of uniting the two kingdoms of England and Scotland. In fact, here in 1616 we find the Tudor myth of Polydore Vergil and Hall in full vigour; only given a new turn by the Stuarts being included within its scope.

Daniel was two years older than Shakespeare. He was of middle class parentage, was educated at Oxford, and lived by the patronage of the nobility and at one time by teaching their children. He was tutor in the Pembroke family in the early 1590's and was patronised by Lord Mountjoy, to whose help in difficult times he was to refer later with gratitude. He was in high repute just before Shakespeare began his second historical tetralogy and he must have commanded respect if not awe through his severe academicism. In some ways he is the earliest English neo-classic writer. Shakespeare probably knew him personally through the Pembroke family and could not have escaped knowing his verses. Contrariwise Daniel could not have escaped knowing, at least by hearsay, Shakespeare's first historical tetralogy.

Daniel published the first instalment of his *History of the Civil Wars between the Houses of York and Lancaster* in 1595. This work was planned in the ambitious form of a long epic poem on a historical subject, on a model of Lucan's *Pharsalia*. It was registered in 1594; and, as Daniel was a painful and slow writer, parts of it may have been in manuscript for a good while before. Any certain similarities between the *Civil Wars* and *Richard II* or *Henry IV* (the substance of which plays was covered in Daniel's first instalment) will imply that Shakespeare was copying Daniel and not Daniel Shakespeare: unless indeed it should turn out that Shakespeare had written his own early version of his second historical tetralogy before he wrote his first tetralogy; in which case some of the debt might be the other way round. The question of debt, however, is of trivial importance compared with the planning of an ambitious poem (unfortunately incomplete) covering the exact extent of Shakespeare's two tetralogies and drawing on the same conceptions of the universe and of history. Daniel begins where Shakespeare begins but he breaks off at a point corresponding to one towards the end of *3 Henry VI*, the point in history where

Warwick through the collapse of Edward IV's French match is about to turn over from York to Lancaster. But in the epistle dedicatory to the 1609 edition he tells us that he planned to end where Shakespeare ended and in so doing makes it plain that he draws his matter from Shakespeare's sources. His plan was

> to show the deformities of civil dissension, and the miserable events of rebellions, conspiracies, and bloody revengements, which followed (as in a circle) upon that breach of the due course of succession by the usurpation of Henry IV; and thereby to make the blessings of peace and the happiness of an established government in a direct line the better to appear. I trust I shall do a grateful work to my country to continue the same unto the glorious union of Henry VII, from whence is descended our present happiness.

Now this is the very accent of Hall's exordium; and when Daniel (like Shakespeare) begins his cycle of history with English prosperity under Edward III and Edward's seven sons, the dependence on Hall is clearer still. Thus Daniel's intention in the *Civil Wars* is precisely Shakespeare's in his History Plays.

In political philosophy Daniel and Shakespeare are identical, although they do not get quite the same emphasis on its different parts. There is, for instance, more cosmic lore in Shakespeare; yet a stanza like this one, pointing to the correspondence between the sickness of the human body and of the body politic, shows Daniel equally aware of it:

> O War, begot in pride and luxury,
> The child of malice and revengeful hate,
> Thou impious good and good impiety,
> Thou art the sole refiner of a state:
> Unjust-just scourge of men's iniquity,
> Sharp easer of corruptions desperate,
> Is there no means but that a sin-sick land
> Must be let blood with such a boist'rous hand?

On the other hand Daniel, writing in narrative, is freer to ruminate and to moralise on political happenings. Thus he can advance alternative motives for a man's act; as when he speculates whether Bolingbroke was sincere when he swore, on landing in England, that he did not seek the throne and concludes that historians have been too rigid in seeking precise cause and effect. Apart from such differences both writers are at one in their sense of history repeating itself, of history educating through the example, of one crime leading to another. There is just the same accent of solemnity in this stanza of Daniel reviewing the reign of Richard II as in the Duchess of Gloucester's speech to Gaunt on the fate of Edward III's sons in *Richard II*:

> In this man's reign began this fatal strife
> (The bloody argument whereof we treat)
> That dearly cost so many a prince his life
> And spoil'd the weak and ev'n consum'd the great;
> That wherein all confusion was so rife
> As memory ev'n grieves her to repeat.
> And would that time might now this knowledge lose,
> But that 'tis good to learn by others' woes.

Like Shakespeare Daniel sees all this misery, however terrible, as the prelude to the great age of the Tudors:

> Yet now what reason have we to complain
> Since hereby came the quiet calm and joy,
> The bliss of thee, Eliza? Happy gain
> For all our losses, when no other way
> The heav'ns could find but to unite again
> The fatal sever'd families: that they
> Might bring forth thee; that in thy peace might grow
> That glory which few times could ever show.

Finally, Daniel shares with Shakespeare the Morality motive of Respublica when he makes an allegorical female figure, the Genius of England, reprove Bolingbroke in his sleep on the first night after he had landed in Yorkshire. He shares with him too such a detail as the metaphor of the prince (in this case Bolingbroke) accepting the homage of his subjects as the ocean receives the tribute of river-water:

> And look how Thames, enrich'd with many a flood
> And goodly rivers, that have made their graves
> And buried both their names and all their good
> Within his greatness to augment his waves,
> Glides on with pomp of waters, unwithstood,
> Unto the ocean, which his tribute craves,
> And lays up all his wealth within that power,
> Which in itself all greatness doth devour;

So flock the mighty, with their following train,
Unto the all-receiving Bolingbroke.

In his choice of incidents Daniel throughout is very close to
Shakespeare. The main differences are that Daniel sticks closer
to his theme of civil war and does not dwell on the more cheerful
events. He must indeed have been aware of this, for he makes
the spirit of Henry V protest that the lessons his poem instils are
solely of what to avoid, and lament that his deeds will soon
perish because there is no one worthy to record them. Daniel is
also closer to history; stopping short of allowing Prince Hal to
kill Hotspur and omitting such a gross distortion of it as Talbot's
capture of Orleans in *1 Henry VI*. He conscientiously records
more of the battles of the Wars of the Roses than Shakespeare
does. On the other hand the resemblances are striking: for
instance the deaths of Talbot and his son are equally spectacular in both poets, while Towton is chosen by both as the
culminating horror of the war, with Henry watching the fray
from a little hill.

In treatment Daniel is very different indeed. He is a rumin-
ative poet with no gift for describing action. His speeches
analysing motives can be excellent and he is good at preparing
the way for action. But he fails at a climax. For instance in
Book Three the first rebellion against Henry IV, worked up by
the Abbot of Westminster, begins excellently, and there is a
magnificent speech by Blunt warning the conspirators of what
their intended action really amounts to: a speech so weighty
and classical as to suggest that Shakespeare owed much to
Daniel in conceiving and executing *Julius Caesar*. But once
action has been decided on, Daniel collapses into flatness:

> And on indeed they went, but, oh, not far:
> A fatal stop travers'd their headlong course;
> Their drift comes known, and they discover'd are:
> For some of many will be false of force.
> Aumerle became the man that all did mar,
> Whether through indiscretion, chance, or worse:
> He makes his peace with off'ring others' blood,
> And shows the King how all the matter stood.

But Daniel's being a smaller poet than Shakespeare does not
mean that he was of no service to him, or to us in appreciating
Shakespeare. Shakespeare's History Plays become fuller and

more authoritative, more truly the national voice when we bear
Daniel's respected and careful poem in mind. For his service
to Shakespeare we must take into account two matters: current
ideas of the epic and contemporary attempts to give them
embodiment. First, the superiority of the epic over every other
literary form was axiomatic in the Renaissance in spite of Aristotle's opinion; and Shakespeare could no more have escaped
the doctrine than he could have escaped the correspondence of
the sun in heaven with the king on earth. Secondly, the idea
of the epic was connected with the idea of patriotism. It was
correct to make your country's history the theme of your epic;
and by achieving an epic in your own tongue you glorified that
tongue and hence the land where it was spoken. Ronsard's
Franciade and Camoens' *Lusiads* combined both functions.
Granted that Shakespeare was not a freak but like other great
poets, he must have been normally ambitious, and, if ambitious,
he would wish to excel in the epic. During the years just before
he wrote his second tetralogy and while he was writing, the
Elizabethan epic was at its height. In 1590 Sidney's *Arcadia* in
its revised form was published: posthumous and incomplete.
It was modelled on Heliodorus' *Aethiopica*, which passed in the
Renaissance for an important book, an authentic prose epic.
In the same year appeared the first three books of Spenser's
Fairy Queen, while the first six books appeared in 1596. Spenser
openly professed himself the Elizabethan Virgil. And lastly
there was Daniel's *Civil Wars*, published in part in 1595 and
added to, presumably, during the years when Shakespeare was
writing his second tetralogy. Now these were the men whose
ideas Shakespeare shared, though he worked in a different
medium. He must have wanted to be one of them, to compete
with them. They would jointly have invited competition, but
Daniel's poem, using Shakespeare's most essential source, Hall,
and treating of identical material, must surely have put it into
Shakespeare's mind to achieve in his own medium the epic
intentions translated into the above three great fragments.
Further, Daniel's failure to animate his material thoroughly
may have encouraged Shakespeare to do better.

In the first tetralogy the Tudor myth and the Morality idea
of Respublica had been the great unifying motives. In the
second the epic idea is added to them. With so grandiose an
expansion of aim we should seek great things in it and we shall
find them.

Hayward's *History of Henry IV*, published in 1599 with a dedication to the Earl of Essex, is known to the common reader only through the trouble that dedication got him into. It deserves a better fate, for as history it carries on the vivid style of More and Cavendish and looks forward to Clarendon. Hayward was further in time from his theme than any of these but by using his imagination and picturing things as if they really happened he can capture much the same effect of proximity. The trouble caused by the dedication is not to the point here; and anyhow the history itself is far from preaching rebellion. The only passage to which exception could be taken is in a speech of the Archbishop of Canterbury urging Henry to return from exile in France, where he cites various precedents for deposing kings. But the context shows the author not to approve of these at all, for he makes Henry justify himself not by these but by "necessity, the tyrant's plea."

> Nay, where necessity doth enforce, it is superfluous to use speech either of easiness or of lawfulness. Necessity will beat through brazen walls and can be limited by no laws.

And Hayward is perfectly orthodox in thinking Henry a usurper.

The importance of Hayward's *History of Henry IV* here is that it is the work of a learned and cultured man and that it deals with history precisely as Shakespeare did. It is not that Shakespeare was Hayward's model, though he does prompt a few passages; it is that both authors express the general conception of history and the special conception of a small period of English history, prevalent among the Elizabethan aristocracy. Here is a passage which at once illustrates the doctrine of rigid cause and effect in history and the pattern in which the Elizabethans saw events from Henry IV to Henry VII. It follows the conjectures of Richard II, shortly to die, on the causes of his own misfortunes. He thinks that his grandfather, Edward III, was incriminated through the violence done to Edward II and that he, the grandson, has suffered in consequence. Referring to Henry IV's disposal of Richard II, Hayward continues:

> King Henry with great discontentment and disquiet held the kingdom during his life; and so did his son, King Henry the Fifth, in whose time by continual wars against the Frenchmen the malice of the humour was otherwise exercised and spent. But his

second successor, King Henry the Sixth, was dispossessed thereof and together with his young son imprisoned and put to death, either by the commandment or connivance of King Edward the Fourth. And he also escaped not free; for he died not without many and manifest suspicions of poison. And after his death his two sons were disinherited, imprisoned, and butchered by their cruel uncle the Duke of Gloucester; who being a tyrant and usurper was lawfully slain in the field. And so in his person, having no issue, the tragedy did end. Which are most rare and excellent examples, both of comfort to them that are oppressed and of terror to violent dealers, that God in his secret judgement doth not always so certainly provide for our safety as revenge our injuries and harms, and that all our unjust actions have a day of payment, and many times by way of retaliation, even in the same manner and measure wherein they were committed.

These are sentiments that have appeared before in this book. It would be tedious to quote other examples of familiar doctrine. I will confine myself to a single parallel with Shakespeare and Hall, Hayward's solemn setting forth of the prosperity of Edward III and his seven sons. It occurs at the very beginning of Hayward's book:

The noble and victorious prince, King Edward the Third, had his fortunate gift of a long and prosperous reign over this realm of England much strengthened and adorned by nature's supply of seven goodly sons.

This passage may fittingly lead on to my next section, on *Richard II*, where the true action begins with a similar exposition.

2. RICHARD II

Richard II is imperfectly executed, and yet, that imperfection granted, perfectly planned as part of a great structure. It is sharply contrasted, in its extreme formality of shape and style, with the subtler and more fluid nature of *Henry IV*; but it is a necessary and deliberate contrast; resembling a stiff recitative composed to introduce a varied and flexible *aria*. Coming after *King John* the play would appear the strangest relapse into the official self which Shakespeare had been shedding; taken with *Henry IV* it shows that Shakespeare, while retaining and using this official self, could develop with brilliant success the new qualities of character and style manifested in the Bastard. *Richard II* therefore betokens no relapse but is an organic part of one of Shakespeare's major achievements.

But the imperfections are undoubted and must be faced. As a separate play *Richard II* lacks the sustained vitality of *Richard III*, being less interesting and less exacting in structure and containing a good deal of verse which by the best Shakespearean standards can only be called indifferent. Not that there is anything wrong with the structure, which is that of *2 Henry VI*, the rise of one great man at the expense of another; but it is simple, as befits an exordium and does not serve through the excitement of its complications to make the utmost demand on the powers of the author. For illustrating the indifferent verse I need not go beyond the frequent stretches of couplet-writing and the occasional quatrains that make such a contrast to the verse of *Henry IV*. It is not that these have not got their function, which will be dealt with later, but that as poetry they are indifferent stuff. They are as necessary as the stiff lines in *3 Henry VI* spoken by the Father who has killed his Son, and the Son who has killed his Father; but they are little better poetically. For present purposes it does not matter in the least whether they are relics of an old play, by Shakespeare or by someone else, or whether Shakespeare wrote them with the rest. They occur throughout the play and with the exception of perhaps two couplets are not conspicuously worse in the fifth act than anywhere else. There is no need for a theory that in this act, to save time, Shakespeare hurriedly began copying chunks from an old play. Until there is decisive proof of this, it is simplest to think that Shakespeare wrote his couplets along with the rest, intending a deliberate contrast. He had done the same thing with the Talbots' death in *1 Henry VI*, while, to account for the indifferent quality, one may remember that he was never very good at the couplet. The best couplets in *A Midsummer Night's Dream* are weak compared with the best blank verse in that play, while few of the final couplets of the sonnets are more than a competent close to far higher verse.

I turn now to a larger quality of the play, of which the couplets are one of several indications.

Of all Shakespeare's plays *Richard II* is the most formal and ceremonial. It is not only that Richard himself is a true king in appearance, in his command of the trappings of royalty, while being deficient in the solid virtues of the ruler; that is a commonplace: the ceremonial character of the play extends much wider than Richard's own nature or the exquisite patterns of his poetic speech.

First, the very actions tend to be symbolic rather than real. There is all the pomp of a tournament without the physical meeting of the two armed knights. There is a great army of Welshmen assembled to support Richard, but they never fight. Bolingbroke before Flint Castle speaks of the terrible clash there should be when he and Richard meet:

> Methinks King Richard and myself should meet
> With no less terror than the elements
> Of fire and water, when their thundering shock
> At meeting tears the cloudy cheeks of heaven.

But instead of a clash there is a highly ceremonious encounter leading to the effortless submission of Richard. There are violent challenges before Henry in Westminster Hall, but the issue is postponed. The climax of the play is the ceremony of Richard's deposition. And finally Richard, imprisoned at Pomfret, erects his own lonely state and his own griefs into a gigantic ceremony. He arranges his own thoughts into classes corresponding with men's estates in real life; king and beggar, divine, soldier, and middle man. His own sighs keep a ceremonial order like a clock:

> Now, sir, the sound that tells what hour it is
> Are clamorous groans, which strike upon my heart,
> Which is the bell: so sighs and tears and groans
> Show minutes, times, and hours.

Second, in places where emotion rises, where there is strong mental action, Shakespeare evades direct or naturalistic presentation and resorts to convention and conceit. He had done the same when Arthur pleaded with Hubert for his eyes in *King John*, but that was exceptional to a play which contained the agonies of Constance and the Bastard's perplexities over Arthur's body. Emotionally Richard's parting from his queen could have been a great thing in the play: actually it is an exchange of frigidly ingenious couplets.

> *Rich.* Go, count thy way with sighs; I mine with groans.
> *Qu.* So longest way shall have the longest moans.

> *Rich.* Twice for one step I'll groan, the way being short,
> And piece the way out with a heavy heart.

This is indeed the language of ceremony not of passion. Exactly the same happens when the Duchess of York pleads with Henry against her husband for her son Aumerle's life. Before the climax, when York gives the news of his son's treachery, there had been a show of feeling; but with the entry of the Duchess, when emotion should culminate, all is changed to prettiness and formal antiphony. This is how the Duchess compares her own quality of pleading with her husband's:

> Pleads he in earnest? look upon his face;
> His eyes do drop no tears, his prayers are jest;
> His words come from his mouth, ours from our breast:
> He prays but faintly and would be denied;
> We pray with heart and soul and all beside:
> His weary joints would gladly rise, I know;
> Our knees shall kneel till to the ground they grow:
> His prayers are full of false hypocrisy;
> Ours of true zeal and deep integrity.

And to "frame" the scene, to make it unmistakably a piece of deliberate ceremonial, Bolingbroke falls into the normal language of drama when having forgiven Aumerle he vows to punish the other conspirators:

> But for our trusty brother-in-law and the abbot,
> And all the rest of that consorted crew,
> Destruction straight shall dog them at the heels.

The case of Gaunt is different but more complicated. When he has the state of England in mind and reproves Richard, though he can be rhetorical and play on words, he speaks the language of passion:

> Now He that made me knows I see thee ill.
> Thy death-bed is no lesser than thy land
> Wherein thou liest in reputation sick.
> And thou, too careless patient as thou art,
> Commit'st thy anointed body to the cure
> Of those physicians that first wounded thee.
> A thousand flatterers sit within thy crown,
> Whose compass is no bigger than thy head.

But .in the scene of private feeling, when he parts from his banished son, both speakers, ceasing to be specifically themselves, exchange the most exquisitely formal commonplaces traditionally deemed appropriate to such a situation.

> Go, say I sent thee for to purchase honour
> And not the king exil'd thee; or suppose
> Devouring pestilence hangs in our air
> And thou art flying to a fresher clime.
> Look, what thy soul holds dear, imagine it
> To lie that way thou go'st, not whence thou com'st.
> Suppose the singing birds musicians,
> The grass whereon thou tread'st the presence strew'd,
> The flowers fair ladies, and thy steps no more
> Than a delightful measure or a dance;
> For gnarling sorrow hath less power to bite
> The man that mocks at it and sets it light.

Superficially this may be maturer verse than the couplets quoted, but it is just as formal, just as mindful of propriety and as unmindful of nature as Richard and his queen taking leave. Richard's sudden start into action when attacked by his murderers is exceptional, serving to set off by contrast the lack of action that has prevailed and to link the play with the next of the series. His groom, who appears in the same scene, is a realistic character alien to the rest of the play and serves the same function as Richard in action.

Thirdly, there is an elaboration and a formality in the cosmic references, scarcely to be matched in Shakespeare. These are usually brief and incidental, showing indeed how intimate a part they were of the things accepted and familiar in Shakespeare's mind. But in *Richard II* they are positively paraded. The great speech of Richard in Pomfret Castle is a tissue of them: first the peopling of his prison room with his thoughts, making its microcosm correspond with the orders of the body politic; then the doctrine of the universe as a musical harmony; then the fantasy of his own griefs arranged in a pattern like the working of a clock, symbol of regularity opposed to discord; and finally madness as the counterpart in man's mental kingdom of discord or chaos. Throughout the play the great commonplace of the king on earth duplicating the sun in heaven is exploited with a persistence unmatched anywhere else in Shakespeare. Finally (for I omit minor references to cosmic lore) there is the scene (III. 4) of the gardeners, with the elaborate comparison of the state to the botanical microcosm of the garden. But this is a scene so typical of the whole trend of the play that I will speak of it generally and not merely as another illustration of the traditional correspondences.

The scene begins with a few exquisitely musical lines of dialogue between the queen and two ladies. She refines her grief in a vein of high ceremony and sophistication. She begins by asking what sport they can devise in this garden to drive away care. But to every sport proposed there is a witty objection.

> *Lady.* Madam, we'll tell tales.
> *Queen.* Of sorrow or of joy?
> *Lady.*   Of either, madam.
> *Queen.* Of neither, girl:
>   For if of joy, being altogether wanting,
>   It doth remember me the more of sorrow;
>   Or if of grief, being altogether had,
>   It adds more sorrow to my want of joy.
>   For what I have I need not to repeat,
>   And what I want it boots not to complain.

Shakespeare uses language here like a very accomplished musician doing exercises over the whole compass of the violin. Then there enter a gardener and two servants: clearly to balance the queen and her ladies and through that balance to suggest that the gardener within the walls of his little plot of land is a king. Nothing could illustrate better the different expectations of a modern and of an Elizabethan audience than the way they would take the gardener's opening words:

> Go, bind thou up yon dangling apricocks,
> Which, like unruly children, make their sire
> Stoop with oppression of their prodigal weight.

The first thought of a modern audience is: what a ridiculous way for a gardener to talk. The first thought of an Elizabethan would have been: what is the symbolic meaning of those words, spoken by this king of the garden, and how does it bear on the play? And it would very quickly conclude that the apricots had grown inflated and overweening in the sun of the royal favour; that oppression was used with a political as well as a physical meaning; and that the apricots threatened, unless restrained, to upset the proper relation between parent and offspring, to offend against the great principle of order. And the rest of the gardener's speech would bear out this interpretation.

> Go thou, and like an executioner
> Cut off the heads of too fast growing sprays,
> That look too lofty in our commonwealth.
> All must be even in our government.
> You thus employ'd, I will go root away
> The noisome weeds, which without profit suck
> The soil's fertility from wholesome flowers.

In fact the scene turns out to be an elaborate political allegory, with the Earl of Wiltshire, Bushy, and Green standing for the noxious weeds which Richard, the bad gardener, allowed to flourish and which Henry, the new gardener, has rooted up. It ends with the queen coming forward and joining in the talk. She confirms the gardener's regal and moral function by calling him "old Adam's likeness," but curses him for his ill news about Richard and Bolingbroke. The intensively symbolic character of the scene is confirmed when the gardener at the end proposes to plant a bank with rue where the queen let fall her tears, as a memorial:

> Rue, even for ruth, here shortly shall be seen
> In the remembrance of a weeping queen.

In passing, for it is not my immediate concern, let me add that the gardener gives both the pattern and the moral of the play. The pattern is the weighing of the fortunes of Richard and Bolingbroke:

> Their fortunes both are weigh'd.
> In your lord's scale is nothing but himself
> And some few vanities that make him light;
> But in the balance of great Bolingbroke
> Besides himself are all the English peers,
> And with that odds he weighs King Richard down.

For the moral, though he deplores Richard's inefficiency, the gardener calls the news of his fall "black tidings" and he sympathises with the queen's sorrow. And he is himself, in his microcosmic garden, what neither Richard nor Bolingbroke separately is, the authentic gardener-king, no usurper, and the just represser of vices, the man who makes "all even in our government."

The one close Shakespearean analogy with this gardener is Iden, the unambitious squire in his Kentish garden, who stands for "degree" in *2 Henry VI*. But he comes in as an obvious foil to the realistic disorder just exhibited in Cade's rebellion. Why was it that in *Richard II*, when he was so much more mature, when his brilliant realism in *King John* showed him capable of making his gardeners as human and as amusing as the grave-diggers in *Hamlet*, Shakespeare chose to present them with a degree of formality unequalled in any play he wrote? It is, in a different form, the same question as that which was implied by my discussion of the other formal or ceremonial features of the play: namely, why did Shakespeare in *Richard II* make the ceremonial or ritual form of writing, found in differing quantities in the *Henry VI* plays and in *Richard III*, not merely one of the principal means of expression but the very essence of the play?

These are the first questions we must answer if we are to understand the true nature of *Richard II*. And here let me repeat that though Richard himself is a very important part of the play's ceremonial content, that content is larger and more important than Richard. With that caution, I will try to explain how the ritual or ceremonial element in *Richard II* differs from that in the earlier History Plays, and through such an explanation to conjecture a new interpretation of the play. There is no finer instance of ceremonial writing than the scene of the ghosts at the end of *Richard III*. But it is subservient to a piece of action, to the Battle of Bosworth with the overthrow of a tyrant and the triumph of a righteous prince. Its duty is to make that action a matter of high, mysterious, religious import. We are not invited to dwell on the ritual happenings as on a resting-place, to deduce from them the ideas into which the mind settles when the action of the play is over. But in *Richard II*, with all the emphasis and the point taken out of the action, we are invited, again and again, to dwell on the sheer ceremony of the various situations. The main point of the tournament between Bolingbroke and Mowbray is the way it is conducted; the point of Gaunt's parting with Bolingbroke is the sheer propriety of the sentiments they utter; the portents, put so fittingly into the mouth of a Welshman, are more exciting because they are appropriate than because they precipitate an event; Richard is ever more concerned with how he behaves, with the fitness of his conduct to the occasion, than with what he actually does; the gardener may foretell the deposition of Richard yet he is far more interesting as representing a static principle of order; when Richard is deposed, it is the precise manner that comes before all—

> With mine own tears I wash away my balm,
> With mine own hands I give away my crown,
> With mine own tongue deny my sacred state,
> With mine own breath release all duty's rites.

We are in fact in a world where means matter more than ends, where it is more important to keep strictly the rules of an elaborate game than either to win or to lose it.

Now though compared with ourselves the Elizabethans put a high value on means as against ends they did not go to the extreme. It was in the Middle Ages that means were so elaborated, that the rules of the game of life were so lavishly and so minutely set forth. *Richard II* is Shakespeare's picture of that life.

Of course it would be absurd to suggest that Shakespeare pictured the age of Richard II after the fashion of a modern historian. But there are signs elsewhere in Shakespeare of at least a feeling after historical verity; and there are special reasons why the age of Richard II should have struck the imaginations of the Elizabethans.

I noted above (p. 188) that at the end of *2 Henry VI* Clifford and York, though enemies, do utter some of the chivalric sentiments proper to medieval warfare. Such sentiments do not recur in *3 Henry VI*, where we have instead the full barbarities of Wakefield and Towton. Shakespeare is probably recording the historical fact that the decencies of the knightly code went down under the stress of civil carnage. But the really convincing analogy with *Richard II* is the play of *Julius Caesar*. There, however slender Shakespeare's equipment as historian and however much of his own time he slips in, he does succeed in giving his picture of antique Rome, of the dignity of its government and of the stoic creed of its great men. T. S. Eliot has rightly noted how much essential history Shakespeare extracted from Plutarch. And if from Plutarch, why not from Froissart likewise?

Till recently Shakespeare's debt to Berners's translation of

Froissart's Chronicle has been almost passed over, but now it is rightly agreed that it was considerable. To recognise the debt helps one to understand the play. For instance, one of the minor puzzles of the play is plain if we grant Shakespeare's acquaintance with Froissart. When York, horrified at Richard's confiscating Gaunt's property the moment he died, goes on to enumerate all Richard's crimes, he mentions "the prevention of poor Bolingbroke about his marriage." There is nothing more about this in the play, but there is a great deal about it in Froissart—Richard had brought charges against the exile Bolingbroke which induced the French king to break off Bolingbroke's engagement with the daughter of the Duke of Berry, the king's cousin. If Shakespeare had been full of Froissart when writing *Richard II* he could easily have slipped in this isolated reference. But quite apart from any tangible signs of imitation it is scarcely conceivable that Shakespeare should not have read so famous a book as Berners's Froissart, or that having read it he should not have been impressed by the bright pictures of chivalric life in those pages. Now among Shakespeare's History Plays *Richard II* is the only one that falls within the period of time covered by Froissart. All the more reason why on this unique occasion he should heed this great original. Now though Froissart is greatly interested in motives, he also writes with an eye unmatched among chroniclers for its eager observation of external things and with a mind similarly unmatched for the high value it placed on the proper disposition of those things. In fact he showed a lively belief in ceremony and in the proprieties of heraldry akin to Elizabethan belief yet altogether more firmly attached to the general scheme of ideas that prevailed at the time. Shakespeare's brilliant wit must have grasped this; and *Richard II* may be his intuitive rendering of Froissart's medievalism.

But there were other reasons why the reign of Richard II should be notable. A. B. Steel, his most recent historian, begins his study by noting that Richard was the last king of the old medieval order:

> the last king ruling by hereditary right, direct and undisputed, from the Conqueror. The kings of the next hundred and ten years . . . were essentially kings *de facto* not *de jure*, successful usurpers recognised after the event, upon conditions, by their fellow-magnates or by parliament.

Shakespeare, deeply interested in titles as he had showed himself to be in his early History Plays, must have known this very
well; and Gaunt's famous speech on England cannot be fully
understood without this knowledge. He calls England

> This nurse, this teeming womb of royal kings,
> Fear'd by their breed and famous by their birth,
> Renowned for their deeds as far from home,
> For Christian service and true chivalry,
> As is the sepulchre in stubborn Jewry
> Of the world's ransom, blessed Mary's son.

Richard was no crusader, but he was authentic heir of the
crusading Plantagenets. Henry was different, a usurper; and
it is with reference to this passage that we must read the lines
in *Richard II* and *Henry IV* which recount his desire and his
failure to go to Palestine. That honour was reserved for the
authentic Plantagenet kings. Richard then had the full sanctity of medieval kingship and the strong pathos of being the
last king to possess it. Shakespeare probably realised that
however powerful the Tudors were and however undisputed
their hold over their country's church, they had not the same
sanctity as the medieval kings. He was therefore ready to draw
from certain French treatises, anti-Lancastrian in tone, that
made Richard a martyr and compared him to Christ and his
accusers to so many Pilates giving him over to the wishes of the
London mob. Shakespeare's Richard says at his deposition:

> Though some of you with Pilate wash your hands,
> Showing an outward pity; yet you Pilates
> Have here deliver'd me to my sour cross,
> And water cannot wash away your sin.

Holy and virtuous as the Earl of Richmond is in *Richard III*, he
does not pretend to the same kingly sanctity as Richard II.
Such sanctity belongs to a more antique, more exotically ritual
world; and Shakespeare composed his play accordingly.

Not only did Richard in himself hold a position unique
among English kings, he maintained a court of excessive
splendour. Froissart writes as follows in the last pages of his
chronicle:

> This King Richard reigned king of England twenty-two year in
> great prosperity, holding great estate and signory. There was

never before any king of England that spent so much in his house as he did by a hundred thousand florins every year. For I, Sir John Froissart, canon and treasurer of Chinay, knew it well, for I was in his court more than a quarter of a year together and he made me good cheer. . . . And when I departed from him it was at Windsor; and at my departing the king sent me by a knight of his, Sir John Golofer, a goblet of silver and gilt weighing two mark of silver and within it a hundred nobles, by the which I am as yet the better and shall be as long as I live; wherefore I am bound to pray to God for his soul and with much sorrow I write of his death.

But Shakespeare need not have gone to Froissart for such information. In an age that was both passionately admiring of royal magnificence and far more retentive of tradition than our own the glories of Richard's court must have persisted as a legend. Anyhow that Shakespeare was aware of them is plain from Richard's address to his own likeness in the mirror:

> Was this face the face
> That every day under his household roof
> Did keep ten thousand men?

The legend must have persisted of this court's continental elegance, of the curiosities of its dress, of such a thing as Anne of Bohemia introducing the custom of riding side-saddle, of Richard's invention of the handkerchief for nasal use. Then there were the poets. Shakespeare must have associated the beginnings of English poetry with Chaucer and Gower; and they wrote mainly in Richard's reign. There must have been much medieval art, far more than now survives, visible in the great houses of Elizabeth's day, illuminated books and tapestry; and it would be generally associated with the most brilliant reign of the Middle Ages. Finally in Richard's reign there was the glamour of a still intact nobility: a very powerful glamour in an age still devoted to heraldry and yet possessing an aristocracy who, compared with the great men of Richard's day, were upstarts.

All these facts would have a strong, if unconscious, effect on Shakespeare's mind and induce him to present the age of Richard in a brilliant yet remote and unrealistic manner. He was already master of a certain antique lore and of a certain kind of ceremonial writing: it was natural that he should use them, but with a different turn, to do this particular work. Thus he makes more solemn and elaborates the inherited notions of cosmic correspondences and chivalric procedure and he makes his ritual style a central and not peripheral concern. Hence the portentous solemnity of the moralising gardeners, the powerful emphasis on the isolated symbol of the rue-tree, the elaborate circumstances of the tournament between Boling-broke and Mowbray, and the unique artifice of Richard's great speeches: speeches which are the true centre of the play but central with a far wider reference than to the mere character of Richard.

In speaking of medieval illuminated books and tapestry I do not wish to imply anything too literal: that Shakespeare had actual examples of such things in mind when he wrote *Richard II*. But it is true that many passages in this play call them up and that unconscious memory of them *might* have given Shakespeare help. Take a passage from one of Richard's best known speeches.

> For God's sake, let us sit upon the ground
> And tell sad stories of the death of kings:
> How some have been depos'd, some slain in war,
> Some haunted by the ghosts they have depos'd,
> Some poison'd by their wives, some sleeping kill'd;
> All murder'd: for within the hollow crown
> That rounds the mortal temples of a king
> Keeps Death his court, and there the antic sits,
> Scoffing his state and grinning at his pomp,
> Allowing him a breath, a little scene,
> To monarchise, be fear'd, and kill with looks,
> Infusing him with self and vain conceit,
> As if this flesh which walls about our life
> Were brass impregnable, and, humour'd thus,
> Comes at the last and with a little pin
> Bores through his castle wall, and farewell king!

Critics have seen a reference here to the *Mirror for Magistrates*, but Chaucer's *Monk's Tale* would suit much better. Death, keeping his court, is a pure medieval motive. Still, these motives were inherited and need imply nothing unusual. But Death the skeleton watching and mocking the king in his trappings is a clear and concrete image that reminds one of the visual arts: and above all the exquisiteness, the very remoteness from what could have happened in an actual physical attempt, of someone boring through the castle wall with a little pin precisely recaptures the technique of medieval illumination. Before the tournament Bolingbroke prays God:

> And with thy blessings steel my lance's point
> That it may enter Mowbray's waxen coat.

That again is just like medieval illumination. When a wound is given in medieval art there is no fusion of thing striking with thing stricken; the blow simply rests in a pre-existing hole, while any blood that spouts out had pre-existed just as surely. This is the kind of picture called up by Mowbray's "waxen coat." Or take this comparison. If anywhere in *Henry IV* we might expect medievalism it is in the description of the Prince performing the most spectacular of chivalric actions: vaulting onto his horse in full armour.

> I saw young Harry, with his beaver on,
> His cuisses on his thighs, gallantly arm'd,
> Rise from the ground like feather'd Mercury,
> And vaulted with such ease into his seat,
> As if an angel dropp'd down from the clouds,
> To turn and wind a fiery Pegasus
> And witch the world with noble horsemanship.

There is nothing medieval here. It is a description recalling the art of the high Renaissance with fused colours and subtle transitions. Set beside it Gaunt's advice to Bolingbroke about to go into exile:

> Suppose the singing birds musicians,
> The grass whereon thou tread'st the presence strew'd,
> The flowers fair ladies, and thy steps no more
> Than a delightful measure or a dance.

Here each item is distinct, and the lines evoke the mincing figures of a medieval tapestry in a setting of birds and flowers.

The case for the essential medievalism of *Richard II* is even stronger when it is seen that the conspirators, working as such, do not share the ceremonial style used to represent Richard and his court. Once again the usual explanation of such a contrast is too narrow. It has been the habit to contrast the "poetry" of Richard with the practical common sense of Bolingbroke.

But the "poetry" of Richard is all part of a world of gorgeous tournaments, conventionally mournful queens, and impossibly sententious gardeners, while Bolingbroke's common sense extends to his backers, in particular to that most important character, Northumberland. We have in fact the contrast not only of two characters but of two ways of life.

One example of the two different ways of life has occurred already: in the contrast noted between the mannered pleading of the Duchess of York for Aumerle's life and Henry's vigorous resolve immediately after to punish the conspirators. The Duchess and her family belong to the old order where the means, the style, the embroidery matter more than what they further or express. Henry belongs to a new order, where action is quick and leads somewhere. But other examples are needed to back up what to many readers will doubtless seem a dangerous and forced theory of the play's significance. First, a new kind of vigour, the vigour of strong and swift action, enters the verse of the play at II. 1. 224, when, after Richard has seized Gaunt's property and announced his coming journey to Ireland, Northumberland, Ross, and Willoughby remain behind and hatch their conspiracy. Northumberland's last speech especially has a different vigour from any vigorous writing that has gone before: from the vigour of the jousters' mutual defiance or York's moral indignation at the king's excesses. After enumerating Bolingbroke's supporters in Brittany, he goes on:

> All these well furnish'd by the Duke of Brittain
> With eight tall ships, three thousand men of war,
> Are making hither with all due expedience
> And shortly mean to touch our northern shore:
> Perhaps they had ere this, but that they stay
> The first departing of the king for Ireland.
> If then we shall shake off our slavish yoke,
> Imp out our drooping country's broken wing,
> Redeem from broken pawn the blemish'd crown,
> Wipe off the dust that hides our sceptre's gift
> And make high majesty look like itself,
> Away with me in post to Ravenspurgh.

The four lines describing by different metaphors how the land is to be restored are not in a ritual manner but in Shakespeare's normal idiom of Elizabethan exuberance. It is not for nothing that the next scene shows the Queen exchanging elegant con-

ceits about her sorrow for Richard's absence with Bushy and
Green. But the largest contrast comes at the beginning of the
third act. It begins with a very fine speech of Bolingbroke
recounting to Bushy and Green all their crimes, before they are
executed. It has the full accent of the world of action, where
people want to get things and are roused to passion in their
attempts:

> Bring forth these men.
> Bushy and Green, I will not vex your souls
> (Since presently your souls must part your bodies)
> With too much urging your pernicious lives,
> For 'twere no charity.

That is the beginning, and the speech goes on to things themselves not to the way they are done or are embroidered. And
when at the end Bolingbroke recounts his own injuries it is with
plain and understandable passion:

> Myself a prince by fortune of my birth,
> Near to the king in blood, and near in love
> Till you did make him misinterpret me,
> Have stoop'd my neck under your injuries
> And sigh'd my English breath in foreign clouds,
> Eating the bitter bread of banishment.

The scene is followed by Richard's landing in Wales, his pitiful
inability to act, and his wonderful self-dramatisation. As a
display of externals, as an exaltation of means over ends (here
carried to a frivolous excess), it is wonderful; yet it contains no
lines that for the weight of unaffected passion come near
Bolingbroke's single line,

> Eating the bitter bread of banishment.

The world for which Bolingbroke stands, though it is a usurping
world, displays a greater sincerity of personal emotion.

Thus *Richard II*, although reputed so simple and homogeneous
a play, is built on a contrast. The world of medieval refinement
is indeed the main object of presentation but it is threatened
and in the end superseded by the more familiar world of the
present.

In carrying out his object Shakespeare shows the greatest
skill in keeping the emphasis sufficiently on Richard, while
hinting that in Bolingbroke's world there is the probability of

development. In other words he makes the world of Bolingbroke not so much defective as embryonic. It is not allowed to
compete with Richard's but it is ready to grow to its proper
fulness in the next plays. This is especially true of the conspirators' characters. Hotspur, for instance, is faintly drawn yet
in one place he speaks with a hearty abruptness that shows his
creator had conceived the whole character already. It is when
Hotspur first meets Bolingbroke, near Berkeley Castle. Northumberland asks him if he has forgotten the Duke of Hereford,
and Hotspur replies:

> No, my good lord, for that is not forgot
> Which ne'er I did remember: to my knowledge
> I never in my life did look on him.

At the beginning of the same scene Northumberland's elaborate
compliments to Bolingbroke show his politic nature: it is the
same man who at the beginning of *2 Henry IV* lies "crafty-sick."
Bolingbroke too is consistent with his later self, though we are
shown only certain elements in his character. What marks out
the later Bolingbroke and makes him a rather pathetic figure is
his bewilderment. For all his political acumen he does not
know himself completely or his way about the world. And the
reason is that he has relied in large part on fortune. Dover
Wilson remarked truly of him in *Richard II* that though he acts
forcibly he appears to be borne upward by a power beyond his
volition. He is made the first mover of trouble in the matter of
the tournament and he wants to do something about Woodstock's murder. But he has no steady policy and having once
set events in motion is the servant of fortune. As such, he is not
in control of events, though by his adroitness he may deal with
the unpredictable as it occurs. Now a man who, lacking a
steady policy, begins a course of action will be led into those
"by-paths and indirect crook'd ways" of which Henry speaks
to his son in *2 Henry IV*. Shakespeare says nothing of them in
Richard II, but they are yet the inevitable result of Henry's
character as shown in that play. It is worth anticipating and
saying that Prince Hal differs from his father in having perfect
knowledge both of himself and of the world around him. Of all
types of men he is the least subject to the sway of fortune.

Another quality shown only in embryo is humour. It is
nearly absent but there is just a touch: sufficient to assure us
that Shakespeare has it there all the time in readiness. It

occurs in the scene where Aumerle describes to Richard his
parting from Bolingbroke.

> *Rich.* And say, what store of parting tears were shed?
> *Aum.* Faith, none for me: except the north-east wind
>   Which then blew bitterly against our faces,
>   Awak'd the sleeping rheum, and so by chance
>   Did grace our hollow parting with a tear.

Richard II thus at once possesses a dominant theme and contains within itself the elements of those different things that are
to be the theme of its successors.

It must not be thought, because Shakespeare treated history,
as described above, in a way new to him that he has lost interest
in his old themes.   On the contrary he is interested as much as
ever in the theme of civil war, in the kingly type, and in the
general fortunes of England.   And I will say a little on each of
these before trying to sum up the play's meaning in the tetralogy
to which it belongs.

Richard II does its work in proclaiming the great theme of the
whole cycle of Shakespeare's History Plays: the beginning in
prosperity, the distortion of prosperity by a crime, civil war, and
ultimate renewal of prosperity.   The last stage falls outside the
play's scope, but the second scene with the Duchess of Gloucester's enumeration of Edward III's seven sons, her account of
Gloucester's death, and her call for vengeance is a worthy
exordium of the whole cycle.   The speeches of the Bishop of
Carlisle and of Richard to Northumberland, parts of which
were quoted near the beginning of this chapter (p. 235), are
worthy statements of the disorder that follows the deposition
of the rightful king.   In doctrine the play is entirely orthodox.
Shakespeare knows that Richard's crimes never amounted to
tyranny and hence that outright rebellion against him was a
crime.   He leaves uncertain the question of who murdered
Woodstock and never says that Richard was personally responsible.   The king's uncles hold perfectly correct opinions.   Gaunt
refuses the Duchess of Gloucester's request for vengeance, the
matter being for God's decision alone.   Even on his deathbed,
when lamenting the state of the realm and calling Richard the
landlord and not the king of England, he never preaches rebellion.   And he mentions deposition only in the sense that
Richard by his own conduct is deposing himself.   York utters
the most correct sentiments.   Like the Bastard he is for support-

ing the existing government. And though he changes allegiance
he is never for rebellion. As stated above, the gardener was
against the deposition of Richard.

As well as being a study of medievalism, Richard takes his
place among Shakespeare's many studies of the kingly nature.
He is a king by unquestioned title and by his external graces
alone. But others have written so well on Richard's character
that I need say no more.

Lastly, for political motives, there is the old Morality theme
of Respublica. One of Shakespeare's debts in *Richard II* is to
Woodstock; and this play is constructed very plainly on the
Morality pattern, with the king's three uncles led by Woodstock
inducing him to virtue, and Tressilian Bushy and Green to vice.
There are traces of this motive in Shakespeare's play, but with
Woodstock dead before the action begins and Gaunt dying
early in it the balance of good and evil influences is destroyed.
Bushy Green and Bagot, however, remain very plainly Morality
figures and were probably marked in some way by their dress
as abstract vices. If Shakespeare really confused Bagot with
the Earl of Wiltshire (according to a conjecture of Dover
Wilson) he need not be following an old play heedlessly: he
would in any case look on them all as a gang of bad characters,
far more important as a gang than as individuals, hence not
worth being careful over separately. Once again, as in the
earlier tetralogy, England herself, and not the protagonist, is
the main concern. Gaunt speaks her praises, the gardener in
describing his own symbolic garden has her in mind. As part
of the great cycle of English history covered by Hall's chronicle
the events of the reign of Richard II take their proper place.
But here something fresh has happened. The early tetralogy had
as its concern the fortunes of England in that exciting and instructive stretch of her history. *Richard II* has this concern too,
but it also deals with England herself, the nature and not
merely the fortunes of England. In *Richard II* it is the old
brilliant medieval England of the last Plantagenet in the authentic succession; in *Henry IV* it will be the England not of the
Middle Ages but of Shakespeare himself. We can now see how
the epic comes in and how *Richard II* contributes to an epic
effect. Those works which we honour by the epic title always,
among other things, express the feelings or the habits of a large
group of men, often of a nation. However centrally human,
however powerful, a work may be, we shall not give it the epic

title for these qualities alone. It is not the parting of Hector and
Andromache or the ransoming of Hector's body that make the
Iliad an epic; it is that the *Iliad* expresses a whole way of life.
Shakespeare, it seems, as well as exploiting the most central
human affairs, as he was to do in his tragedies, was also impelled to fulfil through the drama that peculiarly epic function
which is usually fulfilled through the narrative. Inspired partly
perhaps by the example of Daniel and certainly by his own
genius, he combined with the grim didactic exposition of the
fortunes of England during her terrible ordeal of civil war his
epic version of what England was.

This new turn given to the History Play is a great stroke of
Shakespeare's genius. Through it he goes beyond anything in
Hall or Daniel or even Spenser. Hall and Daniel see English
history in a solemn and moral light and they are impressive
writers. Spenser is a great philosophical poet and epitomises
the ethos of the Elizabethan age. But none of these can truly
picture England. Of the epic writers Sidney in *Arcadia* comes
nearest to doing this. It is indeed only in patches that authentic England appears through mythical Arcadia, but that it
can this description of Kalander's house in the second chapter
of the book is sufficient proof:

> The house itself was built of fair and strong stone, not affecting
> so much any extraordinary kind of fineness as an honourable
> representing of a firm stateliness: the lights doors and stairs
> rather directed to the use of the guest than to the eye of the
> artificer, and yet, as the one chiefly heeded, so the other not
> neglected; each place handsome without curiosity and homely
> without loathsomeness; not so dainty as not to be trod on nor
> yet slubbered up with good fellowship; all more lasting than
> beautiful but that the consideration of the exceeding lastingness
> made the eye believe it was exceedingly beautiful.

This expresses the authentic genius of English domestic archi-
tecture.

Of this great new epic attempt *Richard II* is only the prelude.
What of England it pictures is not only antique but partial:
the confined world of a medieval courtly class. In his next plays
Shakespeare was to picture (with much else) the whole land, as
he knew it, in his own day, with its multifarious layers of society
and manners of living.

3. HENRY IV

In an article on *Structural Unity in the two Parts of "Henry IV"*
R. A. Law maintains that Part Two is a new structure, an un-
premeditated addition. I think so decidedly the other way that
I shall treat the two parts as a single play (as Dover Wilson does
in the *Fortunes of Falstaff*). Indeed Shakespeare almost goes out
of his way to advertise the continuity by keeping the action
patently incomplete at the end of the first part. In IV. 4 the
Archbishop of York is shown preparing for the rebellious action
which is the main political theme of Part Two but which is
almost irrelevant to Part One. In V. 2 there is a probable
reference forward to the second part. Here Worcester refuses
to inform Hotspur of the king's generous consent to confine the
battle to a duel between Hotspur and the Prince and of his
generous offer of a pardon to all the rebels. Worcester distrusts
Henry and probably without reason. Shakespeare was thinking ironically of John of Lancaster's offer of pardon made to the
other rebels in the second part, which, though insincere, was
trusted. And the first part ends with Henry's sending Prince
John and Westmoreland to deal with Northumberland and the
Archbishop; an action which is taken up immediately in the
second part. Finally, one of the most striking anticipations,
pointing to Shakespeare's having planned ahead with much
thought, is the talk between Falstaff and the Prince on justice
in the scene that first brings them in. The Prince has slipped
into the talk of robberies by moonlight an unpleasant reference
to the gallows. Falstaff, not relishing it, seeks to turn the
conversation with

> And is not my hostess of the tavern a most sweet wench?

But the Prince turns the conversation back to the unpleasant
theme. Falstaff again turns the conversation; but the thought
of the gallows is too strong for him and he can't help asking,

> Shall there be gallows standing when thou art king? and resolu-
> tion thus fobbed as it is with the rusty curb of old father antic
> the law?

The Prince does not say no to this. But the questions are not
answered till the end of the second part—indeed they cannot

arise again in the first part because the Prince is not yet king—but there Resolution, or Falstaff and his gang, are indeed fobbed with the rusty curb of the Lord Chief Justice or old father antic the law.

The reason why Law wishes to separate the two parts is that he thinks their motives are different. According to him Part One shows the struggle of the Prince and Hotspur culminating in the Battle of Shrewsbury, while Part Two, in strong contrast, shows the Prince in the background not fighting but fought over, as in the Moralities, by the royal household and the Lord Chief Justice on the one hand and by Falstaff, the epitome of the Seven Deadly Sins, on the other. Law was right in seeing the Morality pattern in Part Two, but wrong in not seeing it in Part One likewise. The struggle between the Prince and Hotspur is subordinate to a larger plan.

The structure of the two parts is indeed very similar. In the first part the Prince (who, one knows, will soon be king) is tested in the military or chivalric virtues. He has to choose, Morality-fashion, between Sloth or Vanity, to which he is drawn by his bad companions, and Chivalry, to which he is drawn by his father and his brothers. And he chooses Chivalry. The action is complicated by Hotspur and Falstaff, who stand for the excess and the defect of the military spirit, for honour exaggerated and dishonour. Thus the Prince, as well as being Magnificence in a Morality Play, is Aristotle's middle quality between two extremes. Such a combination would have been entirely natural to the Elizabethans, especially since it occurred in the second book of the *Fairy Queen*. Guyon is at once the Morality figure fought over by the Palmer and Mammon and the man who is shown the Aristotelian allegory of Excess Balance and Defect in Perissa Medina and Elissa. Near the end of the play the Prince ironically surrenders to Falstaff the credit of having killed Hotspur, thus leaving the world of arms and preparing for the motive of the second part. Here again he is tested, but in the civil virtues. He has to choose, Morality-fashion, between disorder or misrule, to which he is drawn by his bad companions, and Order or Justice (the supreme kingly virtue) to which he is drawn by his father and by his father's deputy the Lord Chief Justice. And he chooses Justice. As in the first part the Aristotelian motive occurs, but it is only touched on. After Falstaff has exchanged words with John of Lancaster about his captive Sir John Colevile, he remains on the stage to soliloquise. He calls John a "sober-blooded boy" and blames him for not drinking sack. John is thus cold-blooded and addicted to thin potations; Falstaff himself is warm-blooded and addicted to strong drink. The Prince is the mean, cold-blooded by inheritance but warmed "with excellent endeavour of drinking good and good store of fertile sherris." Temperamentally he strikes the balance between the parsimony of John and the extravagance of Falstaff. He does the same too in his practice of justice. The justice of John of Lancaster in his cold-blooded treatment of the rebels verges on rigour; Falstaff has no general standard of justice at all; Henry V uses his justice moderately in the way he treats his old companions—at least by Elizabethan standards.

I will develop the structure of *Henry IV* in rather fuller detail. The action of the first part opens with high themes of crusades, chivalry, and civil war. But the Prince is not there, and his father laments that he has not got Hotspur for his son. Soon after his words we see the Prince in Falstaff's company, showing, at least superficially, his inclination to idleness and vanity. When they arrange a robbery, his inclination seems confirmed; yet he will join in with a difference, planning with Poins a joke at the expense of Falstaff. Next there is the quarrel between the Percies and the king; and yet another action is planned, this time rebellion. Hotspur is in the very centre of the plot, unlike the Prince, who is only on the edge of his; he also discloses the exaggeration of his passions. From then on the two actions take their course, with various cross-references; the Prince maintaining his negligent aloofness, Hotspur growing more exclusively absorbed. As the action of the Gadshill robbery closes, the Prince hears of the rebellion and decides to join in it, but with how serious intent we cannot say; his resolve to gain amusement by giving Falstaff a charge of foot shows that at any rate he is not exclusively serious. Vanity having had a long turn, Chivalry must now be allowed to work on the Prince. His father rebukes him, and he promises amendment and his resolution to rob Hotspur of his rebellious honours. But what is his resolution worth when soon after at the tavern in East-cheap he enters with Peto "marching, and Falstaff meets them playing on his truncheon like a fife"? The business of the rebellion proceeds, the rebels raising their forces and Falstaff his ragged company, till the two armies are encamped against each other at Shrewsbury. The crisis occurs in the first scene

of the fifth act, where Worcester comes to the king's camp as
emissary of the rebels. It is important that Falstaff should be
there and that in his presence the Prince should make his choice
for chivalry (to which he actually says he has been a truant) by
offering to settle the whole matter personally in single fight
with Hotspur. Falstaff's speech on honour, which closes the
scene, rounds off the main action of the play, for among other
things it is really the epitaph of his own defeat. There is no
excitement about the Battle of Shrewsbury, for the result has
really been settled by the Prince's decision; but it allows Falstaff to come to life again and to acquire a bogus military
reputation, which will be an important motive of the second
part. In spite of his choice the Prince still finds Falstaff entertaining and backs up his lying claim to have killed Hotspur.
He would have perceived, as the spectator should, how the
Battle of Shrewsbury reversed the episode of Gadshill. At Gadshill the Prince deprived Falstaff of the money he had stolen from
the travellers; at Shrewsbury Falstaff deprived the Prince of
the honour of which he had spoiled Hotspur.

In the second part the military theme of rebellion is continued, but the Prince resigns his share in it to his brother John.
He has proved his worth in chivalry; he must now prove it in
civil life. As in the first part he begins with appearances
against him. He has indulged his inclination to vanity by providing Falstaff with a page, and he has applied military methods
to civil life (as well as indulging his passions) by striking the
Lord Chief Justice. But we learn this by hearsay only: as he
draws nearer to the throne the Prince must be less openly given
to mischief. In compensation, the opposing principles between
which he has to choose are brought face to face, as they never
were in the first part. Thus there are two scenes of sparring
between Falstaff and the Lord Chief Justice. During the first
of these we learn that the Justice has scored a point by having
advised the king to post Falstaff to John of Lancaster's army,
thus separating him from the Prince. In the middle portion of
the play the Morality theme is kept in suspense, while other
important business is transacted. The action broadens to include many phases of English life; Falstaff indulges in adven-
tures that have nothing to do with the Prince; the political
theme of Henry IV's many troubles draws to a close. Shakespeare naturally reassures us that the main action is only in
suspense: for instance in the tavern scene with Falstaff and

Doll Tearsheet the Prince recollects his duties when Peto enters with the news that the king is back at Westminster awaiting news of the Yorkshire rebels. The crisis comes just before the king's death, when the Prince persuades his father that he took the crown from his father's bedside in error, not out of indecent haste to begin a riotous reign. *We* are persuaded too and know that he will accept the rule of the Lord Chief Justice, who committed him to prison, and reject his old companions. Shakespeare knits the end closely not only to the beginning of Part Two but to the whole play. For instance, Falstaff recalls his opposition to his chief enemy and hence the Morality pattern by his last words as he leaves Gloucestershire to salute the new king: "Woe to my Lord Chief Justice." But it is Henry V's words, as he rejects Falstaff, that have the function of gathering the themes together. Henry does not merely preach at Falstaff: every unkind thing he says and every piece of moral advice he gives echo words spoken to or by Falstaff. "Fall to thy prayers" says Henry; and we should think of his earlier words to Falstaff: "I see a good amendment of life in thee, from praying to purse-taking" spoken in the second scene of Part One, and "Say thy prayers and farewell" spoken in a very different tone before the Battle of Shrewsbury. When Henry says

How ill white hairs become a fool and jester,

we should remember (as Falstaff must have remembered) the Chief Justice's words, "There is not a white hair on your face but should have his effect of gravity." And when Henry speaks of the grave gaping for him, we should remember Doll's remark to Falstaff about "patching up thine old body for heaven" and Falstaff's reply of "Peace, good Doll! do not speak like a death's-head; do not bid me remember mine end." These echoes do not make Henry V's speech any kinder but they give it a great deal of point.

The final ratification, through justice administered and chivalric action, of the Prince's two choices is the theme of the next play.

But though *Henry IV* is built on the Morality pattern it is quite without the mental conflict that often marks that pattern, as in *Doctor Faustus*. The action begins at its very latest phase as in *Samson Agonistes* or the *Tempest*. The Prince, though the constant victim of psychological strain, has made up his mind from the start, and any twinges of conscience he feels at his

delay in putting his resolutions into action are minor affairs.
And unlike Samson he is fully aware that he has made up his
mind and is quite spared Samson's pangs of doubt concerning
the final issue. In other words there is not the smallest element
of tragedy in the main action. When we recollect how powerfully Shakespeare had pictured mental conflict in the Bastard
Falconbridge we must conclude that he kept off the tragic
because he wished to do so, not because he was incapable of
dealing with it at this stage of his development. The above
analogy with so superficially different a play as the *Tempest* is
strange. Yet it can be extended. Prospero is like the Prince in
having already chosen: between reason and passion, forgiveness and revenge. And both plays gain their effect by an un-
analysable unity obtained through the subtlest blending of
different strains.

Now the Morality pattern of *Henry IV* will have mainly a
formal or historical interest, if its hero is an insignificant figure.
Of what use thrusting the Prince into the centre, if all the time
we look to left and right at Falstaff and Hotspur? The Prince
as a character has failed to please greatly, because he appeals
less to softer sentiment than Hotspur or Antony, while his im-
puted Machiavellianism is quite without the glamour of the
same quality in an out-and-out villain like Richard III. Yet I
believe that current opinion is wrong and that he can hold his
own with any character in *Henry IV*. Dover Wilson in his
Fortunes of Falstaff deserves gratitude for having helped to redress the balance between the Prince and Falstaff; but as I do
not see the Prince altogether as he does, I will give my version
of him.

The Prince as depicted in *Henry IV* (and what follows has no
reference whatever to Henry V in the play which goes by that
name) is a man of large powers, Olympian loftiness, and high
sophistication, who has acquired a thorough knowledge of
human nature both in himself and in others. He is Shakespeare's studied picture of the kingly type: a picture to which
his many previous versions of the imperfect kingly type lead up:
the fulfilment of years of thought and of experiment. Shakespeare sets forth his character with great elaboration, using both
direct description and self-revelation through act and word.
Though all the subtlety is confined to the second, there is no
important discrepancy between the two versions. And first for
the Prince's character as described from without.

At the end of the first scene in which he appears the Prince
assumes the function of chorus to comment on himself: in the
soliloquy beginning "I know you all." Here he pronounces
his knowledge of his present companions and of what they are
worth and the studied deliberateness of his present conduct.
For his kingly style there is Vernon's description of him to
Hotspur,

> As full of spirit as the month of May,
> And gorgeous as the sun at midsummer,

and of the godlike ease "like feather'd Mercury" with which he
vaults fully armed onto his horse. His father recognises the
comprehensiveness of his mind and passions, when, late in the
second part of the play (IV. 4), he exhorts his son Thomas of
Clarence to cherish his place in the Prince's affections so that
he may "effect offices of mediation" between the Prince's
"greatness" and his other brothers:

> For he is gracious, if he be observ'd.
> He hath a tear for pity, and a hand
> Open as day for melting charity.
> Yet notwithstanding, being incens'd, he's flint,
> As humorous as winter and as sudden
> As flaws congealed in the spring of day.
> His temper, therefore, must be well observ'd.
> Chide him for faults and do it reverently,
> When you perceive his blood inclin'd to mirth;
> But, being moody, give him line and scope,
> Till that his passions, like a whale on ground,
> Confound themselves with working.

But the king is pessimistic. Through the very abundance of his
nature the Prince is as subject to excessive evil as to excessive
good—

> Most subject is the fattest soil to weeds—

and he thinks the signs are that evil will prevail. But Warwick
disagrees, arguing for the power of the Prince's deliberate and
sophisticated nature and his appetite for knowledge:

> The prince but studies his companions
> Like a strange tongue, wherein, to gain the language,
> 'Tis needful that the most immodest word

Be look'd upon and learn'd; which once attain'd,
Your highness knows, comes to no further use
But to be known and hated. So, like gross terms,
The prince will in the perfectness of time
Cast off his followers; and their memory
Shall as a pattern or a measure live,
By which his grace must mete the lives of others,
Turning past evils to advantages.

Something indeed has to be allowed for in all these testimonies.
The Prince in his choric self-comment is concerned first of all
with justifying to an Elizabethan audience this apparent degradation of royalty: hence the powerful emphasis on the rich
compensation for such degradation—

My reformation, glittering o'er my fault,
Shall show more goodly and attract more eyes
Than that which hath no foil to set it off.

Henry not only describes his son but gives the general version
of the princely nature, as can be seen by comparing his words
with Belarius's description of the two princes in *Cymbeline* :

Thou divine Nature, how thyself thou blazon'st
In these two princely boys. They are as gentle
As zephyrs, blowing below the violet
Not wagging his sweet head; and yet as rough,
Their royal blood enchaf'd, as the rud'st wind
That by the top doth take the mountain pine
And make him stoop to the vale.

Warwick is preparing for the rejection of Falstaff as well as
describing the Prince's character. But, for all these reservations, the speakers do combine to testify to the comprehensiveness of the Prince's mind and the deliberateness of his actions.

External testimony, however, is of small account compared
with what is revealed by action and speech; and we must now
consider what sort of person the Prince shows himself. This
means speaking of his relations to some of the other characters,
principally Falstaff. Those who cannot stomach the rejection
of Falstaff assume that in some ways the Prince acted dis-
honestly, that he made a friend of Falstaff, thus deceiving him,
that he got all he could out of him and then repudiated the
debt. They are wrong. The Prince is aloof and Olympian

from the start and never treats Falstaff any better than his dog, with whom he condescends once in a way to have a game. It is not the Prince who deceives, it is Falstaff who deceives himself by wishful thinking. The most the Prince does is not to take drastic measures to disabuse Falstaff; doing no more than repeat the unkind truths he has never spared telling. His first speech to Falstaff ("Thou art so fat-witted . . .") is, as well as much else, a cool statement of what he thinks of him. And the epithet "fat-witted," so plainly the very opposite of the truth in most of its application, is brutally true of Falstaff's capacity for self-deceit. The Prince has a mind far too capacious not to see Falstaff's limitations. In the same scene he plays with him (and with a coolness in full accord with the rejection), when he refers to the gallows. Falstaff dislikes the subject, but the Prince will not let him off. And when later Falstaff tries to attach the Prince to him with "I would to God thou and I knew where a commodity of good names were to be bought," he gets not the slightest encouragement. The Prince just watches and tells the truth. And not in this place alone: it is his habit. He also relishes the ironic act of telling the truth in the assurance that he will thereby deceive: indeed, to such an extent that he once takes big risks and says things which if believed he would have been far too proud to utter. I refer to the episode in the second part (II. 2, at the beginning). This tells us so much of the Prince that it requires close comment.

To understand this scene, we must remember that the Prince has not appeared since the Battle of Shrewsbury, but that he has since been reported to have struck the Lord Chief Justice: the burden of continued chivalrous behaviour at the court has been too great. Thus when he begins "Before God, I am exceeding weary," we naturally conclude that it is of court affairs that he is tired. Poins, with characteristic simplicity, thinks that the Prince's tiredness is but physical and answers with (for him) considerable brightness,

Is't come to that? I had thought weariness durst not have attached one of so high blood.

The Prince at once begins telling the truth about himself which he knows Poins will fail to understand or believe:

Faith, it does me; though it discolours the complexion of my greatness to acknowledge it.

In other words, he does find court affairs exhausting; but he
is genuinely ashamed to have to admit it. Then he adds,

> Doth it not show vilely in me to desire small beer?

meaning by "small beer" such unexacting company as Poins.
Poins misunderstands again, thinking the Prince is talking of
the actual liquor, and answers again with (for him) considerable
brightness,

> Why, a prince should not be so loosely studied as to remember so
> weak a composition.

Misunderstood, the Prince is encouraged to be both more
confidential about himself and to tell Poins just what he thinks
of him.

> Belike then my appetite was not princely got: for, by my troth,
> I do now remember the poor creature, small beer. But indeed
> these humble considerations make me out of love with my great-
> ness. What a disgrace is it to me to remember thy name! or to
> know thy face to-morrow! or to take note how many pair of
> silk stockings thou hast, viz. these, and those that were thy
> peach-coloured ones! or to bear the inventory of thy shirts, as,
> one for superfluity and another for use!

By which the Prince means that he does indeed lack the taste
for royal duties and that it is much more diverting to study
human nature in the shape of that small beer, Poins. And he
goes on to Poins's habits of life, and his illegitimate children.
Poins, simple-mindedly supposing that the Prince's weariness
with his duties has no more depth than his own easy life, asks
how many good young princes would talk so idly when their
fathers were "so sick as yours at this time is." This is a new
turn to the conversation and it gives the Prince an opportunity
for confidences he can count on Poins not to believe or understand:

> *Prince.* Shall I tell thee one thing, Poins?
> *Poins.* Yes, faith; and let it be an excellent good thing.
> *Prince.* It shall serve among wits of no higher breeding than thine.

By this the Prince means that he is willing to say what he is
about to say to people as thick-witted as Poins. Poins, nettled
at the accusation, protests and claims that he can cope with
whatever the Prince has to tell him. Whereupon the Prince

unfolds to him without reserve what he feels about his father. He *is* grieved for him, but, having acquired a bad reputation, any show of grief would be interpreted by the ordinary person as sheer hypocrisy. And so saying he turns on Poins and asks if he is not right on this point of public opinion.

Prince. What wouldst thou think of me, if I should weep?
Poins. I would think thee a most princely hypocrite.

Delighted that Poins has not believed his confession of grief, the Prince continues:

It would be every man's thought; and thou art a blessed fellow to think as every man thinks. Never a man's thought in the world keeps the road-way better than thine. Every man would think me an hypocrite indeed.

He is at once contemptuous of Poins's perception—Poins who had enjoyed his company and who had not the excuse of the general public for knowing nothing of his mind—fascinated at the display of human nature, and relieved at having opened his mind even to some one whom in so doing he completely bewildered.

So much for the Prince's ironic detachment: the characteristic and most attractive side of his deliberate way of acting. His comprehensive nature comes out most brilliantly in an episode that is usually taken as trivial if not positively offensive: the foolery of the Prince and Poins with Francis and the other drawers in the Eastcheap tavern, before Falstaff arrives from the Gadshill robbery. It is a difficult scene, for the editors have not been able to find any meaning in it that at all enriches the play, and the sense of one or two sentences remains obscure. But the general drift should be clear from the Prince's satirical account of Hotspur killing "six or seven dozen of Scots at a breakfast" at the end of the incident and from his own reference to "honour" at the beginning. After what Hotspur has said already of honour earlier in the play it is impossible that there should not be a connection between Hotspur and honour here. The Prince has been drinking and making friends with the drawers of the tavern. He has won their hearts and learnt their ways:

To conclude, I am so good a proficient in one quarter of an hour that I can drink with any tinker in his own language during my

life. I tell thee, Ned, thou hast lost much honour that thou
wert not with me in this action.

In other words the Prince has won a signal victory and great
honour in having mastered this lesson so quickly. It was
Johnson who perceived that the Prince's satire on Hotspur is
logically connected with what goes before and not a mere un-
motivated outburst. But later critics have not given due weight
to that perception. Poins and the Prince have just had their
game with Francis, Poins being as ignorant of the Prince's
true meaning as he was in the scene from the second part just
examined.

> *Poins.* But hark ye; what cunning match have you made with
> this jest of the drawer? Come, what's the issue?
> *Prince.* I am now of all humours that have showed themselves
> since the old days of goodman Adam to the pupil age of this
> present twelve o'clock at midnight.

> *Re-enter* Francis.

> What's o'clock, Francis?
> *Fran.* Anon, anon, sir. *Exit.*
> *Prince.* That ever this fellow should have fewer words than a
> parrot, and yet the son of a woman! His industry is upstairs
> and downstairs; his eloquence the parcel of a reckoning. I
> am not yet of Percy's mind, the Hotspur of the north . . .

Johnson saw that the reference to Hotspur connects with the
Prince's declaration that he is "now of all humours," the entry
and exit of Francis with the Prince's comment being a mere
interruption. The Prince's wealth of humours is contrasted
with the single humour of Hotspur. Once again the Prince says
just what he means but in words that will bear another meaning.
On the face of it his words mean that he is greatly excited, being
ruled simultaneously by every human motive that exists; but
he also means that having learnt to understand the drawers he
has mastered all the springs of human conduct, he has even then
completed his education in the knowledge of men. We can
now understand his earlier talk of honour: he has won a more
difficult action than any of Hotspur's crudely repetitive
slaughters of Scotsmen. Bearing this in mind, we may perceive
things at the beginning of the episode which can easily be

passed over. To Poins's question where he has been the Prince answers:

> With three or four loggerheads among three or four score hogs-heads. I have sounded the very base string of humility. Sirrah, I am sworn brother to a leash of drawers and can call them all by their christen names, as Tom Dick and Francis. They take it already upon their salvation that though I be but Prince of Wales yet I am the king of courtesy.

When the Prince speaks of sounding the base string of humility he uses a musical metaphor. He means in one sense that he has touched the bottom limit of condescension. But he means something more: he is the bow that has got a response from the lowest string of the instrument, namely the drawers. We are to think that he has sounded all the other human strings already: he has now completed the range of the human gamut; he is of all humours since Adam. Now the idea of the world as a complicated musical harmony was a cosmic commonplace, which would evoke all the other such commonplaces. The drawers are not only the base or lowest string of the instrument; they are the lowest link in the human portion of the chain of being and as such nearest the beasts. And that is why the Prince directly after compares them to dogs by calling them "a leash of drawers." At the risk of being accused of being over ingenious I will add that "sounding" and "base" suggest plumbing the depths of the sea as well as playing on a stringed instrument and that there is a reference to Hotspur's boast earlier in the play that he will

> dive into the bottom of the deep,
> Where fathom-line could never touch the ground,
> And pluck up drowned honour by the locks.

It is not for nothing too that the Prince says the drawers think him the king of courtesy. As I shall point out later this is precisely what Shakespeare makes him, the *cortegiano*, the fully developed man, contrasted with Hotspur, the provincial, engaging in some ways, but with a one-track mind.

There remains a puzzle. Why should the Prince, after Francis has given him his heart, and, symbol of it, his penny-worth of sugar (which he wished he could make two) join with Poins to put him through a brutal piece of horseplay? Is not Masefield justified in his bitter attack on the Prince for such brutality? The answer is first that the Prince wanted to see just how little brain Francis had and puts him to the test, and secondly that in matters of humanity we must not judge Shakespeare by standards of twentieth century humanitarianism. In an age when men watched the antics of the mad and the sufferings of animals for sport we must not look for too much. Further we must remember the principle of degree. At the siege of La Rochelle costly dishes were carried into the town under a flag of truce to a Catholic hostage of noble birth, through a population dying of starvation; and such discrimination between classes was taken for granted. It may look strange when Shakespeare in one play represents the beautiful tact of Theseus in dealing with Bottom and his fellows, and in another allows his king of courtesy to be ungrateful and brutal to Francis. But Francis was a base string; Bottom a tenor string, a man in his way of intelligence and substance. Francis could not expect the same treatment. The subhuman element in the population must have been considerable in Shakespeare's day; that it should be treated almost like beasts was taken for granted.

From what I have said so far about the Prince it turns out that far from being a mere dissolute lout awaiting a miraculous transformation he is from the very first a commanding character, deliberate in act and in judgement, versed in every phase of human nature. But he is more than that. When the drawers think him the "king of courtesy" they know him better than his enemy Hotspur and even his own father do. And when Shakespeare put the phrase in their mouths he had in mind the abstract Renaissance conception of the perfect ruler. I will discuss how this conception enters and affects the play.

First, it is not for nothing that Elyot's *Governor* provided Shakespeare with the episode of the Prince being committed by the Lord Chief Justice. True, Shakespeare modified the episode to suit his special dramatic ends; but he must have known that Elyot held up Prince Hal, even during his father's lifetime, as one who was able to subordinate his violent passions to the sway of his reason. If Shakespeare got an episode from the *Governor* concerning his hero, it is likely that in shaping him he would have heeded the class of courtly manual to which the *Governor* belongs and of which Castiglione's *Cortegiano* was the most famous example. Then, there are passages in *Euphues* which are apt enough to the Prince's case. I do not mean that

Shakespeare used them directly, but that, occurring in a conventional didactic book on the education of a typical gentleman, they exemplify the assumptions Shakespeare would have been forced to go on if he meant to picture his perfect prince in accord with contemporary expectation.   Here is Euphues's picture of himself uncorrupted by the vices of Naples, as the Prince was uncorrupted by the vices of London:

> Suppose that Naples is a cankered storehouse of all strife, a common stews for all strumpets, the sink of shame, and the very nurse of all sin: shall it therefore follow of necessity that all that are wooed of love should be wedded to lust; will you conclude as it were *ex consequenti* that whosoever arriveth here shall be enticed to folly and, being enticed, of force shall be entangled? No, no, it is the disposition of the thought that altereth the nature of the thing.   The sun shineth upon the dunghill and is not corrupted; the diamond lieth in the fire and is not consumed; the crystal toucheth the toad and is not poisoned; the bird Trochilus liveth by the mouth of the crocodile and is not spoiled; a perfect wit is never bewitched with lewdness neither enticed by lasciviousness.

And here is Lyly's version, put into the mouth of old Fidus, of the central Renaissance doctrine of the all-round man:

> And I am not so precise but that I esteem it expedient in feats of arms and activity to employ the body as in study to waste the mind: yet so should the one be tempered with the other as it might seem as great a shame to be valiant and courtly without learning as to be studious and bookish without valour.

Now the Prince in addition to skill in arms has a brilliant and well-trained intellect, which shows itself in his talk with Falstaff, of whose extraordinary character the recollection of a good education is an important part.   But the Prince makes not the slightest parade of his intelligence, being apparently negligent of it.   And this leads to another mark of the courtier. This is the quality of *sprezzatura* (which Hoby translates by *disgracing* or *recklessness* and to which *nonchalance* may be a modern approximation) considered by Castiglione to be the crown of courtliness, and the opposite of the vice of *affettazione* (translated by Hoby *curiousness*):

> Trovo una regula universalissima la qual mi par valer circa

questo in tutte le cose umane che si facciano o dicano più che alcuna altra: e ciò è fuggir quanto più si po, e come un asperissimo e periculoso scoglio, la affettazione; e, per dir forse una nova parola, usar in ogni cosa una certa sprezzatura, che nasconda l'arte e dimonstri, ciò che si fa e dice venir fatto senza fatica e quasi senza pensarvi.[1]

Sprezzatura is a genuine ethical quality of the Aristotelian type: the mean between a heavy and affected carefulness and positive neglect. It is in the gift of this crowning courtly quality that the Prince so greatly excels Hotspur. He takes the Percies' rebellion with apparent lightness yet he is actually the hero in it. He gets news of it through Falstaff in the tavern scene after the Gadshill robbery. "There's villainous news abroad" says Falstaff, and goes on to name the different rebels. The Prince, quite unmoved apparently, makes a few idle remarks about Douglas and then goes on to the game of letting Falstaff act his father. Yet at the very end of the scene he lets out his true sentiments with the casual remark, "I'll to the court in the morning." Alone with his father at the court, he is forced by his father's reproaches out of his nonchalance into declaring the full seriousness of his intentions. But this does not stop him in the next scene from relapsing into his apparent frivolity:

Enter the Prince *and* Peto *marching, and* Falstaff *meets them playing on his truncheon like a fife.*

This may be too frivolous for the Italianate courtliness of Castiglione, but Vernon's description of the Prince vaulting with effortless ease onto his horse (quoted above p. 257) is the perfect rendering of it. Finally there is the Prince's nonchalant surrender to Falstaff of his claim to have killed Hotspur and his good-humoured but sarcastic willingness to back up Falstaff's lie:

> For my part, if a lie may do thee grace,
> I'll gild it with the happiest terms I have.

Hotspur both offends against the principle of *sprezzatura* in his

---

[1] I find one rule that is most general, which in this part, me think, taketh place in all things belonging to a man in word or deed, above all other. And that is to eschew as much as a man may, and as a sharp and dangerous rock, too much curiousness and (to speak a new word) to use in everything a certain disgracing to cover art withal and seem whatsoever he doth and saith to do it without pain and, as it were, not minding it. (Hoby's translation.)

blatant acclamation of honour, and is satirised by the Prince for the extreme clumsiness of his would-be nonchalance in the very scene where the Prince takes the news of the rebellion so coolly.

> *Prince.* I am not yet of Percy's mind, the Hotspur of the north; he that kills me some six or seven dozen of Scots at a breakfast, washes his hands, and says to his wife 'Fie upon this quiet life! I want work.' 'O my sweet Harry,' says she, 'how many hast thou killed to-day?' 'Give my roan horse a drench,' says he; and answers 'Some fourteen,' an hour after; 'a trifle, a trifle.'

The Prince here is the complete, sophisticated, internationally educated courtier ridiculing the provincial boorishness of Percy, the Hotspur of the north, much like a character in Restoration Comedy ridiculing the country bumpkin.

This is not to say that Hotspur is not a most engaging barbarian; adorable in the openness and simplicity of his excesses, infectious in his vitality, and well-flavoured by his country humour. The child in him goes straight to the female heart; and when his wife loves him to distraction for all his waywardness, we are completely convinced.

To return to the Prince, as well as fashioning him on the theoretical principles of the kingly character expected by his age, Shakespeare introduces a subtlety of motivation into his mind which if it were legitimate to isolate could quite reconcile one to the habits of the motive-hunting critics of the nineteenth century.

And here let me digress on a danger to modern criticism of Shakespeare. Scholars, having learnt how well versed Shakespeare was in contemporary psychological theory, have been tempted to put the natures of his characters in terms of it rather than in terms of human probability as understood to-day. Miss Lily Campbell, for instance, sees Lear as an embodiment of wrath in old age. He may be; but, once you have thus described him, it is much too easy to assume that this new truth has quite supplanted an old error, when all it has done is to modify an existing accumulation of false and true. That the Elizabethans constructed their characters on rigid, academic, *a priori* suppositions does not mean that they were incapable of first-hand observation. Where they are strange is in the way they combine both methods, or jump from one to another.

Something of this kind occurs in Spenser. He can in the same poem present the most inhuman allegorical abstractions and the terrifying and realistic and truthful picture of the jealous Britomart riding to rescue Artegal from his Amazon captor with looks bent to the ground to hide the "fellness of her heart." When we consider the psychological truth and complexity of the Bastard Falconbridge in *King John* and the inhumanity of the head gardener in *Richard II* we must not be surprised at any extreme of realism or the reverse or of any blending of them in the same character.

The psychological interest of the Prince's character centres in his relations with his father and his youthful apprehension of what it means to be a king. As well as making Hal all that was expected of him as a prince in the days of Elizabeth, Shakespeare entered imaginatively into the predicament in which he found himself as the destined successor of a man who had usurped the crown and thereafter worn himself out in upholding the usurpation. Shakespeare knew the legends of the Prince's wildness and he adopts them; but in so doing he justifies them psychologically by relating them to the conditions in which the Prince was brought up. Having a lively apprehension as well as a powerful nature the Prince would understand his father's troubles and face the terrible fact of the burden of kingship. Added to that was the burden of what his father expected of him. For a youth of his insight the burden was temporarily too great and he had to escape it as best he could: by evasion and revolt. But though he evades the intolerable solemnity of the court, he does no more than postpone a responsibility which fundamentally he knows and accepts. Unable under his father's eye to face being the impeccable prince, he compensates by practising the regal touch among his inferiors and proving himself the king of courtesy. His irony, though practised on so humble an object as Poins, springs from his recognition that the conscientious ruler must always be detached and isolated. His life with Falstaff is at once an escape from a present he cannot face and the incubation of a future which he will surely command. The king's relations with his son come out from his references to Hotspur and from his regrets that the two could not change places. Henry does not understand his son's richer character and mistakenly thinks Hotspur the better man. Nothing could be truer to the working of the human mind than Henry's bewilderment at his son's

behaviour and his consequent attempt to explain it as heaven's
punishment of his own sins.

> I know not whether God will have it so
> For some displeasing service I have done,
> That, in his secret doom, out of my blood
> He'll breed revengement and a scourge for me;
> But thou dost in thy passages of life
> Make me believe that thou art only mark'd
> For the hot vengeance and the rod of heaven
> To punish my mistreadings. Tell me else,
> Could such inordinate and low desires,
> Such poor, such bare, such lewd, such mean attempts,
> Such barren pleasures, rude society,
> As thou art match'd withal and grafted to,
> Accompany the greatness of thy blood
> And hold their level with thy princely heart?

Tell me else, says Henry; and, without pausing to ponder what
the obvious and human reason might be, he issues into bitter
censure of the surface facts of his son's behaviour. And he
goes on to rub in Hotspur's perfections, calling him "Mars in
swaddling clothes" and enlarging picturesquely on his exploits
against Douglas. The Prince, while admiring his father and
sympathising with his difficulties, hates him for holding up
Hotspur as a model. This is why he speaks so satirically of
Hotspur; until, having overcome him, he can afford to let his
natural generosity have scope. When we consider how wonderfully Shakespeare pictured the relations between mother and
son in *Coriolanus*, we need not hesitate to trace the above
motives in the relations between Henry IV and Prince Hal.

So much for the Prince. In speaking of him I have had to
bring in a number of different topics, for he touches the play at
almost every point. I must now enlarge on some of these topics.
I begin with the two other chief characters, Hotspur and Falstaff, both of whom at one time or another have been enlarged
beyond their proper (and really very obvious) provinces, so
as to encroach on the Prince and destroy the balance of
the play.

I fancy there are still many people who regard Hotspur as
the hero of the first part of the play. They are wrong, and their
error may spring from two causes. First they may inherit a
romantic approval for mere vehemence of passion, and secondly

they may assume that Shakespeare must somehow be on the side of any character in whose mouth he puts his finest poetry. For proof of the first error take the frequent habit of reading Hotspur's lines on honour,

> By heaven, methinks it were an easy leap
> To pluck bright honour from the pale-fac'd moon,
> Or dive into the bottom of the deep,
> Where fathom-line could never touch the ground,
> And pluck up drowned honour by the locks,

as the kind of great poetry to which we surrender without reserve. The lines are of course partly satirical at Hotspur's expense; and that Ralph in the *Knight of the Burning Pestle* recites them, on being asked to speak a "huffing part," shows that this was contemporary opinion. Hotspur, however captivating his vitality, verges on the ridiculous from the very beginning, through his childish inability to control his passions. At his first appearance he follows his gloriously vivid and humorous account of the "certain lord, neat and trimly dress'd" demanding the prisoners on the field of battle, an account where he has his passions under control and all his native wit has scope, with his violent description, grotesquely heightened by excessive passion, of the duel between Glendower and Mortimer. From this second description (whose inflation gets overwhelming confirmation immediately after and throughout the rest of the first part) it should be plain that Shakespeare held up Hotspur's excesses to ridicule and never for a moment intended him for his hero. That Hotspur speaks some of the best poetry in the play is undoubted. There is nothing finer, for instance, than Hotspur's account to Blunt before the Battle of Shrewsbury of Henry's past career from the time he was

> A poor unminded outlaw sneaking home

till his present quarrel with the Percies. But to interpret the poetry as a sign of Shakespeare's sympathy with Hotspur's excesses is as wrong as to imagine that Shakespeare approved of Cleopatra's influence on Antony's character because he puts such poetry into her mouth. What the poetry proves is that Shakespeare was much interested in these characters and that he had something important to say through them.

Why then did Shakespeare develop Hotspur's character so highly and put such poetry into his mouth, when a less elaborate figure would have done to symbolise, as was necessary for the play's structure, the principle of honour carried to an absurd excess? It is that he uses him as one of his principal means of creating his picture of England, of fulfilling in a new and subtle way the old motive of Respublica. For though, as said above, Hotspur is satirised as the northern provincial in contrast to that finished Renaissance gentleman, the Prince, he does express positive English qualities and in so doing has his part in the great composite picture Shakespeare was constructing. For all his violent passions, Hotspur is at times very close to life and looks at its concrete manifestations with the same humorous zest as did the Bastard in *King John*. His fits of English passion are utterly opposed to the Welsh dream-world inhabited by Glendower, while Glendower's solemn profession of being given to the arts of poetry and music sting him into an attack on them that is not necessarily in keeping with his nature at all:

> I had rather be a kitten and cry mew
> Than one of these same metre ballad mongers;
> I had rather hear a brazen canstick turn'd,
> Or a dry wheel grate on the axle-tree:
> And that would set my teeth nothing on edge,
> Nothing so much as mincing poetry.

Kittens, ballad mongers, candlesticks and cartwheels, though by no means exclusively English, were very much a part of English life; and Hotspur had noted them and a great deal else with an eye sharp with the zest of the man who adores the solid and reassuring traffic of the everyday world. The forthright Englishman had long been a stock figure in the drama, often contrasted with the effeminate French. There had been Talbot in *1 Henry VI*, Humphrey of Gloucester in *2 Henry VI* and his progeny "blunt Thomas" in *Woodstock*. Hotspur, so live a character as to seem scarcely their kin, does indeed catch up, though he transmutes, the peculiar anglicism of these characters. Shakespeare does not spare "all the faults" of this Englishman yet he makes us "love him still." Similarly though Hotspur teases his wife outrageously, bringing her to the verge of tears with his rebuffs, maddening her with his offhandedness, he yet reassures us of the Englishman's rough kindliness somewhere underneath. There is no real cruelty in his roughness. And when he rates her for "swearing like a comfit-maker's wife," he does in his own (and not indelicate) way make love to her as well as show with what wide-open eyes he passed through the England of which in this play he is so important an expression.

Hot. Come, Kate, I'll have your song too.
Lady P. Not mine, in good sooth.
Hot. Not yours, in good sooth! Heart! You swear like a comfit-
  maker's wife. 'Not you, in good sooth,' and 'as true as I live,'
  and 'as God shall mend me,' and 'as sure as day.'
  And givest such sarcenet surety for thy oaths,
  As if thou never walk'st further than Finsbury.
  Swear me, Kate, like a lady as thou art,
  A good mouth-filling oath and leave 'in sooth'
  And such protest of pepper-gingerbread
  To velvet-guards and Sunday-citizens.
  Come, sing.

If Hotspur is in some way local, very much of an Englishman and contemporary in that he makes us think of Elizabethan and not medieval England, Falstaff enlarges the play, as none of Shakespeare's hitherto had been enlarged, into the ageless, the archetypal. Though richly and grossly circumstantiated, though quite at home in Elizabethan London from court to brothel, he reaches across the ages and over the earth. To Shakespeare as the creator of Falstaff can be applied these words from the most strongly felt of all the paragraphs in Wordsworth's Preface to the *Lyrical Ballads*:

In spite of differences of soil and climate, of language and manners, of laws and customs; in spite of things silently gone out of mind, and things violently destroyed; the Poet binds together by passion and knowledge the vast empire of human society, as it is spread over the whole earth and over all time.

Or one might say that Falstaff was in unseen attendance on Satan in the Garden of Eden to make the first frivolous remark and the first dirty joke, after the Fall. It is surprising that Miss Bodkin did not seize on him for one of her archetypal patterns.

Not that Falstaff is no more than the symbol of the ribald in man. He is a complicated figure combining several functions which it might tax the greatest author to embody in even separate persons.

First (and this has nothing to do with his ribaldry and his lawlessness) he stands for sheer vitality, for the spirit of youth ready for any adventure. He resembles the actual Dr. Johnson, who, when waked in the small hours by Beauclerk and Langton, was delighted to get up and "have a frisk with" them, and the fictitious Pickwick. In all three it is the old or middle age and the gross or portly body that make the youthful vitality so surprising: just as in the *Turn of the Screw* Henry James owes so much of the power with which evil is conveyed to showing it in the minds of children; where it should least be found. Shakespeare did something of the sort when he created Lear: the old man with the passions of a child. But Lear becomes educated; it is the essence of Falstaff in his other parts that he should be incorrigible.

As well as being the eternal child Falstaff is the fool; and I know nothing more to the point than Miss Welsford's last chapter in her book on that topic. Roaring in panic at Gadshill, falling down as if dead before Douglas at the Battle of Shrewsbury, he fulfils the fool's crude function of "mere safety-valve for the suppressed instincts of the bully," instincts common to every member of the audience. But far more often he fulfils the more complicated and more characteristic function of providing by his powers of recovery "a subtler balm for the fears and wounds" of the oppressed. He is kin to Brer Rabbit and Fool Schweik. Not that Shakespeare overworks him in this function, for only once in each part of the play is he thrown quite on the defensive with only his wits to help him: in the first part when the Prince lets it out that it was he and Poins who were the men in buckram, and in the second after the Prince and Poins, having overheard him call the Prince "a good shallow young fellow" and such things, confront him with his words. Having made Falstaff do all that was required in these straits Shakespeare could give him yet another large function.

For not only is Falstaff the passive character who gets away with it when pressed, he is the active impostor and adventurer: not only Schweik but Volpone, not only Brer Rabbit but the *Miles Gloriosus*. Of course Falstaff makes a very different impression from Volpone with his Marlovian ancestry and his grim and bitter excess. But his career like Volpone's is a long series of bluffs and gambles, all brought off till the final crash. He brings off the Gadshill robbery and his pretence of killing Hotspur. He is the adventurer and not the fool when he makes his entry in the second part in new clothes to suit his bogus military reputation, and with his newly acquired page bearing his sword and buckler. He goes on to evade Mrs. Quickly's warrant of arrest and to touch her for a dinner. And he ends the dinner with Mrs. Quickly and Doll devoted to him, while there is every reason to think that he will get rid of the dozen captains who are looking for him and will not "leave the sweetest morsel of the night unpicked." His financial transactions are all in the adventurer's department and they culminate in the bribes he gets from Shallow's pressed men and the thousand pounds he borrows from Shallow himself. Like the fool the adventurer is an eternal stock figure, and we take sides temporarily with him and ultimately against him. We love him to have his day but we admit with decision, if with regret, that his day must end.

But Falstaff embodies something still wider than the adventurer, something more abstract. If from Schweik he goes on to Volpone, he also goes on from the harmlessly comic Vice to the epitome of the Deadly Sins at war with law and order. And he fulfils that last function not only through delightful human action but through precise and academic symbolism. This symbolism is important because, being traditional as well as academic, it is antique and helps greatly to turn Falstaff into the archetypal character that he is. Shakespeare makes Falstaff's part as the symbol of misrule absolutely plain at the very outset. Falstaff's first words are to ask the Prince what is the time of day; to which the Prince answers:

> What a devil hast thou to do with the time of the day? Unless hours were cups of sack, and minutes capons, and clocks the tongues of bawds, and dials the signs of leaping-houses, and the blessed sun himself a fair hot wench in flame-coloured taffeta; I see no reason why thou shouldst be so superfluous to demand the time of the day.

We must not allow the witchery of this prose to distract us here from the thought of other references in Shakespeare to clocks and the divisions of time: from Henry VI's yearning for the shepherd's orderly life—

> So many hours must I tend my flock;
> So many hours must I take my rest;
> So many hours must I contemplate;
> So many hours must I sport myself—

and from Richard II's pathetic image of himself in prison as
the clock worked on by time—

> I wasted time, and time doth now waste me;
> For now hath time made me his numbering clock.
> My thoughts are minutes, and with sighs they jar
> Their watches on unto mine eyes, the outward watch,
> Whereto my finger, like a dial's point,
> Is pointing still in cleansing them from tears.

Henry VI is expressing the regularity of the shepherd's life,
Richard the intolerably regular monotony of his grief. The
Prince is telling Falstaff that his concern is with disorder and
misrule not with order and regularity. And Falstaff blandly
admits it and seeks to attach the Prince to his own side when
he answers:

> Indeed, you come near me now, Hal; for we that take purses
> by the moon and the seven stars and not by Phoebus—

With Falstaff here symbolising disorder, an Elizabethan audience would identify the Prince with Phoebus and know that
Falstaff was trying to undermine his true kingly function of
shining by day. And Falstaff later recalls this conversation when
in the tavern he poses as Henry IV reproving his son and says:

> Shall the blessed sun of heaven prove a micher and eat black-
> berries? a question not to be asked. Shall the son of England
> prove a thief and take purses? a question to be asked.

This is not the only place where Falstaff is academic as well as
amusing. Indeed he utters as many cosmic or scientific
commonplaces as the king himself. His disquisition on sherris-
sack, for instance, is a perfectly correct parody of the physical
organisation of the microcosm and of its correspondence with
another sphere of existence, the body politic:

> A good sherris-sack hath a two-fold operation in it. It ascends
> me into the brain; dries me there all the foolish and dull and
> crudy vapours which environ it; makes it apprehensive, quick,
> forgetive, full of nimble fiery and delectable shapes, which, de-
> livered o'er to the voice, the tongue (which is the birth), becomes
> excellent wit. The second property of your excellent sherris is,
> the warming of the blood; which, before cold and settled, left the
> liver white and pale, which is the badge of pusillanimity and

cowardice. But the sherris warms it and makes it course from the inwards to the parts extreme: it illumineth the face, which as a beacon gives warning to all the rest of this little kirgdom, man, to arm; and then the vital commoners and inland petty spirits muster me all to their captain, the heart, who, great and puffed up with this retinue, doth any deed of courage. And this valour comes of sherris.

Falstaff here makes his sherris act quite correctly after the manner of the humours, which in the form of a vapour could (exceptionally) ascend direct to the brain (to the brain's confusion) or (normally), entering the blood through the liver, create through the medium of vital heat the three kinds of spirit: natural vital and animal. Falstaff also recalls the traditional correspondence between the parts of the human body and the population of the state; in particular that (in Thomas Starkey's words)

like as all wit reason and sense, feeling life and all other natural power, springeth out of the heart, so from the princes and rulers of the state cometh all laws order and policy, all justice virtue and honesty, to the rest of this politic body.

Of course this academic side of Falstaff has more than one job. It makes his antics far funnier, just as it is the gentility of the woman in Burns's poem which, execution apart, gives the louse on her dress half its fun (the other half being that he noticed it in church). But its immediate relevant job is that it helps to elevate Falstaff into the great symbolic figure of misrule or disorder that he is. To be effectively disorderly he must be learned in the opposite of disorder.

As such a symbol Falstaff is much more than a prolongation of the traditional lord of misrule; he stands for a perpetual and accepted human principle. Of this principle George Orwell wrote very agreeably (and for my present argument instructively) in an article in *Horizon* on the *Art of Donald McGill*. The comic postcards of which those going under the name of Donald McGill are typical represent the principle of man's perpetual revolt against both his moral self and the official forces of law and order. They are a modern popular version of the opposition typified for instance by the figures of Dox Quixote and Sancho Panza. Orwell goes on:

If you look into your own mind, which are you, Don Quixote or

Sancho Panza? Almost certainly you are both. There is one part of you that wishes to be a hero or a saint, but another part of you is a little fat man who sees very clearly the advantages of staying alive with a whole skin. He is your unofficial self, the voice of the belly protesting against the soul. He it is who punctures your fine attitudes and urges you to look after Number One, to be unfaithful to your wife, to bilk your debts.

This unofficial self is a stock figure in literature, though in real life he never gets much of a hearing. He gets his hearing largely through ribaldry.

A dirty joke is not, of course, a serious attack upon morality, but it is a sort of mental rebellion, a momentary wish that things were otherwise. So also with all other jokes, which always centre round cowardice, laziness, dishonesty or some other quality which society cannot afford to encourage. The high sentiments always win in the end; leaders who offer blood, toil, tears and sweat always get more out of their followers than those who offer safety and a good time. When it comes to the pinch, human beings are heroic. Women face childbed and the scrubbing brush, revolutionaries keep their mouths shut in the torture chamber, battleships go down with their guns still firing when their decks are awash. It is only that the other element in man, the lazy, cowardly, debt-bilking adulterer who is inside all of us, can never be suppressed altogether and needs a hearing occasionally.

Orwell gets us here pretty close to Falstaff, who, though he stands for disorder, is after all a comic figure and is not solemn enough to represent the Elizabethan notion of chaos; chaos being what the Prince would have represented if he had made the wrong choice. When the Prince calls Falstaff "that villainous abominable misleader of youth, that old white-bearded Satan," he speaks truth only as far as might concern himself. Falstaff's exquisite mendacity about his own character gives us the general truth:

If sack and sugar be a fault, God help the wicked! if to be old and merry be a sin, then many an old host that I know is damned; if to be fat be to be hated, then Pharaoh's lean kine are to be loved. No, my good lord; banish Peto, banish Bardolph, banish Poins: but for sweet Jack Falstaff, kind Jack Falstaff, true Jack Falstaff, valiant Jack Falstaff and therefore more valiant being, as he is, old Jack Falstaff, banish not him thy Harry's company, banish not him thy Harry's company. Banish plump Jack, and banish all the world.

With our virtuous selves we know he is lying; with our unofficial selves we back up the lie, agreeing to call the misleader of youth plump Jack. But only for the moment. We end by banishing the misleader of youth. But it is not the end, for once the misleader of youth has been disposed of, with a "Here we are again" plump Jack reappears; only to be banished again when he becomes too threatening. There is thus no need to be ashamed of having an affection for Falstaff, as long as we acknowledge that we must also cast him out. The school of criticism that furnished him with a tender heart and condemned the Prince for brutality in turning him away was deluded. Its delusions will probably be accounted for, in later years, through the facts of history. The sense of security created in nineteenth century England by the predominance of the British navy induced men to rate that very security too cheaply and to exalt the instinct of rebellion above its legitimate station. They forgot the threat of disorder which was ever present with the Elizabethans. Schooled by recent events we should have no difficulty now in taking Falstaff as the Elizabethans took him.

The things I have treated of so far in this chapter have little to do with *Henry IV* as a pair of plays in a great historical sequence; they concern the plays' innovations. The exception was this: that in the Prince Shakespeare at last completes the many attempts he had made to define the perfect ruler. But there is far more political content than this. Shakespeare indeed carries on (and with sufficient emphasis to give it a place in the background when politics are not the theme) the total historical doctrine I have expounded in the course of this book, and the specific historical theme (the curse incurred through the murder of Woodstock, one of Edward III's seven sons, and not merely passed on but greatly intensified by the murder of Richard) that connects and animates the whole sequence of eight plays from the reign of Richard II to that of Henry VII.

To give a few illustrations of the general historical doctrine first. The finest of all expositions of the principle of history repeating itself and of its being possible to forecast future events on the model of the past is found in the second part of the play.

After Henry has soliloquised on sleep, Surrey and Warwick enter and Henry complains to them of the fluctuating fortunes of the world and how by observing them a man might well quail at the retribution any course of action will bring.

> O God, that one might read the book of fate
> And see the revolution of the times
> Make mountains level, and the continent,
> Weary of solid firmness, melt itself
> Into the sea! and, other times, to see
> The beachy girdle of the ocean
> Too wide for Neptune's hips; how chances mock
> And changes fill the cup of alteration
> With divers liquors! O, if this were seen,
> The happiest youth, viewing his progress through,
> What perils past, what crosses to ensue,
> Would shut the book and sit him down and die.

And he goes on to cite the double alteration or treachery of Northumberland. Whereupon Warwick gives his splendid version (looking forward in cadence to one of the finest passages in *Julius Caesar*, "There is a tide in the affairs of men,") of the doctrine of learning from the past:

> There is a history in all men's lives
> Figuring the nature of the times deceas'd;
> The which observ'd, a man may prophesy
> With a near aim of the main chance of things
> As yet not come to life, which in their seeds
> And weak beginnings lie intreasured.
> Such things become the hatch and brood of time.

Warwick means in the first two lines that in a man's past life there is a pattern, or a sequence of cause and effect, revealing the principle by which events in that past life are governed. If he can once discover that pattern, he can by its analogy forecast coming events. And, as if to indicate the high theoretical tone of these passages, Henry, just before, spoke of the state in terms of the human body:

> Then you perceive the body of our kingdom
> How foul it is: what rank diseases grow,
> And with what danger,.near the heart of it.

The Prince, after he has become Henry V, uses the tradi-

tional equation of the king to the ocean. Hitherto, he says, his
waters have wasted themselves in an idle flow of tides (beating
vainly on the barren shore, we are meant to think), but now
they will take their proper part in the pomp of kingship's ocean
and move with ceremonial majesty:

> The tide of blood in me
> Hath proudly flow'd in vanity till now;
> Now doth it turn and ebb back to the sea,
> Where it shall mingle with the state of floods
> And flow henceforth in formal majesty.

In speaking of civil war, Shakespeare uses the traditional correspondence between the skies and the state, between the eccen-
tric meteors and the rebel peers. Before Shrewsbury Henry
thus admonishes Worcester, one of the emissaries of the rebel
camp:

> Will you again unknit
> This churlish knot of all-abhorred war,
> And move in that obedient orb again
> Where you did give a fair and natural light,
> And be no more an exhaled meteor?

Worcester is bidden cease being a disorderly thing, a meteor or
comet, and become once again a planet revolving round the
sun-king with orderly and predictable motion.

The business of the curse comes in the very first scene and is
sustained throughout each part till Henry's death. Henry
opens the plays by lamenting the recent disturbances and pro-
posing a new crusade. Though an affair of policy, the crusade
was also a penance for Richard's death, carrying on Henry's
last lines in *Richard II*:

> I'll make a voyage to the Holy Land
> To wash this blood off from my guilty hand.

And whenever the crusade is mentioned, as it is several times in
the course of both parts, it should recall the curse and Henry's
unremitting efforts to expiate it. The first scene also gives the
recurring pattern the curse will make. No sooner has Henry
spoken of the crusade than

> all athwart there came
> A post from Wales loaden with heavy news.

That is the pattern: one cruel interposition after another between Henry's hopes and their fulfilment. Yet Henry is a good ruler and is humble before God, confessing before him the crooked ways by which he met the crown. Thus, like Ahab, who humbled himself, he does not incur the utmost doom of the curse in his own person. God limits his punishment to perpetual disquiet and the doom of self-deception. Henry knows he will die in Jerusalem, which he thought meant the Holy Land, and believes that with him the curse will end:

> For all the soil of the achievement goes
> With me into the earth.

Actually Jerusalem turns out to be a room in Westminster, and the curse has scarcely begun its full operation. Further, Henry is deceived about his son and thinks that heaven canalises his punishment into his son's excesses. It is through these that chaos will come again:

> For the fifth Harry from curb'd licence plucks
> The muzzle of restraint, and the wild dog
> Shall flesh his tooth on every innocent.
> O my poor kingdom, sick with civil blows,
> When that my care could not withhold thy riots,
> What wilt thou do when riot is thy care?
> O, thou wilt be a wilderness again,
> Peopled with wolves, thy old inhabitants.

And when Henry is certain of his son's repentance he goes to the other extreme and believes all will be well. But Shakespeare lets us know that the curse is not to be exorcised so easily, that it is only dormant. He makes the Archbishop use the very physical blood of Richard to advertise rebellion. These are Morton's words in the first scene of the second part:

> But now the bishop
> Turns insurrection to religion;
> And doth enlarge his rising with the blood
> Of fair King Richard, scrap'd from Pomfret stones.

And in the same scene Shakespeare expressed through Northumberland's fury at the bad news how ingrained in the rebels is the principle of disorder.

Let heaven kiss earth; now let not nature's hand
Keep the wild flood confin'd; let order die!
And let this world no longer be a stage
To feed contention in a lingering act;
But let one spirit of the first-born Cain
Reign in all bosoms, that, each heart being set
On bloody courses, the rude scene may end
And darkness be the burier of the dead!

These terrible words go quite beyond the partial insurrections of the present to the Wars of the Roses. We should think of the full horrors of Wakefield and Towton, of Margaret's murder of York and of the pageant of father killing son and son killing father.

It remains to support my assertion that in *Henry IV* Shakespeare gives his version of contemporary England, a version allying him to the writers of epic.

Now as the stylistic mark of tragedy is intensity, that of the epic, though tragic intensity may occur, is breadth or variety. And in *Henry IV* there is a variety of style, fully mastered, which is new in Shakespeare and which can hardly be matched even in his later work. This variety contrasts, and I believe was meant deliberately to contrast, with the comparative monotony of *Richard II*. I will mention a few of the styles which Shakespeare practised in these plays.

As a kind of backbone, and corresponding to the high political theme of the plays, is the stately but no longer stiff blank verse used to describe the great happenings which are the main nominal theme. It is the stylistic norm that Shakespeare inherited from the whole series of History Plays he had already written and it is now his absolute servant. One may still call it Shakespeare's official style, but there is not the slightest sense of his using it because he should, and not because he would. It is the perfect correlative of his sincere and solemn heed of the awful and exemplary unfolding of history. Take, for instance, the induction to Part Two, where Rumour tells of the false reports he has spread. It is high-sounding rhetoric; strongly, even violently, metaphorical: and it moves with a gait that is at once ceremonial and consummately athletic:

Open your ears; for which of you will stop
The vent of hearing when loud Rumour speaks?
I, from the orient to the drooping west,

Making the wind my post-horse, still unfold
The acts commenced on this ball of earth.
Upon my tongues continual slanders ride,
The which in every language I pronounce,
Stuffing the ears of men with false reports.
I speak of peace, while covert enmity
Under the smile of safety wounds the world.
And who but Rumour, who but only I
Make fearful musters and prepar'd defence,
Whiles the big year, swoln with some other grief,
Is thought with child by the stern tyrant war,
And no such matter?

It is from this norm that many of the finer passages take their origin: for instance Northumberland's surmise of bad news when Morton enters after the Battle of Shrewsbury:

How doth my son and brother?
Thou tremblest; and the whiteness in thy cheek
Is apter than thy tongue to tell thy errand.
Even such a man, so faint, so spiritless,
So dull, so dead in look, so woe-begone,
Drew Priam's curtain in the dead of night
And would have told him half his Troy was burnt;
But Priam found the fire ere he his tongue,
And I my Percy's death ere thou report'st it—

or Henry V's smooth and Olympian, but powerfully felt, protest that from now on he is quite dedicated to his duty:

The tide of blood in me
Hath proudly flow'd in vanity till now:
Now doth it turn and ebb back to the sea,
Where it shall mingle with the state of floods
And flow henceforth in formal majesty.
Now call we our high court of parliament;
And let us choose such limbs of noble counsel,
That the great body of our state may go
In equal rank with the best govern'd nation.

But there are many passages which depart from the norm and in so doing borrow and repay a virtue which in isolation they would not possess. Hotspur's hearty homeliness gains enormously by being set against Shakespeare's official style: think

for instance of these lines side by side with the passage just
quoted:

> Oh, he is as tedious
> As a tired horse, a railing wife;
> Worse than a smoky house. I had rather live
> With cheese and garlic in a windmill, far,
> Than feed on cates and have him talk to me
> In any summer-house in Christendom.

Moreover in everything Hotspur says there is a quicker speed
and a more abrupt emphasis than in the plays' normal blank
verse. Brilliantly set off by the norm, too, are some passages of
lyrical beauty. Mortimer's words about his Welsh wife have
a Keatsian mellifluousness:

> I understand thy kisses and thou mine,
> And that's a feeling disputation.
> But I will never be a truant, love,
> Till I have learn'd thy language; for thy tongue
> Makes Welsh as sweet as ditties highly penn'd,
> Sung by a fair queen in a summer's bower,
> With ravishing division, to her lute.

And when Lady Percy praises Hotspur, she speaks with a lyrical
fervour that anticipates the praises of Antony in *Antony and
Cleopatra*. Hotspur's honour, she says,

> stuck upon him as the sun
> In the grey vault of heaven, and by his light
> Did all the chivalry of England move
> To do brave acts. He was indeed the glass
> Wherein the noble youth did dress themselves;
> He had no legs that practised not his gait;
> And speaking thick, which nature made his blemish,
> Became the accents of the valiant,
> For those that could speak low and tardily
> Would turn their own perfection to abuse,
> To seem like him: so that in speech, in gait,
> In diet, in affections of delight,
> In military rules, humours of blood,
> He was the mark and glass, copy and book,
> That fashion'd others.

But it is through his use of prose, and of a varied prose, that

Shakespeare creates the fullest range of contrast with his blank verse norm. Indeed, some of the prose has a perfect polish that may go beyond any similar quality in the verse. This prose is the property of the Prince and of Falstaff; it is derived from the best things in Lyly's plays; and it looks forward to the elegancies of Congreve. Like its original and its offspring it is founded on the normal speech-cadence of the most intelligent and highly-educated of the aristocracy. It is simple, but measured and deliberate; and so highly wrought that not a syllable can be altered with impunity. This, for instance, is how the Prince comments on the plan that he and Poins should disguise themselves as drawers to overhear Falstaff:

> From a god to a bull: a heavy descension; it was Jove's case. From a prince to a prentice: a low transformation; that shall be mine. For in every thing the purpose must weigh with the folly. Follow me, Ned.

And these words of Falstaff have the same qualities:

> But Hal, I prithee, trouble me no more with vanity. I would to God thou and I knew where a commodity of good names were to be bought. An old lord of the council rated me the other day in the street about you, sir, but I marked him not: and yet he talked very wisely, but I regarded him not; and yet he talked wisely, and in the street too.

Falstaff commands not only the most exquisite conversational vein, but the Euphuism, of Lyly; and his exhibition of it when he poses as the king reproving the Prince is satirical much in the manner of Congreve exhibiting the affectation of contemporary fashions of speech. But the prose ranges through most ranks of society, through the country gossiping of the two Justices and the plainness of Davy to the Dickensian ramblings of Mrs. Quickly. It embraces a large portion of English life. Taken together, the verse and prose of the play are a stylistic exhibition of most phases of the commonwealth.

The theme of Respublica, now given a new turn and treating not merely the fortunes but the very nature of England, what I am calling the epic theme, is subtly contrived. And the contrivance depends on two conditions: first that the two parts of the play are a single organism, and secondly that we are assured from the start that the Prince will make a good king. By itself the first part does not fulfil the theme of England, which occurs only in hints or patches; by itself the second part with so much business in Gloucestershire would contain an overbalance of provincial England: but treat the two parts as a single play, and the theme of England grows naturally till its full compass is reached when Henry V, the perfect English king, comes to the throne. If we were in doubt about the Prince's decision, we should not have the mental repose necessary for appreciating a static picture of England: we should be obsessed, as we are in *Henry VI*, with the events of civil war; and the troubles of Henry IV would quench our interest in the drone of the Lincolnshire bagpipes or the price of stock at Stamford Fair.

The idea of picturing all England occurred in embryo in *2 Henry VI*, where Shakespeare brings in many social grades. But any coherent picture was out of the question in a play concerned with the progressive disintegration of society. *Henry IV* shows a stable society and it is crowded, like no other play of Shakespeare, with pictures of life as it was lived in the age of Elizabeth. There is nothing archaistic about the Eastcheap tavern and its hostess, about the two carriers in the inn yard at Rochester, about the bill found in Falstaff's pocket, about the satin ordered from Master Dombleton for Falstaff's short cloak and slops, or about the life Shallow liked to think he had led at the Inns of Court: they are all pure Elizabethan. But opinions will differ on how they are to be interpreted. The hard-boiled critics will see no more in them than lively bits of local colour serving to make the heavy historical stuff more diverting to a mixed audience. Those who, like myself, believe that Shakespeare had a massively reflective as well as a brilliantly opportunist brain will expect these matters of Elizabethan life to serve more than one end and will not be surprised if through them he expresses his own feelings about his fatherland. It is also perfectly natural that Shakespeare should have chosen this particular point in the total stretch of history he covered, as suited to this expression. Henry V was traditionally not only the perfect king but a king after the Englishman's heart; one who added the quality of good mixer to the specifically regal virtues. The picture of England would fittingly be connected with the typical English monarch. The details of that picture bear out the notion that Shakespeare deliberately contrived such a connection.

First, it is difficult to deny a deliberate contrast between the play's first scene showing the remoteness of Henry IV from his own people, accentuated by his desire to leave his country for a crusade, and the second scene showing the Prince's easy mixing in the less reputable life of London. The audience would have jumped to it at once that, as in Wilson's *Three Lords and three Ladies of London*, London was now the theme; and they would have identified the Prince with it. But even here Shakespeare will not allow London to usurp everything, witness these words:

> *Falstaff.* 'Sblood, I am as melancholy as a gib cat or a lugged bear.
> *Prince.* Or an old lion or a lover's lute.
> *Falstaff.* Yea, or the drone of a Lincolnshire bagpipe.
> *Prince.* What sayest thou to a hare or the melancholy of Moor-ditch?

And the Prince's soliloquy at the end of the scene, promising that he will exhibit all the proper regal virtues, reassures us that we have been justified, that we have been safe, in identifying the Prince with English life generally. And the process is repeated whenever the Prince condescends to take part in events, in Kent or London. Thus it is that when the Prince is crowned, and even though he is then in anything but a condescending mood, we identify him with the picture of England, then complete.

And there are many things, in which the Prince has no share, that make up this picture. How Hotspur helps in this has been described above; and nowhere more effectively than in the scene in Wales with Glendower and Mortimer. Indeed one of this whole scene's main functions is to create a sense of England through a contrast with Wales. Here not only is the bluff anglicism of Hotspur contrasted with Glendower's Welsh romanticism, but Lady Percy's school-girlish simplicities—"Go, ye giddy goose," and "Lie still, ye thief, and hear the lady sing in Welsh"—are very English and contrast equally with Lady Mortimer's lyricism which Glendower interprets to her husband:

> She bids you on the wanton rushes lay you down
> And rest your gentle head upon her lap.

Thereafter in Part One the theme of England is not greatly developed: it remains in suspense so that it may get full expression in Part Two.

Here, Shakespeare introduces the theme of England just as he did early in Part One: he puts a minutely circumstantiated domestic scene after a scene dealing in a high manner with civil war; political action in the historical past yields to a picture of England to-day. I refer to the conspirators' discussion at York (I. 3) and Mrs. Quickly's attempt to arrest Falstaff (II. 1). To illustrate the skill of Shakespeare's transition, here are some lines from the Archbishop's last speech in I. 3, where the reference to London is both perfectly apt to the business in hand and prepares us for the change to the domestic intimacies of Eastcheap in the next scene:

> What trust is in these times?
> They that, when Richard liv'd, would have him die
> Are now become enamour'd of his grave:
> Thou that threw'st dust upon his goodly head,
> When through proud London he came sighing on
> After the admired heels of Bolingbroke,
> Criest now 'O earth, yield us that king again,
> And take thou this.' O thoughts of men accurst!
> Past and to come seems best; things present worst.

The next scene, and especially Mrs. Quickly, give the answer to the Archbishop's first question and deny the sentiment of the last line. There is something entirely reassuring in Mrs. Quickly's good nature, in her muddled intellect and in her photographic memory of detail. "Thou didst swear to me," she says to Falstaff,

> upon a parcel-gilt goblet, sitting in my Dolphin-chamber, at the round table, by a sea-coal fire, upon Wednesday in Wheeson week, when the prince broke thy head for liking his father to a singing-man of Windsor, thou didst swear to me then, as I was washing thy wound, to marry me and make me my lady thy wife.

Hearing this, we answer that there is a great deal of trust in these times and we are glad to repose in the present. And we accept Mrs. Quickly as the type of all the stupid good-natured women in England. Just as Dogberry and his men reassure us that in *Much Ado* the tragic element will not be allowed to prevail, so Mrs. Quickly reassures us that civil war will yield, as the plays' main theme, to England.

It is in the scenes in Gloucestershire (III. 2; V. 1; V. 2) that the theme of England is completed. But here there is the question of interpretation. Dover Wilson considers these scenes

"a studied burlesque of provincial life and manners for the
hilarious contempt of London spectators," and if he is right
they will be far from creating an epic picture of England. I
think that he is wrong and that his opinion falsifies and im-
poverishes the scenes themselves and goes against the whole
trend of Shakespeare's feelings about the country. Shallow
and Silence may be ridiculous characters; some of the yokels
gathered for recruiting may be pathetic: but these persons are
no more a satire on country England than Nym and Bardolph
are a satire on Elizabethan London. From first to last Shakespeare was loyal to the country life. He took it for granted as
the norm, as the background before which the more formal or
spectacular events were transacted. Shakespeare tells us this;
when he slips in the spring and winter songs after the prolonged
affectations in *Love's Labour's Lost*, or when he inserts the English
realism of Petruchio's country house into the Italianate complexities of the *Taming of the Shrew*. And at the end of his career
he made the wholesomeness of the pastoral life in the *Winter's
Tale* redeem the barren and tortured jealousy of Leontes. Far
from being a satire, the Gloucestershire scenes in *Henry IV*
complete the picture of England and put the emphasis where
Shakespeare meant it to be: on the life of the English country-
side. And that emphasis is given precisely as the Prince
becomes Henry V.

Shakespeare manipulates the matter so delicately that it is
hard to bring forward any neatly tabulated evidence of his
intentions. But it is worth noting two of the hints he gives us.
First, the chief character of the scenes, Justice Shallow, however
ridiculous he is and however much at sea when he leaves the
things he understands, is a good countryman. He knows what
he is doing when he tells Davy to sow the headland with red
wheat; and when he offers Falstaff a pippin "of his own
graffing," we do not question his horticultural skill. And if in
the scene where he first appears he is ludicrous in thinking they
still talk of him as "mad Shallow" at Clement's Inn, he is
genuine enough when he asks the price of a yoke of bullocks at
Stamford Fair. But the context of this question is so much to
the point that it had better be quoted:

Shallow. Jesu, Jesu, the mad days that I have spent! and to see
how many of my old acquaintance are dead!
Silence. We shall all follow, cousin.

Shallow. Certain, 'tis certain; very sure, very sure; death, as the Psalmist saith, is certain to all; all shall die. How a good yoke of bullocks at Stamford Fair?

Shallow's crass simplicity, his dense unawareness of how trite is his moralising and how steep the descent from it, is the most exquisite comedy. And yet Shakespeare uses this passage to express the way he sees life and to strengthen the pattern of the present plays. Shakespeare did indeed see life as a ridiculous but fascinating blend; a blend in the present scene of men dying and bullocks sold in the busy market; while, for the pattern of the play, Shallow speaks his words just after Henry IV has been brought to the point of death: it is in this context that he speaks generally of death and then turns to Stamford Fair, reminding us that it is still flourishing. He tells us what Hardy tells us in a more direct fashion:

> Only thin smoke without flame
> From the heaps of couch grass:
> Yet this will go onward the same
> Though Dynasties pass.

Secondly, there is Davy. The upset in Shallow's house caused by Falstaff's visit must have been great. But Davy is undefeated. Through all the turmoil of unusual hospitality he insists on seeing to the details of his job: the bucket must have a new link; and his friend William Visor of Woncot (though a knave) must not be allowed to suffer at the plea of Clement Perkes. Davy is both administrator and politician, perhaps in his little way the double of Henry IV, and certainly the symbol of the undefeated operating of the country life.

Taken all together, the scenes I have indicated as creating the picture of England (not to speak of the incidental references) include most phases of English life from high to low. The biggest gap is in the middle. Shakespeare says little of the merchant class, in which he had grown up. Perhaps it was this omission that prompted him, when ordered to write again on Falstaff, to choose a middle class setting. There is nothing epic about the *Merry Wives of Windsor*; yet its setting may derive from Shakespeare's epic intentions in *Henry IV*. This omission, however, with its possible result, is incidental. There is enough of England in *Henry IV* and enough confidence in

England to make the two parts Shakespeare's ripe expression of what he felt about his country.

I have used the word epic to describe *Henry IV* but I do not mean that this epithet is merited simply through the English local colour. It is only the intense, the tragic, the agelong that can give the temporary and the local the necessary dignity. Without the eternal character of Achilles the mere life as lived in the *Iliad* would not be raised to epic height. In *Henry IV*, as I have remarked, there is nothing tragic, nothing to correspond to the greatest things in the *Iliad*; but there are other things that serve. First, there are the agelong types, the fool, the adventurer, the "unofficial self," assembled in the character of Falstaff. Secondly, there is the great contrast (typified in the lines of Hardy quoted above) between the theme of civil war, the terrible vicissitudes of high politics, and the theme of the perennial cycles of ordinary life and their persistent rhythms: the cycles of birth and death; and of the seasons with their appropriate tasks, without which man simply cannot exist. Thus it is that the great variety of *Henry IV*, unequalled in Shakespeare, is given a coherence very different indeed from the coherence of Shakespearean tragedy but in its own way not inferior.

4. HENRY V

I have conjectured that Hall's chronicle caught Shakespeare's youthful imagination and impelled him to dramatise the whole stretch of English history from the prosperity of Edward III, through the disasters that succeeded, to the establishment of civil peace under the Tudors. In all the History Plays so far written (*King John* excepted, which is outside the sequence) he had fulfilled his obligation. But in the last three plays he had quite exceeded it by giving, concurrently with the strict historical theme, his epic picture of medieval and of contemporary England. But this excess could not cancel the residue of his obligation. He had created his picture of the great traditional villain king; he had still to create his picture of the great hero king. Richard III had figured in *2* and *3 Henry VI* and had declared his character. But that was not enough. Hall, by incorporating More's life of Richard III, dwells on that king with a special emphasis. Shakespeare fulfils his obligation to

Hall by giving Richard a play to himself, in which his monstrosity is done full justice to. Hall, following the tradition established by Polydore Vergil, makes Henry V the second exceptional figure in his chronicle: the copy-book paragon of kingly virtue, to balance Richard the monstrous pattern of concentrated vice. If Shakespeare was to carry his work through he was obliged to treat Henry like Richard: to allow him a play to himself. There was a personal reason why Shakespeare should now acquiesce in the precedent of Hall: he had finished the theme of England or Respublica and was almost forced to allow a concrete hero to dominate his next History Play.

But Shakespeare also had his duty to the expectations of an Elizabethan audience. Having achieved popularity in showing Henry's youthful dissipation he could not, without scandal, refuse to show Henry in his traditional part of perfect king. And this traditional part contained factors not found in Hall: namely his sudden miraculous conversion when he came to the throne and his pre-eminence among English kings as the bluff hearty man and the good mixer. The legend of his conversion was powerful and of long standing. It began with the chronicler Walsingham, who said that Henry on coming to the throne was turned suddenly into another man, and persisted in the *Famous Victories of Henry V*, where only a miracle can account for the abrupt transition from waster to serious monarch. The tradition of good mixer finds typical expression in the king's dealing with Simon Eyre in Dekker's *Shoemaker's Holiday*.

Here then were two obligations; and they were both impossible of worthy fulfilment. In creating his epic of England Shakespeare had set himself an exacting standard. His political hero, to be worthy of the standard just set, must be the symbol of some great political principle. And there was no principle he could symbolise. The pre-eminently successful political hero in great literature is Aeneas; and it was Virgil's powerful and steady belief in the missionary and civilising destiny of Rome that animated him. England had not yet reached the stage of Virgil's Rome. She had preserved herself, had achieved union, had "rested true" to herself, but she did not yet stand consciously for any wide political idea. The Tudors were successful by personal astuteness rather than by exemplifying any principle. They were not for export, not oecumenical. Thus

Henry V, who could at best stand for Elizabethan political principle, could only fail when great weight was put on him. In other words Shakespeare for his hero was obliged ultimately to choose *homo* not *rex*. It is interesting that Milton did precisely the same when he rejected his political hero Arthur for his universal hero Adam. A further difficulty was that the sophisticated, eminently courtly, and not at all exclusively English character whom Shakespeare had created in Prince Hal had no connection at all with the inhuman copy-book hero of Polydore Vergil.

To fulfil the second obligation in a manner worthy of the plays he had just written was also impossible. The whole point of the Prince's character was that his conversion was not sudden, that he had been preparing with much deliberation for the coming burden. And as for being the hearty man and the good mixer, the Prince may indeed have charmed his audience by the mere fact of his presence at Eastcheap; but his fundamental detachment and persistent irony are quite at odds with the popular conception of a simple forthright energetic man, transparent in character and separated from simple humble souls only by the accident of his exalted position. It would have been too risky to allow him to remain the ironist after he had come to the throne.

Shakespeare came to terms with this hopeless situation by jettisoning the character he had created and substituting one which, though lacking all consistency, satisfied the requirements both of the chroniclers and of popular tradition. No wonder if the play constructed round him shows a great falling off in quality.

Not that Shakespeare jettisoned his old creation without a struggle. He would hardly have begun his play with

> O for a Muse of fire, that would ascend
> The brightest heaven of invention,

if he had felt quite hopeless of his genius soaring into the empyrean, and thus achieving a miraculous solution of the seemingly impossible. And in the first scene where Henry appears (I. 2) and once or twice later Shakespeare does try to invest his hero with a glamour that shall by its sheer blinding power make us insensible to any inconsistencies. The prelates and nobles who incite Henry to great deeds in France speak splendidly:

> Gracious lord,
> Stand for your own; unwind your bloody flag;
> Look back into your mighty ancestors:
> Go, my dread lord, to your great-grandsire's tomb,
> From whom you claim; invoke his warlike spirit
> And your great-uncle's, Edward the Black Prince,
> Who on the French ground play'd a tragedy,
> Making defeat on the full power of France,
> Whiles his most mighty father on a hill
> Stood smiling to behold his lion's whelp
> Forage in blood of French nobility.

Ely reinforces these words of Canterbury with

> Awake remembrance of these valiant dead
> And with your puissant arm renew their feats.
> You are their heir, you sit upon their throne;
> The blood and courage that renowned them
> Runs in your veins; and my thrice-puissant liege
> Is in the very May-morn of his youth,
> Ripe for exploits and mighty enterprises.

These lines not only dazzle us with their brilliance but they place Henry in the grand context of English history and make us forget the subtle personal touches of his previous character. And they do even more. They refer back to a specific passage in *Henry IV*, the reference to May suggesting the description of Henry and his companions before Shrewsbury,

> As full of spirit as the month of May.

It looks as if Shakespeare was trying desperately, by creating casual links between Prince Hal and Henry V, to mask their fundamental discrepancy. Anyhow we cannot but be appeased for the moment; and when Exeter continues with

> Your brother kings and monarchs of the earth
> Do all expect that you should rouse yourself,
> As did the former lions of your blood,

we are still more appeased, for Exeter here takes up Henry's promise, made at the end of the last play, that he will accept his due place among the other monarchs in the ocean of royalty, that his vanity will no longer beat idly on the rocks but that

> Now doth it turn and ebb back to the sea,
> Where it shall mingle with the state of floods
> And flow henceforth in formal majesty.

Further questionings about Henry's character are held off by Exeter's noble commonplace on the order of government being like music:

> While that the armed hand doth fight abroad,
> The advised head defends itself at home;
> For government, though high and low and lower,
> Put into parts doth keep in one consent,
> Congreeing in a full and natural close,
> Like music—

and by Canterbury's splendid comparison of the state to the beehive. But the truth cannot be withheld for ever and out it comes in Henry's speech to the French ambassador about the tennis balls: a speech whose heavy irony and orotundity compare poorly with the Prince's light ironies and truly Olympian grandeur in *Henry IV*. It is not the same man speaking. Later efforts to inflate Henry to greatness are no more successful. His reproof of the traitor, Lord Scroop, at Southampton, is wonderful poetry, possibly the finest thing in the play; yet it is queerly ineffective in its context. The Henry we knew was an unerring judge of human nature and never gave himself away. When he says of Scroop

> Thou that didst bear the key of all my counsels,
> That knew'st the very bottom of my soul,
> That almost mightst have coin'd me into gold,

he speaks gloriously, he may charm us for the moment, but he ultimately bewilders us. He is utterly inconsistent with his old self and with any of the pieces of self that make up his patchwork character in the present play. Nor can one plead that his words are a sententious passage spoken out of character: they are too emotional. One is tempted to suppose (as nowhere else in all Shakespeare's History Plays) that the poet, defeated in the real business of his drama, is drawing on personal experience and filling up the gap with an account of how someone at some time let him, Shakespeare, down. Once again Shakespeare tried to save his play in the scenes before Agincourt. Of

Henry's conversation with Bates and Williams, Johnson wrote that "the whole argument is well followed, and properly concluded." This is a just comment, but the conversation does not get beyond the sober and the rational. It has the chill of Brutus's speech over Caesar's body rather than the warmth of the prose of the previous plays. Henry's following soliloquy "Upon the king!" is splendid poetry and yet somehow extrinsic to the play, a piece of detached eloquence on a subject on which Shakespeare had long meditated with interest and fervour.

Finally, there is a curious reference back to *Henry IV* near the end of the play, as if even then, when the game was lost, Shakespeare was still hankering after continuity with his late masterpiece. It is where Henry, courting Katharine, mentions his skill in vaulting onto his horse fully armed.

> If I could win a lady at leap-frog, or by vaulting into my saddle with my armour on my back, under correction of bragging be it spoken, I should quickly leap into a wife.

Here is a clear reminiscence of the gay description in *1 Henry IV* (quoted p. 257 above) of Prince Hal mounting his horse. But how alien the two passages are: the earlier a brilliant piece of Renaissance painting; the other, with its stalely indecent double-meaning, a piece of sheer writing down to the populace. In spite of these efforts to manufacture connections and of the closeness with which its plot follows on, *Henry V* is as truly separated from the two parts of *Henry IV* as *Richard II* is allied to them.

But I need not deal exhaustively with the play's shortcomings, when they have been set forth in such masterly fashion by Mark Van Doren in his *Shakespeare*. I will rather point out how conscientiously Shakespeare fulfilled his double obligation: to the chroniclers and to his public. If his muse failed to ascend the brightest heaven of invention at least it tried to pay the debts it owed below the sphere of the moon.

First, Shakespeare through the mouth of the Archbishop prolongs the chronicle story of Henry's sudden conversion:

> Never was such a sudden scholar made;
> Never came reformation in a flood
> With such a heady currance, scouring faults.
> For never Hydra-headed wilfulness

> So soon did lose his seat, and all at once,
> As in this king.

To suppose that Shakespeare meant the Archbishop here to be wrong, just as Poins had been wrong, about Henry's true character is to introduce a subtlety quite alien to the rest of the play. Shakespeare is submitting to the popular tradition of the chronicles and going back on his own earlier creation. Another legacy of the chronicle tradition, Henry's rejection of his old companions, had been done justice to in the previous play. Yet Shakespeare is careful to bring it in again when he makes Fluellen say,

> So also Harry Monmouth, being in his right wits and his good judgements, turned away the fat knight with the great-belly doublet.

With this rejection was coupled the election of grave counsellors and the heed Henry gave them. And here Shakespeare pays his debt in full, and once again at his own expense. His Prince Hal had been an eminently self-reliant and self-sufficient young man, one who would never accept the advice of others without subjecting it to the closest scrutiny. In the debate in I. 2 on the French war Henry is a different person. He hardly interposes, much less argues. As a thinker he is quite passive, leaving the business to others. When these have pronounced their verdict, he accepts it without a word of comment but initiates action with

> Call in the messengers sent from the Dauphin.

The perfect courtier in whom intellect and activity was finely balanced has given way to the pure man of action, whose thinking is done for him by his counsellors. His subsequent pedestrian thoughtfulness when he argues with Bates and Williams is inconsistent alike with Prince Hal's brilliant intellect and with the narrow activity he shows both in the scene with his counsellors and his courtship of Katharine. Then the chroniclers (Polydore Vergil and Hall) tell us that Henry was able to learn wisdom by historical precedent. Shakespeare makes his Henry refer to the past history of his country:

> For you shall read that my great-grandfather
> Never went with his forces into France

> But that the Scot on his unfurnish'd kingdom
> Came pouring.

Finally, the chroniclers make much of Henry's piety, and Shakespeare follows them very conscientiously. He pays his debt; but at what a cost. We have only to compare Henry's pious comments on the miraculously low number of English casualties at Agincourt (twenty-five) and his orders for the *Non Nobis* and the *Te Deum* to be sung, with the last scenes of *Richard III* and certain parts of *Hamlet* to recognise how chilly they are. The platitudes of piety can become ultimate statements of overwhelming power if they issue from a worthy context. Occurring as they do here in a play which is constructed without intensity, they can only depress.

Other debts to the chroniclers concern not Henry's character but ideas about history. Before dealing with these I will speak of Shakespeare's fulfilling his debt to his audience by making Henry the hearty king, the good mixer. It was probably his sense of this debt that made him depress Henry's intellectual power in the debate about the French war referred to above. He fulfils it in Henry's familiarity with his "kinsman" Fluellen and his exchange of gages with Williams. But it is in his courtship of Katharine that Henry reaches his full degree of bluffness and heartiness. "I know not," says Johnson, "why Shakespeare now gives the king nearly such a character as he made him formerly ridicule in Percy." Johnson may well ask; for the whole distance between the poles divides the lubberly wooer with his coarse complexion, who "could lay on like a butcher," from the "king of courtesy" of the earlier play.

To revert to the chroniclers, Shakespeare does in *Henry V* keep alive the theme of civil war, but more faintly than in any other of his History Plays. He clearly intended the play to be a splendid interlude, when the ancestral curse was for the moment suspended, figuring in some sort the golden age of Elizabeth. But the curse is not forgotten, for Henry prays before Agincourt that the death of Richard II should not be visited on him then, and he even remembers it when he courts Katharine:

> Now, beshrew my father's ambition! he was thinking of civil wars when he got me: therefore was I created with a stubborn outside, with an aspect of iron.

And the conspiracy of Richard Earl of Cambridge actually re-enacts the theme.

In one historical matter *Henry V* is unique in Shakespeare: its partiality to things Welsh refers obliquely to that side of the Tudor myth (described above pp. 29-32) which Spenser and Warner, among the poets, developed.

> *Fluellen.* All the water in Wye cannot wash your majesty's Welsh plood out of your pody, I can tell you that. God pless it and preserve it, as long as it pleases his grace, and his majesty too!
> *Henry.* Thanks, good my countryman.

I fancy too that Shakespeare spares the French king the ridicule he heaps on the Dauphin, because he was father of Katharine, who, widowed of Henry V, married Owen Tudor and became the ancestress of Henry VII. The French king always speaks with dignity.

I wrote above that *Henry V* was constructed without intensity. It is worth mentioning one or two points in which this is true. After the Archbishop's fable of the bees there is little of the cosmic lore that marks the other History Plays. When Shakespeare's mind was working intensely it was aware of the whole range of the universe: events were not isolated but took place concurrently with other events on all the planes of existence. But the settings of the different scenes in this play are simple and confined. Even the battle of Agincourt evokes no correspondences in the heavens or elsewhere. A second sign of slack construction is the unevenness of the verse. There are passages of flatness among the rhetoric. The rhetoric has been better remembered than the flatness. But take the opening of II. 4 (the first scene showing the French court) up to the arrival of Exeter: it is written in the flattest verse, a relapse into the style of the more primitive parts of *1 Henry VI*; and, though Exeter proceeds to liven things a little, the verse remains lethargic. Nor is there much energy in the verse portions of the play's last scene. A third sign of weak construction is the casualness of the comic scenes. Whereas in *Henry IV* these were linked in all sorts of ways with the serious action, in *Henry V* they are mainly detached scenes introduced for mere variety. The farewell scene of Pistol and the Hostess in London is good enough in itself, but it is quite episodic. It would be unfair, however, not to mention the redeeming brilliance of Fluellen. For sheer original invention Shakespeare never made a better character.

Had the rest of the play backed him up, he would (as his creator probably meant him to do) have filled the place of Falstaff not unworthily.

I fancy, too, that Fluellen helps us to understand Shakespeare's state of mind when he wrote *Henry V*. Fluellen is an entire innovation, like nobody else in Shakespeare before (though many years after he may have begotten the Baron of Bradwardine); and he suggests that Shakespeare was now wanting to do something fresh. Whenever Fluellen, the new character, is on the stage, Shakespeare's spirits seem to rise and he ceases to flog himself into wit or rhetoric. There are other things in the play that suggest Shakespeare's longing for a change. The coarseness of Henry's courtship of Katharine is curiously exaggerated; one can almost say hectic: as if Shakespeare took a perverse delight in writing up something he had begun to hate. Henry's reproof of Scroop, already noted as alien in tone to the norm of the play, has a quality as new as the character of Fluellen; for it is tragic and looks forward to Shakespeare's future bent of mind—

> May it be possible that foreign hire
> Could out of thee extract one spark of evil
> That might annoy my finger? 'tis so strange
> That, though the truth of it stands off as gross
> As black and white, my eye will scarcely see it.

That is one of the tragic themes: the unbelievable contradiction of appearance and reality; felt by Troilus about Cressida, by Hamlet about his mother, and by Othello about Desdemona. It has nothing to do with the matters that have most been the concern of this book: with politics, with patterns of history, with ancestral curses, with England's destiny and all the order of her society. It is a personal and not a public theme.

That Shakespeare was wanting to do something new is not at all to be wondered at. He had written his epic of England and had no more to say on the matter. In writing it he had developed characters of uncommon subtlety and in Prince Hal he had pictured a man, having indeed settled a conflict, but one in whom a genuine conflict had taken place. No wonder if Henry V, traditionally the man who knew exactly what he wanted and went for it with utter singleness of heart, was the very reverse of what Shakespeare was growing truly interested in. And no wonder if in his next great public character, Brutus, Shakespeare pictured a man like Prince Hal in being subjected to a conflict but unlike him in being torn asunder by its operations.[1]

---

[1] These last sentences make suggestions rather like those of Granville-Barker in his essay *From* Henry V *to* Hamlet in *Aspects of Shakespeare*, Oxford 1933. I refer the reader to this excellent essay. But I differ in thinking Prince Hal a much subtler character than Granville-Barker apparently does and look on Brutus as a development from the Prince as well as a reaction from Henry V.

CHAPTER V

Macbeth

In *Henry IV* Shakespeare had successfully depicted in the Prince the true kingly type, but not the ideal reigning king; in *Henry V* he failed to make interesting or consistent what should have been the perfect king in action. He had still to come to terms with that figure. To hold that Shakespeare habitually cried down or satirised the successful man of action by contrasting him with the more interesting but often unsuccessful man of thought—Fortinbras with Hamlet, Anthony with Brutus, Octavius with Anthony—is a mistake. Shakespeare was far too sane and lived in far too perilous a world to underestimate the public and the active virtues. And that he never let the man of action out of mind, though certainly more *interested* in the man of thought, is shown by Guiderius, though so slightly drawn, in *Cymbeline*. But it does seem as if he had to get his man of action, his politically efficient man, put in his proper proportion in the scheme of things. The next version of Henry V was, as Granville-Barker detected, Fortinbras in *Hamlet*. The culminating version, and with it the whole adjustment of politics to life, comes in *Macbeth*. This play, as well as being the last of the great tragedies, is the epilogue of the Histories.

Although an authentic tragedy *Macbeth* treats the body politic differently from the other tragedies. "Scotland" is a more organic part of it than Denmark is of *Hamlet*, Venice of *Othello*, or even Rome of *Coriolanus*. It is a difference that comes out in the propriety of having in the last sentence put Scotland between inverted commas and not the other countries. It is his mother and perhaps Roman ethics that defeat Coriolanus, but it is the body politic as a whole that is the instrument of defeating Macbeth. The personal tragedy of Macbeth, the terrible discrepancy between his virtuous understanding and his corrupt will, his vain conflict with an overruling Providence, and the pervading cosmic theme of disorder seeking to upset the divine order of nature, are all more important than the actual political theme. Yet that theme is the instrument through which Providence works and is one of the motives that combine to make the play so rich. Thus, though *Macbeth* is rightly linked with three other great tragedies in the first place, it is linked in the second with another play, *Richard III*, where likewise the body politic asserts itself against the monstrous individual.

Once linked with *Richard III*, *Macbeth* touches the whole historical context which has been the theme of this book. Its derivation from Holinshed becomes more than a mere convenience in finding plot-material; and it could rightly be called, in one aspect, the finest of all mirrors for magistrates. Indeed Shakespeare seems to imply this last analogy in Macbeth's soliloquy, "If it were done when 'tis done." After saying that he would be willing to cut out the next world, he adds:

> But in these cases
> We still have judgement here: that we but teach
> Bloody instructions which, being taught, return
> To plague the inventor; this even-handed justice
> Commends the ingredients of our poison'd chalice
> To our own lips.

This principle of retribution here and now is the master-theme of the *Mirror for Magistrates*; and Macbeth is entirely at one with that book and with contemporary doctrine in taking historical precedent into account. By *cases* he probably means the actual murders recorded in the chronicles or in the *Mirror*.

But the analogy with *Richard III* goes further. Although very distrustful of elaborate contemporary analogies in Shakespeare's plays, I believe one must give full value to the Elizabethan proclivity to finding examples of history repeating itself. I do not see how Shakespeare's audience could have missed the analogy between the Earl of Richmond in exile at the court of Brittany, jealously watched by Richard III, and Malcolm in exile at the court of England, spied on by the emissaries of Macbeth. The same terror was suffered in England and in Scotland under their respective tyrants. The murder of Macduff's children duplicates that of the princes in the tower; and it is directly after both murders that Providence begins seriously to intervene. At Dunsinane Macbeth's followers desert him exactly as Richard's do at Bosworth. The speeches with which the new kings end the plays are identical in tone. Thus *Macbeth* catches up and includes what had been the most solemn and the most deeply felt of all Shakespeare's political motives: the working out of a crime, the punishment of the villain, and the establishment of the Tudors.

The political theme reaches its full compass in the scene in England, but it is here too that its adjustment to the total world picture is made quite clear. It is a scene of order and stability, which gets much of its effect because it follows, and is interrupted by the report of, Macbeth's culminating crime and supreme act of disorder, the murder of Macduff's family. The English court is stable, corresponding to heavenly stability; and the English king performs his divinely appointed task of healing the "evil." It culminates and ends in Malcolm's words:

> Macbeth
> Is ripe for shaking, and the powers above
> Put on their instruments.

Malcolm and Macduff are the instruments of God's all-inclusive order, now at last beginning to reassert itself. Political action happens to be the means through which something that altogether transcends it chooses to work.

It is in this scene too that Shakespeare finally settled his account with his idea of the good ruler. Malcolm provides little interest in himself but a great deal in what he stands for. He is entirely devoted to the good of his country, he has his personal passions in tight control, he is Machiavellian in his distrust of other men till he is absolutely assured of their integrity, and he is ready to act. He unites in himself the necessary qualities of lion fox and pelican, although somewhat toned down in the leonine part. He is in fact the ideal ruler who has subordinated all personal pleasures, and with them all personal charm, to his political obligations. He is an entirely admirable and necessary type and he is what Shakespeare found that the truly virtuous king, on whom he had meditated so long, in the end turned into. As a subordinate character he fits perfectly in the play and does not risk letting his creator down, as Henry V had done. Or, to put it in another way, he is an instrument, and the lack of interest in the object does not in the least detract from the majesty of the force that puts it to use.

In the course of this book I have pointed to the things Shakespeare shared with his contemporaries, and especially to those things that lie outside the purely dramatic sphere. Thus he shared the conception of history current among the intellectuals of his day; he shared the affection, prevailing in his youth, for the *Mirror for Magistrates*; he shared the impulse to create an epic. By mingling politics with the cosmic and the individual

themes in *Macbeth* he was doing what two of his contemporaries
had already done and, partly, in the same way.   It is true that
nothing in Elizabethan literature matches Shakespeare's epic
picture of England in *Richard II* and *Henry IV*, for here he
invented something and no one was able to follow him.   But
in *Macbeth* Shakespeare did something of the kind Spenser and
Sidney had done.   Politics figure largely in the *Fairy Queen* and
partially in the *Shepherd's Calendar*, but they are subordinate to
the organisation of the cosmos and to the salvation of the individual.   Merlin's prophecies to Britomart are of less moment
than the Garden of Adonis and the repentance of the Red Cross
Knight.   Similarly the defective kingship of Basilius and the
perfect kingship of Euarchus are important parts of *Arcadia* but
they are less important than the personal sufferings of Pamela
and Philoclea in prison, the personal experience of *Astrophel and
Stella*, and the philosophical doctrines of the *Defence of Poetry*.
Macbeth not only is a great tragedy, not only includes the high
political theme with the personal and the cosmic, but it represents its age in showing how all these things should be blended
and proportioned.

Conclusions

AT a time when so much has been said about the principle of order and of the hierarchies in English literature of the Renaissance tradition, it is not likely that anyone will question my conclusion that Shakespeare's Histories with their constant pictures of disorder cannot be understood without assuming a larger principle of order in the background. I hope I have proved by illustration how steadily aware Shakespeare was of that principle throughout his History Plays from the very beginning, and that by this awareness he allies himself to the more philosophical writers of his day.

I do not pretend to be deeply read in the English chronicles, nor have I studied the sources of Shakespeare's Histories with the minute care of a man editing the separate plays. Such detailed study still remains to be fully accomplished; and Boswell-Stone's admirable *Shakespeare's Holinshed* is no longer up to date. But I hope I have settled the general question of where the main ideas about the course of English history from Edward III to Henry VII, current among the educated men of Shakespeare's day, had their origin; and that I have shown one or two undoubted and a number of possible places whence Shakespeare derived both these ideas and his more general philosophy of history.

Again, I have not studied the Chronicle Plays exhaustively. And there is room for a new book on the whole subject. But I have tried to correct one or two notions about them, such as their supposed close connection with the Spanish Armada and their limiting influence on Shakespeare. It becomes more a case of Shakespeare exalting the Chronicle Play than of the Chronicle Play deeply influencing Shakespeare. By singling out some of the plays for special mention I may have seen the class in something of a new perspective. But if the Chronicle Play turns out to be less important in shaping Shakespeare's History Plays, the Morality turns out to be more so, in that it prompted their central theme, that of England or Respublica put in a solemn and highly moral setting.

Though some of my section on the early Shakespeare is conjectural, I hope I have at least strengthened the inclination to take his first plays more seriously.

The three parts of *Henry VI* have been so neglected as works of art on account of mistaken doubts of their authenticity that my criticism of them is bound to be new. They turn out to be far better than is usually reputed. I should like to think I had helped to get them included in the plays of Shakespeare taken into account and enjoyed by the common reader. It is certainly useless to try to appreciate *Richard III* in isolation from the other three plays of the tetralogy. By giving Shakespeare's first historical tetralogy its proper weight one also gets a truer view of his debt to the chroniclers. I have tried to strengthen the new tendency to do justice to Hall as against Holinshed. In these early plays Shakespeare went to both chroniclers for his facts, but Hall is his warrant for the ideas according to which the facts are arranged.

The question of the epic and how far Shakespeare took into account the contemporary ideas of the epic brings with it the general interpretation of the whole series of Shakespeare's Histories. At one time I followed a common opinion in looking on them less as self-sufficient dramas than as experiments in a solemn mode leading him to his true goal of tragedy. Men thought of Shakespeare caught up in his youth by the new and exciting self-realisation of England, in a way deceived into thinking the political theme his true theme, lured on to picturing, as his climax, the perfect king, Henry V. Then, at the culminating moment he realises that the man of action is not his real hero, that his imagined hero has let him down; and, schooled by this experience, he turns to the type of man who fundamentally attracts him, the man whose interests are private not public, whose sphere of thought is the universe and not the body politic. And, let down by his political hero, Shakespeare finds his true outlet in Brutus, Hamlet, and the other great tragic heroes.

I now think this scheme is wrong as a whole, though it contains elements of truth. First, Shakespeare turned the Chronicle Play into an independent and authentic type of drama, and no mere ancillary to the form of tragedy. He did this largely because he grasped the potentialities of the old Morality form, never allowing the personalities of his kings to trespass on the fundamental Morality subject of Respublica. In the total sequence of his plays dealing with the subject matter of Hall he expressed successfully a universally held and still comprehensible scheme of history: a scheme fundamentally religious, by which events evolve under a law of justice and under the ruling of God's Providence, and of which Elizabeth's England was the acknowledged outcome. The scheme, which, in its general outline, consisted of the distortion of nature's course by a crime and its restoration through a long series of disasters and suffering and struggles, may indeed be like Shakespeare's scheme of tragedy; but it is genuinely political and has its own right of existence apart from tragedy. But in addition to this concatenated scheme, Shakespeare in *Richard II* and *1* and *2 Henry IV* gave us his version, which I have called epic, of what life was like in the Middle Ages as he conceived them and in his own day. This version was entirely successful and presents not even a parallel to the form of tragedy. It is one of Shakespeare's vast achievements and it stands unchallengeable: something entirely itself without a jot of suspicion that it ought to be, or ought to lead up to, something else; an achievement sufficient to put Shakespeare among the world's major poets. Nevertheless *Henry IV* led to *Henry V*, a play whose hero was no longer Respublica but Rex, and, once there was a change of hero, the form created by Shakespeare collapsed and the problem of tragedy thrust itself forward. Prince Hal had had nothing to do with tragedy and did not let his creator down; Henry V admitted the problems of tragedy and let his creator down very badly indeed. Thus it is that in a very minor and exceptional way, and at the very end of its exploitation, the History Play served as a transition to authentic tragedy. In *Macbeth* Shakespeare settled the adjustment of the political man of action to the other parts of the tragic world.

Finally I hope this book has served to strengthen the ideas of an educated Shakespeare, and of a poet more rather than less like Dante and Milton in massiveness of intellect and powers of reflection. J. S. Smart said that "Shakespeare intended his works for the same public for which Spenser wrote the *Faerie Queene* and Byrd and others composed their airs." This may be to limit Shakespeare's intentions too much, but it is true as far as it goes and it is not yet widely enough realised. It is certainly borne out by the steady thoughtfulness with which Shakespeare treated his historical themes and by the masterly shaping of most of his History Plays.

It is strange that just when Milton was thought most isolated and uncompromisingly individual the early Shakespeare should have been robbed of his individuality and had his work confounded with that of his fellow dramatists. Milton has since turned out more and more to be the child of his age as well as his unique self. In spite of serious heresies he accepted the prevalent world picture, while in political and ethical thought he followed influential contemporary leads. Examine Shakespeare's early plays unprejudiced by theories of alien authorship, and you find a strong poetic personality of the kind expected in a very great poet: ambitious, concentrated on his art, and already masterful in the way he shapes his material. This double trend of thought is to be welcomed. There is no danger that very great poets such as Shakespeare and Milton should ever be found dull and undifferentiated. To deplore the discovery that they are more normal than was thought is to wish them to be freaks. Such a wish, it cannot be doubted, common opinion will firmly repudiate, rejoicing that our two foremost poets should show themselves, not more private, but more normal and at the same time more comprehensive than had once been supposed.

Notes

page
4. *Lorenzo on music.* M.V. V. 1. 54-88.
   This has been called. By C. H. Herford in his note on the passage in the Eversley Shakespeare.
5. *A specialist in Greek philosophy.* John Burnet in the *Greek Strain in English Literature* (English Association Pamphlet No. 45, 1920).
   The seeds or "germens" of nature. I derive my information from W. C. Curry, *Shakespeare's Philosophical Patterns* (Louisiana State University Press 1937) chapter 2, p. 10.
6. *Angelo and Isabella.* M.M. II. 2. 71-5.
   When Brutus talks of the state of man. J.C. II. 1. 62-9.
   Hamlet's pronouncements. Ham. II. 2. 315-20.
8. *Marlowe's Tamburlaine.* I owe this observation to Willard Farnham, *The Medieval Heritage of Elizabethan Tragedy* (University of California Press 1936) p. 369.
10. *Ulysses's speech on degree.* T.C. I. 3. 75-137.
11. *Sir John Fortescue.* Quotation from Works edited by Lord Clermont (London 1869) I. p. 322.
13. *Sir John Hayward.* Quotation from *David's Tears* (1623) pp. 165 and 168.
13. Quotation at bottom of page is from Hannibal Romei's *Courtier's Academy* translated by I. K., p. 247.
15. *Abridgement of de Sebonde.* Originally in Latin, translated into French by Jean Martin 1550. Quotation translated from book IV chap. 42 of French version.
18. *Lovejoy.* His book is *The Great Chain of Being* (Cambridge, Mass. 1936).
    A book on the hexemeral literature. F. E. Robins, *The Hexaemeral Literature* (Chicago 1912).
19. *Alfred Hart* in *Shakespeare and the Homilies* (Melbourne 1934) pp. 22-3.
21. For Machiavelli I am greatly indebted to J. W. Allen, *A History of Political Thought in the Sixteenth Century* (London 1928) pp. 447-94. Quotation about Calvin and Hooker is from this book, p. 491. I wish to make it plain that in this section I deal with the way the Elizabethans took Machiavelli's historical doctrines not with the influence of Machiavellianism on the Elizabethan drama, which I do not seek to minimise.
22. For Machiavelli and Spenser see E. A. Greenlaw in *Modern Philology*, VII, pp. 187 ff.
    For Raleigh's "atheism" see F. S. Boas, *Marlowe and his*

Circle (Oxford 1929) chap. 4, and M. C. Bradbrook *The School of Night* (Cambridge 1936) chap. 1.

23. Passage from Raleigh's *Sceptic* is in works edited by Oldys and Birch (Oxford 1829) Vol. VIII, p. 551. Passages from his *Maxims of State* are on pages 8-21 of the same volume.

28. For the same process as that described in the first paragraph but within the field of tragedy see Lily B. Campbell, *Shakespeare's Tragic Heroes* (Cambridge 1930) pp. 22 ff.
Hardyng's address to the Duke of York comes in his ninety-eighth chapter.

29. *The Tudor Myth.* For this see especially the two first chapters of E. A. Greenlaw's *Studies in Spenser's Historical Allegory* (Baltimore 1932).

30. *Nor did the house of Stuart upset the myth.* See Roberta F. Brinkley, *Arthurian Legend in the Seventeenth Century* (Baltimore 1932).

32. For Polydore Vergil I have used the Camden Society volumes (period up to the Conquest, *i.e.* books 1-8, London 1846; period from Henry VI to Richard III, London 1844) and where these volumes do not extend the original Latin version in the Basel Edition of 1570.
For Polydore Vergil as historian see C. L. Kingsford, *English Historical Literature in the Fifteenth Century* (Oxford 1913) pp. 191 ff.

33. Quotation translated from Basel Edition, p. 439.

34. *Truce between Edward III and French. Ib.* p. 389.
Richard II and Henry IV. Ib. pp. 424 ff.
Quotation from Camden Edition (1844) p. 137.

35. Quotation, *ib.* p. 82.

36. *Richard II's kidnapping his uncle.* Basel Edition, pp. 421-2.

37. First quotation from Camden Edition (1844) p. 154. Second quotation, *ib.* p. 148. Third quotation translated from Basel Edition, p. 442.
Owen Tudor. Camden Edition (1844) p. 62.

38. Quotation in lines 2 and 3, *ib.* p. 135.
More's *History of Richard III* is most easily accessible in J. R. Lumby's edition (Cambridge 1883).
The episode of Edward IV's widow is in above edition, pp. 25 ff.
Dr. Shaw's sermon. Ib. pp. 63-6.

40. The importance of Hall as historical background of Shakespeare's History Plays was indicated by C. L. Kingsford, *Prejudice and Promise in Fifteenth Century England* (Oxford 1925) pp. 1-21. It was well developed by Greenlaw, *op. cit.* pp. 7 ff. Reference to detailed studies of Shakespeare's debt to Hall will be made later. References are to the 1809 edition.

41. Charles Whibley. In *Cambridge History of English Literature*, III, chap. 15.
45. *Polydore.* Basel Edition, p. 399.
46. Quotation from Hall, p. 19.
    Polydore. Camden Edition (1844) p. 22.
47. Quotations from Hall, pp. 145-6, 256, 248.
    Polydore. Ib. p. 107.
48. *Polydore. Ib.* p. 194.
    Hall. Pp. 382-9.
51. Quotation from Hall, p. 423.
    Quotation from Holinshed, 1587 edition III, p. 655.
    Debate before Henry V's French expedition. Hall, pp. 50 ff.;
    Holinshed, *ib.* pp. 545 ff.
52. *Hall.* P. 145.
53. *Holinshed. Ib.* p. 599.
    Polydore. Ib. p. 24.
    Hall. P. 147.
54. *Holinshed. Ib.* p. 600.
55. *The chief ends of history for the Elizabethans.* For this topic see Lily B. Campbell, *Tudor Conceptions of History in "A Mirror for Magistrates"* (University of California Press 1936).
61. Raleigh's account of the course of English history is in the preface of his *History of the World.*
62. Davies of Hereford's account of the course of English history occurs in *Microcosmos* (1603). Works, ed. Grosart (1878) I, pp. 54 ff.
65. *R. U. Lindabury.* In chapter 12 of *A Study of Patriotism in the Elizabethan Drama* (Princeton 1931).
68-70. Quotations from the Homily in question are on pp. 571, 560, 581, 575-6 of G. E. Corrie's edition of the Homilies (Cambridge 1850).
71. *A Mirror for Magistrates.* The editions up to 1587 (see p. 73) have been edited definitively by Lily B. Campbell (Cambridge 1938) with full introduction on the successive versions of the work and on its authors. References are to pages in this edition. For my treatment of the *Mirror* I have not relied on any other writer but I am glad to find that Willard Farnham in chapter 7 of his *Medieval Heritage of Elizabethan Tragedy* considers it as important in forming Elizabethan tragedy as I do in forming the History Plays of Shakespeare. This importance is confirmed by Howard Baker in his *Induction to Tragedy* (Louisiana State University Press 1940).
73. Quotation on p. 298.
74. Do. pp. 95, 73, 346.
75. Do. pp. 65, 121-2.
76. Do. pp. 280-1, 178, 171.

77. Quotation on pp. 145, 146.
78. Do. p. 214.
79. Do. pp. 244-5, 476.
80. Do. p. 198.
81. Do. pp. 92, 99.
82. Do. pp. 447, 448, 449.
83. Do. pp. 64, 65-6.
84. Do. pp. 65, 178, 412.
85. Do. pp. 391-2, 196.
86. Do. pp. 401, 202.
87. Do. pp. 398-9, 134.
88. Do. pp. 137, 349, 352, 420-1 (italics my own).
89. Do. pp. 272, 359.
93. As *Gorboduc* is available in many editions and as I have indicated in the text where the quotations come from I have thought it unnecessary to give exact references in these notes.
98. *The English Chronicle Play.* For general treatment see F. E. Shelling, *The English Chronicle Play* (London 1902), W. D. Briggs's introduction to his edition of Marlowe's *Edward II* (London 1914), R. M. Smith, *Froissart and the English Chronicle Play* (New York 1915). A new study is overdue. I hope in this section I may have done something to counteract two traditional errors: the importance of the Armada in this class of play and the dominant influence of Marlowe. Briggs's treatment is the most satisfactory.
98-9. *By* 1580 *men began.* See Briggs, *op. cit.* pp. xxvi-xxxix.
99. *Nashe in his Pierce Penniless.* Ed. G. B. Harrison (London 1924) pp. 86-7.
   True Tragedy of Richard III is reprinted in W. C. Hazlitt's *Shakespeare's Library* (London 1875) Part II, Vol. I.
101. *Locrine* in the *Shakespeare Apocrypha* ed. C. F. Tucker Brooke (Oxford 1918). Quotation, IV. 1. 28-43.
102. *Peele.* Ed. A. Dyce. 1828.
   Wilson's play is in Vol. VI of Dodsley-Hazlitt *Old Plays.* Scene and quotation, pp. 447 ff.
103. *Patriotic convention.* For patriotism generally see Lindabury, *op. cit.*
104. Quotation from *Edward I.* Dyce I, pp. 102-3.
105. Quotation from *Pinner of Wakefield*, Churton Collins's edition of Greene (Oxford 1905) Vol. II, p. 216 (lines 1191-1200).
   Edward IV has been reprinted by the Shakespeare Society. Scene between the king and Jane Shore is V. 1.
   Lord Cromwell is in the *Shakespeare Apocrypha.*
   The Queen and Jane Shore. In II. 2 of this part of the play.
106. The *Troublesome Reign of King John* is in Hazlitt's *Shakespeare's*

Library Part II, vol. I and has been edited by E. Rose (Praetorius facsimile). I use edition by F. J. Furnivall and John Munro (London 1913). Quotations, Part 2, Scene 2, 137-141 and Scene 3, 116-9.

True Tragedy of Richard III. Reference to p. 125 of edition cited.

Jack Straw. Ed. H. Schütt (Heidelberg 1901). References to II, 2.

Edward II. References to Marlowe's works ed. C. F. Tucker Brooke (Oxford 1910).

107. Quotations, lines 2333-47, 2591-2, 2627-34.
108. Do. 268, 1132-5, 1655, 1791-5, 2329.
109. *Sir Thomas More* is easiest accessible in the *Shakespeare Apocrypha*, which edition I have used. Quotation, II. 4. 112-9 and 121-35.
110. Do. IV. 5. 69-78, III. 2. 96-8, III. 2. 1-12.
111. Do. I. 3. 64-70.

Edward III is easily accessible in the Temple Dramatists and in the *Shakespeare Apocrypha*. References here to the latter. Quotation, II. 1. 260-6.

112. Do. II. 1. 395-410, II. 1. 34-5, II. 2. 92-9, I. 1. 36-41.
113. Do. III. 1. 105-14, III. 2. 35-7, IV. 3. 29-34.
114. Do. V. 1. 50-5, IV. 4, 127-32, IV. 4. 161.

Woodstock. References here are to Keller's edition. An edition in modern spelling by A. P. Rossiter was published in 1946. *Woodstock* is also in *Elizabethan History Plays,* ed. W. A. Armstrong (World's Classics, 1965).

115. Quotations, II. 1. 11-5 and 18-21, II. 2. 163-4 and 169-75.
116. Do. IV. 3. 87-90, IV. 2. 65-70, V. 2. 181, I. 1. 172-5.
117. Do. II. 1. 54-65.
118. Do. V. 1. 73-5, V. 2. 217-20, IV. 2. 137-49.

In saying that Woodstock is orthodox on matters of civil war and obedience to the king I differ radically from R. M. Smith, *op. cit.* pp. 96-7, who thinks that certain plays of the early 1590's about inefficient kings and rebellions showed a desire to rebel. Even if the authorities may have been nervous about such plays, the plays themselves were harmless enough in sentiment.

119. *Sir John Oldcastle* is in the *Shakespeare Apocrypha*, which edition I use. Quotations, III. 1. 1-5, III. 1. 53-60.
120. *Schücking.* In *Englische Studien* XLVI, pp. 228-51.
121. R. C. Bald, *Addition III of Sir Thomas More* in *Review of English Studies* 1931, pp. 67-9, gives strong reasons for assigning More's speech beginning "It is in heaven" (quoted above, p. 110) to Shakespeare. But he argues on the assumption that, like the 172 lines, it is an addition, the work of the botcher.

120. *Shakespeare's Hand in the Play of Sir Thomas More* by various authors (Cambridge 1923).

120-1. *The players* . . . *"turned to an 'absolute Johannes factotum.'"* A. W. Pollard, p. 5 of *Shakespeare's Hand*.

121. 1593, *the date which* . . . *Ib.* p. 27.
Greg. Ib. p. 48.
Tucker Brooke. In *Shakespeare Apocrypha*, pp. xxi-ii.

122. *Alfred Hart.* In *Shakespeare and the Homilies*, pp. 219-41.
"Lilies that fester . . ." Edward III, II. 1. 451.
Battle of Sluys. Ib. III. 1. 142-82.
W. Keller has written on the debt of *Woodstock* to *Edward II*, *op. cit.* pp. 21-32. Not taking the Morality tradition sufficiently into account, he overestimates this debt.

123. *Old doting greybeards!* Quotation from *Woodstock*, II. 2. 193-200.
Woodstock and the Courtier's horse. Ib. III. 2. 146 ff.
Tucker Brooke. Ib. pp. xxvii-viii.

129. For Shakespeare's debt to Froissart in *Richard II* see J. Dover Wilson's edition of the play, pp. xliv ff. A. P. Rossiter (in a letter to the author) questions the supposed derivation of Shakespeare's Gaunt from Froissart's.

131. Quotation from *2 Hen. VI*, IV. 7. 78-9.
Greene, *Groatsworth of Wit*. Ed. G. B. Harrison (London 1923) p. 43.

132. Quotations, *ib.* pp. 45-6. For Greene's reference to Aesop see Helen P. Scott, *The Upstart Crow, Modern Philology*, Aug. 1927.

133. *A schoolmaster.* For strong support of this notion see J. Q. Adams, *A Life of William Shakespeare* (London 1925) pp. 90-6.
E. K. Chambers, in *William Shakespeare* (Oxford 1930) I. pp. 281 ff.
W. W. Greg, in *The Editorial Problem in Shakespeare* (Oxford 1942) pp. 49 ff.

134. *Courthope.* Quotations from *History of English Poetry* (London 1916) Vol. IV, pp. 458, 462.

135. Smart's plea for an early date for the *Comedy of Errors* is in his *Shakespeare Truth and Tradition* (London 1928) pp. 205-7.
Titus Andronicus. I omit the question of touching up or revision for the 1594 performances. For analogies between this play and *Venus and Adonis* see A. K. Gray in *Studies in Philology* 1928, pp. 295 ff. He argues for revision but of a play not by Shakespeare.

136. *C.E.* I. 1. 16-25.

137. *T. S. Eliot*, in his introduction to Newton's Seneca in the Tudor Translations (London 1927) I, p. xxvii.
Miss Bradbrook, in *Themes and Conventions of Elizabethan Tragedy* (Cambridge 1935) pp. 98-9.

138. *T.A.* II. 2. 88-104.
140. *T.A.* V. 3. 67-76 and 147-8.
142-3. *Lyly,* ed. Warwick Bond (Oxford 1902) II, pp. 205-6 and 210-1.
147. *1 Hen. VI.* II. 5. 63-9.
       2 Hen. VI. II. 2. 18-27.
148. *Rich. III.* III. 3. 9-14.
       Hen. V. IV. 1. 309-14.
149. *Shakespeare's debt to Hall.* See Edleen Begg, *Shakespeare's Debt to Hall in Richard III* in *Studies in Philology* 1935, pp. 189 ff.; Lucille King, *2 and 3 Henry VI—which Holinshed?* in *Publications of the Modern Languages Association* 1935, pp. 745 ff.; and (an important general study) W. Gordon Zeeveld, *The Influence of Hall on Shakespeare's Historical Plays* in *English Literary History* 1936, pp. 317-53. See also A. P. Rossiter's interesting speculations on the supposed discovery of a copy of Hall with Shakespeare's annotations, in the *Durham University Journal,* 1941, pp. 126-39.
151. *1 Hen. VI.* III. 4. 1-12, 16-27.
152. *3 Hen. VI.* II. 5. 21-41.
153. *2 Hen. VI.* IV. 2. 70-5, 78-82 and IV. 10. 18-25.
154. *2 Hen. VI.* III. 1. 147-53, 189-94.
       3 Hen. VI. II. 2. 154-62.
155. *Rich. III.* I. 3. 199-206.
       1 Hen. VI. IV. 4. 47-53.
157. *2 Hen. VI.* II. 2. 10-6.
158. For Shakespeare's debt to Froissart see R. M. Smith, *Froissart and the English Chronicle Play,* and J. Dover Wilson's introduction to his edition of *Richard II.*
161. *Alexander,* in *Shakespeare's Henry VI and Richard III* (Cambridge 1929) pp. 184-5.
162. *Sir Thomas More.* II. 4. 92-6.
164. For a summary of Elizabethan doctrines about the stars see my *Elizabethan World Picture,* pp. 48-55.
165. *1 Hen. VI.* II. 1. 25-7.
166. *Ib.* III. 2. 91-2 and 126 ff.
168. *Ib.* IV. 1. 187-94, IV. 4. 72-6.
170. *Ib.* I. 4. 104-10, IV. 1. 89-110, I. 2. 108-11,
       Holinshed. III. p. 600.
171. *1 Hen. VI.* I. 4. 40-52, V. 3. 54-64.
172. *Ib.* IV. 7. 3-16.
       Rich. III. I. 2. 41-3.
       1 Hen. VI. I. 5. 19.
173. *Ib.* III. 1. 90-1, IV. 2. 9-14.
174. *2 Hen. VI.* III. 1. 147-64.
175. First quotation, *ib.* II. 1. 55-7.

177. *2 Henry VI.* II. 5. 101-3, I. 1. 180-204.
178. *Ib.* I. 1. 239-59.
179. *Ib.* I. 2. 66-7, I. 3. 77, 97-9, 102-3.
180. *Ib.* I. 3. 209-10.
181. *Ib.* II. 2. 69-76.
182. *Ib.* III. 2. 136-40.
183. *Ib.* 153-7.
184. *Ib.* V. 1. 87-105, 157-8.
185. *Ib.* I. 1. 155-7.
186. *Ib.* V. 1. 28-9, I. 1. 214-31.
187. *Ib.* V. 2. 29-45, III. 2. 388-99.
189. *3 Hen. VI.* IV. 6. 68-76, V. 2. 11-5.
191. *In Hall Edward takes an oath,* pp. 291-2.
192. *3 Hen. VI.* I. 4. 66-83.
193. *Ib.* I. 4. 111-42.
194. *Ib.* II. 5. 64-6, 31-4, 103-8.
196. *2 Hen. VI.* V. 1. 213-4.
      3 Hen. VI. III. 2. 174-9, 143.
197. A. P. *Rossiter,* in the *Durham University Journal,* 1938, pp. 44-75.
199. *Rich. III.* I. 4. 136-48.
200. *Ib.* I. 3. 158-60.
203. *Ib.* III. 1. 72-7, 84-8.
204. *Ib.* V. 3. 108-17.
205. *Ib.* I. 4. 69-72, II. 1. 126-32, II. 4. 55-64.
206. *Ib.* IV. 4. 40-3, 25-9, 82-108.
208. *Rants like Judas in the Miracle Plays about to hang himself.* The English version of this is in the thirty-second (fragmentary) play in the Towneley Plays. The Oberammergau Passion Play preserves a German version.
209. *Rich. III.* II. 2. 107-11.
209-10. *Lamb,* in his letter to Lloyd 26 July 1801 and *G. F. Cooke* in "*Richard III*" (1802).
210. *Dowden,* in *Shakespeare: his Mind and Art* (9th Edition, London 1889) pp. 182, 189.
212. *Rich. III.* V. 3. 243-9, 252-6; I. 3. 197-203.
213. *Ib.* 302-3, IV. 4. 182-95.
214. E. K. *Chambers,* in *Shakespeare, a Survey* (London 1925) p. 19.
215. *Holinshed.* Quotation from III, p. 196.
216. *Alexander,* in his *Shakespeare's Life and Art* (London 1939) p. 85. *Dover Wilson,* in the preface to his edition of the play. *Courthope. Op. cit.* p. 466.
217. *1 Hen. VI.* III. 2. 80-3.
218. *Probably in 1594.* I accept Dover Wilson's dating.
219. *John.* V. 4. 33-5, 5. 1, II. 1. 574-82.
220. *Ib.* 589-90, V. 7. 25-7, II. 1. 177-82.

221. *John.* I. 1. 39-43, II. 1. 273.
   Sir Thomas More. II. 4. 54-5.
222. *John.* III. 1. 23-4, V. 1. 12, V. 4. 52-7.
   Dowden. Op. cit. p. 170.
223. *John.* I. 1. 24-6, IV. 3. 45-59.
224. *Ib.* V. 3. 125-34.
225. *Ib.* 139-59.
226. *Ib.* IV. 1. 17-8.
   Masefield. In his comments on the plays in question in his *William Shakespeare* (London 1911).
227. Middleton Murry, in his *Shakespeare* (London 1936) pp. 159-69.
   John. IV. 3. 79, V. 7. 79, V. 2. 128-36.
228. *Ib.* I. 1. 214-5, II. 1. 577-88, V. 7. 70-3.
229. *Mark Van Doren,* in his *Shakespeare* (New York 1939). This book is a series of studies of the separate plays, and all my references can be found in the relevant studies.
   John. II. 1. 191-4, 159-63.
230. *Ib.* III. 1. 114-29, III. 4. 25-35.
231. *Ib.* II. 1. 447-60, 68, 63.
233. *Ib.* IV. 2. 193-202.
234. Dover Wilson dates *Richard II* after *King John,* which dating I accept. See his introduction to *Richard II.*
235. *Ib.* IV. 1. 134-44, V. 1. 55-65.
236. *Ib.* III. 3. 112-6.
   1 Hen. IV. V. 1. 4-5.
   2 Hen. IV. III. 1. 70-9.
238. A good deal has been written on the relations of Daniel and Shakespeare. I accept Dover Wilson's conclusions in his edition of *Richard II,* where the literature on the subject is reviewed.
239. *Daniel.* Quotation from *Civil Wars* IV stanza 46; speculations on Bolingbroke's motives, *ib.* I stanzas 93-9.
240. *Ib.* I stanzas 23, 3, II stanzas 3-4.
241. *Ib.* III stanza 49.
243. *Hayward,* quotations from pp. 144, 287-8.
246. *Rich. II.* III. 3. 34-7, V. 5. 35-8, V. 1. 89-92.
247. *Ib.* V. 3. 100-8, 137-9, II. 1. 94, 96-101.
248. *Ib.* 1. 3. 282-93.
252. *Ib.* IV. 1. 207-10.
252. For Shakespeare's debt to Froissart see notes to pp. 129 and 158.
253. *A. B. Steel,* in *Richard II* (Cambridge 1941).
254. *Rich. II.* II. 1. 51-6, IV. 1. 239-42.
255. *Ib.* IV. 1. 281-3.
256. *Ib.* III. 2. 155-70.

257. *Rich II.* I. 3. 74-5.
1 Hen. IV. IV. 2. 104-10.
Rich. II. I. 3. 288-91.
260. *Rich. II.* I. 3. 37-9.
261. *Ib.* I. 4. 5-9.
264. *R. A. Law,* in *Studies in Philology* 1927.
265. I agree with Dover Wilson in the importance he gives to the
Morality motive in both plays in *The Fortunes of Falstaff*
(Cambridge 1943).
270. *2 Hen. IV.* IV. 4. 30-41, 77-88.
271. *Cym.* IV. 2. 170-6.
274. *The foolery of the Prince . . . before Falstaff arrives, 1 Henry IV.*
II. 4. 1-125.
275. *Johnson.* As Johnson's comment on this passage is omitted
from Walter Raleigh's *Johnson on Shakespeare* (London 1916),
the most accessible place for most of Johnson's criticism of
Shakespeare, I reprint it here :
I am not yet of Percy's mind. The drawer's answer had
interrupted the prince's train of discourse. He was
proceeding thus, *I am now of all humours that have shewed
themselves humours—I am not yet of Percy's mind,*—that
is, I am willing to indulge myself in gaiety and frolick,
and try all the varieties of human life. *I am not yet of
Percy's mind,*—who thinks all the time lost that is not
spent in bloodshed, forgets decency and civility, and
has nothing but the barren talk of a brutal soldier.
277. The passage in Elyot's *Governor* is in Book II Section 6.
(Everyman Edition, pp. 139-40.)
278. *Lyly,* in *ed. cit.* I. p. 193, II. p. 50.
Castiglione, from Book I Section 26.
279. *1 Hen. IV.* V. 4. 161-2.
280. *Lily Campbell,* in chapter on *Lear* in her Shakespeare's *Tragic
Heroes.*
282. *1 Hen. IV.* III. 2. 1-17.
283. *Hotspur's account to Blunt, ib.* IV. 3. 52-105.
284. *Ib.* III. 1. 128-34.
285. *Ib.* 252-62.
286. Enid Welsford, *The Fool* (London 1935).
287. *1 Hen. IV.* I. 2. 1 ff.
3 Hen. VI. II. 4. 31-4.
288. *Rich. II.* V. 5. 49-54.
1 Hen. IV. II. 4. 449-53.
2 Hen. IV. IV. 3. 52-122.
289. *Starkey.* Quotation from *Starkey's Life and Letters* (Early
English Text Society 1878) p. 48.
Horizon, for Sept. 1941.

290. *1 Hen. IV.* II. 4. 516-27.
292. *2 Hen. IV.* III. 1. 45-53, 80-6, 38-40.
293. *Ib.* V. 2. 129-33.
    1 Hen. IV. V. 1. 15-9.
294. *2 Hen. IV.* IV. 5. 190-1, 131-8, I. 1. 200-3.
295. *Ib.* 153-60.
296. *Ib.* I. 1. 67-75, V. 2. 129-37.
297. *1 Hen. IV.* III. 1. 159-64, 205-11.
    2 Hen. IV. II. 3. 18-32.
298. For the importance of Shakespeare's prose in the development of his style generally see G. H. W. Rylands, *Words and Poetry* (London 1928) pp. 144 ff.
    2 Hen. IV. II. 2, end.
    1 Hen. IV. I. 2. 91-8.
300. *Ib.* 82-8, III. 1. 14-5.
301. *2 Hen. IV.* I. 3. 100-8.
    Dover Wilson, in the *Fortunes of Falstaff*, p. 111.
302. *2 Hen. IV.* III. 2. 36-43.
305. *It began with the chronicler Walsingham.* I owe this statement to J. W. Cunliffe's article on the character of Henry V in *Shakespeare Studies* ed. Brander Matthews and A. H. Thorndike (New York 1916).
307. *Hen. V.* I. 2. 100-10, 115-24.
308. *Ib.* 178-83, II. 2. 96-8.
309. *Ib.* V. 2. 142-5, I. 1. 32-7.
310. *Ib.* IV. 7. 48-51, I. 2. 221, 46-9.
311. *Ib.* V. 241-5.
312. *Ib.* IV. 7. 111-5.
313. *Ib.* II. 2. 100-4.
316. *Macb.* I. 7. 7-12.
317. *Ib.* IV. 3. 237-9.
321. *Smart, op. cit.* p. 155.

Index

(No references are made to the plays of Shakespeare that are the main subject of this book.)